Praise for *Mzala Nxumalo, Leftist Thought and Contemporary South Africa*

'In a dispiriting present, these wide-ranging essays reinvigorate left analysis, with many drawing on the work of the communist intellectual and militant Mzala Nxumalo. This reaching back to engage the present means that this volume is an important contribution to sustaining a national left intellectual tradition, a project in dialogue with the best ideas from around the world. Mzala, as he was and remains known, was committed to a non-sectarian approach to building a left project and these essays will be useful to people across the South African left, and elsewhere.'

– Richard Pithouse, scholar, journalist, editor, teacher and activist; author of *Writing the Decline: on the Struggle for South Africa's Democracy* (2016) and editor of *Asinamali: University Struggles in Post-Apartheid South Africa* (2006).

The financial assistance of the National Institute for the Humanities and Social Sciences (NIHSS) towards this publication is hereby acknowledged. Opinions expressed and those arrived at are those of the author and are not necessarily attributed to the NIHSS.

First published by Jacana Media (Pty) Ltd in 2023

10 Orange Street
Sunnyside
Auckland Park 2092
South Africa
+2711 628 3200
www.jacana.co.za

© Individual contributors, 2023

All rights reserved.

ISBN 978-1-4314-3399-5

Cover design by publicide
Editing by Glenda Younge
Proofreading by Debra Primo
Set in Droid Serif Regular 9.5/15pt
Job no. 004094

See a complete list of Jacana titles at www.jacana.co.za

MZALA NXUMALO, LEFTIST THOUGHT AND CONTEMPORARY SOUTH AFRICA

MZALA NXUMALO, LEFTIST THOUGHT AND CONTEMPORARY SOUTH AFRICA

Edited by

Robert J. Balfour

Foreword by

Bonginkosi Emmanuel 'Blade' Nzimande

CONTENTS

Acronyms and abbreviations ix

Acknowledgements xiii

Foreword xv

Introduction: Mzala Nxumalo's ideas in post-apartheid South Africa
Mandla J. Radebe and John Pampallis 1

PART 1: MZALA AND THE NATIONAL QUESTION

1. Radical Left Thought Revival: Mzala's Views and Their Applicability in Contemporary South Africa
   Percy Ngonyama 21

2. The National Question and Exile: Remembering Mzala in London
   Elaine Unterhalter 43

3. Socialism is the Future: Comrade Mzala's Thoughts on the National Question
   Mandla J. Radebe 69

4. The First and Second Transitions and the National Question in South Africa
   Gregory Houston and Yul Derek Davids 97

5. The EFF's Perspective on 'What is the Future of the Left in South Africa in a Global Context?'
   Sam Matiase 129

6. The Dilemma of the Post-1994 Democratic Breakthrough: A Broad Survey of Community Struggles in South Africa
   Noel L.Z. Solani 153

PART 2: COMMUNITY, STATE AND GLOBE: ISSUES, STRUGGLES AND THE POLITICS OF WORK

7. The Challenges of Economic and Social Development in South Africa: Left Perspectives
Alex Mohubetswane Mashilo ... 177

8. Global Economic Imperialism and the Politics of (Under) Development: Street Traders, Domestic Workers and Sex Workers
Pat Horn ... 217

9. Social and Economic Challenges from a Left Perspective
Gunnett Kaaf ... 237

10. After Revisionist Marxism: Reanimating the Critique of Capitalism in South Africa
Bernard Dubbeld ... 255

11. Emerging Powers and the Polycentric World
Vladimir Shubin ... 287

12. Ecocide or Socialism: Ecological Challenges and Neoliberal Capitalist Constrains on Radical Transformation
Rasigan Maharajh and Sigfried Tivana ... 301

Conclusion: The Future of Leftist Thought in a New Century
Robert J. Balfour ... 323

About the Contributors ... 345

Index ... 355

ACRONYMS AND ABBREVIATIONS

AAM	Anti-Apartheid Movement
AIC	African Independent Congress
ANC	African National Congress
ANCYL	African National Congress Youth League
API	American Petroleum Institute
AsgiSA	Accelerated and Shared Growth Initiative for South Africa
B-BBEE	Broad-based black economic empowerment
BIG	Basic income grant
BLF	Black First Land First
BOSCO	Botshabelo Students Congress
BOYCO	Botshabelo Youth Congress (BOYCO).
BRICS	Brazil, Russia, India, China and South Africa
CCETSA	Canon Collins Education Trust for Southern Africa
Comintern	Communist International
COSATU	Congress of South African Trade Unions
CTCP	Confederación de Trabajadores por Cuenta Propia (Nicaragua)
EEA	Employment Equity Act
EFF	Economic Freedom Fighters
GEAR	Growth, Employment and Redistribution Programme
GNU	Government of National Unity

HSRC	Human Sciences Research Council
Idasa	Institute for Democracy
IDWF	International Domestic Workers' Federation
IFES	International Foundation for Elections Systems
ILO	International Labour Organization
IMF	International Monetary Fund
IPP	Independent power producer
ISL	International Socialist League
JIPSA	Joint Initiative for Priority Skills Acquisition
JSE	Johannesburg Stock Exchange
MBO	Membership-based organisations
MDGs	Millennium Development Goals
MK	uMkhonto we Sizwe
NDP	National Development Plan
NDR	National Democratic Revolution
NDS	National democratic society
Nedlac	National Economic Development and Labour Council
NGO	Non-governmental organisation
NGP	New Growth Plan
NSWP	Global Network of Sex Work Projects
NUMSA	National Union of Metalworkers of South Africa
OECD	Organisation for Economic Cooperation and Development
PAC	Pan-Africanist Congress
RDP	Reconstruction and Development Programme
RESA	Research on Education in South Africa
RET	Radical Economic Transformation
SACP	South African Communist Party
SADC	Southern African Development Community
SAIIA	South African Institute of International Association
SOE	State-owned enterprise
SAPOHR	South African Prisoners' Organisation for Human Rights
SASAS	South African Social Attitudes Survey (Statistics South Africa)
SEWA	Self-Employed Women's Association (India)

SEWU	Self-Employed Women's Union
SOAS	School of Oriental and African Studies, University of London
UCT	University of Cape Town
UDF	United Democratic Front
UWC	University of the Western Cape
WASP	Workers and Socialist Party
WIEGO	Women in Informal Employment Globalising and Organising

ACKNOWLEDGEMENTS

The Mzala Centre is gratefully acknowledged as the initiator, host and facilitator of multiple scholarly conferences, from which the academic contributions featured in this book, were drawn. The Centre's role in fostering, supporting and creating a platform for debate and critique of society, the state and the economy, is appreciated.

The National Institute for the Humanities and Social Sciences of South Africa (NIHSS) is gratefully acknowledged for providing funding necessary to support this publication. In particular, the role played by Professor Sarah Mosoetsa is supporting the book, is recognised. It is further acknowledged that the views contained within the book are not necessarily the views of the NIHSS. The NIHSS is also not responsible for any errors or omissions in the book. The NIHSS bears no responsibility for any statement made or opinion expressed in this publication.

The contributions made by Derek Buchler, Nokulunga Ngobese, Jenny Schreiner and John Pampallis towards readiness the initial drafts of the book, are acknowledged with appreciation, as is the support provided by the Mzala Centre at large. Percy Ngonyama who was a valued researcher at the Centre, and who is featured in this book, passed away in early 2019.

This manuscript underwent peer review and was subjected to a rigorous two-step peer-review process before publication, with the identities of the reviewers not revealed to the editor or authors. Where the reviewers recommended revision and improvements, editor or authors responded adequately to such recommendations.

FOREWORD

One of the key declarations from the 2015 founding colloquium of the Mzala Nxumalo Centre for the Study of Southern African Society (popularly referred to as the Mzala Centre) was the need to establish progressive, left and Marxist institutions to research and analyse South African and global realities. This is important, especially as this centre was established in the name of Comrade Jabulani Nobleman 'Mzala' Nxumalo, one of the leading Congress intellectuals of the liberation movement in exile. In order to benefit from Mzala's work, we must continually interrogate, appraise and learn from his contribution to the progress and the challenges that confront our national democratic revolution (NDR).

Such questions are best tackled with input from – and dialogue between – all sections of the progressive movement, including workers, the unemployed, grass-roots community activists, youth and women's organisations and progressive intellectuals. The Mzala Centre has attempted to promote dialogue between these groups to examine and debate the most important issues facing our movement at this point of our history.

The chapters in this book originated from presentations made at three conferences organised by the Mzala Centre. The subjects deal with a wide range of topics, including the new social, economic and political challenges facing democratic South Africa; the need to re-examine the critique of capitalism in the 21st century; the evolving nature of globalisation and neoliberalism and their effect on South Africa since 1994; the continuing poverty and inequality experienced by the country's population and, in some instances, its intensification; the emergence of new classes and social strata, including the black middle class and a growing precariat; the relationship between race, class and community struggles, particularly demands for service delivery by municipalities and public utilities, such as electricity, water and refuse removal; and the ecological challenges under capitalism.

In addition to exploring these issues, a number of chapters provide analyses of various aspects of the national question – that is, the quest for the establishment of a united South Africa, including overcoming the racist and sexist policies of the apartheid regime and its attempts to create and nurture divisions among black people. The highest form of this divide and rule strategy was the bantustan system. This was also one of the principal themes of Mzala's work and was centrally reflected in his most important work, *Gatsha Buthelezi: Chief with a double agenda* (Zed Books, 1988). Bantustans no longer exist in this country, but their undoubted legacy has not received as much attention as it deserves in post-apartheid scholarship.

Strategies of division were not unique to South Africa. Colonial powers have always sought to strengthen their own position as rulers and to weaken resistance among colonised people by creating divisions among them and by widening any divisions that already existed. But nowhere was this strategy implemented with greater resolve or more systematically and brutally than in South Africa.

To fully understand the issues that we face today, many of which are discussed in this volume, it is important that we understand the apartheid era that preceded the advent of democracy. Apartheid – whose lingering impact we still live with but whose nature most of our youth are largely unaware of – was a system of extreme oppression imposed on the black people of South Africa. I encourage all South Africans, and especially the youth, to learn more about it and the struggle against it. This is the system that Mzala, like millions of other South Africans, lived and suffered under, and struggled against – both physically and intellectually. Mzala's writings are an invaluable resource for understanding the struggle, as well as the present dispensation that emerged from and in reaction to it, both its strengths and weaknesses.

In South Africa 'national independence' had been granted by Britain in 1910, but only to the white colonists and their progeny who took over the reins of government and exercised power over all others in order to stabilise colonial control and ensure the continuation of a very profitable source of revenue for British and white South African capitalists. All black people – including Africans, coloureds and Indians – were totally excluded from power. From its earliest days, the liberation movement recognised the bogus nature of this independence and, over time, came to characterise it as 'colonialism of a special type' – a system in which the coloniser and the colonised lived side by side on the same territory.

After 1948, the newly elected National Party government strengthened the oppressive machinery of the state: extending the pass laws; introducing 'Bantu Education'; passing draconian laws to restrict political activities of black people; suppressing workers and their trade unions; and enforcing racial segregation and racial inequality. But more than this, it sought to use the bantustan system to deprive Africans of their very South African nationality and to promote ethno-nationalism. Africans, they argued, were not part of the South African nation but belonged to 10 different nations according to the languages they spoke and the geographical areas that the government set aside for each of them. This applied even to urban dwellers who had never been to those areas but who, nevertheless, were assigned 'citizenship' in one or the other of them. According to the National Party, each of these 'bantustans' – the government would later refer to them as 'homelands' – was to become 'independent' and have its own government; in reality they would all be completely subservient to the white government in Pretoria. The leaders of the bantustans were inevitably people who were prepared to collaborate with the white government in a subservient role. Different forms of governance were developed for other oppressed racial groups – coloureds and Indians, each with their own accommodative leadership – to ensure that that separation and subservience permeated the entire system, albeit in a different form. The Balkanisation of South Africa through the bantustan system was, in fact, Afrikaner nationalism's attempt to resolve the national question – not to build one nation but to break it up into many smaller ones with the white 'nation' holding ultimate power.

The liberation movement saw clearly that this system was nothing but a rationalisation for the continuation of white supremacy and completely rejected it. In response it spelled out in the Freedom Charter its long-held vision of a united, democratic, non-racist and non-sexist South Africa.

Apartheid's vision offered only a fractured country with oppressive structures and practices. History does not determine our present and our future, but it must be kept in mind as we grapple with our current challenges. The insights of Mzala and others like him, and their ways of analysing human interaction, arm us to face the future.

A progressive South Africa looks to the Mzala Centre and other research institutions to make a significant contribution to building one country with a decent life for all its citizens through clarifying and deepening our understanding of the past and the present. The chapters in this volume are part of this effort.

Bonginkosi Emmanuel 'Blade' Nzimande
Minister of Higher Education, Science and Innovation

INTRODUCTION

MZALA NXUMALO'S IDEAS IN POST-APARTHEID SOUTH AFRICA

Mandla J. Radebe and John Pampallis

The post-apartheid South Africa, for which many people such as Nobleman Jabulani 'Mzala' Nxumalo were prepared to lay down their lives, still has far too many unresolved problems and unfulfilled promises, even though significant progress has been made in certain areas. 'Mzala', as he was commonly known, was one of the leading Marxist intellectuals to emerge from the 1976 student uprisings against the apartheid regime in Soweto and elsewhere. Like thousands of other young South Africans, he left South Africa and joined the ranks of the African National Congress (ANC) and the South African Communist Party (SACP). In exile, he engaged actively in the wide-ranging debates within the ANC and SACP, including those associated with the relationship between race, class and gender oppression, and with the national question.

Apart from the well-documented socio-economic challenges characterised by high levels of poverty, inequality and growing unemployment, the 2022 report of the Judicial Commission of Inquiry into Allegations of State Capture chaired by Justice Raymond Zondo painted a grim picture of rampant corruption and lawlessness.

These challenges have become major barriers to the country's developmental agenda and hence its unfulfilled potential.

Although various events, such as the soccer and rugby world cups, have demonstrated possibilities of what could be achieved through national unity, Desmond Tutu's 'rainbow nation', a concept that itself requires further interrogation, has remained a mirage. At the heart of this failure is the unresolved national question (Webster et al, 2017). But what is this national question and why does it remain relevant? Importantly, why are left ideas relevant not only in relation to this question but also to the challenges that besiege South Africa in the era of rampant neoliberalism and the rising tide of narrow nationalism? These questions are even more pertinent in the context of increasing global nationalism and authoritarian capitalism, as characterised by the emergence of leaders such as Donald Trump in the United States, Jair Bolsonaro in Brazil and Narendra Modi in India (Fuchs, 2019).

The 2021 local government elections in South Africa also witnessed the rise of what could be characterised as nationalist and ethno-nationalist parties, such as the Inkatha Freedom Party, the Patriotic Alliance, the Freedom Front Plus and ActionSA, who campaigned along nationalist and ethnic lines by, among others, employing xenophobic messages. Alarmingly, these parties gained positive support at the polls compared to the parties that took a more principled non-racial and inclusive approach in their campaigns. It is perhaps the rise of narrow nationalism that makes issues contained in this book so pertinent. To understand nationalism, we must contend with the national question and the role of community and the state in confronting socio-economic challenges, as well as the global world, in particular the failure of neoliberal capitalism in combating global inequality.

MZALA NXUMALO REMAINS RELEVANT

It is apt that this volume is inspired by Mzala whose praxis remains relevant to this day. From an early age, this native of Ngoje, a small village outside Louwsburg in northern KwaZulu-Natal, demonstrated a burning desire to fight for social justice, one of the themes that underpin this book. His birth in Dundee Hospital in 1955 coincided with major developments in the country. One of these was the Congress of the People, which adopted the Freedom Charter in Kliptown, Soweto, on 26 June 1955. This same document would inspire Mzala and his generation to pursue a struggle for a more just world. By the time Mzala skipped the country in June 1976, he had been involved in various revolutionary activities at institutions from Bethel College and Dlangezwa High School to the University of Zululand. This meant that he was often in trouble with the authorities and hence by the age of 16, Mzala had not only been expelled from Bethel College but also arrested. Prior to this, it was his upbringing by his God-fearing school-teacher parents that exposed Mzala to the struggle literature informed by liberation theology (Radebe, 2022).

As a Soviet Union-trained uMkhonto we Sizwe (MK) soldier, Mzala distinguished himself as a fearless fighter and, fundamentally, as a revolutionary intellectual. Hence, he ranks among the pre-eminent 'intellectual princes' of the ANC (Daniel, 1991). His impressive body of work was published under a variety of noms de plume. Apart from his contribution to the journals of the liberation movement such as *Dawn* and *Sechaba*, his writings include book chapters, articles in academic journals and the book *Gatsha Buthelezi: Chief with a double agenda* (1988). He produced an extensive number of compelling intellectual articles for the *African Communist*, a journal of the SACP, and wrote several articles on the people's war. While in Europe, where he worked for the *African Communist* and the Research on Education in South Africa (RESA) project in London and did a brief stint at *World Marxist Review* in Prague, Czechoslovakia, he also became a public intellectual presenting and commenting on the ANC's perspective on negotiations.

However, it was the national question that engaged him intellectually, including the relationship between the national and class struggle in South Africa, which intrigued him, and he wrote and lectured extensively on the subject. His assertion was that the South African revolution aimed at ending inequality between the nations could only be achieved under socialism (SACP, 1991). While Mzala was proud of his Zulu history and culture, he had no time for narrow ethno-nationalistic politics and, hence, he detested the bantustan system and the quislings at its helm as he believed this stifled the national drive and independence of the African people (Radebe, 2022).

When he succumbed to illness in hospital in London on 22 February 1991, at the tender age of 35, not only did he leave behind his wife Mpho and two young children, his parents and three siblings, but he also left many unfulfilled dreams. His dream in the new South Africa was to become an academic (Radebe, 2022). To this end, his doctoral dissertation was a few months away from submission at the Open University in England, and he had been offered a year-long fellowship at Yale University, where he was to work on a political biography of Oliver Tambo. Professors Gail Gerhart and Tom Karis, renowned American scholars, had passionately motivated for him to come over to Yale. Thus, it is important that Mzala's thoughts be engaged in the manner employed in this volume.

For example, Percy Ngonyama (in Chapter 1 in this volume) reveals Mzala's foresight when he argued in 1981 that some among the oppressed harboured 'bourgeois interests'. Ngonyama links Mzala's contemporary relevance to the current disarticulated wealth distribution, as witnessed in the current black economic empowerment (BEE) scheme introduced at the end of legal apartheid in 1994. Of course, BEE can be traced back to the concept of 'black advancement' of the 1970s when the apartheid regime was under intense international pressure, and desperate to portray economic benefits for black people through foreign investment (see Nzimande, 2007). Nevertheless, BEE is considered part of changing the contradictions characterising South Africa, where political power is in the hands of the majority, but substantial economic power still resides with the same old white capitalist class (see Radebe, 2020).

In this regard, Ngonyama points out that while the politically well-connected have been able to use their patronage network to amass wealth through 'empowerment', this has not 'trickled down' to the masses, who continue to wallow in abject poverty. Gregory Houston and Yul Derek Davids (in Chapter 4 in this volume) articulate the concept of broad-based black economic empowerment (B-BBEE) eloquently in the context of South Africa's first transition, which entailed 'economic transformation that involved addressing some of the racial inequalities characteristic of apartheid'.

Indeed, Mzala's frame of analysis remains pertinent in comprehending the current structure of the economy and attempts at transformation through the creation of a small black corporate petty bourgeoisie aimed at placating the black majority by demonstrating that capitalism was in their interest. All these efforts have been unable to yield the desired outcomes because they are locked into the capitalist system's economic trajectory, which continues to reproduce racialised inequalities (see Radebe, 2020).

This racialised inequality, which is manifested, inter alia, by the unemployed and poor working-class South Africans characterised as 'non-national', who have 'been excluded from glamourised depictions of a South African nation'. This is yet another contemporary relevance of Mzala's thoughts. Several chapters suggest that Mzala's analysis of the national question is still relevant 'insofar as it interrogates conceptions of a nation and the contradictions of nationality in post-apartheid South Africa'. We expand on this point in the next section.

THE NATIONAL QUESTION

It is possible to conclude that the national question has been neglected and perhaps regarded as old school in the post-apartheid democratic South Africa. How, otherwise, can we describe the overt inability of the state and society to deal with the rising tide of xenophobia, racial tensions and sometimes emerging ethnicity. Mkandawire (2009) posits that nationalism and related questions no longer enjoy the favourable attention they received a few decades back, owing to the weakening of the capacity of the nation-state and the emergence of 'cosmopolitan ideologies', among others. Therefore, he argues that concerns relating to the national question have been replaced by discourses on issues such as 'transnationalism, borderlands, globalisation, ethnoscapes, diversity, diasporas, marginality and even "rainbows"' (Mkandawire, 2009). Nevertheless, tensions between race and class, and their concomitant socio-economic manifestations such as inequalities, and between the 'national' and 'social' questions, are not new (Mkandawire, 2009).

However, judging by the rising phenomenon of narrow

nationalism globally, the national question in South Africa has never been more pertinent. The fundamental and elusive question of national unity and independence, and the related question of class within the national liberation struggle (Alexander, 1986), is equally critical. Mkandawire (2009) concurs with the importance of this question and differs with the 'cynicism' of the scholarship that 'tends to occlude political economy'. Inevitably, the fundamental question of class emerges when dealing with the national question, in particular the role of the black working class (Alexander, 1986), which was oppressed as a nation and exploited as a class (Mzala, 1988). Post-apartheid, it is the working class who, after being at the forefront of the national liberation struggle to defeat apartheid, is now being sacrificed 'on the altar of the neoliberal logic of global capitalism' (Mkandawire, 2009).

To fully comprehend the vision of the ANC, which was at the vanguard of the struggle to build a democratic, non-racial and united society, it is imperative to centre this vision on the successes and failures to resolve the national question. How Mzala tackled this question throughout his short but eventful life, argues Unterhalter in Chapter 2 in this volume, can be best understood by tracing his experience of exile. Unterhalter deftly traces Mzala's London experience and invokes their personal interactions in his interaction with the South African exile community in London to frame this question.

As Unterhalter reminds us, while Mzala's views on the resolution of the national question entailed the protection of 'culture and languages as constitutional rights', he emphasised that this should not be 'a continuation of bantustan structures or to privilege particular ethnic affiliations, and where the form of the colonial state and the associated repression is recognised and overturned' (Unterhalter, Chapter 2). Many of his close associates such as Patric Mellet (see Radebe, 2022) argue that Mzala would have been disappointed with the current provincial system, which they regard as a continuation of the bantustan logic. This logic perpetuates narrow ethnic chauvinism, as witnessed in the recent 2022 national conference of the ANC, where campaigns were mobilised along provincial and, inevitably, ethnic lines.

COMMUNITY AND THE STATE

The community and the state are a critical arena for left thoughts. It is in these spheres that these thoughts take shape and manifest. Importantly, it is the interaction between the state, community and market forces that influences, for example, policy formulation and implementation that have a bearing on the lives of the large and expanding precariat (including a large section of those who are unemployed or in the informal sector and those earning below a living wage) and the broader working class (Satgar, 2020). Pat Horn (in Chapter 8 in this volume) writes about the challenges facing the precariat, especially women, in the informal economy. The struggle against apartheid was rooted in community activism and, to an extent, post-apartheid community struggles have continued along these lines (Desai and Wood, 2003). The high incidence of community protests in South Africa should be understood in the context of socio-economic challenges, which include persistent service delivery issues and increased political contestation (Lancaster, 2018). In Chapter 6, Noel Solani unpacks this issue further with a focused analysis on community grievances.

Discourses and ideas in a class-divided society are shaped by the dominant class. In this regard, the capitalist class controls the means of production and important economic aspects such as 'jobs, prices, production, growth, standard of living, and the economic security of everyone' (Lindblom, 1977: 122–3). Thus, government, as a component of the state, is subject to this control too as its 'officials cannot be indifferent to how well business performs its functions. Depression, inflation, or other economic disasters can bring down a government. A major function of government, therefore, is to see to it that business perform their tasks' (Lindblom, 1977: 122–3). Although the state remains a contested terrain, it is the capitalist class that has the upper hand since 'business corporations wield disproportionate influence over the state and, therefore, over the nature of democratic outcomes' (Held, 2006: 171). However, in the South African context, this must take into consideration the role of the black aspirant bourgeoisie – the 'capitalists without capital'. This stratum was part of the nationally oppressed majority and requires financial assistance from the state and the white-dominated private sector (Southall, 2007: 75). Thus, how it relates to and perceives the state is different from that of the historically big corporations.

However, the role of the state in relation to the community must be articulated in a much more nuanced manner in relation to capital. The state is not class neutral but has often been used to impose the interests of the dominant ruling class. To do this, the state requires legitimacy in the eyes of society as a whole. In South Africa, this has meant attempting (only partially successfully) to expand both the monopoly capitalist and petite bourgeois classes to include sections of the black population.

Engels (1875) characterised the state as a product of society, which at a certain stage of development admitted that it had

> become entangled in an insoluble contradiction with itself, that it is cleft into irreconcilable antagonism, classes with conflicting economic interests, might not consume themselves and society in sterile struggle, a power seemingly standing above society became necessary for the purpose of moderating the conflict, of keeping it within the bounds of "order"; and this power, arisen out of society, but placing itself above it, and increasingly alienating itself from it, is the state (cited in Draper, 2011: 252).

Therefore, the left thoughts inspired by Mzala's Marxist–Leninist analysis are relevant when grappling with the plethora of challenges facing society. Many contemporary scholars, such as Sam Matiase in Chapter 5, locate the state at the centre of the resolution of many crises facing the country. Matiase calls for 'a robust, state-led developmental path' to be central in economic development. Capitalism, as Alex Mohubetswane Mashilo postulates in Chapter 7, constitutes the principal contradiction to economic and broader social transformation and development in South Africa. Thus, building a developmental state banking sector, for example, is an imperative.

THE GLOBAL WORLD

Progressive left thoughts occur in a context of a hegemonic global capitalist system that has reproduced various socio-economic challenges for the Global South, a point that Gunnett Kaaf (Chapter 9 in this volume) argues is one of the major challenges facing the Left in contemporary social reality. Hence Bernard Dubbeld's injunction in Chapter 10 that a more robust reading of capital is urgent as a new starting point for the engagement with capitalism. Indeed, capitalism has proven to be robust and agile in reinventing itself. This system constantly evolves and in the 20th century, for example, it reached the 'imperialist stage' characterised by, among others, the concentration of production and the creation of monopolies, the creation of financial capital, the export of capital, the formation of international monopolist capitalist associations, and the completion of the territorial division of the whole world among the biggest capitalist powers (Lenin, 1999: 8).

Not only did imperialism rely on a commitment to uneven economic and political development, but in order to achieve this, it also aggressively expanded through the creation of empires and colonies, with leading Western powers forming alliances and launching fierce struggles that culminated in the two world wars. Within this context, South Africa also had to contend with colonialism of a special type (apartheid) after 1910 when the Union of South Africa was formed (SACP, 1962), the features of which persist to this day. It was on the back of this reality that the national democratic and communist movements were formed globally. These movements, such as the ANC and SACP in South Africa, drew from the international solidarity of similar movements. Although the ANC characterised the adversary as an oppressive white minority, the SACP considered it to be imperialism (Radebe, 2022). This was the genesis, in the South African context, of the concept of the national democratic revolution, which includes elements of both national and class struggles, set against an international backdrop.

Of course, imperialism continues to undergo strategic shifts and in the 1980s, for example, it shifted to neoliberal capitalism. The strategic shifts continue, with contemporary capitalism increasingly taking the form of digital or platform imperialism and colonialism. It is primarily for this reason that leftist ideas must interact with global developments. Some scholars have argued that imperialism is not about to go away and that what we are confronted with instead is the emergence of 'neo-imperialism', a new phase of capitalism with similar objectives as previous ones but buttressed by technological advancements as its critical tools of accumulation. Indeed, the characteristics of neo-imperialism (Cheng Enfu and Lu Baolin, 2021) are some of the principal challenges with which the Left must contend. Linked to this are the dangers of ecological challenges due to neoliberal capitalism, as postulated by Rasigan Maharajh and Sigfried Tivana in Chapter 12 in this volume. Indeed, the capitalist production is not only failing but it has also brought the human species to the brink of an existential crisis.

An important phenomenon in today's world, which must be mentioned, is the rise of China as an emerging superpower, even though this has not been dealt with in this book. China is sometimes characterised in the West as an imperialist country eager to exploit developing countries because its influence and economic activities in the developing world have been spreading. However, China and most of the emerging countries with which it has economic ties deny this. China seeks no obvious political control over other developing countries and places no political conditions in its trade, industrial and financial relations with them. Its economic expansion has not involved political domination; its loans have not been given with political conditions such as those attached by the Bretton Woods institutions and individual Western nations with regard to the adoption of neoliberal precepts such as market-oriented reform policies and reduced state influence in the economy. Chinese investment has also assisted developing countries to build their infrastructure when such assistance was not available from the West.

China's influence in the developing world, however, has not been all benign. Its formidable industrial and export capacity has had a harmful impact on the industrial capacities of many countries with weaker economies. Relatively inexpensive Chinese imports have had a negative effect on local manufacturing, which is unable to compete on price and, usually, on sophistication. Chinese products could also have an effect on the establishment or further expansion of various industries in developing markets. While this may constitute uneven power relations, it cannot be classified as imperialism.

Ironically, the rapid rise of China was partly an unforeseen result of Western neoliberalism because its economic reform policies such as trade liberalisation, the elimination or reduction of tariffs and the deregulation of markets radically expanded the market for low-cost Chinese goods (Boas and Gans-Morse, 2009) across the globe. The relationship between China, imperialism and developing countries, including South Africa, still needs more careful study and analysis.

THE BOOK'S STRUCTURE

The issues discussed earlier are precisely why this volume is timely. All its chapters interact and respond to the pertinent question on the importance of left ideas at this juncture.

In Chapter 1, the late Percy Ngonyama argues that South Africa's post-apartheid democratic dispensation has witnessed a lack of unity among the left forces and a deplorable lack of class critique. Ngonyama posits that, unlike in the struggle years when ideologically grounded open debates were led by the likes of Mzala, the post-apartheid period has witnessed a dearth of class analysis of the current neoliberal capitalist system. Ngonyama explores the contemporary relevance and applicability of Mzala's political views as part of the wider project for left thought renewal. He concludes by pointing out that because Mzala was non-sectarian in his approach to politics, the unity of the Left globally was sacrosanct and a prerequisite for him, and therefore the Left should seek to unite and find common ground to wage a successful struggle against neoliberal capitalism.

In Chapter 2, Elaine Unterhalter explores facets of the exile experience of different South Africans who lived in London in the 20th century. She uses this frame to consider what it might illuminate for Mzala's larger body of work on the national question. Unterhalter's chapter gives a preliminary outline of the history of the South African exile community in London and describes some of her personal memories of conversations with Mzala when he lived there in exile in the late 1980s. These memories are contextualised in relation to some of the socio-cultural relationships of the Left in Britain during that period, most notably the connection with the Anti-Apartheid Movement. The forms of relationships developed during political exile are discussed, together with the difficulties and possibilities of overcoming divisions linked with race and class. This chapter examines the implications of these forms of experience for understanding some of the personal and political aspects of exile and solidarity.

Mzala's major writings and his thoughts on the national question are traced and presented in the context of contemporary challenges by Mandla J. Radebe in Chapter 3. Radebe argues that because Mzala grounded the national and colonial question in Marxism–Leninism, this enabled him to delineate the role of capitalism in the nation-formation process that gave rise to modern nations. This, according to Radebe, enabled Mzala to address the race, ethnicity and class question. He concludes by pointing out that Mzala's vision of a truly united South Africa across racial lines has not materialised, mainly due to the inability of the working class, as the motive force of the revolution, to direct the national liberation struggle to its logical conclusion – socialism.

In Chapter 4, Greg Houston and Yul Davids look at Mzala's argument on how the liberation from apartheid would lead irresistibly towards integration of the different 'nations'. Using Mzala's writings, including his articulation of the role of class at the head of the revolution, they examine how the ANC's first transition – democratising state and society, and meeting basic needs – has impacted on the resolution of the national question. They illustrate how national unity has been undermined by the persistence of various 'nationalisms', as well as the unintended consequences of the transformative agenda during the first transition.

Sam Matiase sheds some light on the importance of the future of the Left in South Africa and in the global context in Chapter 5. Matiase considers a wider political context globally, the unmaking of the pre-1994 dawn of democracy, strong and united left alternative politics, the fragmentation of effective and vibrant grass-roots formations, civic movements and civil society organisations as a result of the creep-in of neoliberal politics and the comfort brought about by the statuses of incumbency of the former liberators, who have shed the Cold War era '-ism' and embraced the bourgeois aspirations and way of life. At the centre of the failures to build a sustainable left alternative, argues Matiase, is essentially, the former liberator's inability to resist the temptations of bourgeois aspirations and, consequently, their betrayal of the dream for a different, more egalitarian and socialist South Africa. In this chapter Matiase posits that the jettisoning of the Reconstruction and Development Programme (RDP) in 1996 in favour of the Growth, Employment and Redistribution (GEAR) policy marked a profound shift away from the RDP model of development towards a free market-oriented and full-blown neoliberal policy trajectory.

In Chapter 6, Noel Solani focuses on the dilemma of the post-1994 democratic breakthrough through the lens of a broad survey of community, because the South African national democratic struggle was rooted in community grievances. He posits that it was in local communities that repression was felt most and so the liberation movements mobilised and organised people based on their own grievances and ideas of what type of society they wanted. In particular, Solani examines the Freedom Charter to reflect on community struggles, both before the advent of democracy and in the era of democracy and the new Constitution. This chapter concludes Part 1.

Part 2, 'Community, state and globe: Issues, struggles and the politics of work' begins with Chapter 7, in which Alex Mashilo unpacks the challenges of social and economic development in South Africa from a left perspective. He explores the implications of the apartheid-era articulation of economic directions pursued post-apartheid. Mashilo argues that while acceding to pressure and unbanning liberation organisations in 1990, FW de Klerk outlined a neoliberal policy regime. Drawing on historical and contemporary Marxist thinking, this chapter critiques the formulation and continuation of the neoliberal trajectory post-apartheid, starting with the 1996 imposition of the GEAR economic policy. Mashilo argues that the capitalist system, as well as its neoliberal iteration, is the principal challenge facing economic and social development in South Africa, consistently producing persistent high levels of inequality, unemployment and poverty, among others. To overcome these and other systemic challenges, the chapter identifies the imperatives facing the Left.

Pat Horn in Chapter 8 takes on the challenge of organising the three categories of women workers in the informal economy. She argues that trade unions worldwide face the challenge of either devising strategies for effectively organising workers in the informal economy, or of remaining helpless to prevent the slow attrition of being reduced to very small, weak organisations as their traditional membership base dwindles to almost nothing. This chapter brings insight into how the workers in the informal economy often find themselves having to organise outside of existing legal frameworks, and how their struggles include demands for the establishment of legal and collective bargaining frameworks that would include them. New approaches, already in practice, are presented on tackling both the organisational challenges and the policy challenges, focusing on the three categories of women workers.

The social and economic challenges from a left perspective stem from two phenomena of contemporary social reality in South Africa, argues Gunnett Kaaf in Chapter 9. The first, according to Kaaf, is the deepening crisis of global capitalism and how it manifests on the local scene, both economically and politically. The second is the weakness of the Left to pose a meaningful challenge to a capitalism that is in deep crisis and to push for social transformation, particularly in the countries on the periphery of global capitalism in the Global South. This chapter analyses these two phenomenal challenges separately, after which Kaaf analyses them jointly and considers the dynamic interplay they express.

This is followed by Bernard Dubbeld's Chapter 10 on revisionist Marxism and the reanimating of the critique of capitalism in South Africa. Dubbeld argues that while contemporary left politics has been successful at diagnosing inequalities, has contributed to progressive legislation and shaped South African social life after apartheid, it has been silent in one important respect. In both the formal academy and in public life more generally, the critique of capitalism – once central to anti-apartheid thinking and activism – has receded in prominence and is neglected or even regarded as *passé* in left politics. This chapter, recognising that theoretically, the revisionist Marxism of the 1970s can no longer adequately explain contemporary conditions and that material changes involving the fragmentation of the working class have contributed to this, argues for renewed attention to a Marxian theory of capitalism, albeit based on a focus on value rather than on class. Such a theory, argues Dubbeld, should be adequate to 21st-century social conditions by showing how value generates inequalities, and could contribute to orienting left politics towards a focus on structural transformation.

In Chapter 11, Vladimir Shubin critiques the term 'emerging powers', which he regards as an expression of Eurocentrism. Shubin questions the belief that the bipolar world, which allegedly existed during the 'Cold War', was replaced by a unipolar one on the threshold of the 1990s. Moreover, Shubin questions the traditional history of the Cold War itself, both its beginning and its end. He also considers the correlation between international and domestic policy, with South Africa and Russia as case studies; in particular he questions the possibility of social cohesion in a class society, when the interests of different strata do not coincide. He ends by considering the present and potential cooperation between South Africa and Russia in BRICS (Brazil, Russia, India, China and South Africa).

In Chapter 12, Rasigan Maharaj and Sigfried Tivana deal with ecocide or socialism – the ecological challenges of neoliberal capitalism. They argue that Mzala's legacy, as a fearless revolutionary and critical intellectual, provides the basis on which to recognise aspects of the contemporary climate crisis as fundamentally premised on the colonial subjugation and expropriation of the peoples and territories of southern Africa. Following the work of Mzala, the authors locate the emergence of the ecological catastrophe in the very processes that forged the contours of racial capitalism and the system of apartheid. They utilise a materialist conception of history to focus attention on the articulation between developments within forces of production, the relations of production that serve to extend and expand capital accumulation, and the consequent environmental relationship with the ecology of southern Africa. Maharaj and Tivana conclude with preliminary discussions about the emerging research challenges in transitioning beyond the corrupt, corporate-state-captured and predatory capitalism currently vested and festering in South Africa.

Finally, Robert J. Balfour concludes the book by considering the implications of fundamental Marxist concepts such as 'class' and 'struggle' in the context of changes in society pertaining to, for example, decolonisation, feminism, and the development of new forms of labour, not always formally part of the formal economy. He further considers insights gained from the book for the revitalisation of leftist thinking, theoretical turns in which the post-human features more prominently in the future of sustainable life on the planet, and the need for new alliances and reorganisation among unemployed, informal and formal organisations.

REFERENCES

Boas, T.C. and Gans-Morse, J. (2009). 'Neoliberalism: From new liberal philosophy to anti-liberal slogan', *Studies in Comparative International Development*, 44(2): 137–61.

Bown, C.P. and McCulloch, R. (2007). 'US trade policy toward China: Discrimination and its implications', in P.A. Petri and S.J. La Croix (eds). *Challenges to the Global Trading System: Adjustment to globalization in the Asia Pacific region*. London: Routledge, pp. 58–82.

Condon, M. (2012). 'China in Africa: What the policy of non-intervention adds to the Western development dilemma', *PRAXIS: The Fletcher Journal of Human Security*, (27): 5–25.

Desai, A. and Wood, G. (2003). 'We are the poors: Community struggles in post-apartheid South Africa', *Labour*, (52): 332.

Draper, H. (2011). *Karl Marx's Theory of Revolution III*, Vol. 2. Delhi: Aakar Books for South Asia.

Edwards, L. and Jenkins, R. (2015). 'The impact of Chinese import penetration on the South African manufacturing sector', *The Journal of Development Studies*, 51(4): 447–63.

Enfu, C. and Baolin, L. (2021). 'Five characteristics of neo-imperialism building on Lenin's Theory of Imperialism in the twenty-first century', *Monthly Review: An Independent Socialist Review*, 73(1): 22–58.

Fuchs, C. (2019). *Nationalism on the Internet: Critical theory and ideology in the age of social media and fake news*. London: Routledge.

Gevisser, M. (2007). *Thabo Mbeki: The dream deferred.* Johannesburg: Jonathan Ball Publishers.

Held, D. (2006). *Models of Democracy.* Cambridge: Polity Press.

Lancaster, L. (2018). 'Unpacking discontent: Where and why protest happens in South Africa', *South African Crime Quarterly*, (64), 29–43.

Lenin, V.I. (1999). *Imperialism: The highest stage of capitalism.* Sydney: Resistance Books.

Lindblom, C.E. (1977). *Politics and Markets: The world's political-economic systems.* New York: Basic Books.

Mkandawire, T. (2009). 'From the national question to the social question', *Transformation: Critical Perspectives on Southern Africa*, 69(1), 130–60.

Mzala, J.N. (1988). *Gatsha Buthelezi: Chief with a double agenda.* London: Zed Books.

Nzimande, B. (2007). 'The ethos of Black Economic Empowerment', in X. Mangcu, G. Marcus, K. Shubane and A. Hadland (eds). *Visions of Black Economic Empowerment.* Johannesburg: Jacana Media, pp. 180–87.

Radebe, M.J. (2020). *Constructing Hegemony: The South African commercial media and the (mis)representation of nationalisation.* Pietermaritzburg: University of KwaZulu-Natal Press.

Radebe, M.J. (2022). *The Lost Prince of the ANC: The life and times of Jabulani Nobleman 'Mzala' Nxumalo.* Johannesburg: Jacana Media.

Satgar, V. (2020). 'The South African precariat, COVID-19 and #BIGNOW', *Global Labour Journal*, 11(2): 173–77.

Southall, R. (2007). 'Ten propositions about black economic empowerment in South Africa', *Review of African Political Economy*, 34(111): 67–84.

South African Communist Party (SACP). (1962). 'The Road to South African Freedom. Programme adopted at the Fifth National Conference of the Communist Party held inside the country', in *South African Communists Speak: Documents from the history of the South African Communist Party 1915–1980.* London: Inkululeko Publications.

Webster, E., Pampallis, K., Mawbey, J. and Cronin, J. (eds). (2017). *The Unresolved National Question in South Africa: Left thought under apartheid and beyond.* New York: New York University Press.

PART 1: MZALA AND THE NATIONAL QUESTION

ONE

RADICAL LEFT THOUGHT REVIVAL: MZALA'S VIEWS AND THEIR APPLICABILITY IN CONTEMPORARY SOUTH AFRICA

Percy Ngonyama

INTRODUCTION

Jabulani Nobleman Nxumalo (henceforth referred to by his most distinguished pseudonym,[1] 'Mzala') has been gone for over 30 years. This esteemed theoretician and prolific writer, member of the African National Congress (ANC) and the South African Communist Party (SACP), and outstanding soldier of uMkhonto we Sizwe (MK), succumbed to illness at a London hospital on 22 February 1991. His body was repatriated to South Africa for burial in his hometown of eNgotshe, Louwsburg, in northern KwaZulu-Natal, as per his wish.

At his funeral, a young Billy Masetlha, representing the African

---

1   Mzala wrote under a number of pseudonyms, including Madoda Tshawe, Ngacambaza Khumalo, Khumalo Migwe and Jabulani Mkhatswa, to mention but a few.

National Congress Youth League (ANCYL), underlined Mzala's unparalleled gallantry and intellectual prowess to more than 1 000 attendees. He called on the mourners and the remaining cadres to emulate Mzala's example and continue the fight: 'Let a thousand Mzalas pick up his spear and march on.'

OR Tambo, the president of the ANC, also used the analogy of the spear in a written message: 'Mzala was a soldier and a scholar. We will pick up his spear and march on to total liberation' (Mtshali, 1991). Speaking in such militaristic terms was common on the passing of a soldier or activist within the context of the ongoing struggle – political, armed and otherwise. Successive speakers lauded Mzala and his selfless contribution to the fight for freedom.

The list of speakers included Geraldine Fraser-Moleketi, who represented the SACP, and Vusi Mavimbela and Shakes Cele, who delivered a message from the ANC's Natal Midlands region on behalf of the late Harry Gwala, who had been prevented from attending by ill-health. Mavimbela stressed Mzala's bravery and heroism on covert military operations in Ingwavuma, an aspect of his life that is often overlooked.

Albeit under vastly changed post-apartheid socio-economic and political conditions, these sentiments have been echoed in recent years by former comrades and leading figures in the Tripartite Alliance, including Bonginkosi Nzimande, Jeremy Cronin, Essop Pahad and 'Peter Mayibuye' (Joel Netshitenzhe) – Mzala's fellow 'June 16 detachment' companion and intellectual contemporary. Emphasis has been placed on Mzala's revolutionary ideas and on the need to revisit some of his major works.

This chapter explores the contemporary relevance and applicability of Mzala's political views as part of the wider project for the renewal of left thought. Mzala was a communist in the Marxist–Leninist tradition, and his views, eloquently articulated in his written work, resonate with many who subscribe to radical left-wing politics, within and outside the organisations to which he belonged. In post-apartheid South Africa, Mzala's name is often mentioned in deliberations about alternatives to the dominant free-market economic model and in arguments for a policy rethink.

Mzala passed away when negotiations for a democratic

transition were in full swing. Contrary to some assertions, Mzala was never vehemently opposed to talks, but he maintained strong views on this route to a solution to the South African racial situation. His passing at such a critical stage of the revolution, at the age of just 35 years, robbed the movement of one of its sharpest young minds. He was an internationalist in every respect, and tributes poured in from different parts of the world. In a message of condolence, the Philippines Communist Party described Mzala as a major 'shaper of Marxist–Leninist thought' (Mtshali, 1991).

Mzala may be gone, but he is certainly not forgotten. There is an extensive archive of his work that not only interrogates issues from within the context of political and historical developments during his lifetime, but also combines a prognosis for a post-apartheid society. It is from this, and from talking with those who knew him, that we can attempt to deduce, in an informed manner, how he would have reacted to the current South African situation.

Mzala, like others who were active in the struggle, in exile and in the underground structures, never lost sight of the main demands of the liberation movement and the nature of the society they were fighting to achieve. The foundations of a post-apartheid South Africa – political and economic – were always present in the exchanges on struggle theory and tactics. During the struggle, activists were always very mindful of what a post-apartheid government should guard against. As early as 1981, Mzala (writing as Madoda Tshawe) sounded a caution to 'the government in waiting', which he expected would be led by the ANC: 'You cannot feed the masses with political slogans when they are starving; they will be used against the new government or perhaps start complaining: the Boers were better than this new government' (Tshawe, 1981a).

This reflection formed part of a much broader examination of the 'national question' and a critique of 'post-independence decadence and narrow bourgeois nationalism' (Tshawe, 1981b). He argued that black people were oppressed as a nation under apartheid, but among the oppressed, there were those who harboured 'bourgeois interests'. After more than two decades of democracy, we have witnessed a number of the formerly oppressed benefitting from 'empowerment' deals. Many politically well-connected people have managed to amass wealth through a patronage network and this has not 'trickled down' to the masses. There is no evidence to suggest that these beneficiaries reward those in their employ any better than before or create decent working conditions, or render adequate and more affordable services to the public. Unwittingly or otherwise, they have become the new oppressors, sometimes in collaboration with their apartheid counterparts.

For a long time, the ANC refuted any suggestion that it had capitulated to capital interests and that its leaders in government and business had gone astray and jettisoned the core values of the struggle. For a variety of reasons, including pervasive infighting and jostling for positions within the organisation, a debate has ensued around this issue. It is now common for senior leaders to speak openly of the unbecoming conduct of some of their comrades. Various internal policy documents and official reports have bemoaned the 'rot', which has manifested in self-enrichment, corruption, arrogance and downright indifference to the plight of the poor. A few days before the ANC's 5th National Policy Conference in 2017, the then secretary-general, Gwede Mantashe, issued a very scathing 'diagnostic' report about the delinquent conduct of some ANC cadres and 'deployees' (Whittles, 2017).

Earlier, in 2006, the deputy general-secretary of the SACP at the time, Jeremy Cronin, denounced the 'foreign tendencies', and the errant behaviour that had infested the movement. Invoking Mzala, he said:

> Government and Party leadership gradually became alienated from the ordinary working people; they formed an elite that ignored the opinions and needs of ordinary people. From the side of the leadership there came the propaganda of success, notions of everything going according to plan, while on the side of the working people there was passivity and disbelief in the slogans being proclaimed by the leadership … the leadership organised pompous campaigns and the celebration of numerous anniversaries. Political life became a move from one anniversary celebration to another (Cronin, 2006).

In this case, Mzala was observing the disintegration in the former Soviet Union. The situation resulted in what Mikhail Gorbachev described as the 'credibility gap' – everything that was proclaimed from the platforms and printed in the newspapers was put in question by the public (Majola, 1988: 96). This quote bears a resemblance to Frantz Fanon's commentary on the conduct of former liberation movements and revolutionaries after independence. Fanon's work on the decolonisation process and postcolonialism is selectively quoted, particularly by bourgeois nationalists. Ahead of the highly contested 52nd ANC conference in Polokwane, Ronald Suresh Roberts disingenuously argued in his pro-Thabo Mbeki book (2007) that the former president was an 'anti-imperialist' Fanonist. This equates to a gross misreading of Fanon's work.

At the time, Mbeki was the head of a government that bore all the characteristics of neoliberalism, with dire consequences for the poor and the working class in general. Fanon (1963: 166) is clear:

> In spite of his frequently honest conduct, the leader, as seen objectively, is the fierce defender ... of the national bourgeoisie and the ex-colonial companies. During the struggle for liberation, the leader awakened the people and promised them a forward march, heroic and unmitigated. Today, he uses every means to put them to sleep and, three or four times a year, asks them to remember the colonial period and to look back on the long way they have come since then.

Worldwide, institutes, centres, foundations and museums dedicated to the memories of historical and revolutionary figures have become common. The Mzala Nxumalo Centre for the Study of Southern African Society, officially launched at the end of 2015, is intended to honour the legacy of Mzala through research on a variety of social issues from a radical left perspective. It also initiates public events to honour Mzala and discuss his revolutionary ideas, including his interrogation of the 'national question', his favourite subject matter and the topic for his unfinished doctoral thesis. Mzala's 'non-racial' position on the national question was in line with the movement's policies, but his stance was radical in the sense that it incorporated an anti-capitalist element. He painstakingly engaged with the concepts of 'race', 'self-determination', 'ethnicity' and 'nation', while not overlooking the importance of 'internationalism' and international proletarian solidarity.

Mzala became an active writer in the late 1970s, a few years after arriving in exile, until the early 1990s. His activism and intellectualism need to be contextualised, historically and politically, and acknowledged. He lived and wrote during a different conjuncture, politically and economically, and his works were read not only nationally, but also on the continent and globally. In addition to the enormous written record that he left behind, his conversations with his contemporaries in academic and political circles, as well as his family and friends, are useful sources and points of reference on his views about events at various periods of his short but productive life. Moreover, transcripts of interviews with Mzala reveal more about the major influences on him and the development of his political ideas. His writing was intended to stimulate debate and contribute to ongoing dialogue on a wide range of topical issues within the movement. Throughout the 1980s, he wrote extensively on the concept of 'insurrection' and the 'people's war'. These were topical and at the centre of debate at this stage of the revolution.

During his troubled stay in Swaziland, around the time of the signing of the 'non-aggression pact' between Mbabane and Pretoria, he managed to infiltrate himself into South Africa for a series of military assignments in Ingwavuma, Natal, which resulted in a number of arrests by the Swazi authorities from the early to mid-1980s. Based on this experience and the groundbreaking developments in South Africa, which included the formation of the United Democratic Front (UDF) and the launch of the Congress of South African Trade Unions (COSATU), he coined the phrase 'cooking the rice inside the pot', a theoretical and tactical evaluation of the progression of the struggle. This phrase became synonymous with his 'insurrectionist' stance and ideas of 'arming the people' for a revolutionary takeover of power.

Joel Netshitenzhe vividly remembers the 'rice and pot'

debate and Mzala's central role in it. This first-hand experience is what sets apart revolutionaries of Mzala's days apart from today's self-styled 'revolutionaries', who fantasise and engage in 'revolutionary phrase mongering' in the comfort of their bourgeois surroundings, and adopt populist phrases in their discourse that are not grounded in any ideology. Mzala's analysis was based on personal experience at the frontlines of the struggle and on extensive archival research, and not on innuendo and speculation.

Years later, from the mid-1980s when it became clear that South Africa's political problems would have to be resolved through negotiation and not 'armed insurrection', Mzala the pragmatist shifted focus and began to engage critically with the idea of negotiation and what the liberation movement should seek to achieve at the bargaining table. His stance did not differ from the ANC's principled position of the possibility of negotiating with the regime.[2] He and others, nonetheless, remained highly sceptical of the regime's intentions for a variety of valid reasons, including the fact that, with resistance escalating, the Botha regime adopted the policy of 'Total Strategy' against what it considered to be a 'Total Onslaught'. This found brutal expression in political assassinations, large-scale detentions and a series of states of emergency.

Changes in the political environment, brought about by the 1994 breakthrough, had implications for the former liberation movement and its cadres who came to govern the country, as this meant that they were no longer 'full-time' freedom fighters. The transition from apartheid to democracy saw a decline in radical left thinking. Reformist, liberal and right-wing commentary dominated the political space and the former cadres enjoyed hegemony on the policy direction of the government.

In the months leading up to the 2017 ANC elective conference, some in the governing party, including very senior government officials, spoke of Radical Economic Transformation (RET) and misappropriated concepts that, arguably, fell within the left political realm. After more than two decades of bourgeois

---

2   The ANC put forward a number of preconditions for negotiations, including the unconditional release of all political prisoners, the lifting of the state of emergency and the return of exiles.

democracy, this should be seen as an acknowledgement of failure. Many on the left considered this to be mere populist rhetoric aimed at garnering popular support in the ANC leadership race.

'Radical', from a left perspective, means getting to the root causes of issues and a complete overhaul of the existing structure. Mzala would have been at the forefront of such an engagement, and exchanges on this and other dominant phenomena in the South African political discourse. He was always willing to engage and would have been disappointed to see the current divisions. Mzala was one of the 'young lions' and he remains an inspiration to many young scholars and intellectuals. How many in the current generation of young activists even bother to read alternative political texts?

Mzala never lived to see the birth of the 'new' South Africa, but he wrote extensively, from an anti-capitalist Marxist–Leninist standpoint, on what a post-apartheid society should look like. In all his work and in one-on-one discussions, Mzala always incorporated a class element, which distinguishes him from 'nationalist' thinkers. Apartheid and colonialism are gone, but their legacy looms large across every sphere of society. In an attempt to deal with this legacy, successive post-apartheid administrations have devised a succession of transformative policies. Arguably, these have either not been successful or have not gone far enough. But the poor have not been docile. Amazing political agency has been demonstrated in renewed militant, community-based struggles for better living conditions, and in demands for access to the now-commodified basic necessities. In some cases, formidable movements have emerged to fight for access to adequate basic needs. Although many of these are not left-wing movements in the radical neoclassical sense, they do call for alternative approaches to economics that consider the aspirations of the people, and policies that put the interests of the marginalised before profit.

During the struggle, a culture of intellectualism was encouraged and it flourished against the backdrop of a well-coordinated 'cadre development' programme. Political education classes, which were at the centre of the theoretical and political development of young comrades, both within and outside the country, disappeared with the dawn of democracy. A wide variety of topics relating to the struggle had been covered in the now-defunct lessons, including the histories of the liberation movement and world revolutions. Essop Pahad, a veteran of the SACP, attributed this absence of political education to the fact that former liberation fighters are now in government departments, in parliament and in the private sector, and have little or no time to organise and conduct political education classes.

Concomitantly, there has been a conspicuous dearth of any analysis of the many failures of the post-1994 dispensation, euphemistically referred to as 'challenges' in elite bourgeois circles. Moreover, in some instances, certain elements have demonstrated utter disregard for the long-standing tradition of allowing dissenting voices – in Maoist terms referred to as enabling 'a thousand flowers to bloom'. Comments about Westernised 'clever blacks', made by then president Jacob Zuma to the House of Traditional Leaders before the 53rd ANC elective conference in Mangaung, were not favourably received in the intellectual sphere: 'Even some Africans, who become too clever, take a position, they become the most eloquent in criticising themselves about their own traditions and everything' (quoted in Pillay, 2014).

Such comments act as a diversion from any critical issues that are raised and are a way of discouraging a critique of the limitations of the government's free market-orientated economic development model and widespread corruption within government and the public sector. Mzala's former comrades are adamant that he would never have condoned such behaviour. He would have spoken out against it, irrespective of where it emanated. He was known for his fearless demeanour and was never scared to challenge any leadership or his peers.

Brian Bunting (1991), a late veteran of the SACP, described Mzala as ever 'loyal to the movement', but critical of bureaucracy, with 'no patience for compromise and fudge'. As a matter of urgency, the left needs to once again produce such true revolutionary intellectuals to counter the neoliberal cultural and political hegemony, to interrogate the character of the post-apartheid state and its implications for the masses, and formulate fresh theories. A malaise has crept into the movement and 'foreign' tendencies have been decried by many stalwarts of the struggle. Increasingly, members are becoming more loyal to individuals and factions than the movement and its struggle values.

Commenting on this sad state of affairs, Mpho Nxumalo, wife, comrade and confidante of the late Mzala, said: 'Mzala was a passionate member of the movement'.[3] Netshitenzhe also commented on Mzala's principled demeanour and said that the movement needed more people of his calibre to help it deal with many of its current challenges, which pose a threat to its survival and influence within society. Jeremy Cronin commented along similar lines and said that 'thousands of Mzalas' are required to work in government departments and state enterprises.

As alluded to earlier, throughout the struggle and at various phases of the resistance, the movement vigorously engaged with a number of tactical and theoretical aspects. For example, in the 1970s to 1980s, the debate centred on the issue of 'insurrection' and the 'revolutionary seizure of political power', a debate that was informed by in-depth analyses of the conditions and developments on the ground in South Africa. The internal resistance was gaining momentum and the apartheid state was increasingly unable to exert full authority over many parts of the country – the 'liberated zones' where organs of people's power had filled the vacuum. This 'revolutionary state' meant that the seizure of power by the oppressed masses was on the horizon, and the exiled movement, working with internal forces, would play the 'vanguardist' role in moving the struggle forward. By the late 1980s, however, the conditions had changed and the dominant theme became negotiations and this became the focus of the struggle intelligentsia.

Mzala made various contributions to these discussions, and these appear under different pseudonyms in the publications of the liberation movement and in academic journals. Proper theorisation and tactical considerations will also emanate from a correct analysis

---

3 Input from the floor at the Future of the Left conference hosted by the Mzala Nxumalo Centre for the Study of South African Society, 8–10 June 2017.

and reading of our present socio-economic and political conditions.

Mzala was very passionate about the 'national question'. This is still a topic for debate nearly 30 years into the new South Africa and more than two decades since Mzala passed away. Within the ANC, views on specific details differed, but there was never disagreement about the development programme for economic and political transformation in a post-apartheid era. The 1955 Freedom Charter was the undisputed blueprint for socio-economic development in a post-apartheid society. Mzala wrote extensively on the Charter, as he saw it as the first step towards the creation of a just society without racial prejudice, where every citizen, in a unitary state enjoyed basic rights and freedom – the antithesis of the 'Balkanisation' of the racist Pretoria regime. It was envisaged that this would create the necessary conditions for the advancement to socialism – a process in which the SACP would play a leading role – the so-called 'second stage' of the revolution.

Following drawn-out negotiations for constitutional change, the movement to which Mzala had dedicated much of his short life was awarded an opportunity, by the majority of South Africans, to govern and bring about a 'better life for all'. In the 1994 elections, the ANC campaigned on the Reconstruction and Development Programme (RDP), which many believed was conceived along similar lines to the Freedom Charter. In 1996, two years into democracy, the RDP was ditched for a neoliberal programme, the Growth, Employment and Redistribution Programme (GEAR), of which the left – including some within the governing alliance – was critical. It was premised on the trickle-down effect of the free market, and critics on the left blamed it for the massive retrenchments, worsening poverty and the lack of service delivery that followed. Sadly – unlike the cultural behaviour during the struggle – this macro-economic policy was imposed from the top, and it was made clear by the new, bourgeois political elite that no discussion would be entertained. Mzala would have been extremely disappointed, not only by this economic policy choice, but also by its unilateral imposition by his former organisation.

The tendency is to blame Jacob Zuma's leadership for 'unintellectualism' and intolerance to open debate. However, the top-down imposition of unpopular policies and suppression of debate began before Zuma became president of the ANC and the country.

Ten years after the introduction of GEAR, government officials argued that there were certain hindrances to the achievement of its key projections and came up with the ambitious Accelerated and Shared Growth Initiative for South Africa (AsgiSA). The latest programme promised to halve poverty and unemployment by 2014, by achieving a 6 per cent annual growth rate between 2010 and 2014, thus meeting the United Nation's Millennium Development Goals (MDGs). The 2010 FIFA World Cup, to be held in South Africa, was supposed to be a major catalyst for this (GCIS, 2010). To achieve these goals, the government launched the Joint Initiative for Priority Skills Acquisition (Jipsa) in 2006 to identify solutions to the major skills shortages constraining the country's ability to meet its economic growth objectives. Suffice it to say that none of these projections were achieved.

During Mbeki's tenure, there was a point at which the economy was growing at just over 5 per cent per annum. Despite the excitement that this generated in elite spheres, this growth did not 'trickle down' to the majority. Nonetheless, with a great degree of complacency, Mbeki (2005) wrote in his weekly column on the ANC's website: 'Is the glass half-full or half-empty?' Certainly, for the majority facing unemployment and destitution, and denied access to life-saving AIDS drugs during an era of AIDS denialism, the glass was undeniably 'half empty'.

In an admission of the failure of these past initiatives to improve the lives of the poor, the Zuma government came up with its own programme: the National Development Plan (NDP), which promised to deliver a 'better life for all' by 2030, based on an expected 6 per cent annual growth rate. This policy has been criticised by many on the left. While it was touted as new and even revolutionary in some alliance circles, it represented no genuine departure from past initiatives premised on the free-market, neoliberal conception of socio-economic development. This type of thinking sees accelerated capitalist growth as the panacea for societal woes.

Just before being ousted from COSATU, the National Union of Metalworkers of South Africa (NUMSA) had voiced serious misgivings about the latest 'neoliberal' macro-economic policy, labelling it a 'right-wing deviation of the Freedom Charter' (NUMSA, 2013). During the 2015 '#FeesMustFall' campaign, militant students, adopting the language of the left, called for access to free quality higher education, which, they argued, was provided for in the Freedom Charter. This call by the student movement elicited much debate and was rejected by some leading figures within the governing party, who argued that nowhere in the Charter was there a provision for free tertiary education.

This has reinvigorated the debate around the Freedom Charter and its clauses, most notably in relation to land redistribution and access to adequate education. Always ready to engage in debate, Mzala would have welcomed this and sought to actively engage, from a radical and revolutionary point of view, with the various dominant positions on the issue. In one of his articles, Mzala noted that the Freedom Charter was not a socialist document, but a revolutionary one, in the sense that its implementation would require the complete overhaul of the prevailing race-based system of rule and the dismantling of the apartheid state apparatus. This would allow for a new, unified post-apartheid nation to emerge.

Mzala saw the Freedom Charter as the first step towards a socialist South Africa. Outside the ANC, other elements of the liberation movement were critical of the Charter and its 'non-racial' character. In the late 1950s, the Pan-Africanist Congress (PAC) separated from the ANC to register its discontent with the adoption of the Charter. On the eve of its 30th anniversary, protestors representing mainly Black Consciousness organisations, under the banner of the New Forum, gathered in Hammanskraal, Pretoria, to adopt the Manifesto of the People of Azania – an alternative document to the Freedom Charter. Mzala published a series of opinion articles in response to these political developments at home, under the theme 'The Freedom Charter is our lodestar'. These were highly critical of the forum and its 'alternative' to the Freedom Charter. Disagreements between individuals from different political traditions over the Charter still continue in South Africa today.

THE NATIONAL QUESTION: RACE AND CLASS PERSPECTIVE

In one of his polemical articles, Mzala asserts that no other issue has been more central to debate within the liberation movement than the national question – particularly within the left-leaning sections of the liberation movement. From the late 1920s, the SACP acknowledged the link between race and class in South Africa and sought to create the necessary connections between the struggle against racial oppression and class oppression, resulting in the adoption of the 'Black Republic Thesis'. The national question continues to be at the centre of debate in the democratic era. As in the past, there are diverse opinions on its exact nature and its resolution, and on concepts such as nation, race and ethnicity.

Mzala is famous for his book, *Gatsha Buthelezi: Chief with a double agenda*, published in 1988. For several reasons, it became a useful propaganda tool for both the forces of liberation and those aligned with Buthelezi. For the former, it was proof of the chief's collaborationist position. For the latter, it reinforced notions that members of the ANC were hell-bent on slandering the good name of Buthelezi because they were jealous of him. However, it is useful to view the book not as some kind of obsession with Buthelezi, but as part of Mzala's long-standing intellectual interest in the national question. He had begun writing and publishing analytical articles on solutions to the South African situation in the late 1970s. These articles and the book were aimed at stimulating and contributing to the debate on topical issues within the movement.

About a decade before the publication of the monumental *Gatsha Buthelezi* (1988), Mzala published some critical polemical pieces about Buthelezi and his use of ethnic chauvinism and Zulu nationalism for political mobilisation. The captivating subtitle of the book emanated from Mzala's argument that Buthelezi had a 'double agenda' – he claimed to be anti-apartheid, yet was actively involved in perpetuating the racist system by participating in its administration. Today, it could be argued that the former liberation movement has its own double agenda, in the sense that it condemns globalisation and imperialism, but participates in organisations driving these processes on a global scale, including the International Monetary Fund, the World Bank, the World Trade Organization and the World Economic Forum. Moreover, the policies they have devised and are ardently implementing are in compliance with the fiscal discipline provisions of imperialist global capitalism.

Unfortunately, ethnicised and racialised politics has once again reared its ugly head within our society as a result of competition for scarce resources. There has been a tendency to blame minorities, other ethnic groups and foreigners for poverty, crime, unemployment and other socio-economic woes, instead of making the necessary connection with the pro-rich economic model that is fuelling these problems (Hassim *et al*, 2008). These divisions are a stumbling block for the proletarian unity and solidarity that Mzala propagated. He argued that the working class should unite against their common enemy, regardless of their background. Internationalism, strives for the unity of the proletariat as a class, because their material conditions and interests coincide – irrespective of national growth (Mzala, 1988: 17–18). Mzala was fully aware that 'narrow nationalism' was not just a phenomenon among 'bourgeois nationalists', as the working class could also demonstrate these tendencies: 'Theoretically speaking, the successful struggle against exploitation requires that the working class be free of narrow nationalism' (Mzala, 1988: 18).

Even within the governing party, with its proud traditions of non-racism and democracy, certain elements have uttered statements that stand to only reinforce racism, xenophobia and ethnicity (*TimesLIVE*, 2017), and political discourse has become riddled with divisive racial and ethnic stereotypes. Misperceptions that Africans, or particular ethnic groups, are more important than others and have shared destinies, pose fresh threats to notions of unity and social cohesion. Mzala saw Inkatha's 'tribal orientation and origin' as constituting a grave danger to the 'national unity of the oppressed' and the exploited classes, and a stumbling block to the genuine resolution of the national question. Mzala, writing as Ngacambaza Khumalo, similarly considered that the 'narrow, chauvinist and ethnocentric' nature of Inkatha's character undermined the national unity advocated by the liberation movement. He also argued that the belief that the Zulu people were an important group around which national unity should be forged, was similar to the Afrikaner belief that they were a 'chosen people' of God. He considered Inkatha's 'militant and pseudo revolutionary' stance to be counter-revolutionary and it stood to further complicate the future resolution of the national question (Khumalo, 1978: 97).

Mzala was also critical of the Pan-Africanist and Nationalist views on the national question, which he saw as 'exclusionary' and based on the false notion that certain groups shared similar aspirations. His main criticism was that these tended to ignore the class interests within groups. He argued that the black proletariat endured oppression as part of the 'oppressed nation' but was also exploited under the racially based capitalist system, which relied on their unskilled cheap labour. He asserted:

> The correction of economic injustice lies at the very core of solving the national question. It is thus understandable that the doubly oppressed and doubly exploited black working class should constitute a distinct and reinforcing layer in the national liberation struggle. Furthermore, it is the need to ensure that the liberation struggle contains a strongly organised working class that constitutes the principal reason behind the alliance of the ANC and SACP ... At the same time, we must strictly distinguish from the tendency towards national exclusiveness which is a drive by the bourgeois elite amongst the oppressed to take over the role of the new exploiter (Mzala, 1988: 17).

We are already witnessing elements of this, where 'white capitalism' is regarded with disdain and the black capitalist class is seen as inherently well-meaning and capable of addressing and understanding South Africa's socio-economic woes. While there may appear to be contestations between the exploiters from different racial groupings, ultimately the aim of both is to increase profit at the expense of the poor, the majority of whom are black, given our well-documented recent history of dispossession and racial oppression. In the months leading up to the 2010 FIFA World Cup held in South Africa, former national chairperson of the Young Communist League, David Masondo, made this point very clear (Ngonyama, 2010: 168–86).

Mzala was a staunch believer in internationalism and international working-class solidarity, which distinguishes his politics from that of bourgeois nationalists. He argued that the working class should seek to forge links with other working-class individuals, even beyond their borders, since they had similar aspirations and little connection with their national ruling elites. Under capitalist globalisation, 'international solidarity' has taken on a whole new urgency. Capital and production have become globalised. Solidarity among the 'toilers of the Earth' is now greater than before, and effect should be given to the slogan 'Workers of the world unite'. There are, however, serious obstacles to unity and solidarity. Xenophobia and ethnicity loom large and are beloved by the ruling elite as an effective, yet silent tool to divide and rule.

Mzala saw potential for unity and solidarity in the South African working class, for both blacks and whites. He foresaw this unity as unfolding as follows:

> To have complete trust in white workers, the black workers must be convinced that the white workers are no longer infested with the national chauvinism of such as Arrie Paulus, PW Botha or Magnus Malan and that they place fraternity with black workers above the privileges they obtain from the white bourgeoisie (Mzala, 1988: 18).

This would have been a very controversial statement within the context of politics in the 1980s.

An important pillar of the debate around the national question was the concept of self-determination. In South Africa, a range of views on this emerged. Some saw self-determination as Verwoerdian and bantustan notions of separating the many 'nations' into independent self-governing territories. Writing a few years earlier, Mzala sought to deal with this concept and his take contrasted sharply with that of bantustan and apartheid thinking. He wrote: 'National self-determination does not mean territorial secession, separation, fragmentation or formation of small states. It means the right to self-determination for a single South African nation within the whole of South Africa' (Mzala, 1988: 26). This was a clear critique of apartheid's Balkanisation policies. Mzala distinguished between 'revolutionary nationalism' and 'reactionary nationalism', which he also referred to as 'petty bourgeois national opportunism'.

With the Freedom Charter at the centre of development planning and eradication of the legacy of apartheid and colonialism, he argued that:

> The solution of the national question in South Africa can only proceed from the integration of the two nations, under conditions of total equality, into a single South African nation. The fusion of these nations, it is perceived, will only proceed systematically if the exercise is headed by the working class (Mzala, 1988: 26).

Mzala strongly believed in the power of a united working class and its potential to change things and transform society for the better. That his former comrades, in the seat of government for more than two decades, have not implemented the Freedom Charter to its fullest – yet are conversely the drivers of an extreme, pro-rich version of neoliberal capitalism – would surely make him turn in his grave.

CONCLUSION

I have argued for unity among left forces and deplored the lack of a class critique. There is a common enemy: the neoliberal capitalist system. And as the SACP's song, *Thibela ma bourgeois*, suggests, it is the bourgeoisie that we need to be wary of and not like-minded anti-capitalist formations (Ngonyama, 2006).

Despite the well-documented 'neo-Stalinist' tendencies of some of his comrades, Mzala was non-sectarian in his approach to politics. For him, solidarity among left forces, nationally and globally, in the fight against the inhumane system of capitalism, was sacrosanct and a prerequisite. The left remains fragmented and has failed to evade the demon of sectarianism. This is not just a South African phenomenon. Ideally, the left should seek to unite and find common ground. Moreover, as Italian Marxist Antonio Gramsci argued, the bourgeoisie's hegemony is not only achieved through violence, but also through other factors such as culture, ideology and consciousness. Thus, the left should look to find constructive and practical methods of countering the dominant bourgeois ideology and culture.

Mzala and others were engaged in a struggle to change their world under their inherited material conditions and much analysis and theorisation went into their work. Today, as the left forces seek to transform the current world for the better, they are presented with possibilities and limitations that could be overcome through dialogue and comradeship. New grassroots movements that emerged after the fall of apartheid are waging struggles against neoliberalism, but the vanguard has not been fully supportive of them. However, it is encouraging to see serious discussion about linking up these struggles, and even the possibility of forming a united left, anti-capitalist front. In this situation it is critical to guard against the use of the divide-and-rule tactics of both the old and new bourgeoisie.

As Oliver Tambo and Billy Masetlha said in their tributes to Mzala at his funeral, if we are to achieve any progress in the fight against capitalist domination, a new generation of cadres must pick up the spear that was left behind by Mzala and others in the radical left tradition, and continue the fight for a humane world, where people's basic needs supersede the capitalistic desire for the maximisation of profit at all costs.

REFERENCES

Bunting, B. (1991). 'Death of Mzala Nxumalo'. London: Liberation Archives – University of Fort Hare (LAUFH). LMR/035/0121.

Cronin, J. (2006). 'Blank pages in history should not be allowed: The role of revolutionary intellectuals'. Address given at the 15th anniversary of Mzala's death, Galeshewe, Kimberley, 25 February 2006.

Fanon, F. (1963). *The Wretched of the Earth*. New York: Grove Weidenfeld.

Government Communications and Information System (GCIS). (2010). Africa 2010: Economic Opportunities.

Hassim, S., Kupe, T., Worby, E. and Skuy, A. (eds). (2008). *Go Home or*

Die Here: Violence, xenophobia and the reinvention of difference in South Africa. Johannesburg: Wits University Press.

Khumalo, N. (1978). 'The compromising role of Inkatha', *The African Communist,* 74 (Third Quarter): 94–99.

Majola, S. (1988). 'Perestroika and class struggle: A comprehensive review of Mikhail Gorbachev's book, *Perestroika: New thinking for our country and the World'*, *The African Communist,* 113 (Second Quarter): 91–106.

Mbeki, T. (2005). 'Is the glass half-full or half-empty?' ANC.org.za.

Mtshali, F. (1991). 'Mzala laid to rest'. University of Fort Hare, Liberation Struggle Archives, London Mission (LM), Box 35, Folder 121.

Mzala, J.N. (1988). 'Revolutionary theory on the national question in South Africa', in M. van Diepen (ed.). *The National Question in South Africa.* London: Zed Books.

Ngonyama, P. (2006). 'The Ideological Differences within the Tripartite Alliance: What Now for the Left?' Durban: Centre for Civil Society. Available at: http://ccs.ukzn.ac.za/default.asp?3,28,11,2835 (Accessed 25 April 2023).

Ngonyama, P. (2010). 'The 2010 FIFA World Cup: Critical voices from below', in P. Alegi and C. Bolsman (eds). *South Africa and the Global Game: Football, apartheid and beyond.* London and New York: Routledge, pp. 168–86.

National Union of Metal Workers of South Africa (NUMSA). (2013). 'The National Development Plan: Mixed bag, or downright neoliberal proposals for South Africa?' NUMSA critical analysis and rejection of the NDP. Available at: http://www.numsa.org.za/admin/assets/articles/attachments/00119_the_ndp_mixed_bag_or_do wnright_neoliberal_proposals_for_south_africa1.pdf (Accessed 25 April 2023).

Pillay, V. (2014). 'Seven ways you know you're an African', *Mail & Guardian Online,* 14 October. Available at: mg.co.za/article/2014-10-14-seven-ways-you-know-youre-an-african-according-to-jacob-zuma (Accessed 25 April 2023).

Roberts, R.S. (2007). *Fit to Govern: The native intelligence of Thabo Mbeki.* Johannesburg: STE Publishers.

TimesLIVE (2017). 'You are fuelling Xenophobia', *TimesLIVE,* 17 July.

Available at: https://www.timeslive.co.za/politics/2017-07-17-you-are-fuelling-xenophobia-sahrc-warns-deputy-police-minister/ (Accessed 25 April 2023).

Tshawe, M. (1981a). 'Letter to the Editor', *Sechaba*, 28 June.

Tshawe, M. (1981b). 'The national question', *Sechaba*, 6 June. Available at: http://www.historicalpapers.wits.ac.za/inventories/inv_pdfo/A2675/A2675-4-01-jpeg.pdf (Accessed 25 April 2023).

Whittles, G. (2017). 'Premier League fails to block scathing diagnostic report', *Mail & Guardian Online*, 30 June. Available at: https://mg.co.za/article/2017-06-30-premier-league-fails-to-block-scathing-diagnostic-report-at-policy-conference (Accessed 25 April 2023).

TWO

THE NATIONAL QUESTION AND EXILE: REMEMBERING MZALA IN LONDON

Elaine Unterhalter[1]

In the late 1980s I was working with Mzala (Jabulani Nobleman Nxumalo) and Thozamile Botha for Research on Education in South Africa (RESA) in a small office in London. RESA was a project led by Harold Wolpe, linked to the University of Essex and the African National Congress (ANC). RESA conducted research on education in South Africa, as it was and as we might wish it to be. Our office was partitioned out of a larger suite, rented from the British Defence and Aid Fund for Southern Africa, which later became the Canon Collins Education Trust for Southern Africa (CCETSA). Three desks

---

1   My thanks to Jenni Karlsson for initially asking me to record my recollections of working with Mzala, and to Ireen Dubel, Christabel Gurney, Margaret Ling, Rosa Crawford and Joe Crawford for detailed, in-depth and insightful comments on a draft of this chapter and how to develop the analysis, together with very useful suggestions of further material to consult. The chapter was further developed drawing on material in Mandla Radebe's biography, and I thank him for the chance to see the manuscript before publication. My sincere appreciation to Robert Balfour for encouragement and many useful pointers of ways to develop and deepen the argument.

were squeezed into a tiny corridor of an office, crammed with books, papers and very early computers. There were no windows and as the office was quite close to the main door of the CCETSA office, we were constantly looking up as visitors to CCETSA came and went. It was difficult to work, jammed together in such a small space, so much of the time we talked. The fragments of our discussions give some idea of the lived experience of exile, and of how different the experiences of fellow South Africans were across boundaries of race, class and history. Trying to reach back to that moment, I think of all three of us as positioned on different ledges, with things swirling below and around us, trying to reach across and find words that might create links. But solidity through joint projects needed to be built to hold up the words, the ideas and people they connected. We lacked time to do this or maybe I misunderstood the significance of what Mzala was encouraging me to do with the time we had. Although each of us had come down a different road to that small space, our work and our ideas about it, oriented us to big horizons. I think, sitting together in that windowless office, we tried to make our connection and our actions a bit more substantial, so that the ideas were better anchored in some understanding of what was important to us and why. But the difficulties were enormous.

In this chapter I want to reflect on some of the implications of that attempt to connect, drawing out some of the aspects of exile, and of Mzala's responses to them, that I glimpsed in those interactions through RESA. The discussion is an attempt to explore what some of these experiences of exile might illuminate within Mzala's larger body of work on the national question. I have organised the chapter in three parts. The first section outlines some features of the social and political relationships of the group of South Africans who lived in exile in London from the 1960s to the early 1990s, when many began to return. The second section draws on some of my memories of conversations with Mzala in the late 1980s. It gives a personally inflected flavour of some of the experiences of exile, some of the issues under discussion and some of the perspectives Mzala formulated. In this section I try to contextualise some of these remembered conversations in relation to some of the socio-cultural relationships of the Left in London in the 1980s. The last section attempts to connect the fragments of remembered conversations with Mzala, his thinking about the national question and some analysis of political exile and solidarity.

SOUTH AFRICANS IN EXILE IN LONDON

London has been a centre for political exiles from many countries over centuries. Some areas of London have particular associations with exile groups, and there are plaques on the houses where a number of particularly prominent political exiles lived. These include Karl Marx, who lived in London from 1849 until his death in 1883, first in a very poor area in the centre of the city, home to many immigrant families from other parts of Europe, and later in a more comfortable middle-class area, because of support from Friedrich Engels, whose family owned a factory. Vladimir Lenin also lived in London for stretches between 1902 and 1905, staying in the central areas of the city where tenement housing, small workshops and offices were crowded together. He, like Marx, made use of the British Museum Library, which was centrally located, admitted men and women of all classes to the reading room, and was a warm place to work (Holmes, 2014).

These examples highlight aspects of the peculiar mix of Britain. While it was more liberal than other European countries and allowed political activists to live without imprisonment, it did not prevent spying on or other forms of harassment of political exiles, who were also excluded from certain jobs and educational opportunities. In the 19th century, London was a huge economic and political hub, with probably the largest concentration of capital and military power anywhere in the world. It was a city of vast contrasts and divisions of wealth and poverty. Social separation, marked by class, gender, ethnicity, race and religion, was clearly evident in where people lived, how they socialised, the work they did, and the cultural associations they made. Much of the economy of London was tied to the extensive empire Britain ruled, and this required trained administrators to work within the legal framework of the British Empire in the early decades of the 20th century. Highly educated men from India, such as Jawaharlal Nehru and Muhammad Ali

Jinnah, and Jomo Kenyatta and Seretse Khama from Africa, were brought to London for training. While studying in the heart of the Empire, these men developed many important critiques of Empire, which would emerge in the new post-colonial states they helped to establish.

South Africans coming to London travelled down similar routes of passage, partly connected to the networks of family, friends, faith or work, framed by the Empire, sometimes drawing on links with groups like the Brotherhood Movement, London's black community and left organisations, and partly attracted by the possibilities of education. Some were involved in building associations that critiqued the colonial relationships of the 19th and early 20th centuries, such as the League Against Imperialism and the series of Pan-African conferences that culminated in the 1945 Pan-African Congress in Manchester.

These affiliations formed the backdrop against which a later generation of political exiles from apartheid came to London. In retrospect, in the light of the current inhumane treatment of almost all asylum seekers and refugees seeking to come to the United Kingdom, it seems remarkable how open the British authorities from the 1950s were to the admission of undocumented South Africans, who left illegally or were forced out by banning orders or exit permits. A number were given residence rights although some were known members of the South African Communist Party, and Britain had an anti-communist foreign policy position.

A full history of the different periods of South African migration to the United Kingdom and their connection to one another has not yet been written. There are two historical monographs that analyse some of these processes. Robert Skinner (2010) provides some of the history of the liberal humanitarian antecedents of the Anti-Apartheid Movement (AAM), founded in the 1960s, and some of the connections between political exiles and Christian transnational networks. Mark Israel's study (Israel, 1999), based on interviews with 75 South African political exiles living in London and the south of England, mainly those who arrived in the 1960s and 1970s, charts processes of migration, identity and conflict with the apartheid state. Articles by David Killingray (2009) and Hakim Adi (2012) provide an overview of the range of Pan-African thinkers and political activists that congregated in London, some of whom had important connections with members of the South African exile community. In some ways, partly because of the different demographics under investigation, the connections between the secular political left, in Israel's analysis, the Christian liberal left in Skinner's, and the Pan-African left in Adi's and Killingray's, do not completely mesh, although all were facets of a particular group of South Africans drawn together by a shared view of what they were against. An issue of contemporary relevance is whether and in what ways they were able to examine closely what might divide them, and why and how a range of changing ideas and relationships might shape the kinds of connection that could be made, illuminating some meanings of solidarity.

No overview history of South African exiles in London weaves together the many threads of dislocation, difference, aspiration and adaptation that were part of my recollection of the period that Mzala lived through. Nonetheless, there are substantial sections in a range of biographies, autobiographies and memoirs[2] that distil some of the political, economic, social and cultural activities of the South African exile community from the 1960s to the early 1990s. There are in-depth treatments of some of the social relationships built or put under strain among families and friends (for example, Bernstein, 1994; Suttner, 2003; Slovo, 2004; Altschuler, 2008). The significance of this group of exiles for the formation of the Anti-Apartheid Movement (AAM) and the form of political organisation it developed is highlighted in a substantial body of work (for example, Gurney, 2000; 2009; Skinner, 2009). A number of studies draw out the international networks built up by groups of South African exiles in relation to

---

2 This is a preliminary list of biographies, autobiographies and memoirs of South Africans who lived for a period in London, which provide treatment of the issue of the social, cultural, economic and political relationships associated with exile: Hilda Bernstein, Denis Brutus, Yusuf Dadoo, Barry Feinberg, Ruth First, Barry Gilder, Dennis Goldberg, Adelaide and Walter Hain, Peter Hain, Baruch Hirson, Denis Hirson, Rica Hodgson, Hazel Hutchinson, Paul Joseph, Ronnie Kasrils, Norma Kitson, Deborah Levy, Norman Levy, Miriam Makeba, Hugh Masekela, Bloke Modisane, Thabo Mbeki, Lewis Nkosi, Arthur Nortje, Jabulani Nxumalo, Aziz Pahad, Ronald Segal, Wally Serote, Anthony Sher, Archie Sibeko, Gillian Slovo, Joe Slovo, Oliver and Adelaide Tambo, Ben Turok, Desmond Tutu, Ann Marie and Harold Wolpe, and Donald Woods.

understanding issues such as the politics of sport (Llewellyn and Rider, 2020), the women's movement (Unterhalter, 2000; Manicom, 2016), international communist solidarities (Sapire, 2009; Thorn, 2009), and campaigns against the arms trade (Skinner, 2009; Moraes, 2021). A major focus has been some of the ideas developed about the fragility of ideas of home (Gready, 2003; Clingman, 2013), and the feeling that black South Africans experienced of being outsiders in South Africa under apartheid, a sense amplified and reconstituted in exile (Modisane, 1963; Gready, 1994; Lombardozzi, 2007). A major theme is the physical and symbolic violence associated with exile, which disrupts ideas of time, space, home and belonging (Israel, 1999; Dovey, 2004; Dalamba, 2006; Thorpe, 2020). The articulations formulated or attempted between national and transnational understandings have been looked at mainly in terms of ideas (Dubow, 2017; Bethlehem, 2018; Unterhalter, 2019; Llewellyn and Rider, 2020) rather than the lived experience of these processes, although a number of biographical and autobiographical works bring out how travel, money, hospitality and work opportunities were arranged by transnational networks, connecting communist parties (Joseph, 2019; Radebe, 2022) or cultural industries (Feldstein, 2013). A small body of work looks at how race and the politics of race, anti-colonialism and the diaspora connected with some of the political relationships of South African exiles, leading to strong connections and deep friendships (Israel, 1999; Killingray, 2009; Werbner, 2010; Williams, 2015).

It can be seen that the scholarly work on South African exiles in London highlights that there was not one single exile community, but a constellation of different groupings, loosely held together by a sense of where they had come from, a place of division and oppression, but in which, from different viewpoints, much hope was invested for change. The symbolic and ideal forms of that hope bumped up against material and social relationships in complex ways. Ngonyama (2017: 84) writes that Mzala's perspective on the national question was one where he distinguished between 'narrow nationalism', focused on self-serving processes of accommodation with injustice, and 'revolutionary nationalism', which wove together elements of 'anti-capitalist and internationalist proletarian solidarity'. Radebe (2022) gives a detailed account of how Mzala's ideas were formed and reformed through conversations and writing in the homes and work places of ANC members in London, and how conversations in pubs, at speaking engagements, and over research projects, sparked his interest, leading him to pose probing questions with regard to many facets of the politics of the times. A question I want to consider is which parts of his distinctive position on the national question, which he developed in some of his writings, might have been due to his experience of exile in London, and why? These complexities help to frame some of my recollections of Mzala's location in the setting of the South African exile community in London.

MZALA AND REFLECTIONS ON EXILE

Mzala had a wonderful talking style. His eyes sparkled. He picked up an idea and played on it, like a musical instrument, so our discussions ranged widely. They were not just about the topic we were working on – the politics of apartheid education.[3]

Mzala did not tell me where he had been born, but I knew he knew northern KwaZulu-Natal, where I had worked at the Charles Johnson Memorial Hospital in the early 1970s as an English teacher.[4] I told him about the history of the Nqutu district, which I had researched from historical records for my PhD. He listened and clearly knew a great deal more than I did about the local politics of the area, alliances and land disputes. I have paged through his 1988 book on Gatsha Buthelezi (Mzala, 1988) to see if he had recorded an anecdote that I had told, him about a meeting Buthelezi had attended in July 1974 in Nqutu. I remembered that Buthelezi had shared the

---

3 For some accounts of the RESA project and the work it did, see the biography of Harold Wolpe (Friedman, 2015), chapters in the edited collection on Harold Wolpe's political and intellectual contribution (Reynolds, Fine and Van Niekerk, 2019), and two edited collections with chapters by some of the people who worked on the project (Unterhalter *et al*, 1991; Unterhalter, Wolpe and Botha, 1991).

4 Mzala was born in the hospital at Dundee in Northern Natal, his family home was at Ngoje, and his primary schooling at Louwsburg (Radebe, 2022), all areas not too far from Charles Johnson Memorial Hospital.

podium with a local official from the Bantu Affairs Department, and how incongruous this had seemed given Buthelezi's persona in the press at the time as a spokesperson against apartheid. It seemed to me the attention of the people at the meeting was fractured, not simply supportive or dismissive. This incident is not in the book, but many other facets of that complex story are. Looking at Mzala's controversial book across the space of more than 30 years, its detail and richness of analysis is striking. In an age of soundbites and quick judgements, this extensive piece of discussion, closely argued with a wealth of detail, makes compelling reading.

Mzala must have been working on the manuscript at the time we sat talking together in the RESA office, which may be why I recollect our discussions about Nqutu. But one aspect of many exile experiences, which comes through more clearly in the autobiographies and memoirs than the more analytic accounts, is how many different strands and projects wove through people's lives, and how moving about between offices, meetings and a 'day job' or a particular project meant multiple relationships were interwoven with experiences of loneliness and dislocation. My memory was that Mzala was a research officer at RESA in the late 1980s, but in preparing this chapter, I looked through some of the old RESA reports and Mzala was not listed in that role. Ngonyama (2017) records, and Radebe (2022: 175) confirms, he was registered for a PhD at Essex University. In that capacity he may have been attached to our project. He would often get a telephone message and have to rush off to a meeting, so he was clearly doing many jobs in a single day. The biographic note on his book (Mzala, 1988) describes him as 'a former law student at the University of Zululand', who 'has worked for several years in the ANC Research Department in Lusaka, Zambia'. In his 1990 review article in the *Journal of Southern African Studies* on how to understand the crisis of the South African state (Mzala, 1990), no formal affiliation is given. The fragility of the written record regarding Mzala's work on RESA and in the South African community in exile in London signals something about the impermanence of exile lives, as well as the way in which Mzala's scholarly acuity seemed to somehow rise above this.⁵ His work is detailed, in depth, critical. He writes on the paradox of Buthelezi's agenda and the multi-facetedness of the crisis of the South African state in the late 1980s. His capacity to understand contradiction and complexity might have been nurtured through having to hold it together while living in many different spaces. A number of the memorialising accounts analysed by Ngonyama (2017) recall how Mzala relished argument and critique, and Radebe (2022) extends and deepens this theme. In my reading there is something distinctive about the way in which Mzala clearly formulates and defends a key line of argument. This is evident if one looks closely at how the analysis is built up in some of his key pieces of writing, as well as the substance of the points made.

In his study of Buthelezi (Mzala, 1988), both the subtitle of the book, *Chief with a double agenda*, and the opening sentence, 'Chief Gatsha Buthelezi is the most controversial black politician in South Africa' (Mzala, 1988: 1), set up the issue of a puzzle. The first two chapters deepen the question and the ambiguity. How can Buthelezi be both a man of peace and involved with repression of student protest at the Ngoye campus of the University of Zululand? How could he work within and help to shape the apartheid-created bantustans yet claim a position as a critic of that process? Mzala's analysis of this paradox takes us back to the colonial conquest of the Zulu Kingdom, and the ways in which chiefs were appointed in the service of apartheid. Thus, Buthelezi and the position he occupies did not merely arise – they are the products of political relationships formed over a long period.

Mzala examines the way in which Buthelezi engaged with the apartheid authorities (chapters 4–6) and some of the political organisation he undertook to establish Inkatha. Then he looks at the way in which this movement was used to carry out assassinations

---

5 Radebe's (2022) chapters on Mzala's life in London provide details and incidents, recall some of the themes of discussion and debate emerging in Mzala's writings, and the recollections of family and friends. But there is much more to be explored to bring out the texture of the relationships in play, and the significance of the work Mzala did, despite or because of this impermanence and diasporic mixing.

for the apartheid regime and sow racial division between Africans and Indians (chapters 7 and 8). In the final chapters he picks up key political issues of the 1980s in South Africa – the formation of COSATU and the issue of sanctions – and takes apart Buthelezi's position on the working class and the political economy of South Africa. In the penultimate chapter, Mzala counterposes his view on the national question to that of the federal constitution proposed by Buthelezi's Ulundi Accord of 1984.

Mzala argues for a liberated South Africa, where provincial autonomy is formulated through a constitutional process, not as a continuation of Bantustan structures; where culture and languages are protected as constitutional rights, not in order to privilege particular ethnic affiliations; and where the form of the colonial state and the associated repression is recognised and overturned. He maps the profound economic changes that are needed and that 'every vestige of apartheid and racial oppression will be scrupulously removed from every field of state service and public life' (Mzala, 1988: 225). He sketches the extensive education and training that are needed, together with the guarantees required for freedom of thought and of the press, and the high levels of popular mobilisation that this entails (Mzala, 1988: 225–26). Thus, we see Mzala, in the arc of his argument looking closely at a problem, detailing its history, drawing out some contemporary significance and postulating a position that looks beyond Buthelezi's 'take' on the national question. Mzala formulates an alternative horizon, and populates it with different ideas.

The scholarly achievement of Mzala's study of Buthelezi did not come out of nowhere. The range of books, journal and newspaper articles read, together with the interviews conducted, and the refinement of ideas, clarified through meticulous discussion, would be commended in any scholarly monograph, but for this to have been accomplished alongside Mzala's life as an activist is remarkable. Considerable work must have been expended in bringing the book together and taking it through publication, over and above the clear line of analysis developed.

John Daniel of Zed Press, whom Mzala thanks particularly for his help in preparing the book for publication (Mzala, 1988: vii), had met

Mzala when he was working in Swaziland. John Daniel was looking to 'publish progressive work largely on the Third World by scholars and activists from the Third World' (quoted in Ngonyama, 2017: 90). While Mzala's project for a study of Buthelezi neatly met Daniel's objectives, the ways in which Mzala formulated a particular position on the national question, which drew in many internationalist currents, must have drawn from his experiences in exile, not just in London but also in many countries in Africa and Europe.

Enormous organisational labour was entailed in producing a book in the period before computers. The material culture entailed sheaves of paper typed on noisy typewriters, messily corrected and arduously retyped. The impermanence of place would have made the process even more difficult. Mzala (1988: vii) acknowledges that many people helped with the book, but coordinating and completing it must have taken considerable effort and commitment.

Zed Press was a small left-wing publisher. The acknowledgement of the support from John Daniel, together with the recognition on the back cover of the significance of this book by three eminent scholars on South Africa – Shula Marks, Wally Serote and Ronald Segal – provides evidence of the range of political networks to which Mzala was connecting in London in the 1980s and the broad current of ideas from which he drew. There was a strong left presence in publishing in Britain at the time, with many specialist imprints, journals and newspapers, and a wide array of left/liberal publications. Reading and research were not unusual activities for left activists, as the expansion of enrolment and employment in universities only began after 1991. In the 1980s there were few academic jobs but many small and medium research and publishing organisations. A number of activist organisations focusing on South Africa had research or information wings and employed South African exiles and British left activists. The International Defence and Aid Fund and the AAM have been most documented (Gurney, 2000; Herbstein, 2004; Gurney, 2009; Williams, 2015), but there were a host of others linked to the black publishing industry, solidarity with the Southern Africa Frontline States, opposition to South Africa's nuclear industry, and campaigns on women's health, to note but a few. Providing information about conditions in South Africa, which was overlooked by defenders of the UK government's support for apartheid, was a key area of engagement.[6]

It is important to understand something of the context of 1980s Britain under the Conservative governments of Margaret Thatcher. It was a period of enormous political, economic, social and educational change, when some of the consequences of extreme deprivation and police harassment of working-class and black communities periodically erupted in explosive confrontations on the streets of many cities. The British government's support for the Botha regime in Pretoria was, to some extent, constrained by the politics of the Commonwealth, the political moves associated with the Lancaster House talks on Zimbabwe and the alliances built by the AAM (Onslow, 2009; Gurney, 2009), but Thatcher's cordial relationship with Botha and the government's refusal to impose sanctions on South Africa was fuelled by Cold War politics, the continued importance of trade and investment in South Africa to the British economy, and overt support for a politics of white rule. This chimed well with domestic political and economic strategies. Thatcherism entailed a ruthless attack on the trade union movement. Switching the British economy from a focus on industrial production – and support for the jobs and communities engaged with this work – to establishing the City of London as a globalised centre of finance and orienting the economy to a huge expansion of employment in the service sector, brought enormous and painful changes in the culture and relationships of work. In addition, Thatcherism was associated with a new political-ideological move that linked the culture of the free market with a socially conservative politics of the white (nuclear) family and an English notion of the nation (Hall and Jacques, 1983).

The 1980s was a period of harsh defeat for the Left in Britain, but also one marked by new ways of organising, analysing, and attempting to build solidarities (Rowbotham *et al*, 2014; Davis and McWilliam, 2018; Hall, 2021). The Left was widely dispersed through trade unions, women's groups, lesbian and gay activists, environmental groups, solidarity movements with national liberation struggles, the anti-nuclear movement, communist and socialist parties, anarchist

---

6   For some of the range of activities, see the oral history accounts assembled on the Forward to Freedom website. Available at: https://www.aamarchives.org/

collectives, arts and cultural groups, and anti-racist mobilisation, to name but a few. The Labour Party's control of significant political centres, such as the Greater London Council, led to reassessments of how to work with local government in some areas. In many areas, local level mobilisation on race focused on black communities' experiences of police brutality, and of discrimination in work, housing, health and education. There were moments of unification of the Left around projects to challenge Thatcherism, support the trade unions' defence of jobs, protect decent work conditions and oppose the build-up of nuclear weapons, and southern Africa was one issue that united various anti-Thatcher constituencies. Left organisations coalesced at key moments in taking solidarity action on southern Africa, such as the 1984 opposition to Botha's visit to Britain, when black groups took a lead, the 1985–1986 campaign for sanctions associated with a huge demonstration in November 1985, and the 1988 'Nelson Mandela: Freedom at Seventy' campaign. Support took many forms. Trade union branches were the biggest group of organisations affiliated to the AAM: the trade union movement underwrote the parlous finances of the AAM, and the large Manufacturing, Science and Finance Union (MSF) guaranteed the AAM overdraft. Local authorities boycotted South African goods and named streets and housing estates for Nelson Mandela. During the miners' strike, Women Against Pit Closures affiliated to the AAM. Key events like the miners' strike of 1984–1985 and the huge Campaign for Nuclear Disarmament (CND) demonstration of 1983 also brought these many different groupings together. These moments of coalescence were connected with events in South Africa by a number of activist scholars, close to the AAM and the ANC, whose works drew out links between the de-industrialisation of Britain, the changing global economy, the significance of South African mineral production and the anti-communist politics of the Botha regime (Fine and Rustomjee, 2018; Hall, 2021). But, while there were moments of coalescence for left politics in the United Kingdom, there were also many forces fragmenting alliances – falling trade union membership as jobs disappeared, the Labour Party losing repeated elections, and a range of bitter disputes raging within the Communist Party.

Thus, while it is not surprising that Mzala, living in this milieu, should draw on research and writing as part of his political engagement, what is distinctive is the depth and seriousness of his scholarly focus and his very particular concern with the national question as an issue of historical and contemporary significance. His perception was that South African activist scholars in the liberation movement had a key contribution to make in analysing the contemporary moment, outlining its colonial history, and showing the persistence of colonial relationships, as exemplified by Buthelezi. Colonialism, he wrote, had robbed black South Africans of their land, dictated their economic subjugation, robbed them of their wealth and denied them the right to govern themselves (Mzala, 1988; 1990). This sense of an arc of history, reaching into the past but bending towards justice for all oppressed people in Africa, and supporting the formation of a national, democratic state, appears to resonate with the experience of exile, a vantage point that, for all its pain and dislocation, may make clearer some of the larger patterns of time past and still to come.

I remember some of Mzala's stories, told with a light touch, although the events in themselves signalled moments that were anything but frivolous. I had a small car and was a nervous driver. We were on our way to a meeting at Harold Wolpe's house and the petrol gauge read empty. The choice was to look for a petrol station and be late for the meeting, or to try to get to the meeting but possibly run out of petrol.

'Take the risk,' Mzala said; 'turn off the engine as you go down the hills.' He said that he had once been in a plane with other comrades that had had to make a forced landing in Libya. They had fastened their seatbelts and hoped for the best. The plane had bumped and juddered, but they landed safely. I felt reassured – and we got to the meeting. Maybe it was his tone. There was much I did not ask. Why had they been forced to land in Libya? What had happened next? Why were we so distant with each other about big events, even though we spent our days working together in that small office?

Thinking back over the space of 30 years, I have tried to answer this question. Modisane (1963) writes about the attraction and isolation he felt in encounters with white liberal intellectuals, the ways in which he felt positioned by them and how exile amplified that sense of exclusion. The pain of the recollection centres on what Mzala may have felt in response to my silence, as well as a sense of anger at my inadequacy. This may be linked to the ways in which a culture of secrecy was associated with exile experiences, as is so poignantly evoked in a number of memoirs (Slovo, 2009; Levy, 2018). Silence and the different race and class experiences of South Africa and London, twisted personal and professional relationships away from the solidarity we tried to build in other ways. Silence and secrecy were partly protective, because apartheid agents did operate in London, but silence could also work to dampen creative enquiry. Looking back, I feel that I did not use words and our time together well enough. I had read Modisane and many other trenchant accounts of racialised relationships and their excluding resonance. Although the ANC was a non-racial movement and RESA was a project explicitly working to overcome racial inequalities in South African education, a kind of everyday, lived solidarity was hard. The history I carried was not only where I had been born and studied, but also how much I needed to understand to be open to learn. I think Mzala was talking into that gap, urging me to take a risk and listen better. It is more than 30 years since Mzala died, and I am only now closely reading his work.

Many of the writings on South Africans in exile in London evoke the ferment of ideas, emotions, connections and friendships. A few comment on the differences of where we had come from, where and how we were living in exile and how we saw our futures. I think this feeling of being together and apart was part of the texture of conversations I remember with Mzala. We shared many interests and yet it was hard to go below the surface. He must have been perplexed by how little I knew, and possibly hesitant about how to point this out. The complexities of diaspora affiliations and divisions have been a theme in much literature about exile, and have been noted in studies of particular diasporas (Segal, 1996; Knott and Mcloughlin, 2010). Pat McFadden (2020) writes about the ways in which transformative ideas about gender among anti-apartheid activists in exile were coopted, and this re-evokes for me a sense of critical doubt, which was part of the conversations of the 1980s. The ways in which the national question shaped the kinds of connections that were and were not made among South Africans exiles is a theme picked up in Mzala's (1990) discussion of works on the South African transition. For him, unravelling the gaps in arguments made by key commentators on this conjuncture, illuminates how location and context can shape ideas. How to build and sustain solidarity, given all the areas of hesitation and difference, the often keenly fought battles over interpretation of the national question, is a central theme in his 1990 examination of how to understand the transition moment.

If we look closely at the argument made in his commentary on the South African crisis (Mzala, 1990), we see him posing a main question about what stage the South African revolution was at, and whether a post-apartheid government in the future[7] would have a political and economic programme capable of bringing the crisis to an end and generating economic prosperity for the whole population (Mzala, 1990: 564). In reviewing three books that grapple with this issue – by Alex Callinicos, Billy Cobbett and Robin Cohen, and John Suckling and Landeg White – he takes each apart for failure to appreciate what he argues is historically specific about South African capitalism and the struggles against it, highlighting the roots of that specificity in a history of race and colonisation. The dynamics of this argument have been much debated (for example in Webster and Pampallis, 2016), and its particular contours and detail of the forms of the issue raise a number of themes regarding solidarity, and how to develop the political culture of solidarity in a democratic national state. The subtext of the analysis in the article is the point Mzala makes in his final paragraph. Here he writes that an analysis of economic, political and social conditions is not an exercise to be pursued merely for academic interest. For him it is key that the liberation movement, and some of the researchers within it, should be actively engaged in these scholarly debates, not merely as observers, but as formulators of policy that may, in future, become the government policy in the post-apartheid South Africa.

---

7   The article was written before the South African transition, but looked forward to the issues to be raised in that process of transition.

'Herein lies the significance of the endeavours that have gone into the writing of these books' (Mzala, 1990: 578). Solidarity is, thus, supporting exiles in the work they have set themselves.

A long and distressing conversation we had over many hours one day was about HIV. Mzala had published some articles questioning the origins of the virus (Nxumalo, 1988a; 1988b). In our conversation he raised many points about the colonial history of Africa, the ways in which controls over health were linked with controls over people; how 'big pharma' was not simply benign. These were compelling arguments and he had many facts, figures and stories. I was shaken because I had only a simple way of thinking about illness and treatment, and the numbers and suffering involved. I had not connected the many accounts of the ravages of the virus with the larger political economy background.

That connection, between the personal and the political, was something with which Mzala seemed to live. I think that he did not dichotomise these relationships, and I think that might have been how and why he finished both his 1988 book and his 1990 article with political vision statements. To have a personal politics was the point. I have written down these fragments of memory trying to evoke something of Mzala's qualities for readers who did not know him. Decades after his death, part of me wanted to return the compliment to Mzala of the generous gift of detail, the humour and rigour of analysis that inflects his well-remembered voice. In concluding, I also want to try to pick up some of the threads of our unfinished conversations about home, the national question, and solidarities, and to think about what light the meaning of political exile might cast on those themes.

POLITICAL EXILES AND A PERSPECTIVE ON THE NATIONAL QUESTION

Ashwini Vasanthakumar's (2021) study of the ethics of political exiles draws out how exiled individuals and groups, despite their own dislocation and difficulties, play a vital ethical role in relation to the countries from which they come. They can, she argues, be 'rescuers and representatives, nation-builders and peace-makers, and witnesses to the suffering they have left behind' (Vasanthakumar, 2021: 2). She shows how political exiles can activate and sustain solidarity networks, and hold powerful actors to account. Using a wide range of media, they can give voice to marginalised perspectives.

Vasanthakumar acknowledges the significant contribution of many prominent political exiles, but the main part of her argument concerns exile communities and representatives who are not high profile. Mzala can be read as occupying a dual position: although he was prominent, during the 1980s he was not very high profile outside the liberation movement. Although, as Ngonyama (2017) and Radebe (2022) show, he was close to a number of leading political figures in the ANC in exile, he was, in some ways, writing for an audience beyond the ANC and the SACP. As a writer, he published not just in the publications of the ANC and the SACP, but also in academic journals on African and Southern African Studies, and in his monograph published by Zed Press. The final chapters of Radebe's biography outline the projects he was planning in the United States in the last years of his life. While the implications of his work have taken some decades to emerge, partly because of the different claims made regarding how to interpret different facets of his writing (Ngonyame, 2017; Houston, 2020; Mkodzongi and Rusenga, 2021; Radebe, 2022), with hindsight, some significant aspects of his voice can be discerned as a representative, a witness and a builder for solidarity. Using Vasanthakumar's (2021) notion of the exile's responsibility to give voice, we could view Mzala as wishing to take this position of bearing witness, through academic publication, as a key act to invite and express solidarity. The perspective from exile portrays South Africa's long history and the clear principles that delineate the desired future. In contrast to Buthelezi's vision of the national question, centred on a particular parochial ethnicity, Mzala affirms:

> The Natal *Indaba* does not even come near to the basic[s] enshrined in the Freedom Charter, and which represent the aspiration of the overwhelming majority of the South African people. It is these principles that the future constitution must enshrine. Then, and only then, can it be said that South Africa has undergone a fundamental political change (Mzala, 1988: 226).

The sense of possibility and frustration for political exiles in relation to established disciplines in the social sciences and arts emerges in a number of studies, which highlight both the achievements and the positioning of political exiles as outsiders, often with fragile job security and access to publication (Ash and Sollner, 2002; Zeleza, 2006; Roninger, 2020). Some political exiles have had enormous intellectual influence, shaping the study of history, literature, linguistics, economics, religion, cultural disability and gender studies. Key figures in the 20th century who have shaped whole disciplines include political exiles from Nazi Germany who went to the United States, such as Hannah Arendt, Theodore Adorno, Herbert Marcuse and Albert Hirschman. Political exiles from colonial and postcolonial oppression who are associated with major intellectual movements include Paulo Freire, Edward Said and Mahmood Mamdani. To these one could add some names of South African political exiles, such as Sol Plaatje or Vic Finkelstein, who made significant contributions while living in London, by giving voice and bearing witness, despite the terrible sense of separation from home they experienced (Finkelstein, 1993; Shakespeare and Watson, 1997; Willan, 2019). This capacity to read across seems to be a form of solidarity that some political exiles have refined acuity to realise. This reaching between different settings at home and elsewhere is another feature of Mzala's scholarship, driving his notion that engaging the national question was a process of making an international movement as 'the struggles of the peoples of the rest of Africa and those of South Africa against colonialism and for freedom are one and indivisible' (Mzala, 1988: 223).

There are many facets of Mzala's work that resonate with this analysis of the ethics of exile. In his two largely academic pieces of writing (Mzala, 1988; 1990) we see him holding powerful actors, both politicians and theorists, to account for the implications of their words. While there are points of the political moment in 1990 that he misjudged, and much that he tragically overlooked in trying to understand HIV, a strong sense of the ethics of responsibility, and the rigour needed in thinking about this, is evident. A number of the historical accounts of the political moves made by the ANC in exile draw out arguments about a balance of forces, of who was around the table (Lissoni, 2009; Lodge, 2021). Mzala's analysis is not about a politics of positions, but about a searching examination of who says what and why, and with what consequences. This is not a discussion about ideas detached from political realities, but it is also not a discussion about pragmatics that lacks a moral compass or a sense of the importance of representation. His idea of home and the national question is always inflected ethically, but that ethics comes at a cost. A powerful passage from Edward Said evokes some of the many layers around the interpretation of Mzala's writing:

> Exile is strangely compelling to think about but terrible to experience. It is the unhealable rift forced between a human being and a native place, between the self and its true home: its essential sadness can never be surmounted. And while it is true that literature and history contain heroic, romantic, glorious, even triumphant episodes in an exile's life, these are no more than efforts meant to overcome the crippling sorrow of estrangement. The achievements of exile are permanently undermined by the loss of something left behind forever (Said, 2003: 173).

In Mzala's writing, and through the fragments of my recollection, I see him formulating a position on the national question within which there is a powerful sense of making a form of representation against estrangement. Time is highly significant, and it is possible the perspective from exile shaped this. His writing takes a wide angled look at three centuries of history, the dangerous present and a clearly defined future. Words and the organisation of ideas provide ways to take account of and connect personal, local, national, diasporic, global, social, economic, linguistic and health inequalities. The challenge of living with these multiple layers is enormous, as are the costs. Going into exile, taking the risk and the loss, but nonetheless talking, thinking and writing through the pain, was a courageous, ethical engagement oriented to challenging many forms of injustice and trying to bring about change. The injustices we talked about remain as profound, as do the possibilities of acts of solidarity.

REFERENCES

Adi, H. (2012). 'African political thinkers, Pan-Africanism and the politics of exile, c. 1850–1970', *Immigrants & Minorities*, 30(2-3): 263–91.

Altschuler, J. (2008). 'Re-remembering and re-imagining relational boundaries: Sibling narratives of migration', *Annual Review of Critical Society*, 6: 26–43.

Ash, M.G. and Söllner, A. (eds). (2002). *Forced Migration and Scientific Change: Emigre German-speaking scientists and scholars after 1933*. Cambridge: Cambridge University Press.

Bernstein, H., (1994). *The Rift. The exile experience of South Africans*. London: Jonathan Cape.

Bethlehem, L. (2018). 'Restless itineraries: Antiapartheid expressive culture and transnational historiography', *Social Text*, 36(3): 47–69.

Clingman, S. (2013). 'Looking from South Africa to the world: A story of identity for our times', *Safundi*, 14(3): 235–54.

Dalamba, L. (2006). 'Writing against exile: A chronotopic reading of the autobiographies of Miriam Makeba, Joe Mogotsi, and Hugh Masekela'. Doctoral dissertation, University of KwaZulu-Natal.

Davis, J. and McWilliam, R. (eds). (2017). *Labour and the Left in the 1980s*. Manchester: Manchester University Press.

Dubow, S. (2017). 'New approaches to high apartheid and anti-apartheid', *South African Historical Journal*, 69(2): 304–29.

Gready, P. (2003). *Writing as resistance: life stories of imprisonment, exile, and homecoming from apartheid South Africa*. Lanham, MD: Lexington Books.

Feldstein, R. (2013). 'Screening anti-apartheid: Miriam Makeba, "Come Back, Africa"', *Feminist Studies*, 39(1): 12–39.

Fine, B. and Rustomjee, Z. (2018). *The Political Economy of South Africa: From minerals–energy complex to industrialisation*. London: Routledge.

Finkelstein, V. (1993). 'The commonality of disability', in J. Swain, V. Finkelstein, S. French, and M. Oliver (eds). *Disabling Barriers: Enabling environments*, London: SAGE Publications, pp. 9–16.

Gready, P. (1994). 'The South African experience of home and homecoming', *World Literature Today*, 68(3): 509–15.

Gurney, C. (2000). '"A great cause": The origins of the Anti-Apartheid Movement, June 1959–March 1960', *Journal of Southern African Studies*, 26(1), 123–44.

Gurney, C. (2009). 'The 1970s: The Anti-Apartheid Movement's difficult decade', *Journal of Southern African Studies*, 35(2): 471–87.

Hall, S. and Jacques, M. (eds). (1983). *The Politics of Thatcherism*. London: Lawrence and Wishart, p. 19.

Hall, S. (2021). *The Hard Road to Renewal: Thatcherism and the crisis of the Left*. London: Verso Books.

Holmes, R. (2014). *Eleanor Marx. A life*. London: Bloomsbury Publishing.

Houston, G. (2020). Jabulani 'Mzala' Nxumalo: revolutionary intellectual', in V. Reddy, N. Bohler-Muller, G. Houston, M. Schoeman and H. Thuynsma (eds). *The Fabric of Dissent: Public intellectuals in South Africa*. Cape Town: Best Red, pp. 391–95.

Israel, M. (1999). *South African Political Exile in the United Kingdom*. London: Palgrave Macmillan.

Jones, D. and Plaatje, S. (1970 [1916]). *A Sechuana Reader*. London: Gregg.

Killingray, D. (2009). 'Rights, land, and labour: Black British critics of South African policies before 1948', *Journal of Southern African Studies*, 35(2): 375–98.

Knott, K. and McLoughlin, S. (eds). (2010). *Diasporas: Concepts, intersections, identity*. London: Zed Books.

Levy, D. (2018). *Things I Don't Want to Know: On writing*. London: Bloomsbury Publishing.

Lissoni, A. (2009). 'Transformations in the ANC External Mission and Umkhonto we Sizwe. 1960–1969', *Journal of Southern African Studies*, 35(2): 287–301.

Llewellyn, M.P. and Rider, T.C. (2020). 'Dennis Brutus and the South African Non-Racial Olympic Committee in Exile, 1966–1970', *South African Historical Journal*, 72(2): 246–71.

Lodge, T. (2021). *Red Road to Freedom. A history of the South African Communist Party* Johannesburg: Jacana Media.

Lombardozzi, L.M. (2007). 'Journeying beyond Embo: The

construction of exile, place and identity in the writings of Lewis'. Doctoral dissertation, English, Media and Performance Studies, University of KwaZulu-Natal.

Manicom, L. (2016). 3. 'Afastada Apprehensions: The politics of post-exile location and South Africa's gendered transition', in A. Heitlinger (ed.). *Émigré Feminism: Transnational perspectives.* Toronto: University of Toronto Press, pp. 30–66.

McFadden, P. (2021). 'Through 500 years African women have fought for freedom'. Interview. Available at https://capiremov.org/en/interview/patricia-mcfadden-african-women-have-fought-for-freedom/ (Accessed 20 April 2023).

Mkodzongi, G. and Rusenga, C. (2021). 'The idea of a "rainbow nation" and the persistence of agrarian injustices in post-apartheid South Africa', in S.J. Ndlovu-Gatsheni and B. Ngcaweni (eds). *The Contested Idea of South Africa.* London: Routledge, pp. 206–23.

Modisane, B. (1963). *Blame Me on History.* London: Thames and Hudson.

Moraes, R.F.D. (2021). 'Transnational activism and domestic politics: Arms exports and the anti-apartheid struggle in the UK–South Africa relations (1959–1994)', *Foreign Policy Analysis*, 17(4): 21. DOI:10.1093/fpa/orab023

Mzala, J.N. (1990). 'Is South Africa in a revolutionary situation?' *Journal of Southern African Studies*, 16(3): 563–78.

Mzala, J.N. (1988). *Gatsha Buthelezi: Chief with a double agenda.* London: Zed Books.

Ngonyama, P. (2017). '"Comrade Mzala": Memory construction and legacy preservation', *African Historical Review*, 49(2): 72–101.

Nxumalo, J. (1988a). 'AIDS: Misinformation and racism', *Sechaba*, July.

Nxumalo, J, (1988b). 'AIDS: The imperial connection', *Sechaba*, September.

Onslow, S. (2009). '"Noises off": South Africa and the Lancaster House Settlement, 1979–1980', *Journal of Southern African Studies*, 35(2): 489–506.

Plaatje, S. (1916). *Native Life in South Africa.* London: King & Son.

Radebe, M. (2022). *The Lost Prince of the ANC. The life and times of Jabulani Nobleman 'Mzala' Nxumalo.* Johannesburg: Jacana Media.

Reynolds, J. Fine, B. and Van Niekerk, R. (eds). (2019). *Race, Class and the Post-apartheid Democratic State*. Pietermaritzburg: University of KwaZulu-Natal Press, pp. 213–40.

Roniger, L. (2020). *European and Latin American Social Scientists as Refugees, Émigrés and return-migrants*. London: Palgrave Macmillan.

Rowbotham, S., Segal, L., Wainwright, H. and Patel, P. (2014). 'After Thatcher: Still trying to piece it all together', *Soundings*, 56(56): 137–53.

Said, E., (2003). *Reflections on Exile and Other Essays*. Cambridge, MA: Harvard University Press.

Sapire, H. (2009). 'Liberation movements, exile, and international solidarity: An introduction', *Journal of Southern African Studies*, 35(2): 271–86.

Segal, R. (1996). *The Black Diaspora: Five centuries of the black experience outside Africa*. London: Macmillan.

Shakespeare, T. and Watson, N. (1997). 'Defending the social model', *Disability & Society*, 12(2): 293–300.

Skinner, R. (2009). The Anti-Apartheid Movement: Pressure group politics, international solidarity and transnational activism', in N. Crowson, M. Hilton and J. McKay (eds). *NGOs in Contemporary Britain: Non-state actors in society since 1945*. London: Palgrave Macmillan, pp. 129–46.

Slovo, G. (2009). *Every Secret Thing: My family, my country*. London: Hachette UK.

Suttner, R. (2003). 'Culture(s) of the African National Congress of South Africa: Imprint of exile experiences', *Journal of contemporary African Studies*, 21(2): 303–20.

Thorpe, A. (2021). *South African London*. Manchester: Manchester University Press.

Thörn, H. (2009). 'The meaning (s) of solidarity: Narratives of anti-apartheid activism', *Journal of Southern African Studies*, 35(2): 417–36.

Unterhalter, E. (2021). '"Sol Plaatje and UCL": Alternative histories of education and international development'. Blog series, Centre for Education and International Development, University College London. Available at: https://blogs.ucl.ac.uk/ceid/2021/01/11/alternative-histories-of-education-and-international-development-004-unterhalter (Accessed 20 April 2023).

Unterhalter, E. (2019). 'Articulation and a theorisation of educational change: Reflections on Harold Wolpe's work on South Africa', in J. Reynolds, B. Fine and R. van Niekerk (eds). *Race, Class and the Post-apartheid Democratic State.* Pietermaritzburg: University of KwaZulu-Natal Press, pp. 213–40.

Unterhalter, E. (2000). 'Gendered diaspora identities: South African women, exile and migration, *c.*1960–1995', in S. Ali, K. Coates and W. Wa Goro (eds). *Global Feminist Politics. Identities in a changing world.* London: Routledge, pp. 107–25.

Vasanthakumar, A. (2021). *The Ethics of Exile: A political theory of diaspora.* New York and Oxford: Oxford University Press.

Werbner, P. (2010). 'Many gateways to the gateway city: Elites, class and policy networking in the London African diaspora', *African diaspora*, 3(1): 131–58.

Willan, B. (2018). *Sol Plaatje. A life of Solomon Tshekisho Plaatje, 1876–1932.* Johannesburg: Jacana Media.

Williams, E. (2015). *The Politics of Race in Britain and South Africa: Black british solidarity and the anti-apartheid struggle.* London: Bloomsbury Publishing.

Zeleza, P.T. (2006). 'The disciplinary, interdisciplinary and global dimensions of African Studies', *International Journal of African Renaissance Studies*, 1(2): 195–220.

THREE

SOCIALISM IS THE FUTURE: COMRADE MZALA'S THOUGHTS ON THE NATIONAL QUESTION

Mandla J. Radebe

INTRODUCTION

The national question has been among the hotly contested and complex topics within the South African national liberation movement since the formation of the African National Congress (ANC) in 1912. This debate is at the heart of the content of the South African struggle and the nature of the society it has sought to build, post-apartheid. In the 1980s, one of the primary interlocutors in this debate was Mzala Nxumalo, an activist and intellectual of the ANC and South African Communist Party (SACP). He is remembered for his passionate discussions on this topic. In an obituary statement following his untimely death, the SACP described him as someone who was 'endlessly fascinated and intrigued by the national question, and wrote and lectured extensively on the relationship between the national and class struggle in South Africa'. He regarded ending inequality between the nations as the main aim of the South African revolution, which 'could only be achieved under socialism' (SACP, 1991).

According to Mpho Nxumalo (cited in Radebe, 2022), Mzala's wife and a fellow activist, the national question was 'foremost' to him. His articulation of the national question was linked to 'ensuring an uninterrupted shift towards socialism' (Mellet in Radebe, 2022). Although not dogmatic in his articulation, Mzala was innovative in his application. For example, some of the research he conducted was on the origins of the southern African Bantu people (Nzimande in Radebe, 2022), with the primary purpose of debunking the ethno-nationalistic tendency, as manifested in the apartheid government's bantustan policy (Nxumalo, 1992).

Mzala engaged the national question using historical materialism, which enabled him to investigate concretely the class character of the society in question and the historical conjuncture under which oppression and exploitation occurred (Shivji, 2019). This chapter traces his major writings on the national question with the view to presenting his thoughts in the context of contemporary South Africa's myriad challenges. It begins by tracing his thoughts on the national question from a historical perspective, presenting his views on various tendencies such as the colonialist, liberal, nationalist, Africanist and Marxist–Leninist perspectives.[1] This chapter also analyses Mzala's thoughts on the role of capitalism in the process of nation-formation.

But Mzala primarily used Marxism–Leninism to comprehend the national question. In this regard, this chapter interacts with his thoughts on the role of white communists in the national question, the question of the right to self-determination, the link between the national and class struggle and the importance of working-class internationalism. Lastly, in his quest to unravel the national question, Mzala interacted with the concept of non-historic nations

---

1 Writing on parties, factions and tendencies in Britain, Rose (1964: 37–38) described a political tendency as 'a stable set of attitudes, rather than a stable group of politicians. It may be defined as a body of attitudes expressed in Parliament about a broad range of problems; the attitudes are held together by a more or less coherent political ideology. One may speak of right-wing and left-wing tendencies within both British parties because of the extent to which political differences in this country may be placed along a single left-right axis.' The concept of tendencies used in this chapter is precisely this one.

put forward by Marx and Engels (1974). Inherent in this analysis is the problem of ethnicity that was prevalent in South Africa due to the separation policy practised by the apartheid regime, which manifested in the bantustan policy, among others. The section on the 'National question from the South African historical perspective' unravels the major tendencies that Mzala identified in the writing of the South African history as he sought to understand the national question more deeply. It is through this that he grounded the evolution of the national question in South Africa.

The section on 'Capitalism and nation-formation' presents Mzala's demonstration of the centrality of capitalism in the nation-formation process that gave rise to modern nations. Linked to this, the section titled 'Marxism and the national question' examines how Mzala grounded the national question, both theoretically and ideologically. Marxism–Leninism enabled him to unpack the character of colonial oppression. Thus, he perceived the role of white communists as revolutionary in organising the black working class to resolve the national question. Mzala advanced a strong case for the right of the oppressed to self-determine – a right that he regarded as being at the heart of addressing the colonial question (Mzala, 1988). Marxism–Leninism clarified his view on the national and class struggle and the resolution of the national question.

Another dimension that is inherent to such an analysis is his perspective on working-class internationalism and the national question. He grounded the South African struggle in this context.

In the section 'Non-historic nations and the national question', Mzala's thoughts on the dynamic problem of ethnicity emerge. To Mzala, the unity of the oppressed and the exploited working class was paramount when dealing with the national question. In the final analysis, while Mzala made an important contribution to theorising the South African revolution, his vision of a united South Africa across racial and class lines has not materialised. Part of the problem has been the failure on the part of the national liberation movement to allow the working class, the motive force of the revolution, to lead the revolution to its logical conclusion – socialism.

THE NATIONAL QUESTION FROM THE SOUTH AFRICAN HISTORICAL PERSPECTIVE

One of the ways in which Mzala engaged with the national question was through surveying the writing on the history of South Africa. As is to be expected and given the history of the country, the understanding of the national question is varied, and the debate around it can be characterised into three broad categories: the left, the centre and the right. On the broad left position are the 'four foundational traditions', which include Marxism–Leninism, the Congress tradition, Trotskyism and Africanism (Webster and Mawbey, 2017). At the centre is the liberal tendency, while on the right is the narrow ethnic tendency, as embodied by Afrikaner nationalism. Of course, a more nuanced approach is necessary since 'there are also distinctive challenges arising from Afrikaner nationalism's implementation of the bantustan policy, as well as the rise of Inkatha and Zuluness, the New Left, black consciousness, feminism and liberal constitutionalism' (Webster and Mawbey, 2017: 2).

However, Mzala thought that this multiplicity of understandings was no excuse for ignorance. Notwithstanding the contested theories, he expected everyone who interacted with this important question to demonstrate rigour. He thought that South Africa's contested history had direct implications for the formulation of policies that sought to resolve problems posed by the national question (Nxumalo, 1992). Mzala grounded his perspective by identifying what he regarded as major tendencies in the writing of South Africa's history and their impact on the national question.

The colonialist tendency

The first major tendency that Mzala identified was the colonialist tendency, which he thought was contemptuous of Africans and whatever they had achieved in the past. Afrikaners were key to this tendency. They disputed the Africans' claim to South Africa and they were supported in this by some historian, such as Theal (1897), who sought to deny that Africans were the indigenous people of the country. According to Visser (2004), Afrikaners interpreted their own history as a bitter struggle for self-preservation and fulfilment in the face of the hostile forces of nature and the African peoples they encountered in the country. However, Afrikaners regarded the British as their true oppressors and opponents and saw them as sympathisers of the Africans in their struggle against the Boers (Visser, 2004). In this tendency, Theal's (1897) writing became the foundation of the Afrikaner ideology, which politicians such as Hendrik Verwoerd found useful, decades later. Hence, Mzala argued, for both Theal and Verwoerd, 'Africans had no right to claim the whole of South African territory as belonging to them' (Nxumalo, 1992: 15). But regardless of who is writing, the historical question 'of [to] whom South Africa belongs, is the first and central issue in the presentation of the national question in this country' (Nxumalo, 1992: 15).

The emergence of the National Party (NP) as a political force, when it took over government in 1948, affirmed this ongoing contestation of the country and its history. To consolidate its ideological and material stranglehold on the country, the NP articulated an Afrikaner-biased historiography, which sought to create the impression that African tribes such as the Tswana, Zulu and Venda were nations that came to South Africa about the same time as the white colonial settlers. This was done to advance their notion of rule, and the oppression of the African people was part of resolving their interpretation of the national question. 'If blacks had no prior claim to the whole of the South African territory,' argued Mzala, 'then they had no right to self-determination in the whole country' (Nxumalo, 1992: 17). Based on this strategy of dispossession, and divide and rule, the NP came up with schemes such as the bantustans.

The liberal tendency

Second, there is the liberal tradition in the South African historiography. In this tendency, South Africa was considered to constitute a single nation, with the whites making up the core while blacks had to be integrated on the basis of meeting particular standards. This was a marked departure from the apartheid ideologists, who considered South Africa as comprising many nations that had to be kept apart (Nxumalo, 1992). In this liberal tradition, four historians – Macmillan (1927, 1928, 1975), De Kiewiet (1937, 1941), and Wilson and Thompson (1969) – demonstrate a common approach to the national question (Nxumalo, 1992). For example, Macmillan (1927) advocated for the extension of the franchise to blacks. However, this was not a universal but a qualified franchise, where 'White South Africa must carry its child races along with it on the way to progress' (Nxumalo, 1992: 21). Similarly, De Kiewiet (1937), and Wilson and Thompson (1969) ignored the national demands of the oppressed people and pretended that they enjoyed national equality with whites.

In fact, Mzala's views are a continuation of a negative assessment of Wilson and Thompson's 1969 book, *The Oxford History of South Africa*, Volume 2, by intellectuals located within the liberation movement. In his 1971 review in the *African Communist*, Lerumo concurs with the view that there was

> no real inkling to be gained from this book of the heroic strivings of the majority of the South African people, their labour and liberation movements; nor that these movements are the key to the future, the only real opposition, their vision of our country, the Freedom Charter, the only alternative to the monstrous edifice of tyranny and racialism created by imperialism and its proteges in Southern Africa (Lerumo, 1971: 126).

Lerumo was aggrieved by the fact that the editors of the book segregated

> the political expression of the aspirations of four-fifths of the South Africans into a single, non-essential, chapter is evidence of the extent to which they, perhaps not consciously, have betrayed the purpose proclaimed at the outset of their first volume: to produce a whole history of the whole people of South Africa (Lerumo, 1971: 125).

However, scholars outside of the liberation movement regarded the book as part of an emerging trend that sought to 'emphasize the role of Africans in South African history' by highlighting 'interaction' between different races and groups in South Africa (Wright, 1975: 456–57). These reviews, just like the book itself, seemed to be blind to the muted voices of the oppressed majority.

Nevertheless, this tendency moves closer to Mzala's Marxist articulation of nation-formation in that it identifies the centrality of the economy. However, it still regarded whites as constituting the principal elements of the country and hence, in the minds of liberal scholars, the national question was resolved by the 1910 formation of the Union of South Africa, which united the white groups in the country (Nxumalo, 1992). Within a liberal white perspective, Africans were not important in terms of rights or belonging, but only in terms of labour or servitude. Hence, the dependence of whites on black labour was 'the greatest social and economic fact' in 19th-century South Africa (De Kiewiet, 1937, in Nxumalo, 1992: 26).

While liberal historians emphasised race co-operation (Egan, 2012), some thought of South African liberalism as patronising because it regarded 'the civilisation of the natives' as not equal to their integration 'into the colonial system on equal footing with the settlers'. This liberalism perceived the natives as inferior to whites by nature and, hence, they needed to be civilised (Maloka, 2014: 35). Thus, the decision by the liberals to join the Union of a white nation not only betrayed the Africans in their quest for self-determination, but also exposed the ultimate liberal standpoint on the South African national question. Because of the liberals' notion of multiracialism, their South African history begins when whites meet blacks. What transpired prior to this was not considered important. Thus, historians such as Wilson and Thompson (1969) ignored oral history in their account of the South African past. Instead, liberal historians such as De Kiewiet argued that prior to the arrival of whites, Africans were 'savages with no government' who were always prone to violence (De Kiewiet, 1937, in Nxumalo, 1992: 26). Although this tendency raised important issues, including the development of a single economy (whether real or not) as important in producing a single nation, it ignored the fundamental question of self-determination by the oppressed (Nxumalo, 1992).

Within the same parameters, and in unravelling the national question from a historical perspective, Mzala deemed it necessary to go beyond the limitations of the 'empiricism and idealism' that neglected oral history. In articulating historical materialism in an attempt to reach a concrete understanding of the national question, Mzala argued that 'the level of historical research that would help us penetrate the overall social complex, the social totality, is theoretical analysis of both the modes of production and socio-economic formations of various epochs of social developments' (Nxumalo, 1992: 32). Nevertheless, the emergence of the liberal tendency in the writing of the South African history represents an important stage of progress from the colonial tendency, which had distorted and ignored the existence of African people. The nationalists sought to build on this tendency to assert the role of Africans in the South African history.

The nationalist tendency

This tendency called for, among other things, South African history to be written by Africans because no matter how sympathetic the Europeans may be, they could not be entrusted with such a task (Nxumalo, 1992). This is not to say that all history written by Africans was inherently objective and progressive; for example, Silas Modiri Molema's (1920) work, *The Bantu, Past and Present: An ethnographical and historical study of the native races of Africa*, relied heavily on Eurocentric sources and, therefore, it fell victim to the influence of colonialist and liberal historians (Nxumalo, 1992). In some quarters, Molema's work is regarded as part of the efforts to assert an Africanist outlook and resist Westernisation (Nombila, 2018). Another African who succeeded in publishing was Mangena Fuze (1922). His work, *Abantu Abamnyama, Lapho Bevela Khona*, was translated into English in 1979 as *The Black People and Whence They Came*. However, just like Molema, he fell into the trap of relying on colonialist sources and, thus, repeated their myths (Nxumalo, 1992).

However, it is through the writings of African nationalists that crucial information about South Africa's national question emerged. For example, it is through the writings of Sol Plaatje (1916, 1930) that the existence of two nations – the oppressed and the oppressor

– was made clearer. In his book *Native Life in South Africa*, Plaatje (1916) provided an account of the origins of the 1913 Natives Land Act and 'made a devastating description of some of its immediate effects' (Nxumalo, 1992: 38). It is from the writings of the liberation movement, as discussed earlier, that one can see a clear link between democracy and the national question. This emerged through the writings of ANC and Communist Party activists who articulated the 'principle of the majority rule as the only logical answer to the solution of the colonial and national question' (Nxumalo, 1992: 46).

The Africanist tendency

In the 1940s, an Africanist tendency emerged through leaders such as Anton Lembede (1945), who espoused 'some basic principles of African Nationalism'. This was defined as a spirit of self-determination, and this liberation could only be driven by Africans themselves (Nxumalo, 1992).

However, this tendency can be traced to Pan Africanism, which originated in the United States, driven by activist scholars such as WEB Du Bois (1919, 1921) (Shepperson, 1962; Chennells, 1997). In South Africa, this Africanist tendency can be traced back to 'The regeneration of Africa' speech delivered by Pixley ka Isaka Seme, a future ANC president, at New York's Columbia University in 1906 (Dunton, 2003). The challenge Mzala had with this tendency was its inability to connect the relationship between national and class oppression. For him, class was integral to the national question, not just during the anti-colonial struggle, but also fundamental in analysing and comprehending precolonial societies. He was concerned by what appeared to be the African tendency's idealistic characterisation of these societies, to the extent that social and ethnic dimensions were discussed without incorporating class analysis.

In his analysis of contemporary developments, Mzala located the bantustans in the economic interests of the colonialists and perceived the role of black bourgeoisie as pivotal in supporting the system. However, he made a distinction between the bantustan bourgeoisie and the petty-capitalist stratum that emerged organically in the South African capitalist economy. He argued that the latter stratum's political and economic ambitions for national equality and mobility were frustrated by a glass ceiling constructed by apartheid policies. Subsequently, it realised that its immediate fate lay with the national liberation movement. Indeed, the objectives of the national liberation movement embodied the interests of all strata within the nationally dominated and oppressed majority, including the black petite bourgeoisie and the emerging black bourgeoisie (Slovo, 1988). On the other hand, the black bantustan bourgeoisie was cultivated deliberately by the apartheid regime to play a collaborationist role (Nxumalo, 1992).

Nevertheless, Mzala regarded the Africanist tendency as lacking coherence and consistency when it came to class analysis of the social base of nationhood. Mzala argued that, instead of engaging all the social and ethnic elements of the national question in South Africa,

> the Africanist tendency takes an African continental perspective, leaving South Africa's national problem unsolved, and finds satisfaction in engaging in the debates about mere name-calling, whether South Africa should be called Azania or South Africa. (Nxumalo, 1992: 56).

The Marxist–Leninist tendency

It was the Marxist–Leninist tendency that Mzala regarded as having made a comprehensive analysis of the national question. 'Jack and Ray Simon's *Class and Colour in South Africa*, as well as Francis Meli's *South Africa Belongs to Us*, has proved that it is within this ideological terrain that most of the answers to the questions posed by South African historiography, as well as by the problems of presenting the national question; find some initial ... answers' (Nxumalo, 1992: 59). Notwithstanding claims that Marxism was weak on the national question (Davis, 1976), with progressive organisations such as the South African Labour Party basing their black membership on condition of meeting some racist qualifications, including the 'upholding' of 'white standards' (see Lodge, 2021), it is Marxism, brought to South Africa by the white settler community, which ultimately offered creative analysis to the national question (Drew, 2018). Thus, Mzala presented the ANC/SACP alliance and their theory on nation-formation as essential in the presentation of the national question and in unravelling the relationship between the class and national struggle.

CAPITALISM AND NATION-FORMATION

Capitalism was central in the birth of modern nations. It was at the heart of the nation-formation process and its rise engendered a common economic life. This process eliminated the scattered state of production and fostered political concentration which, according to Marx and Engels (1962: 72), 'lumped together into one nation' what were hitherto independent provinces that were connected by mere alliance (Hoffman and Mzala, 1990: 413). The development of 'modern' nations was linked to the capitalist mode of production, as articulated by Lenin (1966: 72), as 'an inevitable product, an inevitable form, in the bourgeois epoch of social development' (Hoffman and Mzala, 1990: 413).

Therefore, the assertion by colonialist historians, who sought to reduce a nation to merely a cultural community, was incorrect. In fact, this was idealistic because it portrayed the nation as a 'non-historic category' whose existence was dependent on a community of people with a common culture. Lenin characterised this as a 'psychological' conceptualisation of nationhood (Hoffman and Mzala, 1990). For Mzala, it was important to appreciate that economic factors gave rise to the creation of nation-states. However, this was not the case in South Africa and, therefore, it was opportunistic for the apartheid regime to characterise bantustans as nation-states. Capitalism, as far as Mzala was concerned, had not produced a single nation-state in South Africa.

Nevertheless, it could have been possible for capitalism to produce a nation-state in South Africa had it not been for the imposition of ethnic separation, since there were 'favourable factors for integration that were created by the development of capitalism on South African soil' (Hoffman and Mzala, 1990: 414). The rise of modern nations can be attributed to the imperative of supply and demand of the capitalist economy. The bourgeoisie needed domestic markets to accumulate capital, but more importantly, the bourgeoisie could not exploit wage labour and consolidate its economic interest without a state. As already indicated, it was the liberal and the Marxist tendencies that connected the South African national question with capitalism, although the liberals vacillated on the question of self-determination of the nationally oppressed black people, who were also exploited as a class. To this end, nation-building must be considered as a political process integral to the bourgeois democratic revolution (Hoffman and Mzala, 1990).

MARXISM AND THE NATIONAL QUESTION

Marxism has made an important contribution to the concept of 'nations' by unravelling the fundamental question of oppression and self-determination. Mzala employed Marxism to analyse colonial oppression. He saw Marxism as an irreconcilable enemy of all national oppression, fighting for national equality and the self-determination of nations. Marxism, for Mzala, supported the liberation struggle of the colonial people against the oppressive imperialist bourgeoisie (Migwe, 1983).

National oppression and class exploitation, for him, had to be linked to capitalism. Thus, the emergence of nations had to be understood in the context of the rise of capitalism. The development of nations, he argued, had been driven by the economic factor (Mzala, 1988). During this process, economic ties led to the creation of internal markets, which in turn led to the emergence of settlements of communities in territories – a process that was accompanied by the formation of common languages for communication and national conscience (Mzala, 1988). This is in line with Lenin's articulation of the nation-formation process, later emphasised by Stalin, that in the precapitalist period, elements of nationhood, such as language, territory and common culture, did not fall from the skies but most likely became a reality during the epoch of rising capitalism, 'with its national market and its economic and cultural centers' (Stalin, 1929: 5).

Therefore, Mzala was of the view that the 'Marxist definition of a nation, concrete and historical character, rejects any timeless or abstract theory that wholly divorces a nation from its essential material root, that is from its social essence in human history' (Mzala, 1988: 32). With this historical emergence of nations, capitalism used nationalism to submit the class interests of the workers to their class rule (Mzala, 1988). As Lenin (1914) argued, these were essentially bourgeois nations. However, Mzala was cautious of engaging with history in a static and mechanical manner. For example, the limitations of the role of language in nation-formation, as enunciated by Stalin (1929), were found wanting when countries such as Germany, with a common language, produced two nations.

For Mzala, the national question had to be understood in the context of various epochs and developments that shaped the country's history. Therefore, not only was 1652 important, in that it marked the arrival of the first white settlers in South Africa, but so was the 1910 formation of the Union of South Africa, which essentially set in motion the creation of a white nation. On the other hand, the 1912 formation of the ANC equally set in motion the creation of an African nation. These nation-formation processes were along similar lines to the European context linked to the development of capitalism (Mzala, 1988). However, the intentions of these nation-formation processes were different. While the formation of the Union sought to consolidate the white nation's grip on power and domination, economically and culturally, the formation of the ANC was driven by the imperative of self-determination and the ending of the subjugation of Africans by regaining political and economic independence.

Mzala (1988) argued that it was primarily capitalism that united Africans in South Africa. Through the process of capitalist production, various African ethnic groups and tribes met and ultimately developed their own national consciousness. This led to the formation of the national liberation movements and aspirations to build their own nation-state of South Africa, their native land. The nationalism of the African people was not an abstraction, but concrete and material, informed by their race position in the country's wealth – and the entire superstructure[2] (Mzala, 1988).

---

2   Marx's base and superstructure metaphor articulates that the economic base or the current 'mode of production', influences the superstructure, which comprises 'the surface elements of society such as law, ideology, culture' (Spence, 2009: 212).

White communists and the national question in South Africa

The South African liberation struggle owes part of its success to the role played by the white communists, most of whom arrived in the country in the late 19th century as artisans. Many belonged to labour and socialist organisations in their countries of origins and thus 'became the first organisers of the labour movement' in South Africa (Mzala, 1988: 36). Communists played a major role in most effective campaigns by black South Africans, especially in the 1940s and 1950s. Campaigns such as the Defiance Campaign were a culmination of this influence, where workplace trade union and community activism were fused in the same people (Lodge, 2021). However, to understand the role of white workers in the national question, it is important to appreciate their location in the South African capitalist economy. Mzala went back to Slovo (1976) to argue that the white worker was not just getting crumbs 'but had a seat at the table of the capitalist class helping in the domination of the black working class' (Mzala, 1988: 38). He also found parallels with Marx's articulation of the hostility between the English and the Irish working classes, where the English workers regarded themselves as 'a member of the ruling nation' (Marx 1870), thus reducing themselves to a capitalist tool.

Similarly, in the South African context, a dichotomous relationship between black and white workers emerged. A progressive section of white workers elevated the conflict between labour and capital, while national oppression was an important factor for black workers. In essence, the national question was a more sensitive matter for black workers, whereas it was not a fundamental political question for white workers, and hence it was neglected (Mzala, 1988). A reactionary tendency among white workers was further exposed during the 1922 Rand Revolt with their infamous slogan, 'Workers of the World Unite for a White South Africa' (Breckenridge, 2007: 242). The upside to this unfortunate turn of events is that it exposed to white communists the importance of the national question (Mzala, 1988).

To an extent, this attitude by white workers remains with trade unions such as Solidarity (*Solidariteit*) often siding with capital on the national question, precisely because they have historically benefitted from the oppression and exploitation of black workers. Solidarity was spawned by the historical race division within the working class and Afrikaner nationalism of a sovereign Afrikaner *volkstaat* (people's state). Thus, it has resisted labour and political reforms that seek to redress the apartheid legacy by 'joining forces with right-wing political parties, demonstrations and strikes' (Visser, 2007) with the primary objective of preserving the apartheid racial privileges. The emergence of the International Socialist League (ISL) in 1915 could be characterised as a turning point in working-class politics in South Africa. Here, again, Mzala saw a close link between the national and class question. He regarded the ISL's role as important in that it sought to unite the working class across racial lines by calling for the freedom of Africans (Mzala, 1988). For Mzala, these communist pioneers were inspiring in their solution to the national question, which they regarded as being tied to the socialist struggle. 'With the emancipation of labour from capital, the black worker, it was hoped, would then rise to a position of equality with his white counterpart. Great hope was vested in the revolutionary potential of that section of white workers which pledged its unqualified support for socialism' (Mzala, 1988: 46).

The right to self-determination

The nation-formation process goes beyond producing a state that is 'functional' for capital. With democracy comes a momentum that also threatens the interests of the bourgeoisie since the state consists of both the capitalist and the working classes. The state cannot be abstracted from the economy and hence 'nation-formation acquires its coherence and legitimacy as the struggle for self-determination and democracy' (Hoffman and Mzala, 1990: 416). Mzala perceived the national question as a class question, which could not be fully comprehended outside the class rule. Thus, he ascribed to the communists, the lucid articulation of self-determination.

The Communist International (Comintern) resolution on the national and colonial questions was crucial since, for the first time, this matter was elevated from being just a country-specific issue to an international question. Hence, for Mzala, Lenin's intervention on the national and colonial questions was critical and this was the perspective that had to be considered in the South African context. To this end, the existence of the oppressor and oppressed nations in South Africa had to be considered in the context of imperialism. Therefore, the colonial question had to be addressed by dealing with the fundamental question of the right of the oppressed to self-determination (Mzala, 1988).

Lenin's view, that to achieve socialism, communists from the oppressor nations had to fight for the right of the oppressed nations, was important for Mzala. Of course, within both the oppressor and the oppressed nations there were class dynamics, mainly premised on the exploitation of the working class by its national bourgeoisie. Thus, the

> Comintern's formulation of the South African national question thesis elevated the importance of the right of the oppressed to self-determination. The 'black republic' thesis must, therefore, be understood in this context. The Comintern's intervention for the SACP to prioritise and advance the struggle for national liberation, which must precede the social transformation, became the foundation of the SACP's policy on the national question (Mzala, 1988).

However, the concept of self-determination was not without controversy or contestation. For example, Rosa Luxemburg regarded Lenin's approach as 'Utopian' (Page, 1950: 350). She argued that it was 'a veritable perversion of socialism to regard present-day capitalist society as the expression of this self-determination of nations' (Luxemburg, 1976: 289). Nevertheless, Lenin's articulation

> would be central to how the South African revolution would define the relationship between the national and class struggle (Mzala, 1988).

The national and class struggle

For Mzala, the resolution of the South African national question was premised on the class content of the national liberation struggle. He argued that national liberation would be incomplete if it did not proceed to socialism. On these bases, he defended the nationalism of the ANC in that it should 'not be confused with the classical drive by the elitist group among the oppressed people to gain ascendency so that they can replace the oppressor in the exploitation of the mass' (Mzala, 1988: 51). He regarded the ANC as having been able to maintain the integration of national and economic emancipation, because it was alive to the reality that while Africans suffered national humiliation, they were also deprived of their right to the country's wealth. Thus, 'the correction of economic injustice lies at the very core of solving of the national question' (Mzala, 1988: 51).

Mzala argued that the national question should not be treated merely as a historical basis but rather as a class basis. In his articulation of a socialist-oriented national liberation, he postulated that while bourgeois liberals forget that the national liberation struggle was just the first stage of a social revolution, 'Marxists consider the socio-economic base of national oppression and the solution of the national question in a revolutionary way that will end in victory for the working class' (Mzala, 1988: 51). Although not advocating for a crude stagism, Mzala was conscious of the reality that a social revolution was not an event that could be won in a single victory. On the contrary, this entailed a series of stages of tackling various problems, with the ultimate objective being the 'expropriation of the bourgeoisie' (Mzala, 1988: 51).

To his mind, waging a socialist struggle on the terrain of the national liberation struggle was informed by the democratic content of nationalism against colonial oppression. For Mzala, this in no way meant support for a tendency towards 'national exclusiveness' of the bourgeois elite among the oppressed, who would take over as new exploiters (Mzala, 1988: 51). While Mzala acknowledged the importance of socialists' commitment to national democracy, he was conscious of the limitations of the national bourgeoisie. Thus, he invoked Lenin:

> To throw off oppression is the imperative duty to the proletariat as a democratic force, and is certainly in the interests of the proletarian class struggle, which is obscured and retarded by bickering on the national question. But to go beyond these strictly limited and historical limits in helping bourgeoisie nationalism means betraying the proletariat and siding with the bourgeoisie (Lenin, 1914, cited in Mzala 1988: 52).

This could be considered as one of the dilemmas facing contemporary South African socialists and their alliance with the national bourgeois movement. While the ANC, with the help of the communists and the working class, was central in throwing off oppression and proceeding to implement progressive policies to transform the country, it remains a nationalist movement. To this end, its programmes such as the Growth, Employment and Redistribution (GEAR) policy, an orthodox macro-economic policy that stressed deficit reduction and a tight monetary policy, combined with trade liberalisation (Weeks, 1999), have been bourgeois nationalist in character and the organisation has demonstrated an inability to decisively end class exploitation. Yet, owing to historical ties, communists have felt compelled to support the ANC, based on the minimalist programme to transform society. By so doing, the communists have risked co-option into this 'bourgeoisie nationalism' and are thus 'betraying the proletariat' (Lenin, 1914).

Working-class internationalism and the national question

Mzala was convinced that the South African revolutionary theory on the national question was aligned with the epoch of the transition from capitalism to socialism. To this effect, he would not have agreed with the new theories emerging from the ANC, such as the national democratic society (NDS). The NDS regards the national phase of the struggle as the end, without addressing the capitalist structure of the economy on which the unequal wealth distribution that shapes the South African national question is premised. Mzala conceded that the national movements inspired by the formation of nation-states because of capitalism were bourgeois in content. However, he believed that their character had been altered by the rise of the working class at their helm, and that this changed their social content and their attitudes to the national question (Mzala, 1988).

He regarded the solving of the national question as contingent on the working class taking the lead against national oppression and class exploitation. However, he perceived this to be based on class consciousness, free from narrow nationalism. In this way, the working class would not side with its own national bourgeoisie against the working class of other nations. If that were to happen, he argued, it would weaken international solidarity and divide the working class. In the context of the South African revolution, Mzala regarded the national question as requiring emphasis on the unity of black and white workers so that they are not diluted by narrow nationalism. Nevertheless, the basis for this to occur would involve the appreciation by the white working class that it would never free itself from capitalist exploitation until black people were free from white supremacy. 'Furthermore', he argued, 'the unity of black and white workers will remain a pipe-dream unless white workers recognize the right of Blacks to self-determination' (Mzala, 1988: 53).

For Mzala, the content of the national question depended on the class that raised it. But, as mentioned, he was against any form of nationalism that bred hostility between workers of different nations or nationalities. Instead, he argued for the unity of the working class and regarded anything less to be 'petty bourgeois national opportunism' (Mzala, 1988: 54). The ANC and the SACP, according to Mzala, had articulated a solution to South Africa's national question that was premised on the integration of the two nations – the oppressor and the oppressed nations – into a single South African nation on condition of total equality. Fundamentally, this integration would 'proceed systematically if the exercise is headed by the working class' (Mzala, 1988: 54). He considered the working class to be the motive force of this process:

> If the aim of the South African revolution is not only to end the inequality between the black and white nations, but also between

African, Indian, Coloured, Afrikaner and English nationalities, and the racial hostility that goes with that national hostility, it is also to bring these nations and nationalities into a single South African nation without any national or racial privileges. To achieve this aim, it is necessary to organize the only class that is capable of achieving this kind of revolution – the working class (Mzala, 1988: 54).

Mzala was convinced that, by organising the working class in this fashion, the national democratic revolution to socialism would proceed uninterruptedly. To his mind, it was impossible to redress and abolish national inequalities under capitalism. This task, Mzala thought, was tantamount to abolishing classes, just as Lenin (1916) had argued that the capitalist transformation to socialism could only occur when the proletariat create the possibility of abolishing national oppression. However, the smoothness of this transition, according to Mzala, was dependent on the class at the head of the revolution (Mzala, 1988).

NON-HISTORIC NATIONS AND THE NATIONAL QUESTION

In applying Marxism to the national question, Mzala could not escape engaging with the concept of 'non-historic nations'. His thoughts on this topic are best captured in his 1990 paper, jointly written with John Hoffman. In their analysis of the national question, Marx and Engels (1974) characterised those nation states that were produced by capitalism in 19th century Europe as progressive, while condemning as 'non-historic' those nationalities that they regarded as constituting a barrier to capitalist progress. This dismissive and derogatory characterisation of the 'non-historic-nations' has been regarded as embarrassing by Marxists (Hoffman and Mzala, 1990). While admitting that the 'non-historic nations' formulation was problematic, Hoffman and Mzala (1990) believed that there was some valid and viable rationale behind it. They regarded the formulation as having significant relevance in the examination of the national question in South Africa.

The problem of ethnicity

Mzala's posture on ethnicity was also influenced by historical materialism. He found value in Lenin's (1914) characterisation of the 'exaggeration' of ethnic factors as the substance of bourgeois nationalism. Hence, he regarded the ethnic policies of the colonial apartheid rulers as a strategy to prevent Africans from forming their own African nation. Through this strategy, South Africa would continue to be a 'white nation' with the Africans fragmented in smaller pieces of impoverished homelands. In this way, Indians and coloureds, who constitute part of South Africa, remained 'until 1983 in a kind of ideological limbo' (Hoffman and Mzala, 1990: 423). In such an environment it becomes imperative to develop a cogent conceptualisation to distinguish between 'authentic and illusory nations, and between ethnically based nationalities and a democratic structured nation, [otherwise] no meaningful challenge to apartheid is possible' (Hoffman and Mzala, 1990: 423). The unity of the oppressed and the exploited working class was central to Mzala's analysis of the national question.

He could not fathom how the Afrikaners, and whites in general, could be regarded as constituting a South African nation. To do so would be to deny the existence of the majority black people in the country. Moreover, he argued, 'their very existence as colonial nationalities' was premised precisely on their 'denial of the African peoples the right to self-determination and democracy' (Hoffman and Mzala, 1990: 424). On the other hand, the various African ethnic communities in South Africa could not be regarded as separate nations 'since a historico-economic examination of their existence demonstrates that they are nationalities from which an African nation was forged' (Hoffman and Mzala, 1990: 424). This African nation developed because of capitalism in South Africa. But until that point, the various ethnic communities constituted a perfect example of Engels' characterisation of 'non-historic nations' as, in their individual existence in the bantustans, they stood 'as a barrier to the full consolidation of a South African nation' (Hoffman and Mzala, 1990: 424).

However, in defining a nation, various tendencies are apparent, such as ethnic nationalism, which is perceived as an 'organic folk-community which would immerse the individual in the unbroken chain of tradition' (Kohn, 1955: 34). The liberal tendency is antithetical, given its focus on things such as individual and property rights, the significance of equality before the law, the equal participation of citizens in political and social life, etc (Massey, Hodson and Sekulić, 2003). A liberal conception of nationalism regards the limit of 'governmental power' while securing civil rights by creating a 'rational civil society' (Kohn, 1955: 29). However, Mamdani (2021) posits that liberal theory 'embraced one group identity, the nation, unconditionally', its claim to have eschewed group identity in favour of individual agency notwithstanding. However, a conceptualisation of the nation such as Mamdani's (2018), in his characterisation of 'citizen' and 'subject', fails to appreciate the role of capitalism and hence the class antagonism that emerges therein. A nation ought to stand on democratic pillars rather than ethnicity and, thus, the South African revolution's primary task was to unite these multiple nationalities into a single democratic nation-state. This, while considering the whites, Indians and coloureds as minority national groups who are entitled to play a full and equal role in the building of the new nation (Hoffman and Mzala, 1990).

CONCLUSION

What is evident in Mzala's writing, and crucial for consideration when engaging with his work, is the fact that his praxis, and thus frame of analysis, were firmly located within a Marxist–Leninist national liberation movement. His thoughts were grounded in the classical Marxist tradition, in particular, what is perceived to be an economic determinist perspective in articulating consciousness and ideology (see Polanyi, 2001). It is, therefore, unsurprising that his choice of scholarly collaborators such as John Hoffman, who later became his supervisor for his doctorate, were steeped in classical Marxism. Perhaps Mzala's fights with Harold Wolpe, his initial doctoral supervisor, who insisted, inter alia, that Mzala drop the rigid line he had adopted on the national question, could be understood in this context (see Radebe, 2022).

Not that Mzala was oblivious to other Marxist traditions, as witnessed in his frustration with the *African Communist*'s refusal to accept Pallo Jordan's article on the basis that it was not its task to 'undertake reappraisal of Trotsky and Trotskyism but rather to develop Marxist–Leninist thought in Africa' (Radebe, 2022: 223). In fact, Mzala was critical of the *African Communist* and its record of 'unmitigated intolerance of those Marxist positions that were questioning the legitimacy of the Soviet practice' (Radebe, 2022: 297). Nevertheless, his association and location limited his interactions with other traditions in his writings, for obvious reasons. Absent from his writings was consultation with Eurocommunism and the British 'New Left' theorists who engaged similar topics, including national identity, such as Tom Nairn and even older Marxists outside the Lenin tradition like Gramsci.

In any event, through his writings, Mzala considered the major obstacle to national unity in South Africa as the nationalism of the oppressor nation. Indeed, almost 30 years after the democratic breakthrough, the oppressor nation, both the far right and the liberals, has actively and subtly resisted national unity, which it perceives as a threat to its ill-gotten privileges. Even its working class, through labour unions such as Solidarity, has opted to side with their national bourgeoisie in resisting social transformation, precisely because, as white workers, they had a seat in the national oppression of black people. This resistance has played into the hands of narrow ethno-nationalists within the formerly oppressed, as can be observed in the rise of narrow populist organisations such as the Economic Freedom Fighters (EFF) and the Black First Land First (BLF).

Although Mzala's views were pivotal in the conceptualisation of the South African nation post-apartheid and the post-apartheid democratic dispensation has sought to build a united South African nation, there is little doubt that Mzala's vision has floundered. This is because the revolutionary movement jettisoned the critical pillars of working-class leadership at the helm of the national liberation movement and, as a result, the national liberation movement has failed to build on its gains and proceed towards socialism, which would be a cornerstone in resolving South Africa's national question. Of course, the ANC has never pretended to be a socialist organisation, its stance as a disciplined force of the left notwithstanding. And equally, as Nzimande (2004) once posited, it has never been anti-socialist either. As Luxemburg (1976) argued, self-determination is impossible in a bourgeois democratic society. The black working class remains subalternised, with little to no self-determination to speak of.

Part of the solution rests on a non-racial working class solidarity at national level, where there is mobilisation of collective resources (Burawoy, 2019), and at the international level, as recently witnessed in the United Kingdom and the United States where efforts to draw attention to 'the dynamics, structures, inequalities, and contradictions of capitalism as the systemic core of neoliberal globalization and ruling class privilege and power' have been made (Maher, Gindin and Panitch, 2020: 1). In the final analysis, it is only through socialism as a building block towards a classless society that true self-determination of the working class is possible.

REFERENCES

Breckenridge, K. (2007). 'Fighting for a white South Africa: White working-class racism and the 1922 Rand Revolt: The 1922 Insurrection and Racial Killing in South Africa, Jeremy Krikler: Book review', *South African Historical Journal*, 57(1): 228–43.

Burawoy, M. (2019). 'Painting socialism: Working-class formation in Hungary and Poland', in S.G. McNall (ed.). *Bringing Class Back In: Contemporary and historical perspectives.* London: Routledge, pp. 311–30.

Chennells, A. (1997). 'Plotting South African history: Narrative in Sol Plaatje's Mhudi', *English in Africa*, 24(1): 37–58.

Connor, W. (1978). 'A nation is a nation, is a state, is an ethnic group is a ...', *Ethnic and Racial Studies*, 1(4): 377–400.

Davis, H.B. (1976). *The National Question: Selected writings of Rosa Luxemburg.* New York: Monthly Review Press.

De Kiewiet, C.W. (1937). *The Imperial Factor: A study in politics and economics.* eBook (2022). London: Routledge. https://doi.org/10.4324/9781003306832

Drew, A. (2018). 'Marxist theory in African settler societies: Algeria and South Africa'. Available at: http://www.africanstudies.uct.ac.za/sites/

default/files/image_tool/images/327/2018/Drew-Marxism-African.pdf (Accessed 20 April 2023).

Dunton, C. (2003). 'Pixley ka Isaka Seme and the African renaissance debate', *African Affairs*, 102(409): 555–73.

Egan, A. (2012). 'South African liberalism and South African history: An ongoing challenge', *Focus*, (65). Available at: https://hsf.org.za/publications/focus/focus-65/04.%20A_Egan%20-%20South%20African%20Liberalism%20and%20South%20African%20History.pdf (Accessed 20 April 2023).

Fuze, M.M. and Cope, A.T. (1979). *The Black People and Whence They Came: A Zulu view*. Pietermaritzburg: University of Natal Press.

Hoffman, J. and Mzala, N. (1990). 'Non-historic nations' and the national question: A South African perspective', *Science & Society*, 54(4): 408–26.

Khumalo Migwe [Mzala] (1983). 'Karl Marx and the colonial question', *African Communist*, 94 (Third quarter).

Kohn, H. (1955). *Nationalism: Its meaning and history*. Princeton, NJ: D. Van Nostrand.

Kunovich, R.M. and Hodson, R. (1999). 'Conflict, religious identity, and ethnic intolerance in Croatia', *Social Forces*, 78(2): 643–68.

Lembede, A.M. (1945). 'Some basic principles of African Nationalism', *Ilangalase Natal*.

Lenin, V.I. (1966). 'The working class and the national question', *Collected Works*, 19, pp. 91–92.

Lenin, V.I. (1916). 'The socialist revolution and the right of nations to self-determination', *Collected Works*, 22, pp. 143–56.

Lerumo, A. (1971). '*The Oxford History of South Africa, Vol. II: South Africa, 1870–1966*. Edited by M. Wilson and L. Thompson. Book review', *African Communist* (0001-9976), 47, p. 122.

Lodge, T. (2021). *Red Road to Freedom: A history of the South African Communist Party 1921–2021*. Johannesburg: Jacana Media.

Luxemburg, R. (1976). *The National Question: Selected writings by Rosa Luxemburg*, Vol. 24. New York: New York University Press.

Maloka, E. (2014). *Friends of the Natives: The inconvenient past of South African liberalism*. Durban: 3rd Millennium Publishing.

Mamdani, M. (2021). 'The nation-state and its minorities: Some questions on reading Madhav Khosla, India's Founding Moment', *Global Intellectual History*, 8(1): 1–6.

Mamdani, M. (2018). *Citizen and Subject: Contemporary Africa and the legacy of late colonialism*. Princeton, NJ: Princeton University Press.

Marx, K. and Engels, F. (1974). *On Colonialism*. Moscow: Progress Publishers.

Macmillan, W.M. (1927). *The Cape Colour Question: A historical survey*. London: Faber & Gwyer.

Maher, S., Gindin, S. and Panitch, L. (2020). 'Class politics, socialist policies, capitalist constraints', in L. Panich and G. Albo (eds). *Beyond Market Dystopia: New ways of living, Socialist Register 2020*, p. 56.

Migwe, K. (1983). 'MK soldiers viewpoint – Let is organise', *Dawn*, 7(6): 12–14.

Molema, S.M. (1920). *The Bantu, Past and Present: An ethnographical and historical study of the native races of South Africa*, Vol. 5. Edinburgh: W. Green & Son.

Massey, G., Hodson, R. and Sekulić, D. (2003). 'Nationalism, liberalism and liberal nationalism in post-war Croatia', *Nations and Nationalism*, 9(1): 55–82.

Mzala, J.N. (1988). 'Revolutionary theory on the national question in South Africa', in M. Van Diepen (ed.). *The National Question in South Africa*. London: Zed Books: pp. 30-55.

Nombila, A.W. (2018). 'Reading the idea of nation, Pan-Africanism and globalization in the thought of Dr Silas Modiri Molema', *Journal of African Union Studies*, 7(2): 149–61.

Nxumalo, J. Mzala. (1992). *The National Question in the Writing of South African History: A critical survey of some major tendencies*, DPP Working Paper, 22. London: Development Policy and Practice Research Group, Open University.

Nzimande, B. (2004). 'An ANC U-turn, or the Progressive Consolidation of a Majority Left Consensus?'. Available at: https://numsa.org.za/2004/09/an-anc-uturn-or-the-progressive-consolidation-of-a-majority-left-consensus/ (Accessed 20 April 2023).

Page, S.W. (1950). 'Lenin and self-determination', *The Slavonic and East European Review*, 28(71): 342–58.

Plaatje, S.T. (1921). *Native Life in South Africa: Before and since the European War and the Boer Rebellion*. London: PS King and Son.

Polanyi, K. (2001). *The Great Transformation: The political and economic origins of our time*. Boston, MA: Beacon Press.

Radebe, M.J. (2022). *The Lost Prince of the ANC: The life and times of Jabulani Nobleman 'Mzala' Nxumalo*. Johannesburg: Jacana Media.

Rose, R. (1964). 'Parties, factions and tendencies in Britain', *Political Studies*, 12(1): 33–46.

SACP. (1991). 'A tribute to Mzala'. Available at: http://www.sacp.org.za/main.php?ID=2313 (Accessed 14 December 2021).

Shepperson, G. (1962). 'Pan-Africanism and "Pan-Africanism": Some historical notes', *Phylon (1960–)*, 23(4): 346–58.

Shivji, I.G. (2019). 'Sam Moyo and Samir Amin on the peasant question', *Agrarian South: Journal of Political Economy*, 8(1-2): 287–302.

Slovo, J. (1988). 'The South African working class and the national democratic revolution'. South African Communist Party. Available at: https://www.marxists.org/subject/africa/slovo/1988/national-democratic-revolution.htm (Accessed 20 April 2023).

Spence, C. (2009). 'Social accounting's emancipatory potential: A Gramscian critique', *Critical Perspectives on Accounting*, 20(2): 205–27.

Stalin, J. (1929). 'The national question and Leninism', *PRISM: Political and Rights Issues and Social Movements*, 286.

Visser, W. (2007). 'Labour and right-wing extremism in the South African Context: A historical overview', *ITH-Tagungsberichte*, Vol. 41. Available at: http://academic.sun.ac.za/history/downloads/wvisserlabour.pdf (Accessed 14 December 2021).

Visser, W. (2004). 'Trends in South African historiography and the present state of historical research'. Paper presented at the Nordic Africa Institute, Uppsala, Sweden, 23 September 2004. Available at: http://sun025.sun.ac.za/portal/page/portal/Arts/Departemente1/geskiedenis/docs/trends_sahi storiography.pdf (Accessed 14 December 2021).

Webster, E. and Mawbey, J. (2017). 'Revisiting the national question', in E. Webster, K. Pampallis, J. Mawbey and J. Cronin (eds). *The Unresolved National Question in South Africa: Left thought under apartheid and beyond*. New York: New York University Press.

Weeks, J. (1999). 'Commentary. Stuck in low GEAR? Macroeconomic policy in South Africa, 1996–98', *Cambridge Journal of Economics*, 23(6): 795–811.

Wright, H. (1975). 'Monica Wilson and Leonard Thompson (eds). *The Oxford History of South Africa. Vol. 2* (Book review)', *The American Historical Review* (0002-8762), 80(2): 456.

FOUR

THE FIRST AND SECOND TRANSITIONS AND THE NATIONAL QUESTION IN SOUTH AFRICA[1]

Gregory Houston and Yul Derek Davids

INTRODUCTION

Jabulani 'Mzala' Nxumalo was one of a number of South Africans who grappled with the issue of the national question (No Sizwe, 1979; Jordan, 1988; Pahad, 1988; Wolpe, 1988; Carrim, 1996; Dexter, 1996; Jara, 2006; Suttner, 2011; Alexander, 2012; Jordan, 2012;). In this chapter, his theorisation of the national question in South Africa is used as the basis for an analysis of the impact of the ruling African National Congress's (ANC's) first transition – democratising state and society and meeting basic needs – towards the resolution of the national question. Data from the South African Social Attitudes Survey of the Human Sciences Research Council (HSRC) is used to illustrate how national unity has been undermined by the persistence

---

1 This is an updated version of a paper presented at the inaugural colloquium of the Mzala Nxumalo Centre for the Study of South African Society: 'South Africa today: To what extent has the country achieved the goals of the liberation struggle?' 8–9 April 2016, Redlands Hotel and Conference Centre, Pietermaritzburg.

of various 'nationalisms', as well as the unintended consequences of the transformative agenda during the first transition. This is followed by a review of the ANC's notion of a second transition – socio-economic transformation over the next 30 to 50 years – in the context of the ongoing challenges faced in the resolution of the national question.

THE NATIONAL QUESTION IN SOUTH AFRICA

In his most detailed discussion of the national question, Mzala (1988) argued, on the one hand, that capitalist development in South Africa gave rise to unity among African workers, and 'built national consciousness and a desire towards the formation of their own national state over the whole of South Africa'. He added that the 'nationalism of the oppressed black people in South Africa ... is a reflection of the black people's concrete material conditions in the colour-defined position they occupy in relation to the wealth of the country, the political institutions of administration, education, etc.' (Mzala, 1988: 40). On the other hand, the white settler population had 'systematically conquered the territory and subjected the indigenous inhabitants to political oppression and economic exploitation'. This had resulted in a 'division of South Africa into oppressor and oppressed nations'.

For Mzala, the only way the national question could be resolved was through the right of the oppressed to self-determination. He concludes that, for the ANC and South African Communist Party (SACP), 'the solution of the national question in South Africa can only proceed from the integration of the two nations, under conditions of total equality, into a single South African nation' (Mzala, 1988: 54). This, he argued, will occur once 'the people of South Africa liberate themselves from apartheid oppression', at which time 'they will gravitate irresistibly towards integration'.

After 29 years of democracy, national unity remains elusive in South Africa and liberation did not open the way for the gravitation towards integration. According to Mazibuko Jara (2006), there are several reasons for this, including the fact that national liberation in South Africa did not lead to a transition from capitalism to socialism, as Mzala had expected. Mzala's treatment of the national question did not accommodate the transition stage of the National Democratic Revolution (NDR). Indeed, his expectation was that the NDR would 'proceed uninterruptedly to socialism'. For Mzala (1988), it was only through the abolition of classes that national inequality could be abolished, which was not possible under capitalism.

In addition, Mzala – and the ANC and SACP – paid very little attention to the impact of apartheid on the development of racial identities among the white, coloured[2] and Indian[3] communities during that era. The Nationalist Party's (NP) concept of nationhood restricted qualification to membership of the nation to specific characteristics and aspects such as culture, language, race, etc. From the outset of its rule in 1948, it embarked on a systematic programme to separate the race groups in all aspects.

By contrast, the concept of nationhood derived from African nationalism – an inclusive nationhood in which race, colour, religion, etc. would be irrelevant – was based on territory, as opposed to race or ethnicity. This is embodied in one of the clauses of the ANC's Freedom Charter, drafted in 1955: 'South Africa belongs to all who live in it, black and white.' At the time Mzala wrote his article on the national question in the late 1980s, Africans, coloureds, Indians and white democrats had been drawn into a united struggle against apartheid. The most significant factor that facilitated the increasing participation of minority populations in the anti-apartheid struggle was the formation of the United Democratic Front (UDF) in 1983. By the end of the decade, the anti-apartheid struggle had touched virtually every coloured and Indian community in the country and, increasingly, coloured, Indian and white people had been drawn into organisations affiliated to the ANC-aligned UDF. It appeared that some degree of integration had occurred during the course of the struggle.

---

2 Several scholars have written about the development of coloured identity in the Western Cape. These include Adhikari (1992), Goldin (1987), Jung (2000) and Lewis (1987). Adhikari (1992) claims that a coloured identity had developed in the Western Cape by the 1880s.

3 Scholars who have examined Indian identity include Singh and Vawda (1988), Arkin, Magyar and Pillay (1989), Freund (1995), Moodley (1975), Pachai (1971), and Vahed and Desai (2010).

However, soon after the unbanning of the ANC and SACP in February 1990, it became clear that there was an emerging realisation among coloureds, Indians and whites that their interests were 'threatened by the African National Congress's programmes and statements rather than in some way accommodated'.[4] Jakes Gerwel (1991) identified the problem as one arising from the fact:

> that apartheid did create separate social entities and that people do have what we sometimes in Congress jargon used to call nationality feelings around those issues ... I think there was an assumption that the non-racialism which we saw as an anti-apartheid expression in the resistance period translates itself equally positively into organisational membership ... In the resistance period, it was around the non-racial opposition to apartheid that the nationally oppressed groups came together. Now we are talking about preparing to govern and people think in a different mode about that.[5]

It is at this stage that it became clear that members of minority groups were beginning to think of the future in terms of their racial identities. Thus, instead of the irreversible gravitation towards integration that Mzala had predicted – which had increasingly taken place during the course of the liberation struggle and reached unprecedented heights during the 1980s – racial identities began to play an increasingly important role during the early 1990s.

NATIONAL IDENTITY IN THE POST-APARTHEID ERA

During the democratic era, racial identities remain entrenched. This is demonstrated by data drawn from the South African Social Attitudes Survey (SASAS), a cross-sectional survey series conducted

---

4 Interview with Rory Riordan conducted by Padraig O'Malley, 8 August 1991, The O'Malley Archives, Nelson Mandela Foundation. Available at: https://omalley.nelsonmandela.org/omalley/index.php/site/q/03lv00017/04lv00344/05lv00511/06lv 00543.htm (Accessed 20 April 2023).

5 Interview with Jakes Gerwel conducted by Padraig O'Malley, 16 September 1991, The O'Malley Archives, Nelson Mandela Foundation. Available at: https://omalley.nelsonmandela.org/omalley/index.php/site/q/03lv00017/04lv0 0344/05lv00511/06lv 00600.htm (Accessed 20 April 2023).

annually by the HSRC since 2003. The survey series consists of nationally representative probability samples of South African adults aged 16 years and older living in private households. Each SASAS round consists of a sample of 500 population census enumeration areas (EAs) as primary sampling units, stratified by province, geographical sub-type and majority population group. A split sample design is used, with two different questionnaire versions, each being administered to 3 500 target respondents in order to accommodate increased thematic content. The survey series aims to explain the interaction between the country's changing institutions, its political and economic structures, and the attitudes, beliefs and behaviour patterns of its diverse populations (Roberts, Kivilu and Davids, 2010; Roberts, Weir-Smith and Reddy, 2011). Use is made of data drawn from the 2003 to 2020 SASAS rounds.

The starting point is to assess the degree of national unity in South Africa, beginning with levels of pride in the nation. From 2003, the SASAS series asked respondents whether they agreed, neither agreed nor disagreed, or disagreed with the following statement: 'I would rather be a citizen of South Africa than of any other country in the world.'

Figure 4.1: Levels of national pride in being a South African by race, 2003 to 2018 (% saying agree and strongly agree)

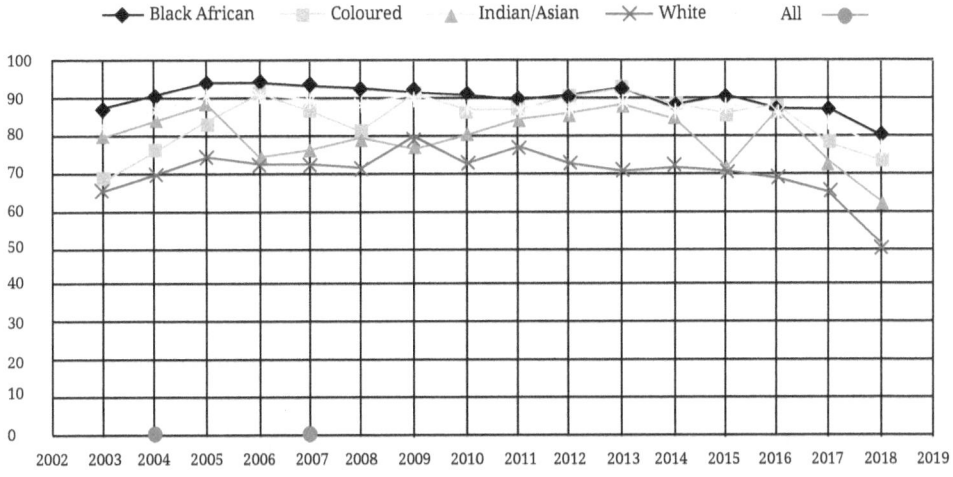

Source: HSRC SASAS 2003–2018
Notes: The 2004 and 2007 values are imputed midpoint figures.

Levels of pride in being South African were above 80 per cent (those saying agree and strongly agree) for all race groups from 2003 to 2017 (Figure 4.1). It is only in 2018 that national pride slipped below the 80 per cent mark when 76 per cent of South Africans indicated that they 'would rather be a citizen of South Africa than of any other country in the world'. However, the disaggregated results showed that in 2012 about 91 per cent of Africans, 90 per cent of coloureds and 86 per cent of Indians felt that they 'would rather be a citizen of South Africa than of any other country in the world', while only 73 per cent of whites felt this way. This pattern is repeated from 2003 to 2018, although levels of national pride across all race groups dropped substantially from 2015 to 2018 (Figure 4.1).

It is clear that there are significant differences in levels of national pride among the different race groups. However, it would be important to cross-tabulate the attitudinal findings against class to see if intensity of 'narrow nationalism' correlates with relative social advantage. Use is made here of data from the 2020 SASAS round on the attitudes of people who self-identify as lower class, working class, middle class, upper middle class, and upper class.

The 2020 SASAS survey round show that levels of pride in being South African declined further to around 75 per cent (Figure 4.2). But national pride was highest among those people who considered themselves lower class (78 per cent) and working class (77 per cent), and lowest among those who considered themselves upper middle class (62 per cent) and upper class (52 per cent). About 72 per cent of people who considered themselves middle class indicated that they 'would rather be a citizen of South Africa than of any other country in the world' (Table 4.1). There is some correlation between the attitudes on this issue of people who believe they belong to a particular class with the attitudes of people who belong to a particular race group. Thus, the higher up the class hierarchy, the lower the level of pride in being South African, which mirrors the hierarchy in levels of national pride of race groups that occupied particular positions in the racial hierarchy that existed during the apartheid era.

Figure 4.2: Levels of national pride in being a South African by class, 2020 (% saying agree and strongly agree)

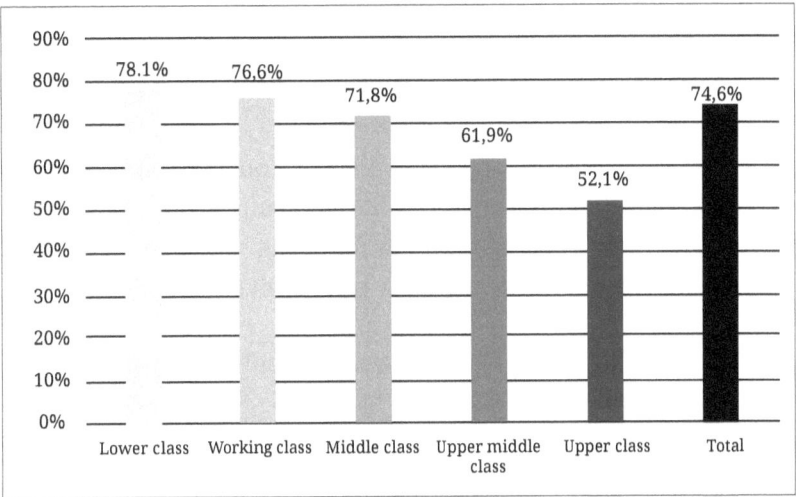

Source: HSRC SASAS 2020

Self-identification is a key indicator of progress towards the development of national unity in the country. Government Communications made use of the Future Fact Mindset Surveys to determine self-identification among South Africans between 2004 and 2012.

Table 4.1: National self-identification, 2004–2012

	2004	2007	2008	2009	2011	2012
As an African	18.4	25.8	32.6	30.2	30.8	29.1
As a South African	52.8	52.6	45.7	54.1	50.8	52.4
By race	4.1	9.9	11.3	7.1	9.1	8.8
By language group	13.6	2.6	3.1	1.9	3.7	4.1

Source: Future Fact Surveys (2004, 2007 to 2009, 2011 and 2012)

Around half of the respondents in the Future Fact Surveys conducted between 2004 and 2012 call themselves 'South African'. There was no change to this level of self-identification between 2004 and 2012, with the level marginally lower in 2012, at 52.4 per cent. Although only a fraction of the respondents categorised themselves according to race, the number was substantially up from the 4.1 per cent of 2004 to 8.8 per cent in 2012. There was, however, a notable drop in self-identification in terms of language group between 2004 and 2012, from 13.6 per cent to 4.1 per cent.

National unity in a highly diversified country relies on trust between the different race groups. Respondents to the SASAS series were asked if they agreed with the following statement: 'People of different racial groups do not really trust or like each other.'

Figure 4.3: Belief that people of the different race groups do not really trust or like each other by race, 2003–2018 (% saying agree and strongly agree)

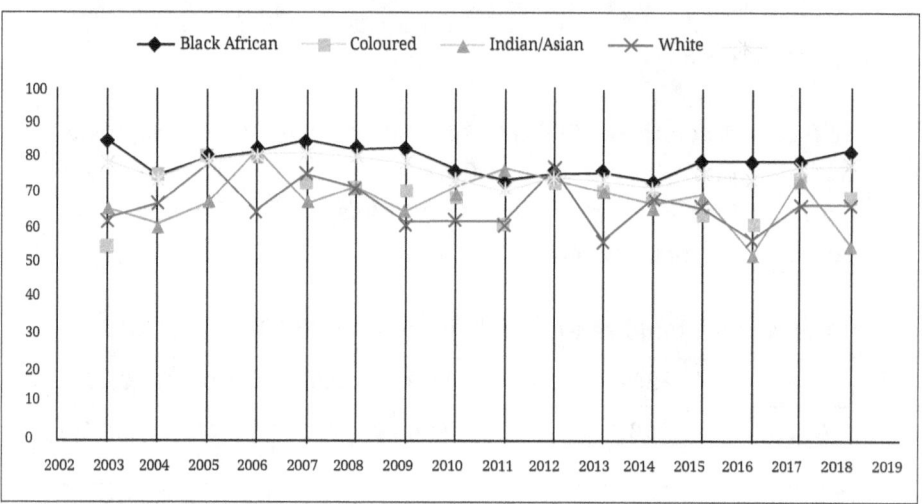

Source: HSRC SASAS 2003–2018
Notes: The 2004 and 2007 values are imputed midpoint figures.

In the HSRC surveys conducted in the period between 2003 and 2018, the overwhelming majority of South Africans of all race groups felt that people of different race groups do not really trust or like each other. This feeling is high among members of all race groups (73 per cent in 2008) and higher on average among Africans (75 per cent) than the other race groups (coloureds – 65 per cent; Indians – 65 per cent; and whites – 64 per cent) during this period.

The belief among all South Africans that people of different race groups do not really trust or like each other declined to 65 per cent in 2020 (Figure 4.4). However, in that year, about 68 per cent of people who considered themselves lower class and 68 per cent who considered themselves working class felt this way. Close to 60 per cent of people who considered themselves middle class, 62 per cent who considered themselves upper middle class and 56 per cent who considered themselves upper class felt that people of different race groups do not really trust or like each other. Once again, there appears to be a clear difference in beliefs between the classes and a correlation between class and race group attitudes.

Figure 4.4: Belief that people of the different race groups do not really trust or like each other by class, 2020 (% saying agree and strongly agree)[6]

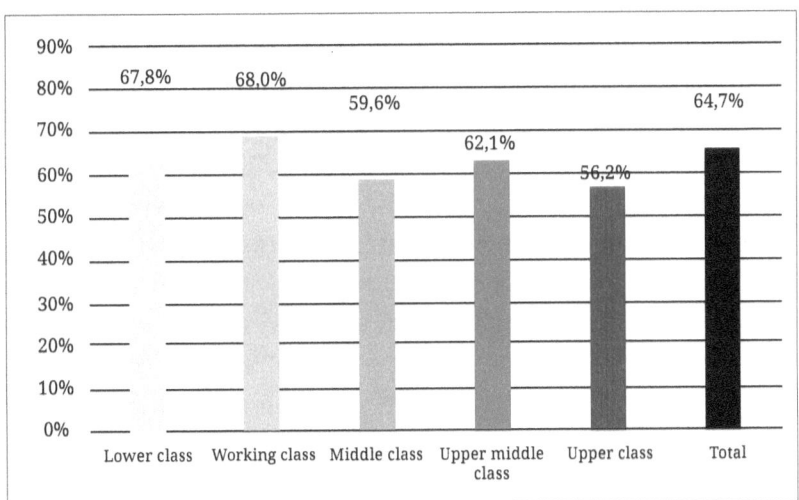

Source: HSRC SASAS 2020

If trust or positive feelings about members of other race groups are indications of social cohesion in diverse societies, the data suggest that the potential for resolving the national question in South Africa is dismal. This then begs the question: What factors, if any, account for these developments during the first democratic transition?

---

6   The 2009 SASAS round did not include the question on trust between the different races. An average figure derived from the other nine years was used for 2009.

THE FIRST TRANSITION

In this section, data from the HSRC SASAS series and other surveys are used to indicate the effect of the first transition on the national question in South Africa. The ANC identified the first transition as consisting of two key elements: democratising state and society; and meeting basic needs (ANC, 2012). The former involved introducing a universal franchise, based on one person, one vote, which was inaugurated with the historic founding elections on 27 April 1994. This led to the election of the first non-racial parliament; the establishment of a Government of National Unity, followed by successive ANC-led administrations, which included people of all race groups; and the transformation of state machinery. The latter led to a change in the doctrines, composition and management style of the civil service, the judiciary, the army, the police and intelligence service. Most importantly, the transformation of state machinery involved a change in the racial composition of all state institutions, which had been dominated by whites during the apartheid era.

At the beginning of 1994, only 2 per cent, 1 per cent, 3 per cent and 5 per cent of managers in the public service were African, coloured, Indian or women, respectively. White males dominated the upper echelons, while African workers, who constituted 70 per cent of public service workers, were located largely in categories defined as unskilled. The transformation of state machinery was aimed at reversing the systematic exclusion of black people and women from senior positions in the public service (Muthien and Houston, 2002: 78).

However, the period of the first transition has been characterised by extensive criticism of the democratic government. For instance, the media often critically draws attention to government failures in areas such as education, the breakdowns in the criminal justice system, non-delivery in the health and hospital sectors, deteriorating infrastructure and so on. Attention is often drawn to specific government departments that are plagued by mismanagement, corruption and a failure of financial systems. Some of the general failures of the public service include poor governance, a lack of accountability, a lack of transparency, incompetent and under-qualified officials, widespread corruption and massive failures in planning, budgeting and implementation. The consequences are service delivery failures, massive under-spending by government departments, negative audit opinions and significant cases of unauthorised, irregular and fruitless and wasteful expenditure, inadequate planning, budgeting and implementation, and numerous cases of fraud and corruption involving senior public officials (Kanyane, Houston and Sausi, 2013).

The transformation of state machinery has impacted differently on the different race groups. This is reflected in the SASAS series by levels of trust in the national government. Figure 4.5 indicates levels of trust in government among the different race groups from 2012 to 2018.

Figure 4.5: Levels of trust in national government by race, 2012–2018 (% saying trust and strongly trust)

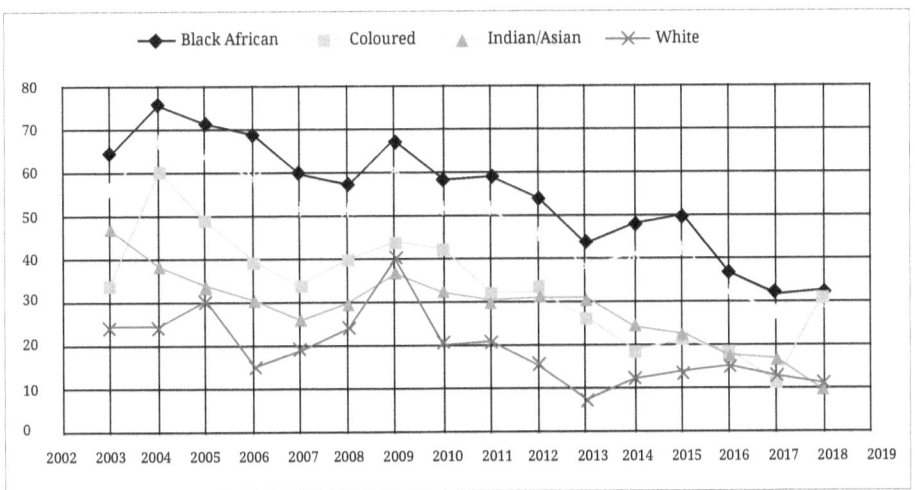

Source: HSRC SASAS 2003–2018
Notes: The 2004 and 2007 values are imputed midpoint figures.

There are significant differences in levels of trust in the national government among the different race groups. While trust in government was 54 per cent for Africans in 2012, coloured and Indian trust in government was 33 per cent and 32 per cent, respectively, and trust in government among whites was 16 per cent (Figure 4.5). These levels of trust were consistent across all race groups from 2003 to 2018. In other words, between 2003 and 2018, Africans displayed higher levels of trust in national government compared to coloured, Indian and white South Africans. What is also interesting to note is that all levels of trust in national government declined between 2003 and 2018 (Figure 4.5).

Trust in the national government among all South Africans had declined to under 33 per cent in 2020 (Figure 4.6). In the same year, while trust in government was above 36 per cent among people who considered themselves lower class, about 7 per cent of people who considered themselves upper class trusted the national government. Just under 36 per cent of people who considered themselves working class trusted the government, while 28 per cent who considered themselves middle class and just above 26 per cent who considered themselves upper middle class felt this way. Thus, the higher up the class hierarchy, the lower the level of trust in government, which mirrors the hierarchy in levels of trust of race groups that occupied particular places in the apartheid racial hierarchy.

Figure 4.6: Levels of trust in national government by class, 2020 (% saying trust and strongly trust)

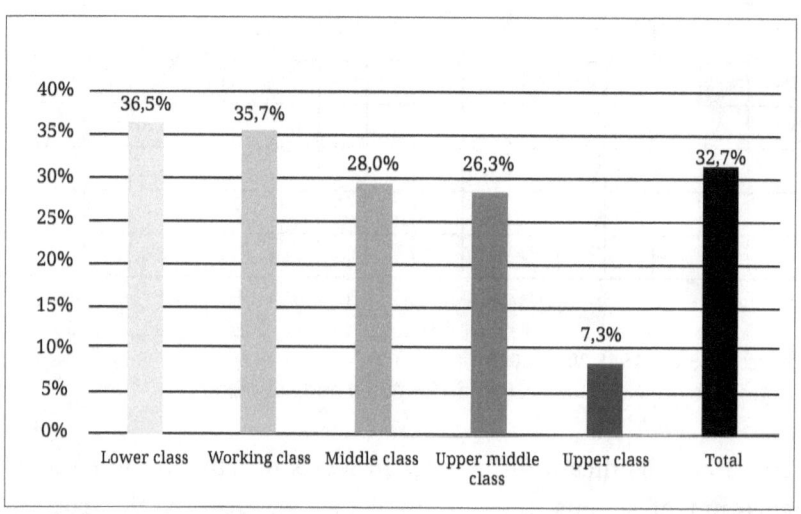

Source: HSRC SASAS 2020

The first transition included economic transformation, which primarily involved addressing some of the racial inequalities that were characteristic of apartheid. Among the most important of these were measures to address equality in employment, that is, the Employment Equity Act (EEA), and equality in ownership and control of big business through broad-based black economic empowerment (B-BBEE).

The basic idea behind the EEA was to achieve equity in the workplace by promoting equal opportunity and fair treatment in employment through the elimination of unfair discrimination; and implementing affirmative action measures to redress the disadvantages in employment experienced by designated groups to ensure their equitable representation in all occupational categories and levels in the workforce. In particular, the application of affirmative action measures meant that companies with more than 50 employees had to ensure that suitably qualified employees from designated groups – Africans, Indians, coloureds, women and people with disabilities – had equal employment opportunity and were equitably represented in all occupational categories and levels of the workforce.

The basic idea behind the policy of B-BBEE was to offer economic opportunities to the black population – that is, Africans, Indians and coloureds – that were not available prior to the advent of majority rule. The strategies used by the policy to try to stimulate economic expansion and equality in the population include encouraging ownership of business and property, incentives to take on management roles, offering schemes for the development of the skills essential in securing employment, and preferential procurement of goods and services.

The HSRC SASAS series has included a question on affirmative action every year since 2003. Table 4.2 provides data on support for affirmative action by members of the four different race groups between 2007 and 2018.

Support for affirmative action has been generally high among Africans between 2007 and 2018 (Table 4.2). On the other hand, support for the policy among coloureds and Indians – the other two race groups included as beneficiaries of affirmative action – has been relatively low. Support among coloureds has ranged from a low of 24 per cent (percentage saying they agree and strongly agree) in 2006 and a high of 44 per cent in 2008. Similarly, support among Indians ranged from 15 per cent (2015) to 39 per cent (2017). The low level of support for the policy among members of these two race groups may be a result of perceptions that Africans are the main beneficiaries. In contrast, white support was below 25 per cent for most years besides 2017 when it reached 34 per cent (those saying they agree and strongly agree with the affirmative action policy). However, it is evident that support for affirmative action was lowest among whites for all survey years (2007 to 2018) (Table 4.2). This is a reflection of the resistance to a policy that favours other race groups at the expense of whites.

Table 4.2: Support for affirmative action by race, 2007–2018 (% saying agree and strongly agree

	Black African	Coloured	Indian/ Asian	White	All
2007	78	34	27	19	66
2008	76	44	36	18	66
2009	76	26	21	22	64
2010	75	30	23	22	64
2011	73	31	25	18	62
2012	73	41	36	9	60
2013	69	25	24	13	58
2014	79	27	15	21	67
2015	78	25	30	14	66
2016	72	24	26	17	61
2017	76	27	39	34	66
2018	74	25	22	19	63

Source: HSRC SASAS 2003–2018

In 2020, support for affirmative action was highest among people who considered themselves lower class (73 per cent) and lowest among people who considered themselves upper class (27 per cent) (Figure 4.7). Just over 54 per cent, 55 per cent and 51 per cent of people who considered themselves working class, middle class and upper middle class, respectively, were in favour of affirmative action. Close to 63 per cent of all South Africans supported these policies, which is similar to the level of support in 2018. There is a similar correlation between levels of support for affirmative action in class and race groups that exists in the correlation of levels of trust in government among these two groups.

Figure 4.7: Support for affirmative action by class, 2020 (% saying agree and strongly agree)

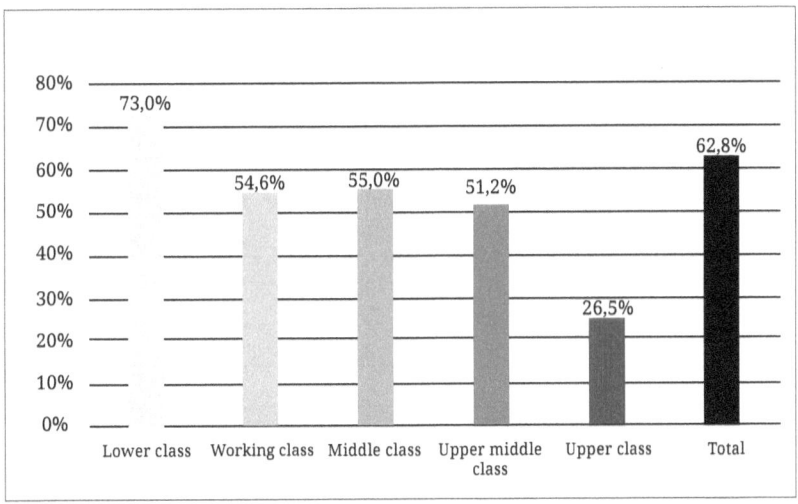

Source: HSRC SASAS 2020

The second key element of the ANC's first transition, meeting basic needs, focused on improvements in the living conditions of the people, especially the poor. The Reconstruction and Development Programme (RDP) underpinned the post-apartheid government's initial efforts to meet social needs during the first transition. Through the RDP, the ANC-led government hoped to meet the need for jobs, land, housing, water, electricity, telecommunications, transport, a clean and healthy environment, nutrition, health care and social welfare. This was to be achieved through programmes to redistribute land to landless people, introducing compulsory education, building houses, providing clean water and sanitation, electrifying homes and providing access for all to affordable health care and telecommunications (Muthien and Houston, 2002).

Perceptions of improvements in their lives among members of the various race groups are useful indicators of the impact of this aspect of the first transition on the different race groups. In the SASAS questionnaires between 2003 and 2018, respondents were asked the following question: 'In the last five years, has life improved, stayed the same or gotten worse for people like you?'

Figure 4.8: South African's perceptions that life has improved for various race groups by race, 2003–2018[7] (% saying life has improved)

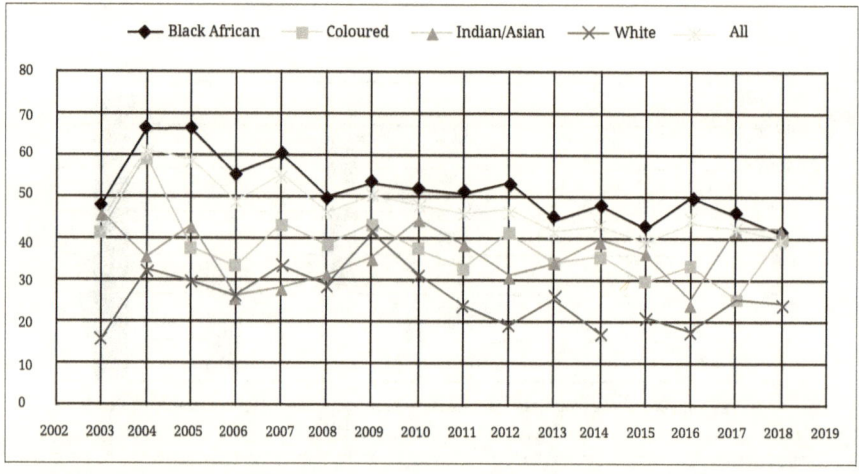

Source: HSRC SASAS 2003–2018

Between 2003 and 2018, African people were generally more positive about life in the previous five years than coloureds, Indians and, in particular, whites (Figure 4.8). On average, just under half of the African respondents felt that their lives had improved, with about 67 per cent feeling this way in 2005. For whites, however, only about a quarter (30 per cent) experienced improvements in their lives. During the same period, on average, about 33 per cent of whites felt that their lives had worsened, while the average figure for Africans was about 8 per cent. On average, about 24 per cent of coloureds and

---

7   The figures are based on the respondents who agreed or strongly agreed to the statement that in the last five years, life had improved for people like them.

22 per cent of Indians felt that their lives had become worse.

In 2020, the perception that life had improved for their race groups in the previous five years was highest among people who considered themselves upper middle class (46 per cent) and lowest among those who considered themselves upper class (21 per cent) (Figure 4.9). However, there was also a low level of belief among people who considered themselves lower class (22 per cent) that life had improved for their race group in the previous five years. In addition, only 32 per cent of people who considered themselves working class and 29 per cent of those who considered themselves middle class felt this way in 2020. Although there appears to be a correlation between the attitudes of whites and the upper class on this issue, there appears to be no correlation between the attitudes of African people in the period 2003 to 2018 and the attitudes of people who considered themselves lower class, working class or middle class in 2020 on life improving for their race groups. This suggests that there have been significant improvements for some black people who have moved into the upper middle class, and less improvement for many others who remained in the lower classes.

Figure 4.9: Perceptions that life has improved for various race groups by class, 2020 (% saying life has improved)

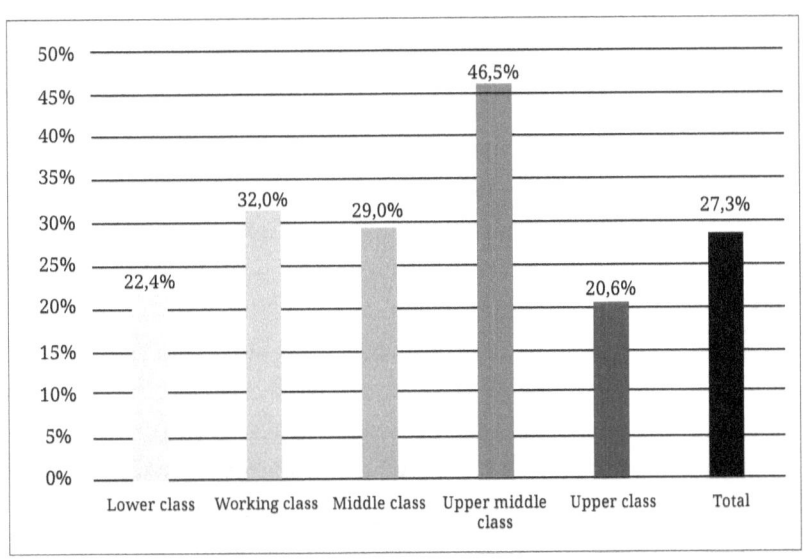

Source: HSRC SASAS 2020

Another indicator of the impact of the first transition on the different racial groups is their perceptions of progress being made in the country. The SASAS questionnaires from 2003 to 2018 included the following question: 'Generally speaking, do you think that things in this country are going in the right direction or going in the wrong direction?'

Figure 4.10: Country going in the wrong direction by race, 2010–2018 (% saying in the wrong direction)

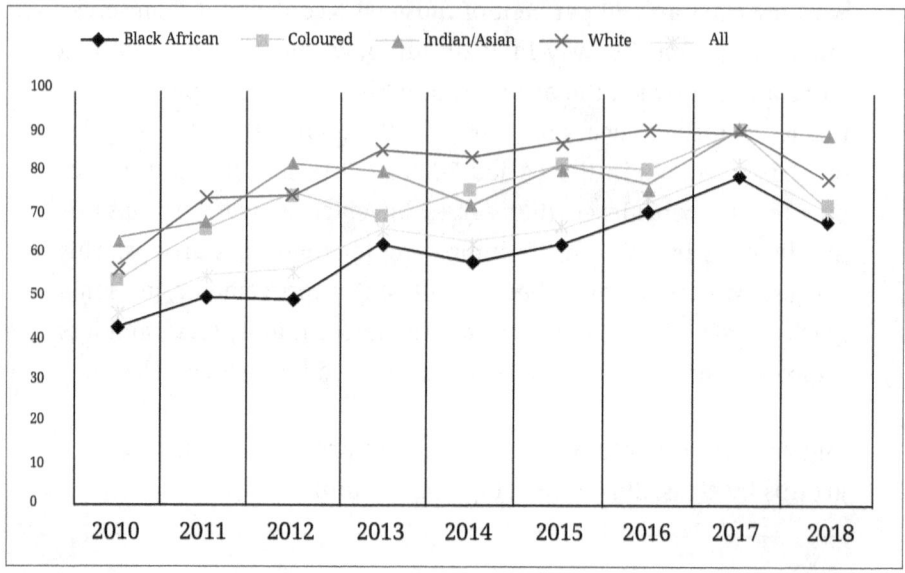

Source: HSRC SASAS 2003-2018

Large proportions of respondents of all race groups felt that the country was moving in the wrong direction (Figure 4.10). While 59 per cent of Africans felt this way in 2014, more than 76 per cent of coloureds, 73 per cent of Indians and 84 per cent of whites felt that there was no progress in the country. This pattern is almost consistent from 2010 to 2018. However, it is clear that there was a general increase among all race groups from 2010 to 2018 who felt that South Africa was going in the wrong direction (Figure 4.5).

In 2020, 70 per cent of people who considered themselves lower class, more than 68 per cent of people who considered themselves working class and just above 72 per cent of people who considered themselves middle class felt that the country was moving in the wrong direction (Figure 4.11). Close to 62 per cent of those who considered themselves upper class felt this way. By contrast, just above 58 per cent of people who considered themselves upper middle class felt that there was no progress in the country. Again, there is evidence here that black people who have moved into the upper middle class have been the main beneficiaries of the first transition among black people, and that many others have been left behind.

Figure 4.11: Country going in the wrong direction by class, 2020 (% saying wrong only sometimes)

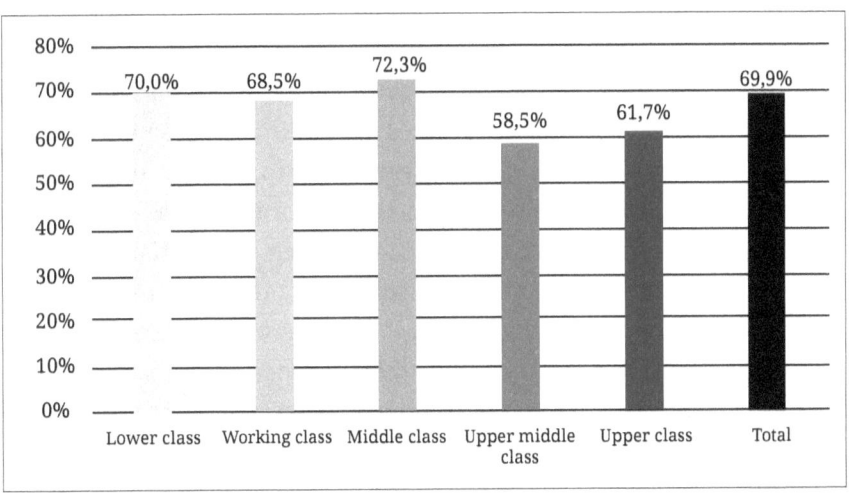

Source: HSRC SASAS 2020

The data presented indicates significant differences in perceptions among the four race and five class groups in South Africa on the impact of the processes aimed at the democratisation of state and society and meeting basic needs during the first transition. Generally, the impact has been positive for the majority of Africans, while the impact has been negative for coloureds, Indians, and whites in particular. It has been most positive for the upper middle class, and most probably those black people who have been the main beneficiaries of the policies that underpinned the first transition. It appears that the first transition had the effect of exacerbating the conditions that undermine national unity, instead of contributing to the resolution of the national question. Indeed, it could be argued that there has been a reversal of the gains made during the course of the struggle in this regard.

Unfortunately, the first transition has led to a situation in which there is no shared feeling of belonging among all race and class groups, no shared sense that all groups are engaged in a common enterprise, and a feeling among members of certain minority groups and of the lower classes that they do not have the same life opportunities as members of the majority group and upper classes. Perceptions of unequal opportunities for the different racial groups have been a major factor behind the resurgence of racial identities among members of the coloured, Indian and white communities in the post-apartheid era.

According to Mohamed Adhikari (2005: 176), 'It has become commonplace for Coloured people disaffected with the new South Africa to express their disgruntlement by lamenting that "first we were not white enough and now we are not black enough".' Adhikari adds that, 'Besides accentuating their interstitial position within a transforming South African racial hierarchy, the phrase very neatly captures coloured people's perennial predicament of marginality.' Another view of the existence of perceptions of unequal opportunities among minority groups in post-apartheid South Africa is put forward by Daniel Hammett (2008: 652) in the following terms:

> Within communities who see themselves as excluded from citizen rights and policies of redress, a perception of un-entitlement is developing among those believing themselves to be marginalised from equity policies, distanced from political influence and, ultimately, excluded from citizenship rights.'

Hammett (2008) draws attention to a number of other areas in which coloureds feel excluded or marginalised from the benefits of the new democracy. Among the most important of these are job opportunities, education and training opportunities, and housing. Likewise, Adhikari (2005: 179) lists limited job opportunities for the coloured working class, the poverty faced by this sector of the coloured population and the limited provision of basic services such as housing, electricity and sanitation to the coloured working class during the democratic era.

On the other hand, the loss of privileges is felt most sharply by the white community. Most importantly, the democratisation of state and society has resulted in a major shift in the racial composition of parliament, the cabinet, the judiciary, the civil service, the army, the police and the intelligence service. In effect, political control shifted from a white minority regime to a democratic one, in which Africans were the majority. Also, economic transformation during the first transition was aimed at a radical restructuring of an economy that was dominated by whites.

THE SECOND TRANSITION AND THE NATIONAL QUESTION

In 1988, Mzala argued that:

> The ANC maintains that the drive for national emancipation is integrally bound up with the struggle for economic emancipation. The oppressed in South Africa have suffered more than national humiliation: they have been deprived and poverty and starvation has been their life experience. The correction of economic injustice lies at the very core of a solving of the national question (Mzala, 1988: 51).

In 2012, the ANC released a discussion document on the second transition (ANC, 2012: 4). It stipulated that the ANC had concluded the 'first transition with its focus on democratisation', and that there was a need for 'a vision for a second transition that must focus on the social and economic transformation of South Africa over the next 30 to 50 years'. The socio-economic transformation during the second transition is considered necessary because the first transition 'proved inadequate and even inappropriate for a social and economic transformation phase' (ANC, 2012: 35). Most importantly, the apartheid economy remains more or less intact. Above all else, however, the ANC identified the task of overcoming poverty, unemployment and inequality as priorities during the second transition. The ANC focused on this task as the link between the resolution of the national question and social and economic transformation during the second transition.

In the discussion document, the ANC drew attention firstly to enduring poverty, which is overwhelmingly located in black communities. The ANC also noted that the persistently high rates of unemployment and growing under-employment were major factors behind the slow growth in per capita income among blacks in general. It added that income distribution by race was highly skewed in favour of whites, and that this was an important 'indicator of the national question and socio-economic progress' (ANC, 2012: 18). For instance, African and coloured income levels in 2008 were still only 13 per cent and 22 per cent, respectively, of white per capita income, while the income gap for Indians had narrowed to 60 per cent of those of whites. The discussion document included a discussion of progress in expanding the black middle class and black ownership and control of the economy.

The document called for, among other things, deracialisation of ownership and control of wealth, management and the professions; an efficient market, free from racial and gender exclusions that characterised apartheid colonialism; and land and agrarian reform and rural development, including land redistribution and assistance to emergent and small-scale farmers and cooperatives.

Recognition was given in the document to the fact that many whites still feel threatened by transformation and the consequent need to engage with various strata and interests within the white community on the ANC's national vision. The ANC also recognised that white capital would have to be a critical part of consensus on a socio-economic transition. It was necessary, therefore, to engage and struggle to ensure that the ANC's vision forms the basis of national consensus.

In its 8 January statement for 2013, the National Executive Committee of the ANC stipulated that it was committing itself to bringing about socio-economic freedom as it entered 'the second phase of the transition from apartheid colonialism to a national democratic society'. Attention was drawn to the skewed patterns of ownership of the economy, and it was noted that decisive action was 'required to thoroughly and urgently transform the economic patterns of the present in order to realise our vision for the future' (ANC, 2013). Included in this was the opening up of space for more black people and women to participate in the economy, as employees, as creators of jobs and, importantly, as owners of the means of production. The ANC promised to speed up the process of land reform, including replacing the principle of 'willing buyer, willing seller', which has not sufficiently addressed the problem, with the 'just and equitable' principle when expropriating land for land-reform purposes.

In May 2014, addressing the public at the Union Buildings after his inauguration as president, Jacob Zuma stated that: 'Today marks the beginning of the second phase of our transition from apartheid to a national democratic society.' He added that economic transformation, guided by the National Development Plan, would take centre stage. In terms of ownership and control of the economy, Zuma promised that the ANC-led government would improve the implementation of the employment equity and black economic empowerment laws, as well as land restitution and redistribution and other forms of empowerment.[8]

Several changes in employment equity, B-BBEE and land ownership legislation have been introduced since Zuma's address in an effort to increase the pace of transformation. Of note here are the amendments to the EEA, effective from 2014. These make provision for the imposition of fines on companies that have more than 50 employees for non-compliance with their obligation to prepare and/or implement an employment equity plan or submit an annual employment equity report. Companies that do not comply with the EEA requirements may be issued with a fine for non-compliance, ranging between R1.5 million and/or 2 per cent of annual turnover, whichever amount is greater, for first offences, and R2.7 million or 10 per cent of annual turnover, whichever amount is greater, for multiple offenders.

---

8   Address by President Jacob Zuma on the occasion of his inauguration as fifth President of the Republic of South Africa Union Buildings, 24 May 2014, Pretoria. Available at: http://www.thepresidency.gov.za/pebble.asp?relid=17449 (Accessed 20 January 2023).

In 2014, amendments were introduced to the B-BBEE Act, while the Codes of Good Practice on BEE were amended in 2015. These amendments included, among others:

- removing the discretion that state organs and public entities previously held by making it compulsory for them to apply the B-BBEE Codes or relevant sector codes of good practice gazetted in terms of the B-BBEE Act when awarding licences and authorisations, and procuring goods and services;
- introducing the provision in the B-BBEE Act that in the event of any conflict between the Act and any other law in force immediately prior to the date of commencement of the amended B-BBEE Act, the Act will prevail if the conflict relates to a matter dealt with in the B-BBEE Act;
- codifying fronting as an offence and the introduction of penalties for contravention, including penalties such as fines up to 10 per cent of turnover and imprisonment;
- establishing a BEE Commission with the power, among other things, to oversee, supervise and promote adherence to the B-BBEE Act, to receive and investigate complaints relating to BEE and to maintain a registry of major BEE transactions; and
- introducing new compliance targets that are more difficult to achieve and maintain and the addition of new measurement criteria for the skills development, preferential procurement and supplier development elements (Pillay, 2016).

The ANC-led government also took several other steps to increase black ownership of the economy. This included the release of its Black Industrialists Policy in 2016. The policy provides for up to R50 million in financial support to black industrialists who present projects that require an investment of at least R30 million. In addition, regulations to the Preferential Procurement Policy Framework Act, No. 5 of 2000, included provisions that favour tenders that will benefit black-owned or black-women-owned companies (Pillay, 2016).

However, despite the introduction of measures aimed at improving the implementation of affirmative action policies, coloured and Indian South Africans remained sceptical about the benefits of these policies for them. As indicated in Table 4.2, coloured support for these policies between 2014 and 2018 ranged from 24 per cent (2016) to 27 per cent (2014 and 2017), while Indian support fluctuated dramatically between 15 per cent (2014) and 39 per cent (2017) and then 22 per cent in 2018.

Finally, the ANC embarked on several steps to introduce a change in policy with regard to land ownership and redistribution. This has probably been the most controversial issue impacting on the national question in recent times. The first step the ruling party took in this regard was to adopt a resolution at its 54th National Conference in 2017 that 'the ANC should, as a matter of policy, pursue expropriation of land without compensation'. It then proceeded to bring this about by appointing a parliamentary committee after the 2019 elections to amend Section 25 of the Constitution, which allowed for compensation that is fair and equitable for land that is expropriated. A draft Constitution Eighteenth Amendment Bill was then developed and published for public comment, stipulating that 'a court may ... determine that the amount of compensation is nil', that the nil rand compensation must (still) be 'just and equitable' and, lastly, that national legislation must be enacted spelling out the 'specific circumstances where a court may determine the amount of compensation is nil' (Van Staden, 2020: 171–73).

Opposition to the Bill and land expropriation without compensation came from several quarters, including the opposition Democratic Alliance (DA) and the liberal Free Market Foundation. The latter argued that the Bill replaces the entrenched section 25 right to property 'with uncertainty'. It added that the proposed amendment in the Bill could create a situation where 'any future government may whimsically decide to change the circumstances for nil compensation', including 'targeting political opponents and their supporters, targeting the property of particular foreign nations, and/or targeting religious and/or ethnic minorities' (Free Market Foundation, 2020: 10). The DA opposed any threat to property rights that the amendment of the Constitution suggested on principle, while pointing out that the section of the Bill 'on nil compensation, in particular, is open to abuse by government and requires far more precision in the wording and definitions'. It added: 'The Bill also does not adequately address the expropriation of property other than land, despite a vague allusion to intangible property in the definitions' (DA, 2019: 49).

The De Klerk Foundation argued that by 2019, significant harm had already been caused 'to the South African economy, investment, food security and agricultural production' in the period since the resolution adopted by the ANC in 2017 (De Klerk Foundation, 2020: 2). The right-wing AfriForum grounded its opposition to land expropriation without compensation as follows:

> It is clear that the South African government's push for expropriation without compensation is founded in racist sentiment and a distortion of history. It is also clear that the so-called hunger for land is largely non-existent – particularly with regard to agricultural land. Furthermore, it is clear that land reform has already been disastrous to the extent that it has been executed in South Africa. While the primary targets of this policy are clearly white farmers, the primary victims might just as well be the very people that the South African government claims to represent (AfriForum, 2019: 6).

While the other organisations posit their opposition to the policy in more general terms, AfriForum is explicit that the objective would be to expropriate land from white farmers. This policy thus entrenched another line of fracture between the race groups in South Africa, and another challenge to a resolution of the national question.

It is evident that as the process of economic transformation gains momentum, a deepening of racial antagonism will occur, particularly as whites increasingly lose their privileged position in the workplace and in terms of ownership of land and in the economy, thus adding to the existing challenges around the resolution of the national question.

CONCLUSION

Several lessons should be drawn from the experiences during the first transition. Above all else, there is a need to deracialise economic redress for the reasons given by many of the critics of this programme. Most importantly, it has fostered divisions within the black community between Africans, on the one hand, and coloureds and Indians, on the other; it has benefitted the elite among blacks, and it has given rise to resistance on the part of whites (Southall, 2004; Alexander, 2007; Hammett, 2008; Habib and Bentley, 2008: xi; Dupper, 2008: 303; Ndletyana, 2008: 95). None of these can assist in a project that leads to integration.

According to Friedman and Erasmus (2008: 67), although most SASAS findings indicate white resistance to racial redress policies, the problem lies in the way the policies are framed in racial terms. They argue that there is the likelihood of less resistance if the measures to address racial inequalities were phrased as anti-poverty measures, rather than as a means of reversing racial power and privilege. The emphasis on poverty, unemployment and inequality in the second transition is a good basis for this. Second, the quest to meet basic needs must address the needs of all, where all South Africans can feel that they are experiencing improvements in their lives.

However, Mzala's notion of racial integration cannot take place in a capitalist economy and particularly in a situation where steps undertaken to achieve equality come at the expense of one or the other race group. It would take a major leap for South African whites to realise that the future relies on their willingness to give up certain aspects of privilege. However, the resurgence of racial identities in the democratic era and the feeling among most whites that the future is not bright makes this very unlikely. On the other hand, there is increasing frustration with the rate of social and economic transformation in South Africa among members of the black majority. The deracialisation of economic redress in areas where this is possible without dramatically affecting racial redress would go a long way to focusing redress on those who need it most, people in the lower classes, while removing those features of it that deepen racial antagonism. This would be a major step in the process of building social cohesion and a positive step in the resolution of the national question that Mzala desired.

REFERENCES

Adhikari, M. (2005). *Not White Enough, Not Black Enough: Racial identity in the South African coloured community*. Athens OH: Ohio University Press.

Adhikari, M. (1992). 'The Sons of Ham: Slavery and the making of coloured identity', *South African Historical Journal*, 27: 95–112. DOI:10.1080/02582479208671739

African National Congress (ANC). (2012). 'The Second Transition: Building a national democratic society and the balance of forces in 2012'. A discussion document towards the National Policy Conference, Version 7, as amended by the Special NEC, 27 February 2012. Available at: http://www.anc.org.za/docs/discus/2012/transition.pdf (Accessed 10 February 2023).

AfriForum. (2019). 'Expropriation without compensation: A disaster in waiting'. Available at: https://afriforum.co.za/wp-content/uploads/2019/08/Expropriation-without-compensation.pdf (Accessed 10 June 2021).

Alexander, N. (2012). 'The unresolved national question in South Africa', in J. Na'eem. (ed.). *Pretending Democracy: Israel, an ethnocratic state*. Johannesburg: Afro-Middle East Centre, pp. 199–216.

Alexander, N. (2007). 'Affirmative action and the perpetuation of racial identities in post-apartheid South Africa', *Transformation: Critical Perspectives on Southern Africa*, 63: 92–108. DOI:10.1353/trn.2007.0013

Arkin, A.J., Magyar, K.P. and Pillay, G.J. (1989). *The Indian South Africans: A contemporary profile*. Pinetown: Owen Burgess.

Carrim, Y. (1996). 'The national question in post-apartheid South Africa: Reconciling multiple identities', *African Communist*, 145 (3rd Quarter): 49–58.

De Klerk Foundation. (2020). Submission on the Draft Constitution Eighteenth Amendment Bill, 2019. Available at: https://cfcr.co.za/index.php/en/document-library/ (Accessed 11 June 2021).

Democratic Alliance (DA). (2021). Democratic Alliance Shadow Cabinet Update. Available at: https://cdn.da.org.za/wp-content/uploads/2021/02/11074253/DA-Shadow-Cabinet-Report.pdf (Accessed 9 June 2021).

Dexter, P. (1996). 'Marxism and the national question in a democratic South Africa', *African Communist*, 145: 59–66.

Dupper, O. (2009). 'The beneficiaries of affirmative action', in O. Dupper and C. Garbers (eds). *Equality in the Workplace: Reflections from South Africa and beyond*. Cape Town: Juta.

Free Market Foundation. (2020). Submission to Parliament on the draft Constitution Eighteenth Amendment Bill, 2019. Available at: https://www.freemarketfoundation.com/dynamicdata/documents/20200207-submission-on-constitution-eighteenth-amendment-bill-2019.pdf (Accessed 5 June 2021).

Friedman, S. and Erasmus, Z. (2008). 'Counting on "Race": What the surveys say (and do not say) about "race" and redress', in A. Habib and K.A. Bentley (eds). *Racial Redress and Citizenship in South Africa*. Cape Town: HSRC Press, pp. 33–77.

Freund, B. (1995). *Insiders and Outsiders: The Indian working class of Durban, 1910–1990*. Portsmouth, NH: Heinemann.

Goldin, I. (1987). *Making Race: The politics and economics of coloured identity in South Africa*. Cape Town: Maskew Miller Longman.

Habib, A. (2004). 'Preface', in A. Habib and K.A. Bentley (eds). *Racial Redress and Citizenship in South Africa*. Cape Town: HSRC Press.

Hammett, D. (2008). 'The challenge of a perception of "un-entitlement" to citizenship in post-apartheid South Africa', *Political Geography*, 27(6): 652–68.

Hendricks, C. (2005). 'Debating coloured identity in the Western Cape', *African Security Review*, 14: 117–19. DOI:10.1080/10246029.2005.9627597

Jara, M.K. (2006). 'The national question post-apartheid: Western Cape lessons and challenges for socialist theory and practice'. Paper presented at the Harold Wolpe Memorial Trust's Tenth Anniversary Colloquium, 'Engaging Silences and Unresolved Issues in the Political Economy of South Africa', Cape Town, 21–23 September.

Jordan, P. (2012). 'A century of struggle: The nation and class', *New Agenda*, 45 (First Quarter).

Jung, C. (2000). *Then I Was Black: African political identities in transition*. New Haven, CT: Yale University Press.

Kanyane, M.H., Houston, G.F. and Sausi, K. (2013). 'State of South

African public service in the context of macro socio-economic environment', *Journal of Public Administration and Governance*, 3(1). DOI:10.5296/jpag.v3i1.3267

Lewis, G. (1987). *Between the Wire and the Wall: A history of South African 'Colored' politics.* New York: St Martin's Press.

Moodley, K.A. (1975). 'South African Indians: The wavering minority', in L. Thompson and J. Butler (eds). *Change in Contemporary South Africa.* Berkeley, CA: University of California Press, pp. 250–280.

Muthien, Y. and Houston, G. (2002). Transforming South African state and society: The challenge of constructing a developmental state', in A.I. Samatar and A.I. Samatar (eds). *The African State: Reconsiderations.* Portsmouth, NH: Heinemann, pp. 53–99.

Ndletyana, M. (2004). 'Affirmative action in the public service', in A. Habib and K.A. Bentley (eds). *Racial Redress and Citizenship in South Africa.* Cape Town: HSRC Press, pp. 77–98.

Nxumalo, M.N. (1988). 'Revolutionary theory on the national question in South Africa', in M. van Diepen (ed.). *The National Question in South Africa.* London: Zed Books, pp. 30–55.

Pachai, B. (1971). *The South African Indian Question, 1860–1971.* Cape Town: Struik.

Pahad, E. (1988). 'South African Indians as a national minority in the national question', in M. van Diepen (ed.). *The National Question in South Africa.* London: Zed Books, pp. 86–95.

Pillay, V. (2016). 'Recent changes to the BEE landscape', *Golegal*, 16 April. Available at: https://wwwgolegal.co.za/changes-bbbee-act/ (Accessed 11 June 2021).

Republic of South Africa. (2015). *Development Indicators 2014.* Pretoria: Department of Planning, Monitoring and Evaluation. Available at: *http://www.poa.gov.za/news/Pages/ DEVELOPMENT%20INDICATORS%202014%20final.pdf*/DPME%20 Indicators%202013.pdf (Accessed 9 June 2021).

Roberts, B., Weir-Smith, G. and Reddy, V. (2011). 'Minding the gap: Attitudes toward affirmative action in South Africa', *Transformation*, 77. DOI:10.1353/trn.2011.0047

Roberts, B., Kivilu, M. and Davids, Y.D. (2010). *South African Social Attitudes 2nd Report: Reflections on the Age of Hope.* Cape Town: HSRC Press, pp. 1–367.

Singh, R. and Vawda, S. (1988). 'What's in a name? Some reflections on the Natal Indian Congress', *Transformation*, 6: 1–21.

Sizwe, N. (1979). *One Azania, One Nation: The national question in South Africa*. London: Zed Press.

Southall, R. (2004). 'The ANC and black capitalism in South Africa', *Review of African Political Economy*, 31: 313–28. DOI:10.1080/0305624042000262310.

Suttner, R. (2011). 'Revisiting the National Democratic Revolution: The "National Question"'. Paper presented at the departments of Sociology, Anthropology and Development Studies seminar, University of Johannesburg.

Vahed, G. and Desai, A. (2010). 'Identity and belonging in post-apartheid South Africa: The case of Indian South Africans', *Journal of Social Sciences*, 25: 1–12.

Van Staden, M. (2020). 'Property rights and the basic structure of the Constitution: The case of the Draft Constitution Eighteenth Amendment Bill', *Pretoria Student Law Review* 14(2): 169–93.

Wolpe, H. (1989). 'Race, class and the apartheid state', *Apartheid & Society*, 13(2): 125–26. DOI:10.1177/030981688903800112.

FIVE

THE EFF'S PERSPECTIVE ON 'WHAT IS THE FUTURE OF THE LEFT IN SOUTH AFRICA IN A GLOBAL CONTEXT?'

Sam Matiase

The Mzala Nxumalo Centre's conference in 2017 aimed to consider the question, 'What is the future of the left in South Africa in a global context'. The conference made profound theoretical contributions to many of the most pertinent debates facing the left in South Africa and in a global context. That noted, a revolutionary party is needed to achieve a socialist revolution, because of the low and uneven levels of development and consciousness among members of the society in South Africa, in particular those engaged in various forms of struggles for a new world order.

The central purpose of this chapter is to reflect on the question: 'What is the future of the left in South Africa in a global context?' To explore this, three main aspects are discussed. The first is to consider what Marxist–Leninist essentials are necessary for the left and socialist forces to mobilise and lead fundamental changes in society. Reference is made to the unprecedented wave of electoral victories by leftist parties and the so-called populist presidential candidates in Latin America.

Second, this chapter traces the challenges and pitfalls to attaining the ideal of socialism, and what has gone wrong. This ideal seems to have been betrayed by the Left, particularly in South Africa where social and economic transformation has not occurred to the extent or depth anticipated or hoped for since 1994.

Third, it seeks to identify and explain how the revival of the Left could be fostered by cultivating a socialist culture and value systems, and by creating viable alternatives to the liberal model of capitalism in South Africa and the world.

MARXISM AND THE DEMISE OF THE LEFT IN THE POST-LIBERATION STRUGGLE STATE

Marxism teaches us that, 'the revolution cannot go forward and achieve its goals without a vanguard organisation able to guide the people in all its battles and on all fronts'. Any organisation in pursuit of its revolutionary agenda has to engage in a number of battles ranging from the ideological, political and cultural to the economic and intellectual fronts.

For this reason, a revolutionary party has to build its organisational, political and intellectual capacity to successfully engage in this battle of ideas. First and foremost, as Lenin (1917) points out, it is essential to have a revolutionary party capable of leading and providing organisational, political and ideological guidance to its cadres and to the working class.

While this is true, Tony Cliff (1973) submits that, 'If the working class were homogeneous ideologically, there would be no need for leadership (or organisations in any form), but the objective possibility of revolution will not wait until all reach a class-conscious intellectual level.' Therefore, the objective reality that Cliff talks about requires that the working-class must be made aware of their revolutionary tasks. The subjective aspect of this chapter, by way of the question – What is the future of the Left? – is an attempt to bring about this awareness. This chapter considers the issues affecting the future of the Left, what might have gone wrong with the Left and the challenges it faces today.

What is the future of the Left and what should be done to resurrect it? These are inextricably related questions and presuppose that there *is* a future for socialism. Rather than offering a critique of capitalism, this chapter attempts to answer the question on the future of the Left. In the process, it illustrates how prospects of a successful future for the Left have been obliterated by those who proclaim 'Socialism is the future, build it now!'" because they are complicit in the abuses associated with capitalism, such as spectacular consumerism, accumulation and exploitation.

In South Africa, as Vishwas Satgar observes, 'the emergence of a new generation of black economically empowered (BEE) and tenderpreneur politicians and invidivuals with political links, has firmly embedded the ANC and its alliance partners into patronage politics, state-led class formation, crony capitalism and widespread corruption'. It is the formation of this new petite bourgeois class that has led to 'tenderisation' of the state and the 'Guptarisation' of state procurement under the former president, Jacob Zuma (Satgar, 2011). The complicity of the adherents, mainly within the ranks of the ANC-SACP-COSATU, is palpable in its manifestation of these tendencies.

When the ANC-SACP-associated think tank, the Mzala Centre, called for a conference to discuss the future of the left, the question arises: 'Why are they avoiding a familiar and well-known concept, 'socialism', in favour of an obscure concept, however relevant it might be in revolutionary circles?'

I referred to this question as 'tricky' because only a prophet can hazard a guess as to either the future of the Left or of socialism. Joe Slovo (1990) asked this question in the most profound and direct way: 'Has socialism failed?' And, he argued, 'if socialists are unable to come to terms with this reality [question], the future of socialism is indeed bleak'. Slovo raised the question of how, 10 years later at the beginning of the 21st century, leftist formations had evolved in Latin America in particular.

Slovo's question is relevant in the 21st century, which has witnessed an unprecedented wave of electoral victories by leftist parties and the so-called populist presidential candidates in Latin America. This wave started in 1998, when Hugo Chavez was elected president of Venezuela and was evident more recently in 2006, when a former revolutionary leader, Daniel Ortega, and the Sandinista National Liberation Front returned to power in Nicaragua, while a left-thinking economist, Rafael Correa, became president in Ecuador (Levitsky and Roberts, 2011).

Leftist alternatives emerged or were strengthened in the 2000s, even in countries where they did not capture or win the presidency, such as Mexico, Colombia, Peru, Costa Rica and Honduras, albeit with a minimal presence. All of these represent hope, notwithstanding the considerable right-wing influences in the electoral politics of countries such as Brazil.

The rise of the Left was an interesting turn of events in a region where political and economic liberalism was buttressed hugely by US imperialist hegemony. This appeared triumphant at the end of the Cold War with the collapse of the Soviet bloc, the demise of statist and socialist development models, and the rise of the so-called Washington Consensus around free market or neoliberal economic policies.

According to Williamson (1990) and Edwards (1995), the US-style capitalist democracy appeared to be the only dominant force in the region and globally in the 1990s. It was during these troubled times that former liberation movements and labour movements went into retreat and revolutionary alternatives seemingly foreclosed, as historical rivals to liberalism from both populist and leftist traditions accepted market reforms and capitulated. In the eyes of many, despite the rise of leftist governments in Latin America, the Left had all but vanished and succumbed to US-style reforms.

One must acknowledge the hazards of trying to offer an opinion on something 'so recent in time and distant in space' (Herbert Aptheker in *The Truth About Hungary*, 1957), but it is worth reflecting on the crisis with which the Left is now faced, even if this must be done hesitantly where concepts such as 'the left' are vague and potentially confusing.

Therefore, in the light this, I prefer to simply refer to socialism, rather than creating conceptual confusion about the Left vis-à-vis socialism, the reason being that when the Soviet Union collapsed, I cannot remember the intellectual giants of the revolution at the time – such as Harry Gwala, Joe Slovo and Pallo Jordan – referring to the collapse or failure of 'the Left'. The question that gripped revolutionaries at the time was whether socialism had failed, while the question of whether the Left had failed never arose. I was asked to participate in the opinion-making process of something close to what Herbert Aptheker (1957) called 'the ordeal of careful scrutiny'. This is, essentially why I leave the question to the imagination of the reader. It is also important to recognise that the old socialist formations have not survived. The last 23 years have seen a near-complete obliteration of the 'real' left formations in South Africa, while simultaneously giving rise to new ones. To this extent, the Economic Freedom Front (EFF) Founding Manifesto observes that:

> The Congress-aligned left-wing formations have been swallowed into reform politics of patronage and will never regain integrity to pursue real working-class struggles any time soon. The organised left has been swallowed by the state, and is currently at the forefront of justifying the rapacious and callous theft of public funds by the (then) incumbent president of the republic.

The resilience of capitalism and neoliberalism can in part be attributed to the weakness of socialist politics and formations internationally. In the South African context, the ANC-SACP-COSATU alliance has in many ways contributed to efforts to undermine – if not fragment – the emergence of or the unity of the left forces.

The tragic death of the Left – comprising a group of genuine revolutionaries who once displayed great heroism, daring and genuine revolutionary devotion – was not due, however, to the 'inevitability of capitalism' (Rothschild, 1994) or adverse circumstances, but came about through the group's readiness to embrace bourgeois aspirations, and their leaders' justification of opulent lifestyles, not unrelated to the theft or abuse of state resources. This, more than the Left's failure to organise the working class, becomes the most debilitating example of betrayal. Although the working class and the poor still have the will to organise, there is a dire and desperate need for principled leadership.

As paradoxical as it may seem, it is axiomatic that a true and genuine liberation inextricably lies in the abolition of the existing mode of production that is responsible for the adverse social and economic circumstances of the working class and the poor. Therefore, the solution lies in crafting and pursuing a revolutionary strategy for the creation of a caring society without the existing capitalist exploitative social relations and ownership of the means of production. The answer, sadly, does not lie in a reformist strategy that seeks integration within the existing dominant relations of production. It requires a robust, state-led developmetal path in which the state plays a decisive and catalytic role in directing economic development and growth through enabling and encouraging the private sector to play its part.

How can 'revolutionaries' who have settled comfortably into the existing exploitative social order, and who have no intention of its wholesale transformation, bring about a socialist revolution? These are the same people who, under the spell of neoliberalism, have drawn themselves and the whole society into a consumerist Western culture.

I should like to be permitted one liberty in the art of careful scrutiny: to say that any argument that seeks to build a caring society within the framework of capitalism amounts to reformism, which neglects the very structural conditions that produce exploitation. Reform is a strategy that naturally includes the pursuit of reforms of every kind – economic, social and political – within the framework of capitalism. Are we involved in the national democratic revolution or a struggle to reform the existing social order, which seems perpetual in its longevity? Fukuyama argued that, unlike the weaknesses of the communist–totalitarian left regimes of Latin America, Eastern Europe and the Soviet Union, East Asia, which sought to impose socialist systems, 'liberal principles in economics – the free market – have spread and succeeded in producing unprecedented levels of material prosperity' (Fukuyama, 1992). Therefore, if we are involved in a national democratic revolution, our primary objective should be the abolition of the existing social relations.

It is strongly argued that:

> the social revolution requires the concentration of the decisive productive forces in the hands of the people. It does not need a

change in the ownership of property but its annihilation, not the smoothing over of class antagonisms, but the abolition of classes, not the improvement of existing society but the foundation of a new one (Mthukwane, 2018, 1).

This is why Lenin argued that:

> we cannot move out of the bourgeois-democratic revolution boundaries of the Russian revolution, but we can vastly extend these boundaries and within these boundaries we can and must fight for the interests of the working people, for its immediate needs and for conditions that will make it possible to prepare its forces for the future complete victory (Lenin, VI).

This is a poignant and telling observation about not only the future of the Left, but also that of socialism in South Africa and globally. We should be careful of not allowing ourselves and the Left, its formations and structures, as well as those who fight for economic emancipation, to be co-opted or assimilated by a predatory political elite at the expense of the genuine aspirations of the poor working class.

If the organised Left (the SACP and COSATU) has not been able to resist the enticement of the corrosive influence of bourgeois aspirations and political incumbency, is the EFF able to do this? Can this organisation avoid being co-opted and assimilated and exemplify the principled leadership needed by the working class?

Returning to the question of the future of socialism, it is apposite to refer to the thinking and the wisdom of one of the great sons of Africa, Chris Hani. Hani, the former Secretary-General of the SACP, would have been eminently suited to answer this question at a time when world socialism faces its worst ideological and legitimacy crises. While the question may arise as to whether there is any ideology today that is more resilient and durable than capitalism, evidence suggests otherwise. I shall revert to Hani later, but wish to reflect more on the question itself, especially in the context of what is occurring in contemporary South Africa. An honest assessment of socialism today might conclude that it is in ideological intensive care. The question is: What are the chances that it will come out alive?

This can be deduced from the manner in which the question has been framed: 'What is the future of the Left?' We are afraid to talk openly about socialism under democracy, when there was no shame about openly debating socialism before, even under apartheid. Why is this the case today?

The question, as well as the need for conferences to discuss it, constitutes a recognition that today socialism faces its worse crisis in history. In the 19th century, Karl Marx proclaimed that the spectre of communism was upon the world. In making this proclamation, he never doubted that socialism was the future and the force to be reckoned with, as the spectre of communism was on the horizon and its time had come. The question that gripped his mind was: How does socialism become the logical reality to save humanity from the barbarism of capitalism? However, almost 150 years later, the future of socialism remains inextricably linked to the future of the Left.

THE LEFT AND THE ECONOMY

The question about the future of the Left is, thus, also a question about the crisis (of purpose, relevance and agency) that has produced the crisis for socialism. As suggested earlier, the weaknesses of socialism are not externally, but internally, induced. The real enemy of socialism are none other than those who profess to be its followers – but who are socialists by day and capitalists by night – and who are exposed routinely in the narratives about state capture? For them, socialism is no different from witchcraft or superstition – they mistakenly still believe that the masses can be inspired by an ideology that is negated by the actions of its adherents.

By embracing neoliberal economic policies, the ANC-led alliance has effectively gone full cycle. Through BEE and other forms of economic empowerment of historically disadvantaged individuals, the left has degenerated into cronyism. Successive democratically elected governments have endorsed mutually beneficial relations between its officials, in collusion with corrupt and politically connected individuals.

The 'Guptarisation' of South Africa's political leadership and the advent of 'tenderpreneurship' was preceded by a neoliberal policy called Growth, Employment and Redistribution (GEAR), a macro-economic strategy of government, that saw a significant shift towards the free-market system and firmly anchored the economy in the capitalist system.

According to COSATU, the canon of neoliberalism and liberal thinking in South Africa was epitomised by GEAR. GEAR was designed to address strategic flaws contained in the Reconstruction and Development Programme (RDP), as the democratic government could not deliver what it said it would through the RDP. As a result of these internal contradictions within the ANC-SACP-COSATU alliance, the then Minister of Finance, Trevor Manuel, presented GEAR as a macro-economic framework in June 1996. The strategy sought to place the South African economy on a new path, which was inconceivable given its limitations. Initially, it was thought that GEAR would boost the country's economy to above 3 per cent, but the economy has struggled to reach this target (COSATU, 2001).

In the discussions at the time, COSATU held the view that the country needed a new growth path to respond to the twin challenges of rapidly rising poverty and suffering, and mass unemployment and inequality. This was premised on the realisation that the existing growth crisis had deep structural roots located in the particular combination of capitalism and apartheid that had shaped the present society and economy. Unfortunately, COSATU's growth path was ultimately not endorsed by the ANC due to the anti-working-class ideological shifts that were underway and held sway within the leadership of the governing party.

This shows how at the moment of 'liberation', the levers of state power came to be 'geared' in neoliberal capitalism. Proponents of GEAR justified it on the basis that it gave effect to the realisation of the RDP. GEAR's primary principle was that economic growth must occur first, and then employment would follow, and once employment had increased, the distribution of income would improve. This causal and cascading structure based on neoliberalism has evidently and spectacularly failed, not only in South Africa but also elsewhere. This loss of the battleground led COSATU to raise the following question in 2001: 'How do we account for the shift to the right in economic policy, especially after 1996?' The answer was that there was a hostile change in the balance of forces in that white capital had successfully won sections of the formerly oppressed into its ranks; linked to this was the emergence of a so-called 'patriotic', bureaucratic bourgeoisie that used its access to the state to expand the emerging black capitalist class.

The emergence of these sections from among the ranks of the formerly oppressed meant that the hegemony of the working class was being eroded by forces that sought a deracialised form of capitalism, with no interest in the long-term objective of building socialism. As argued, the working class lost the battleground and everything shifted towards the right in a neoliberal orientation manifestly in favour of capital.

It is clear that while political democracy has been deepened in many respects, it is in the field of the economy and ideology that the working class has suffered. In class terms, democracy has benefitted those who own economic resources rather than the working class and the poor. The EFF correctly characterises this by asserting the following:

> [T]he neoliberal policy fundamentals adopted to please the international financial institutions, which found expression in the Growth, Employment and Redistribution (GEAR), Accelerated and Shared Growth Initiative of South Africa (AsgiSA), and the National Development Plan (NDP) will never solve South Africa's development problems and will instead continue to expose it to unfair global competition, which will result in the strangling of potential economic activities in the country. The global economic crisis will also further worsen the economic conditions of South Africa, which is heavily dependent on exporting primary commodities (EFF Founding Manifesto, 2013).

Decisions about the nature and pattern of capital accumulation, social and economic policy, legal institutions and cultural expressions, political practice and the administration of state affairs are still biased towards capitalist class interests. To a large extent, the state remains insensitive to the plight of the working-class majority; the classical example here is how the state swiftly responded and brutally dealt with striking Lonmin's mineworkers in 2012, killing 34 of them, in what is notoriously known as the Marikana massacre (Workers and Socialist Party, 2013).

The following structural challenges have deepened since the introduction of the macro-economic strategy of GEAR in 1996, and they underline the problems associated with the capital-friendly, neoliberal policies of the post-1994 growth path:

- The means of production and power remain concentrated in white capitalist hands. The Johannesburg Stock Exchange (JSE) is still dominated by a few large firms; 50 per cent of the JSE is concentrated in six companies. And more than 80 per cent is made up of large banks and companies engaged in the core of the minerals-energy-complex. Estimated black ownership of JSE-listed companies ranges between 1.6 and 4.6 per cent.
- In 2001 COSATU claimed that control of the economy is still in white hands: top management and senior managers of major corporate companies continue to be predominantly drawn from the white population (COSATU, 2001). By 2021 the economically active white South Africans made up just 8.8 per cent of the total economically active population, but held 66.2 per cent of top management positions in the private sector (Kosser, 2022: 1).
- Redistribution of income has not occurred and this is accompanied by a decline in the real incomes of African households; income inequality has increased and black households have become poorer and poorer (COSATU, 2001).
- The incidence of poverty remains high; although government's social grant system has increasingly mitigated against households' exposure to extreme poverty, more than 57 per cent of individuals in South Africa are living below the income poverty line (COSATU, 2001).
- The persistence of and increase in unemployment among Africans and the general population was worsened by the outbreak of the COVID-19 pandemic. A broad and expanded definition of the unemployment rate puts unemployment in the country at about 46,6 per cent. This means that almost half of the economically active population have no jobs.

- The youth unemployment rate is now 66.5 per cent under the narrow definition, which is surely a recipe for social and political unrest. Further, this is a massive waste of human resources, which could be mobilised for development. The rate of participation of Africans in the labour force is 42 per cent and for whites, 68 per cent because of continued structural racial domination and exclusion.
- The crisis in education persists and the quality of education is declining. The children of the poor remain trapped in inferior education with wholly inadequate infrastructure (Mlatsheni and Rospabe, n.d).

The persistence of these fault lines points to an urgent need for a shift in class power relations in order to lay an appropriate political context for a thorough transformation of South African society. Evidence shows that although democracy has deepened through one person, one vote, it is not enough. No policy shift will automatically emerge unless it is preceded by a shift in class power relations in society. The following section explores how the present political configuration of South Africa's economy exacerbates legacies of privilege, as well as control along racial and class lines.

Political power in the control of the post-1994 government is meaningless because it has not been used to win the battles that began during the wars of dispossession. Instead, the post-1994 government has played an active role in reproducing the inequalities and imbalances of the past by not doing anything to transform the economy, opting instead for superficial changes through BEE. As the statistics used earlier indicate, neoliberal policies adopted and embraced by the post-1994 government have worsened the conditions of the poor, and ossified the structural unemployment and inequalities designed by colonial and apartheid South Africa. Vestiges of apartheid and colonial economic patterns, ownership and control remain intact, despite the attainment of political freedom through the liberation struggle. What is apparent, though, is that political freedom without economic emancipation is meaningless. In this regard, the following sections explore the alternatives to historical leftist formations.

THE LEFT AND CRITIQUES OF SOCIALISM AS LIVED EXPERIENCE

It is against this background that the EFF's opening statement, under the preamble of its Founding Manifesto, begins with: 'Our decision is to fight for the economic emancipation of the people of South Africa, Africa and the world.' It further articulates the current state of affairs by underlining:

> Our indignation at the continued economic domination of the people of South Africa and the extreme exploitation of the black working class explains where we come from, where we are, what our mission is, what our character is, and what is to be done to emancipate the black people of South Africa, the working class in particular, from economic bondage. The solutions we provide represent a coherent ideological tradition and draw inspiration from developments around the world on what has been done to advance the development and betterment of people's lives in the aftermath of the defeat of colonialism and against imperialism (EFF's Founding Manifesto, 2013).

Chris Hani had the following insights to share concerning the future of socialism:

> Socialism is not about big concepts and heavy theory. Socialism is about decent shelter for those who are homeless. It is about water for those who have no safe drinking water. It is about health care; it is about a life of dignity for the old. It is about overcoming the huge divide between urban and rural areas. It is about a decent education for all our people. Socialism is about rolling back the tyranny of the market. As long as the economy is dominated by an unelected, privileged few, the case for socialism will exist (Hani, 1992).

An ideology can never magically inspire the masses unless its adherents practise it. Unfortunately, it seems that socialists in the late 20th and early 21st centuries have been oblivious to this lesson and seem not to want to practise socialism; instead, their practices make a mockery of its ideals. The age-old saying, 'ye shall know them by their actions,' is apposite. The masses are fully aware of the evils of capitalism and yearn for a better life. The masses are quite aware that there is no ethical consumption under capitalism and that is not the answer to the ecological, environmental, economic and socio-political crises facing humanity.

Capitalism is a philosophical system that promotes the spirit of individualism and private ownership, with greed at its core, so it is not surprising that corruption is so pervasive in this system – even though voodoo socialists deny it. What is paramount in capitalism is that the well-being and desires of individuals stand above the common good. The ethos, norms and values that have permeated the fabric of society for many centuries are those engendered by this philosophy. Yet our socialists deny it (Moqejwa, 2014). The taste for spectacular consumerism is unaffordable, even to most of those who subscribe to it. This is borne out by the record levels of individual debt in South Africa, paired with a culture of 'tenderpreneurship' (Workers and Socialist Party, 2014). According to the Workers and Socialist Party (WASP), tenderpreneurship is masked as a way to empower previously disadvantaged individuals; it has, however, become one of the most deleterious banes of the new South Africa.

There is nothing concrete being offered to the masses in line with the socialist vision. How do we ensure that MaKhumalo in the rural area can relate to the socialist vision? In practical terms, how is socialism going to change her living conditions in the rural area? These questions that go directly to the common good, point to a future for the Left beyond theory and rhetoric.

The neoliberal capitalists and the Hellen Zilles (*Business Day*, 2019) of this world would answer by saying that colonialism provided piped water to the masses. Certainly, when Hani raised this point, he was not envisioning the current decadent capitalist social order as being the ultimate solution to the plight of the working class. This is an important distinction, between services provided as commodities by the capitalist social order, and socialism. Furthermore, the doubling of inequalities in South Africa over the past 20 years bears testimony to this. The point made by Hani must never be mischievously viewed as negating the importance and role of theory as the material force. What is clear from Hani's testimony, cited earlier, is that the case for socialism – but never for the Left – will always exist for as long as the masses are homeless, poverty-stricken and hungry. I accordingly submit, in agreement with Hani, that socialism has never and will never fail. However, as argued in this chapter, the socialists have failed socialism. No ideology is worthy if its adherents fail to practise it.

The key question remains: in this critical historical era, are there are viable alternatives to bourgeois ideology – considering that even those who are critical of it, enjoy its benefits? Current critiques of capital risk being crowded out by bourgeois voices, even if the excesses of neoliberalism are evident in, for example, the crisis concerning climate change, driven as this is by a long history of industrialisation and extraction, which have destroyed the environment. This raises the fundamental question as to whether those advocating the socialist vision in South Africa have a strategy that can be employed to strengthen the socialist culture. It is contested that there is nothing visible on the horizon to pose as a real challenge to the capitalist philosophy and way of life.

It is my view that members of the Communist Party in South Africa have been absorbed into bourgeois culture. As George Bush, the former US president, famously said: 'They talk left, but walk right.' Their party leaders fool the masses about the spectre of communism that is about to happen, while acting as levers in the hands of capital, to entrench capitalism. The political commentator Vera Kharuzhaya (quoted in Atwood, 1985) correctly characterised this breed of communist as 'bourgeois communists', because they live and act like capitalists, while occasionally singing the praises of socialism to fool the masses.

The dominance of capitalism does not mean that it cannot be challenged. This could be achieved by growing the socialist culture in a practical way. It seems that a majority of people, due to illiteracy, cannot relate to an abstract concept of socialism. It is only when socialism becomes a practical reality that the masses will realise its virtues.

All powerful philosophies have grown because their proponents lived and practised them. Capitalism is powerful today because both its adherents do not merely theorise, write and talk about its virtues, they live and practise it. They, like Professor Robert Heilbroner, a luminary of the New York New School (cited by Slovo), have raised their glasses to toast the victory of capitalism. According to Heilbroner, capitalism organises the material affairs of humankind more satisfactorily than socialism. Most former liberators, the ex-nomenklatura of our times, share Heilbroner's views.

If anything, capitalist 'success' illustrates that practice is key to grow the socialist culture. The importance of practising what one preaches is self-evident. Great revolutionaries, including Karl Marx, died as 'paupers' because they were dedicated to the betterment of the lot of the ordinary people. Can this be said of the latter-day communists, who are pseudo-socialists, while purporting to be the disciples of Marx? The converse appears to be true.

One of the greatest contemporary revolutionaries, who practically demonstrated how to serve the people, was Thomas Sankara (1949–1987). It was his steadfast adherence to the socialist conviction and determination to cultivate proletariat culture that attracted the wrath of his enemies. Sankara was living evidence that any worthy ideology cannot only be preached but must also be practised. Principled and exemplary living would set the general framework for meaningful and principle-centred societal transformation. Over the last 30 years, South African society has undergone only the 'deracialisation' of capital as opposed to real transformation that promotes the common good. A transformed society is reflected in the attitudes, behaviours, conduct and language of its people and leaders.

The reality of these unsustainable bourgeois aspirations, and the dangers brought about by them, is not a new phenomenon. It was highlighted in 1968 in an essay by an 18-year-old Chinese high school student, Yang Xiguang. The essay gained notoriety because Xiguang argued that the major conflict in China was not between Mao's supporters and enemies, nor between China's proletariat and former wealthy (aristocratic feudal lords), but rather between a 'red capitalist class' (akin in many respects to a 'new patriotic class') on the one hand, and the masses of the Chinese people, on the other. He wrote:

> At present over 90 percent of our high-ranking officials have formed into a unique class – the red capitalist class ... it is a decadent class impeding historical progress. Its relationship with the people has changed from that of leaders and followers to rulers and ruled, to exploiters and exploited, from equal, revolutionary camaraderie to oppressors and oppressed. The class interests, prerogatives, and high income of the red capitalist class is built upon repression and exploitation of the masses of the population (Yang Xiguang, 1968: 3).

This statement led to his imprisonment for 10 years, just as many have been banished from the ANC (people such as Bantu Holomisa and Julius Malema), from the SACP (such as Dale T. McKenly and Mazibuko Jara) and from COSATU (trade union leaders such as Joseph Mathunjwa, Irvin Jim and Zwelinzima Vavi) for openly criticising the neoliberal agenda and the direction taken by the former liberation movement.

The EFF's Founding Manifesto underscores a similar situation and argues that,

> While the legalistic forms of colonial-apartheid domination have been eroded 20 years ago, the economic system that marginalised, oppressed and exploited the black majority is still intact, with a few individuals benefiting, but only because they have been co-opted to portray a wrong picture that all is and will be well in our country (EFF's Founding Manifesto, 2013).

It is these few individuals that are benefitting from a system based on the super-exploitation of the black majority; this was a class that the late Chris Hani warned us about when he said: What I fear is that the liberators emerge as elitists ... who drive around in Mercedes Benz, and use the resources of this country ... to live in palaces and to gather riches (Chris Hani, 1992).

Sadly, and true to Hani's prophetic nightmare, 29 years later, the elitist class of former liberators, the ex-nomenklatura, who 'have tainted the noble ideal of socialism through their rapacious greed to a point where few would now invoke an attempt to return to an ideology that was once a driving force for revolutionary change'

(Sullivan, 2002). To this point, the working class the world over, has turned to capitalism as a new force for social change. This, unfortunately, is the situation of the armchair critics of capitalism in South Africa today. They are occasionally involved in theoretically critiquing capitalism while enjoying its benefits. They curse the forbidden tree, yet eat its fruits. The following section explores key aspects of capitalism's 'success'.

The success of capitalism is due to the fact that its adherents live and practise it as they staunchly believe in it. They practise its core principles, key among which is private property ownership and individualism. These two principles mean that the advancement of the individual interest is the defining feature and way of life in a capitalist society. The advancement of the common good in general is subordinate to those of the individual.

Unlike capitalism's focus on greed and individualism, a true revolutionary is always fighting for the common good of the community and not the advancement of the self. It was indicated earlier that some poor people, through the inducement of capital, end up harbouring bourgeois aspirations. When revolutionaries assimilate, they become prisoners of capital, and become conflicted when defending revolutionary principles lest they offend the master of patronage and thereby risk losing jobs, tenders and status. South Africa is also not immune from global influences. On the contrary, this local dominance of capitalism is a replica of the global trend. This does not mean, however, that this dominance is beyond being challenged or critiqued.

The pervasive dominance of capitalism is a reflection of its revolutionary nature, which has been well noted by its protagonists in the past. It is unfortunate that there is no noteworthy ideology that even remotely challenges this dominance in the South African society today – despite some elements who claim to be the ordained ideological opponents of capitalism.

In reflecting on the argument put forward in this chapter, it is important to make the following observations: First, we live in a world dominated by capitalist hegemony and culture. Second, the working class is unable to challenge this hegemony, partly because it harbours bourgeois aspirations and, given the chance, would embrace them. Third, the socialist culture could be developed through the practise of principles such as sacrifice, humility, love for the people and simplicity, among others. Fourth, a true revolutionary would never aspire to a bourgeois lifestyle. Fifth, a true revolutionary, through practical revolutionary practice, would negate any capitalist hegemony and cultivate a socialist culture. Sixth, there is a need for the Left, if it takes itself seriously, to unite.

Mzala Nxumalo (Ngonyama, 2012), whose life and work are celebrated in this volume, penned an essay titled 'Cooking the rice inside the pot: A historical call in our times' (1985). Borrowing from Lenin, he wrote, 'It is not enough to call ourselves the vanguard contingent, we must act in such a way that all other contingents recognise and are obliged to admit that we are not tailing behind semi-spontaneous mass upsurges but are marching in the vanguard.' This raises the questions: Which position is the Left occupying in the struggle today? Is it taking the vanguard or the rear-guard, or it is comfortably tailing the semi-spontaneous mass protests, without taking its potential leadership role seriously?

According to Leon Trotsky, the question formulated by Lenin – Who shall prevail? – is a question of the correlation of forces between the international Left and the world's revolutionary proletariat, on the one hand, and on the other, international capital and its bourgeois hostile forces, which are ranged against the struggle for socialism. In its essence, Lenin's question is not only a military one, but more of an economic one. It is in the economic terrain of struggle that the question becomes more urgent and relevant.

The collapse of communist states, or their reinvention in the form of state capitalism (for example, China) does not alter the relevance and usefulness of Marxism for understanding a world that, more than ever, has been shaped by class conflict and the struggles of the oppressed people against corporate power, nor has it shaken the values and commitment of those on the side of workers, unions, minorities, national liberation, peace, women, the environment and human rights. Still, what has happened to socialism represents both a theoretical challenge to Marxism and a practical challenge to the future prospects of anti-capitalist struggles and the triumph of a socialist victory.

A FUTURE BEYOND THE CAPITALIST MIRE

My final remark on the question of the future of socialism takes its cue from the opening statement in that, unless the Left takes up the task of cultivating a socialist culture, it has no future. Capitalism represents the culmination of economic and political dominance on a world scale. This right-wing triumphalism partly explains why the later revolutionaries in our country have fully embraced bourgeois aspirations and rationalised their bourgeois lifestyles. This must be rejected, however, by cultivating a unifying socialist culture.

It is critical that the Left confront the harsh realities of working-class fragmentation in the neoliberal era, which has hugely undermined the traditional base for socialist politics. Left parties have, on countless occasions, failed to transform institutions such as the media and reactionary organs of the repressive regimes, which has left their governments vulnerable to internal or external destabilisation. Laying hands on these state organs without transforming them, fails to appreciate what a Gramscian scholar, Lucio Oliver says when he describes the state as 'the vehicle for hegemony in political and civil society' (quoted in Levitsky and Roberts, 2011). As the experience of the Latin American presidential victories and, to a lesser extent, European left governments has revealed: winning governmental power and not state power, and all power in all its aspects, cannot in any way be equated with control over the state as a whole.

To sustain governmental power in a world political system dominated by capitalism requires that left governments internalise at least three critical structural constraints of electoral or governmental power (Buxton *et al*, 2021): First, there is the need to maintain governmentality, which is the capacity to engage the capitalist world order in a manner that maintains popular and electoral support. Second, winning public office does not necessarily provide the Left with hegemony over other state institutions such as the military and civil service and, therefore, cannot guarantee control over hard power. This has the potential to limit the range of political options available. Third, left governments must govern in the context of a neoliberal civil society, in which the working class is fragmented and is largely individualist rather than socialist.

Attaining hegemony over civil society therefore requires a significantly deeper process than merely achieving electoral power. This does not diminish the importance of winning electoral or governmental power, because attaining the latter is one method available in a bourgeois, capitalist system of governance (Buxton *et al*, 2021). While this approach is important, left parties should appreciate that being in government does not mean being in charge; they would be well advised to heed the counsel of Gabriel Hetland, who calls for competing for government power while simultaneously deepening democracy at the level of consciousness, and organisation and building powerful movements outside the formal structures of the state (Buxton *et al*, 2021).

The Left must rise to the occasion and also be conscious of the dilemmas and the potential sins of incumbency and the inherent tendencies of leaning towards electoralism, which is the pursuit of electoral goals above all other concerns. It is the job of a theoretically conscious and informed Left to organise against such dangers while not collapsing into reactionary abstentionism.

This is the only viable and practical way to build and finally attain hegemony over civil society for a new relook into the role of the Left and the future of socialism in South Africa and internationally. Reconstruction is urgent and this is what the working class and poor masses of the world look forward to. All international radical Marxists and socialist activists, of all nations, must step forward and become consumed by the need to mobilise, organise and agitate the people to work towards bringing about an alternative, a new world system and a desirable future for working-class people – a system that is based on socialist propositions and which requires the defeat of imperialism and capitalism.

REFERENCES

Aptheker, H. (1957). *The Truth about Hungary*. New York: Mainstream Publishers.
Atwood, M. (1985). *The Handmaid's Tale*. New York: Random House.
Bhorat, H. (2006). Youth unemployment and education in South

Africa. Harold Wolpe Memorial Trust Dialogue, 2 February, Cape Town.

Buxton, N., Barrett, P., Chavez, D. and Ramand, P. (2021). 'The New Politics Conference 2021: Democratic Socialism in Global Perspective'. Report of the Conference organised by the Transnational Institute (TNI) and the Havens Wright Center for Social Justice.

Cliff, T. (1973). 'Reprint from the International Socialist Tradition: Lenin and the Revolutionary Party', *International Socialist Review*, 5: 34–38.

COSATU. (2001). 'A Growth Path towards Full Employment'. COSATU booklet.

Economic Freedom Fighters (EFF). (2014). 'EFF Founding Manifesto: Radical movement towards economic freedom in our lifetime'. Available at: https://effonline.org/wp-content/uploads/2019/07/Founding-Manifesto.pdf (Accessed 14 April 2023).

Cosser, K. (2022). 'Race and private sector ownership in South Africa: three viral claims investigated', *Africa Check*, 6 Dec. 2022.https://www.polity.org.za/article/race-and-private-sector-ownership-in-south-africa-three-viral-claims-investigated-2022-12-06 2-7 (Accessed 16 May 2023).

Edwards, S. and Edwards, A.C. (1995). *Monetarism and Liberalization: The Chilean experiment*. Chilcago, IL: University of Chicago Press.

Fukuyama, F. (1992). *The End of History and the Last Man*. New York: The Free Press.

Hani, C. (1992). *Voices of Liberation*. Pretoria: Human Sciences Research Council. ResearchGate.

Havens Wright Center for Social Justice. (2021). *New Politics Conference, 2021: Democratic Socialism in Global Perspective*. Rosa Luxemburg Stiftung and Latin American, Caribbean and

Hetland, G. (2021). 'In and against the state', in N. Buxton, P. Barrett, D. Chavez, and P. Ramand (eds). *The New Politics Conference 2021: Democratic socialism in global perspective*. Report of the Conference organised by the Transnational Institute (TNI) and the Havens Wright Center for Social Justice.

Iberian Studies Program. Available at: https://www.tni.org/en/publication/new-politics-conference-2021 (Accessed 14 April 2023).

Jordan, P. (2014). 'Who's left in the post-1994 conjuncture? Debate on the Left', *New Agenda, South African Journal of Social and Economic Policy*, No. 54. Available at: https://hdl.handle.net/10520/EJC162418 (Accessed 13 April 2023).

Kapp, L. (2013). 'The responses of trade unions to the effects of neoliberalism in South Africa: The case of COSATU and its affiliated unions'. Dissertation, University of South Africa.

Lehulere, O. (2003). 'The road to the right: COSATU economic policy in the post-apartheid period', in F. Barchiesi and T. Bramble (eds). *Rethinking the Labour Movement in the 'New South Africa'*. London: Routledge.

Lenin, V.I. (1999 [1917]). *Imperialism: The highest stage of capitalism*. Introduction by D. Lorimer. Sydney: Resistance Books.

Levitsky, S. and Roberts, K.M. (2011). *The Resurgence of the Latin American Left*. Baltimore, MD: Johns Hopkins University Press.

Mlatsheni, C. and Rospabé, S. (2002). 'Why is youth unemployment so high and unequally spread in South Africa?' Development Policy Research Unit Working Paper 02/065. University of Cape Town.

Moqejwa, K. (2014). 'Philosophy of praxis: Cultivating the socialist culture'. Unpublished.

Mthukwane, N.D. (2018). 'Is the liberation struggle over?' Northern Cape News Network. Southern African Freelancers Association. Available at: https://ncnn.live/is-the-liberation-struggle-over/ (Accessed 12 April 2023).

Nxumalo, M. (1985). 'Cooking the rice inside the pot: A historical call in our times'. Available at: www. https://amadlandawonye.wikispaces.com (Accessed 14 April 2023).

Rothschild, E. (1994). 'Adam Smith and the invisible hand'. Papers and Proceedings of the Hundred and Sixth Annual Meeting of the American Economic Association (May 1994), *The American Economic Review*, 84(2): 319–22.

Satgar, V. (2011). 'Reclaiming the South African dream', *Red Pepper*, 28 December. Available at: https://www.redpepper.org.uk/reclaiming-the-south-african-dream/ (Accessed 14 April 2023).

Slovo, J. (1990). 'Has socialism failed?' Available at: https://www.sahistory.org.za/sites/default/files/Has%20Socialism%20Failed%20

by%20Joe%20Slovo.pdf (Accessed 14 April 2023).

Sullivan, S. (2002). *Marx for a Post-Communist Era: On poverty, corruption and banality.* London: Routledge.

Havens Wright Center for Social Justice. (2021). New Politics Conference. 2021: Democratic Socialism in Global Perspective. Rosa Luxemburg Stiftung and Latin American, Caribbean, and Iberian Studies Program. Available at: https://www.tni.org/en/publication/new-politics-conference-2021 (Accessed 14 April 2023).

Trotsky, L. (1936). *The Revolution Betrayed: What is the Soviet Union and where is it going?* New York: Pathfinder Books. Available at: https://www.marxists.org/archive/trotsky/1936/revbet/ (Accessed 12 April 2023).

Workers and Socialist Party (WASP). (2013). 'After Marikana: What way forward for the mineworkers?' International Socialist Alternative. Available at: https://socialist.org.za/campaigns/after-marikana/ (Accessed 11 April 2023).

Williamson, J. (1989). *Latin American Adjustment: How much has happened?* Peterson Institute for International Economics. Digitised by the University of California.

Xiguang. Y. (1968). 'Whither China. A radical complaint against the emerging establishment.' First Published in English as 'Whither China?', translated in American Consulate General, Hong Kong's *Survey of China Mainland Press*, no. 4190, pp. 1–18. Available at: https://www.marxists.org/subject/china/documents/whither-china.htm (Accessed 11 April 2023).

SIX

THE DILEMMA OF THE POST-1994 DEMOCRATIC BREAKTHROUGH: A BROAD SURVEY OF COMMUNITY STRUGGLES IN SOUTH AFRICA

Noel L.Z. Solani

INTRODUCTION

In the 1950s, as part of mobilising the masses to fight for freedom against oppression, the liberation movements came up with a slogan, *'Amandla'*. When uttering this word, a person would clench their fist, signalling the power of unity. The people would, in return, shout in unison, *'Ngawethu'*. This slogan took us to the 1994 democratic breakthrough in South Africa. *Amandla* or 'power to the people' was aimed at inculcating the idea in the masses that it was within their power to liberate themselves. It was also to impress upon the working classes that the growth of the economy of this country was made possible through their labour. In short, a consciousness was created among the masses that no one but themselves was able to alleviate the pain of the conditions of their existence.

This chapter aims to examine the contribution of the slogan to the democratic breakthrough. It further aims to examine to what extent it impressed upon generations of people the power that lay in their hands; over decades, this was expressed through community struggles, industrial action and mass demonstrations. For these purposes, historical documents will be examined, together with the promise of the slogan that expressed the desire of the people. The impact of policy decisions, such as the Reconstruction and Development Programme (RDP) of 1993, the Growth, Employment and Redistribution (GEAR) policy of 1996, and the National Development Plan: Vision 2030 (NDP) of 2011, will be examined. The period of focus for this analysis will be 1994–2017 because the first 23 years of democratic rule gives us enough historical evidence to understand the challenges that confront the democratic project of the post-apartheid South Africa.

HISTORICAL BACKGROUND

The slogan *'Amandla'* expressed in tangible ways the demands of the people in one of the first historical documents adopted by the mass of South Africans aligned to the Congress Alliance – the Freedom Charter, which was adopted on 25 and 26 June 1955 at the Congress of the People held in Kliptown, Soweto. The preamble of the Charter states:

> We the people of South Africa, declare for all our country and the world to know: that South Africa belongs to all who live in it, black and white, and that no government can justly claim authority unless it is based on the will of the people.

The 1996 South African Constitution, Act No. 108 of 1996, expresses this sentiment:

> We, the people of South Africa,
>
> Recognise the injustices of our past;
>
> Honour those who suffered for justice and freedom in our land;

> Respect those who have worked to build and develop our country; and
>
> Believe that South Africa belongs to all who live in it, united in our diversity.

The first clause of the Freedom Charter asserts this view when it says, 'The People Shall Govern!' and continues:

> Every man and woman shall have the right to vote for and to stand as a candidate for all bodies which make laws;
>
> All people shall be entitled to take part in the administration of the country;
>
> The rights of the people shall be the same, regardless of race, colour or sex;
>
> All bodies of minority rule, advisory boards, councils and authorities shall be replaced by democratic organs of self-government.

The 1993 Interim Constitution gave practical effect to these desires and, therefore, at last, the people were able to govern and elect their own representatives. Before this event, the only solution they had at their disposal was unity of purpose and fighting for their rights. These struggles were led mainly by the Congress Alliance, although other formations were fighting for civil rights, as explained in Andre Odendaal's book, *The Founders* (2012). As Jack and Ray Simons pointed out in *Class and Colour in South Africa* (1983: 610), these struggles occurred because of the 'contradictions between the dynamic potential of a multi-racial labour force and the straitjacket of racially segregated institutions; between the dominant collective role of Africans in the economy and their exclusion from the centre of power'. This brings us closer to another longstanding demand of the people, which is given expression by clause seven of the Freedom Charter: 'There Shall be Work and Security!'. It goes on to state that:

> All who work shall be free to form trade unions, to elect their officers and to make wage agreements with their employers;

> The state shall recognise the right and duty of all to work, and to draw full unemployment benefits;
>
> Men and women of all races shall receive equal pay for equal work;
>
> There shall be a 40-hour working week, a national minimum wage, paid annual leave, and sick leave for all workers, and maternity leave on full pay for all working mothers;
>
> Miners, domestic workers, farm workers and civil servants shall have the same rights as all others who work;
>
> Child labour, compound labour, the tot system and contract labour shall be abolished.

Both the Interim Constitution and the Constitution of the Republic of South Africa infuse these aspirations contained in the Freedom Charter. However, community struggles continue to reflect the race and class nature of the South African society. In *Development: Dilemmas in post-apartheid South Africa* (Freund and Witt, 2010: 4), this is attributed to the historical nature of development, where the 'consequences of the past are still with us and because of patterns of accumulation in the South African economy [which is] still ploughing the furrows laid down during its classical period of industrialisation'.

The rate of unemployment and the economy that is being scaled down in traditional employment sectors has made it difficult to quantify any gains made by the post-apartheid government in impoverished areas. Community struggles are a product of dreams that seem forever to be deferred, even though the Freedom Charter and the Constitution of South Africa clearly give expression to them.

The housing problem remains unresolved and this is unlikely to change in the foreseeable future. This is not a new problem, especially for the black majority (meaning African, Coloured and Indian citizens). This is precisely why, even in the 1950s, the Freedom Charter talked about decent housing for people in areas in which they choose to live. When the Government of National Unity (GNU), led by the African National Congress (ANC), came into power in 1994, a huge housing backlog existed for the majority of the population. Then the population of South Africa was estimated at fewer than 40 million people. In 2011, according to the last census, the population stood at 55 million. Mary Tomlinson (2015) explains the housing situation as follows:

'Since 1994, the government has provided more than 2.5 million houses and another 1.2 million serviced sites. Over the same period, the housing backlog increased from 1.5 million to 2.1 million units. The number of informal settlements has gone from 300 to 2 225.'

For the period 1994 to 2015, the housing subsidy for the poor increased from 1 per cent to 3.8 per cent of the Gross Domestic Product (GDP) (Tomlinson, 2015). It is quite evident that what makes the eradication of informal settlements problematic is the dependence of a large number of the youth and adult population on state grants. Most of them cannot provide even the basic necessities for themselves, due to a scarcity of jobs and an economy that seems unable to yield growth that is congruent with that of the population.

In 1994, during the first democratic elections in South Africa, the ANC and its alliance partners – the South African Communist Party (SACP) and the Congress of South African Trade Unions (COSATU) – were united under the banner of the RDP. The ANC election manifesto, as a result, was based on the principles of the RDP document (1994), a product of broad consultation by the ANC with civil society organisations and the trade union movement. The RDP acknowledged that poverty continues 'to exist side by side with modern cities' in South Africa; and that, 'the economy was built on systematically enforced racial divisions in every sphere of our society'. Therefore, both the ANC's 1994 election manifesto and the RDP recognised that: 'No political democracy can survive and flourish if the masses of our people remain in poverty, without land, without tangible prospects for a better life. Attacking poverty and deprivation must therefore be the first priority of a democratic government.' The manifesto puts it as follows:

> Democracy means more than just a vote. It must be measured by the quality of life of ordinary people – men and women, young and old, rural and urban. It means giving all South Africans the

opportunity to share in the country's wealth, to contribute to its development, and to improve their own lives.[1]

Clearly, what the RDP and the ANC's first election manifesto articulated was not new. As we have seen, these priorities were already articulated in the Freedom Charter in 1955. These remained relevant because they reflected not only the aspirations of the majority of the people, but also the material conditions and experience of the working class. When the ANC came into power, as the majority in government, it amplified these through the GEAR policy plan, approved by cabinet in 1996, with a vision that sought:

- a competitive, fast-growing economy that creates sufficient jobs for all work seekers;
- a redistribution of income and opportunities in favour of the poor;
- a society in which sound health, education and other services are available to all; and
- an environment in which homes are secure and places of work are productive.

In the post-GEAR policy period, a number of policy proposals by the government sought to address the same issues experienced by poor and lower middle-class communities. The Accelerated and Shared Growth Initiative for South Africa (AsgiSA), the New Growth Path (NGP) and more recently the National Development Plan (NDP) all seek to achieve the same goals as the Freedom Charter. The RDP did as well, plus the myriad policy formulations by the government, with differing emphases placed on various aspects by different departments. The NDP has its 15 outcomes, and every department is supposed to contribute to the success of a particular outcome, similar to other plans that aim to 'eliminate poverty and reduce inequality by 2030'.[2]

---

1 ANC (1994). National Election Manifesto. Available at: http://www.anc.org.za/content/1994-national- elections-manifesto (Accessed 12 September 2022).
2 Available at: https://www.poa.gov.za/news/Documents/NPC%20National%20 Development%20Plan%20Vision%20203 0%20-lo-res.pdf (Accessed 12 November 2022).

However, from the GEAR policy to the NDP, all seem not to have achieved the ultimate goals of eradicating poverty and unemployment and thus restoring dignity to the masses of South Africans. The GEAR policy drew the most criticism from the ANC's alliance partners. This makes it necessary for us to review some of the responses to the GEAR policy. Before that, it is important to note that some have defined the RDP as:

> a set of critical analysis of social circumstances in South Africa that showed no way forward in terms of emphasis or priority and no basis for independence from the larger context of a fiscally constrained economic policy, that from the beginning allowed only limited space for attacking those circumstances (Freund and Witt, 2010: 9).[3]

For COSATU (1997), GEAR was untenable because, in their view, it made South Africa a friendly environment for investors from countries 'with very poor workers' rights and records'. It further argued that the policy called on the 'government to reduce on social spending, thereby accelerating the rate of unemployment' (COSATU, 1997). In short, COSATU (1997) saw GEAR as 'essentially an anti-working-class economic programme and a setback in [the] struggle for socialism'. In Chapter 7 in this volume, Alex Mashilo expatiates the views expressed by COSATU in a rather more forceful manner when he argues that, 'to many in the left, the adoption of GEAR amounted to a turn to the right [since it] advanced neoliberal economic policy measures'. The objectives that COSATU envisaged in GEAR were similar to those already stipulated in GEAR, except for the explicit ones that COSATU had wanted GEAR to reflect:

- working-class control of strategic companies such as banks;
- ensuring greater state control over the economy; and
- that all steps taken are part of a process leading to a socialist society, democratically controlled by the workers.

---

3   COSATU 6th National Congress Resolutions, 16–19 September 1997. Available at: http://www.COSATU.org.za/show.php?ID=2156 (Accessed 14 November 2022).

The last point made in the COSATU resolutions, concerning the development of a socialist society, is the most critical for policy formulation in South Africa. If this issue is not directly confronted, and is moved around in all government policies, no consensus can exist about the direction in which the country must move. The tension that exists in the alliance between the ANC, COSATU and the SACP is caused by different opinions about which direction the country should take. Instead of confronting issues directly, both the SACP and COSATU tend to focus their attention on the nature and character of the ANC's leaders. At times, it seems there is a plea from these partners for the ANC to push for a left agenda, and to remind all members, followers and supporters of the ANC to be clear on the multiclass nature of the ANC as an organisation.

Organisations on the left should, in my view, focus on building a socialist society and preparing the South African electorate, through education, about what socialism can mean for them. An alliance of left-wing organisations is required at this stage to fight the struggles of the working class, focusing on commonalities rather than ideological differences. In short, pragmatic programmes by left organisations should be at the forefront.

The tension around the GEAR policy could be compared to the way the Freedom Charter was received in 1955: to some members of the ANC, the Charter was the ultimate policy position, while to socialists, it articulated minimum demands. The Deputy Secretary of NUMSA, Karl Cloete, articulated this as follows: 'For NUMSA, the Freedom Charter remains a transitionary programme which could lay the basis to develop and advance a working-class programme that must open up the space and forward march to a socialist agenda' (Cloete, 2015). Therein lies the dilemma of post-apartheid South Africa. The SACP and COSATU had similar views on the GEAR policy and further argued that, even if it yielded economic growth, it would be jobless growth. The debate centres on, and is judged by, how it achieves the aim of 'economic growth and transformational development' or 'jobless economic growth', which is unable to reduce or eliminate the rate of poverty in South Africa. As shown below, the unemployment rate in South Africa since 1994 has been consistently above 20 per cent, which suggests deeper issues than mere policy formulations;

these are probably also systemic and need to be uprooted for the economy to yield the expected results. At this point, there is the need to take heed of Friedrich Engels (2009 [1903]: 33):

> [A]ll successive historical conditions are only places of pilgrimage in the endless evolutionary progress of human society from the lower to the higher. Every step is necessary and useful for the time and circumstances to which it owes its origin, but it becomes weak without justification under newer and higher conditions which develop little by little in its own womb, it must give way to the higher form, which in turn comes to decay and defeat.

Race, while it continues to be a relevant analytical tool, has to share space increasingly with class as the gap between rich and poor widens in South Africa. The primary terrain of conflict is becoming that of class antagonism, a by-product of an individual's economic standing in society. Having conquered racial antagonism since apartheid began in 1948, and colonial struggles before then, it was inevitable that class struggles would emerge in South Africa after liberation. Lenin (1975: 17) once stated that 'in any society the strivings of some of its members run counter to the striving of others', and Marx, in *The Communist Manifesto* (1848), succinctly stated that 'the history of all hitherto society is the history of class struggles'.

True to their prophetic words, in South Africa, the outcomes of the liberation struggle did not do away with class, and instead a new class of black bourgeoisie emerged. Most of the time, this dichotomy is articulated with great 'surprise' and popularly described as, 'the rich are getting richer, while the poor are getting poorer'.[4] The Jacob Zuma presidency of the ANC and his leadership of the country exposed this diminishing racial interest and increasing class interest in society. The marches to both Parliament and the Union Buildings as a show against corruption and against the March 2017 release of Pravin Gordhan and Mcebisi Jonas from their Treasury

---

4   COSATU Press Statement, 17 January 2017. Available at: http://www.COSATU.org.za/show.php?ID=12318; also, 5th National Policy Conference, 30 June–5 July 2017, International Relations Policy Discussion Document of the ANC.

responsibilities, were supported by all races – seemingly because they felt that the threat to the economy and possible downgrading of the South African economy to 'junk' status threatened their savings and economic standing.

This increasing class interest found resonance primarily in the urban centres of the country, where there is a growing bourgeoisie. The black middle class has increasingly come to find less in common with their fellows, even though historically all black people had been oppressed together based on their race. The main components of segregation and apartheid – 'restrictions on permanent urbanisation, territorial separation of land ownership, and the use of traditional institutions as providers of social services and means of social control and, along with other mechanisms of labour coercion ... the system of migrant labour, which characterised South Africa's road to industrialisation' (Wolpe, 1972: 427) – no longer exist and have been dismantled. The evidence of this is seen in the ever-increasing informal settlements in urban spaces.

In Pretoria in 2017, this antagonism played itself out between residents of Mahube Valley, an informal settlement in Mamelodi, and bond owners. Residents of this suburb, which by all appearances is a black middle-class community, demanded the settlement be abolished and accused its members of stealing electricity and water. The solution of the then mayor, Solly Msimang, was to promise that he would build a wall to separate the two communities (Mitchley, 2017). His suggestion was similar to that effected by the world powers when Berlin was divided after World War II. Such a local 'solution' would very likely further increase antagonism between the two groups concerned.

Two other incidents demonstrated this transformation and the increasing class nature of contemporary South Africa. The first was the Marikana massacre, which took place on 16 August 2012, the result of collusion between the ruling class and the new emerging black capitalist class, as demonstrated by correspondence between the ministers of police and mineral resources and energy, and the chairperson of Lonmin Platinum Mine. The second is the loss of some of the metros by the ruling party, the ANC, to the opposition coalition led by the Democratic Alliance (DA) in the 2016 local government elections. Historically, the DA was a party of the capitalist class and the English bourgeoisie. However, recent events demonstrate the evolution of the DA and the support it is gaining from the poor and working-class communities arising from disaffection with the ruling ANC, primarily owing to service delivery issues and corruption.

In analysing the revolution of 1848, Lenin said, 'it revealed the various classes of society in action. The shooting down of the workers by the republican bourgeoisie in the June days of 1848 in Paris finally established the fact that the proletariat alone is socialist by nature' (Lenin, 1975: 80). Perhaps the question needing to be asked is: Has South Africa, through the Marikana massacre, reached its Paris moment? Has the time come for the review of the alliance between the ANC and the party of the proletariat? Or, stated differently, is the alliance the cause of a dilemma or the causative factor creating the conundrum?

Perhaps there is a strong need for South Africans to engage broadly in a debate around what type of society is needed, with a congress comprising all political formations and civil society organisations to come up with policy guidelines to address the basic needs of the poor, the unemployed and the working class. In such a conference, the question of continuing with a capitalist society and moving towards a socialist society must be confronted head on. A serious analysis of the global economic crisis of 2008, which was caused by a financial meltdown as the result of a coalition within the United States financial sector, and that had a grave impact on developing world countries, forces us to ask questions about the viability of justice under a capitalist economy. In chapter 10 of this book, Gunnet Kaff challenges the dominant view of the 2008 financial meltdown and argues that, 'the deepening crisis of global capitalism did not start in 2008 with the great recession that resulted from the financial meltdown but goes further to the 1970s'.

The decades of democratic rule in South Africa, with all the good intentions of the state, have demonstrated the stubbornness of dealing with and reducing levels of poverty in our country. With each policy change, the levels of unemployment remained high, between 23.3 per cent in 1999 and 27.7 per cent in 2017, according to Statistics South Africa. Of course, within the intervening years, the rate has fluctuated, but has always been above 20 per cent. This puts at risk the state affordability of other social services that the government provides. If the situation is not radically altered, the number of poor will increase tremendously and thus put further strain on state coffers. The end result will be an increase in protests within the country and a state that cannot afford to assist the most vulnerable of its citizens. When this happens, the dream will not only be deferred, but will be negated. Although this is recognised by both the proponents of socialism and capitalism in South Africa, there are very different views about how to address the challenge.

It would seem that the ever-increasing community struggles in South Africa are a result of the structure of our economic system, which is unable to address persistent levels of unemployment. Stated differently, all efforts by the government to address the inequalities of the past are incapable of dealing with the high demand for services, using the available resources. A few historically disadvantaged individuals who have succeeded in the economic system and been absorbed as captains of industry through black economic empowerment (BEE) are just a drop in a sea of poverty. They give false hope that, with hard work, there is the possibility of making it. It would seem that the material conditions of the people are teaching them differently and the lesson they are learning is that their conditions can be changed only if they fight for certain minimum benefits, which is well known by the ruling class, both in government and on the opposition benches. The ANC and the SACP characterise this as the National Democratic Revolution (NDR), whose aim is the destruction of apartheid structures and the raising of living standards for the people.

These are some of the reasons why community protests continue to increase instead of decreasing, with people demanding improvement in their living standards today. They colloquially voice this as, 'we voted'. This means that the masses understand democracy as a vehicle to alleviate their suffering and bring about a better quality of life. Their voting has to change the conditions that they were born into, those of grinding poverty, deprivation and inequality.

CIVIL SOCIETY MOBILISATION AND PROTESTS IN SOUTH AFRICA

Community struggles in South Africa were always and continue to be 'located in the socio-economic system' (Brewer, 1986: 283) that is embraced by the state. The difference in protests from the 1940s up to the early 1990s was in their opposition to the racial nature of the South African society, where whites were, by design, more privileged than blacks (that is, Africans, Indians and coloureds). In this context, black South Africans had many struggles to fight for, some of them being the right to vote on a common voters' roll, the right of assembly, and all other human rights currently enshrined in the South African Constitution.

These struggles were concretely organised around the demand for decent housing, toilets, roads, equal pay for equal work, decent health care and the abolition of Bantu education, etc. This means, broadly speaking, that certain legislation that formed the pillars of white supremacy was targeted, such as the Group Areas Act, No. 41 of 1950, the Reservation of Separate Amenities Act, No. 49 of 1953, and the Bantu Education Act, No. 47 of 1953. In other words, community struggles took both the character of national struggles and local struggles that were rooted in the rejection of apartheid laws. The community struggles, workers' struggles and students' struggles of the post-apartheid era are a continuation of people's desire for better living and working conditions, which have a direct impact on the affordability of tertiary education in South Africa. For example, organisations such as Abahlali baseMjondolo (translating as Shack Dwellers' Movement) are continuing the struggles that were, in the past, led by civic organisations. These struggles are about basic necessities, which include decent houses, latrines, clean water and electricity, which the middle strata of society now take for granted.

Walsh (2008: 255) informs us that in '2005 alone, there were 10 000 protests in South Africa'. By 2017, the numbers of protest marches had tripled, but statistics alone do not illustrate their causes and effects. Let us reflect on some of the protests that took place in 2017 alone. Vuwani residents in Limpopo continued their struggle against being incorporated into the Malamulele Municipality from the Makhado Municipality. Each protest had a ripple effect, which spread to schools and businesses. At the root of their refusal to be incorporated into Malamulele was the perception, real or imagined, that if they were incorporated, they would be deprived of services. At Riverlea in Johannesburg, residents demanding houses burned a Rea Vaya bus and public amenities. In Wolseley, outside Cape Town, people in informal settlements had their shacks demolished by the Witzenberg Municipality, and their response was similar to that demonstrated in other areas, when they retaliated by attacking public buildings. They did this too in Ikamvalihle, Gqeberha, when the municipality forcefully removed residents from the municipal land they occupied. Similarly, in the City of Cape Town, people vandalised a community centre as a result of forced removals from municipal land in Endlovini, near Monwabisi Beach, in Khayelitsha. In Middelplaas, Mpumalanga, the community protested when a child fell into a pit toilet and nearly died. With each year that passed, the police violence towards protesters intensified, including incidents such as the brutal killing of Andries Tatane on 13 April 2011 at Ficksburg in the Free State.

An analysis of these protests indicates close similarities with those of the 1980s. The difference between the post-apartheid protests, however, is in their nomenclature – they are called 'service delivery protests', but in the 1980s, they were called community protests. The second difference is that, in the 1980s, the system promoted differences, whereas in the post-apartheid era, the state is aware of the difficulties and the living conditions experienced by these communities. An added motivation to protest is that those who are in informal settlements know that there is a better life, because they have seen the state constructing houses with proper infrastructure. Most importantly, they are aware that the Constitution of the country is on their side, as evidenced in the Grootboom case. Here, the court ruled that, the 'state was obliged to take positive action to meet the needs of those living in extreme conditions of poverty, homelessness or intolerable housing'.[5]

---

5   *Government of the Republic of South Africa and Others vs Grootboom and Others*, 2001 (1) SA 46 (cc).

The common denominator in some of these protests, especially those that take place in border towns, such as Matatiele and Merafong, is their refusal to be incorporated into area A from area B. The reasons given for this refusal are not political, but have to do with perceived better services provided in area B, as already indicated. In the case of Matatiele, where protests have been about being incorporated back into KwaZulu-Natal from the Eastern Cape, this may cost the ANC dearly. The coalition between the ANC and the African Independent Congress (AIC) at Ekurhuleni may change the power dynamics if the ANC consistently refuses to play ball. This will be of interest in understanding contemporary South African politics, for a party formed to agitate for a particular course and in a different province would have a political impact in another province, in this case in Gauteng. It also reflects Gauteng as a melting point for all South Africans and from all provinces, ever since the discovery of gold in what was historically called the Transvaal. The AIC, which is dominated by those who favour the reincorporation of Matatiele into KwaZulu-Natal, may collapse the coalition if the ANC government does not address their demand to their satisfaction. After a long lull on the matter, on 28 October 2020, Lulama Ntshayisa of the AIC raised the matter in parliament with the Deputy Minister of Cooperative Governance, Parks Tau, when asking an oral question. In this debate, Tau responded that the matter was being managed by the ANC and the AIC. Up to today, it remains on the agenda of engagement between the two parties.

The drivers for political protest are clear; they are motivated by the material conditions experienced by the majority of people. It would seem that the solutions offered have run their course. Communities no longer trust the government when it says they must have patience and faith, as development will ultimately reach them. Explanations about insufficient resources to address their basic needs no longer make sense to them. This is exacerbated by daily reports of the misuse of funds by various government departments and at different levels. The R240 million spent by the Department of Public Works on security features at former president Jacob Zuma's home did not help to reassure the poor and the working class that the coffers of the state were inadequate to address the triple evils of poverty, unemployment and inequality with immediate effect.

It should be mentioned, however, that protest in the past few years has not been a feature confined to the South African experience. The global economic environment, which primarily affects the working class and the poor, is continually affecting the world's poor in adverse ways. Price increases affect food, school fees, university tuition, medical expenses and, as cannot be emphasised enough, quality housing. These protests are a direct reaction to these conditions. The student protests in South Africa, in what eventually became known as #FeesMustFall, are symptoms of the global economic system that prioritises profits over the well-being of the people.

These struggles cannot be divorced from community struggles and worker struggles for better working conditions and a living wage. They are directly linked. The protests against e-tolls in Gauteng are an indicator of the middle class also feeling the economic meltdown, as they are squeezed from all sides through direct and indirect taxation. As the economic situation deteriorates, it threatens their home bonds and the status of their children at school, many of whom attend private institutions. They experience their household income shrinking, for all practical purposes and in real terms.

The argument has been put forward here that the problems faced by South Africa seem to be structural and systemic. By this it is meant that the economic system seems to not benefit the most vulnerable in society. This then raises questions about the current political and economic structures being able to deliver on the needs of the poor, even under the most favourable conditions. Probably, the question that needs interrogation is whether the South African economy is structured in a way that can deliver on social goods and eliminate unemployment and poverty? Or, borrowing from Gramsci, has the time arrived to seriously revisit and analyse 'the forms of political power, the concrete relations between social classes and political representation, and the cultural and ideological forms in which antagonisms are fought and regulated' (Gramsci in Forgacs, 2000: 189) in the South African context?

In so doing, the electoral system also needs to be revisited. This is because experience indicates that the proportional representation system promotes the dictatorship of the party, rather than the rule of the people, through elected representatives. Perhaps for South Africans to regain their power and fulfil the desires of that famous slogan, '*Amandla*' or 'power to the people', a constituency-based electoral system would be preferred at this time in history. Communities would be able to hold both their parliamentary representatives and councillors directly responsible for decisions made for them and could punish them in the next elections if their demands were ignored. This does not necessarily mean, in a constituency-based system, that the electorate could not punish politicians; but if they do so, it could impact the whole political party, in which there could still be men and women whom they wish to retain as their representatives. A case in point is the Johannesburg Municipality where the ANC was punished by the electorate, not because of any wrongdoing on the part of the councillors, but for the decisions taken by national government, such as e-tolls and other scandals affecting certain leaders of the ANC at a national level. It should be noted that at the level of local government – unlike at the national government level – there is a hybrid governance system where a portion of seats are allocated to the parties and the rest are contested in wards. In practice, this makes no difference, because as soon as the ward councillors are elected and take the oath, the parties they campaigned under take over and they are required to pay allegiance to that party. In short, the spirit of the electoral system as a whole lends itself to a particular ethos. This assertion is made taking note of the reality that, even independent candidates, once they are elected have to forge partnerships with particular parties to have any impact. Without those alliances, they are powerless and they know it.

In other words, while the major problem lies with policies that seem to fail the majority, the electoral system indirectly contributes by taking the power away from the people and putting it squarely in the hands of political formations. For example, until recently, at the national level, the South African electoral system did not cater for independent candidates standing for election if their ideas and views did not find resonance with any of the current political parties. For progress to take place and for power relations to be changed, an individual needs to be held accountable – someone who cannot hide behind the cloak of a collective. When individuals are dressed in the colours of a party and are not answerable directly to the constituencies they represent, they tend to vote as a block and approve decisions that may have a direct negative impact on society and the constituencies they purport to represent.

CONCLUSION

Although the Constitution and some legislative Acts are pro-poor, the government is unable to meet the demands and aspirations of working-class and poor communities because of the way in which the economic system is organised. The dominant view that advocates for privatisation and liberalisation of the economy as drivers of growth seems to have gained hegemony. However, experience over the past 29 years has shown that, even when the South African economy was growing, this did not result in job creation or the reduction of poverty levels. On the contrary, the captains of industry and major economic actors continued to benefit at the expense of the workers.

This leaves us with a number of important questions. First, how can we change society for the better? How do we address the challenges of poverty and unemployment, which, in turn, lead to huge inequalities? Second, are there alternative economic systems that could improve the conditions of the poor? Third, can our existing parliamentary formations lead these struggles or has the time come for left organisations to be more assertive and lead the struggle for economic freedom and a society free from abject poverty and disease? There has definitely been an increase in the number of protest movements. For the most part, the grievances they communicate are relevant and justified, but who is leading these protests and to what ideological end?

The SACP and COSATU are the largest left formations in the current conjuncture and are in alliance with the ruling party in South Africa. Given this dynamic, are they in a position to lead the struggles of the poor and the workers? Is the vanguard of the working class in touch with grass-roots structures that are leading these organisations? Are the cadres of the SACP armed with an advanced revolutionary theory about the participants, and even the leaders of these struggles? I am not suggesting that the ANC is incapable of leading the national democratic struggle; however it is a multi-class organisation, and as such cannot lead a socialist struggle. This is the responsibility of the SACP and other left organisations. The mere fact that the government has been unable to reduce the rate of unemployment illustrates a deeper, structural problem in our economy, as I have argued.

My aim is not to cast aspersions on the ANC. Over the past 23 years, it has mainly succeeded in uniting South Africans under the banner of non-racialism, reconciling the country into a common citizenship and ushering in one of the world's most human rights-oriented constitutions. Under difficult economic conditions, it has succeeded in creating and sustaining a safety net for the poor and deprived through state grants. These are achievements that cannot be denied, yet poverty, inequality and unemployment persist.

REFERENCES

African National Congress (ANC). (2017). 'International Relations Policy Discussion Document of the ANC'. Presented at the 5th National Policy Conference, 30 June–5 July.

African National Congress (ANC). (1994). *The Reconstruction and Development Programme*. Johannesburg: Umanyano.

Brewer, J.D. (1986). 'Black protest in South Africa's crisis: A comment of Legassick', *The Royal African Society*, 85(339), April: 283.

Cloete, K. (2015). 'Freedom Charter still relevant in the struggle for a socialist SA', *Politicsweb*, 11 November. Available at: http://www.politicsweb.co.za/opinion/freedom-charter-still-relevant-in-the-struggle-for (Accessed 14 April 2023).

Congress of South African Trade Unions (COSATU). (2017). Press Statement (17 January 2017). Available at: http://www.COSATU.org.za/show.php?ID=12318

Congress of South African Trade Unions (COSATU). (1997). COSATU 6th National Congress Resolutions, 16–19 September, 1997. Available at: http://www.COSATU.org.za/show.php?ID=2156 (Accessed 14 April 2023).

Engels, F. and Marx, K. (2009 [1903]). *Feuerbach: The roots of the socialist philosophy*. Translated by A. Lewis. New York: Mondial, pp. 3–33.

Freedom Charter, as adopted at the Congress of the People at Kliptown, Johannesburg, on 25 and 26 June 1955.

Freund, B. and Witt, H. (eds). (2010). *Development Dilemmas in post-apartheid South Africa*. Pietermaritzburg: University of KwaZulu-Natal Press, p. 4.

Gramsci, A. in D. Forgacs (ed.). (2000). *The Antonio Gramsci Reader: Selected writings, 1916–1935*. New York: New York University Press.

Lenin, V.I. (1975). *On Marx and Engels: Workers of all the countries unite!* [Collection of seven articles written between 1895 and 1919]. Peking: Foreign Language Press.

Marx, K. and Engels, F. (1848). 'The Manifesto of the Communist Party'. Published in 1969. *Marx/Engels Selected Works, Vol, 1*. Moscow: Progress Publishers, pp. 98–137.

Mitchley, A. (2017). 'Tshwane Mayor wants to build wall to separate clashing communities', *News24*, 22 June. Available at: https://www.news24.com/SouthAfrica/News/tshwane-mayor-wants-to-build-wall-to-separate-clashing-communities-20170622 (Accessed 14 April 2023).

National Planning Commission, The Presidency, Republic of South Africa. (2012). National Development Plan, 2030: Our future – Make it work. Available at: https://www.poa.gov.za/news/Documents/NPC%20National%20Development%20Plan%20Vision %202030%20-lo-res.pdf (Accessed 14 April 2023).

Odendaal, A. (2012). *The Founders: The origins of the ANC and the struggle for democracy in South Africa*. Johannesburg: Jacana Media.

Simons, H.J. and Simons, R.E. (1983). *Class and Colour in South Africa: 1850–1950*. London: Idaf, p. 610. Now available at ANC Books On-Line.

Tomlinson, M.R. (2015). 'Why can't we clear the housing backlog?' *The Policy Bulletin of the Institute of Race Relations*, 4(20), 6 October.

Walsh, S. (2008). 'Uncomfortable collaborations: Contesting constructions of the poor in South Africa', *Review of African Political Economy*, 35(116), June: 255–79.

Wolpe, H. (1972). 'Capitalism and the cheap labour power in South Africa: From segregation to apartheid', *Economy and Society*, 1(4): 425–56.

Cases

Government of the Republic of South Africa and Others vs Grootboom and Others, (2001). (1) SA 46 (cc).

PART 2:
COMMUNITY, STATE AND GLOBE: ISSUES, STRUGGLES AND THE POLITICS OF WORK

SEVEN

THE CHALLENGES OF ECONOMIC AND SOCIAL DEVELOPMENT IN SOUTH AFRICA: LEFT PERSPECTIVES

Alex Mohubetswane Mashilo

CAPITALISM AND THE NEOLIBERAL AGENDA

Capitalism is the principal contradiction to economic and broader social transformation and development in South Africa. This colonially imposed mode of production was the foundation on which colonisation and apartheid oppression occurred and is the base on which the legacy of the era of oppression continues.

To decolonise the country, the colonially imposed mode of production has to be replaced, through a revolution, with a qualitatively different, caring mode of production. This would serve the needs of the people, as opposed to a system that puts profits and private capital accumulation before the people. To this end, there is a monumental struggle to be fought, considering not only the problems of internal dimensions such as the persisting legacy of colonial and apartheid oppression, but also external dimensions. For instance, imperialism has had an enormous influence on the affairs of South Africa. Especially in the policy space, imperialism forms the external dimension of the remaining structural problems that stand in the way of complete freedom after the liberation struggle achieved South Africa's April 1994 democratic breakthrough. With the capitalist mode of production as its base, imperialism has taken the place of colonialism.

In their latest iteration of the capitalist mode of production, imperialist forces and their networks of intellectuals and policy-makers have developed neoliberalism over the past few decades, predating South Africa's 1994 democratic breakthrough. Neoliberalism was officially incorporated into the country's policy framework post-1994 from 1996 through the government's undemocratic adoption of the economic policy called Growth, Employment and Redistribution (GEAR).

When the government introduced GEAR as non-negotiable, thus adopting it undemocratically, it bypassed the National Economic Development and Labour Council (Nedlac), which comprises its own representatives and those of organised labour, organised business and the organised community constituency. Nedlac was established in terms of the Nedlac Act (1994), which granted it the power to consider all significant changes to social and economic policy in South Africa's democracy. Nedlac consultation, in terms of the Act, must be done with the purpose of seeking consensus and concluding agreements on matters pertaining to social and economic policy. In contradiction, GEAR was introduced without following this process.

The greatest challenge currently facing the left in South Africa is, therefore, to intensify the struggle to achieve a revolution against the exploitative capitalist mode of production, and its global imperialist regime and neoliberalism, to safeguard democratic national sovereignty, and fight for revolutionary transformation and development to meet the material needs of the people, the majority of whom are working class and poor.

Against this background, this chapter explores the implications of the apartheid era's articulation of economic directions pursued post-apartheid. The evaluation focuses on the neoliberal policy articulation in 1990 by the last president of the apartheid regime, Frederik Willem de Klerk. The chapter offers a critique of the formulation and continuation of neoliberal policy post-apartheid, with reference to GEAR and later the Accelerated and Shared Growth Initiative for South Africa (AsgiSA), by drawing on historical as well as contemporary Marxist thinking. In addition, this chapter assesses the challenges facing the left and makes suggestions regarding what ought to be done, emphasising the importance of forging broader left unity and learning from historical experiences.

NEOLIBERAL POLICY DEVELOPMENT AND THE LEGACY OF APARTHEID

The neoliberal policy regime imposed through GEAR contained elements to which the apartheid regime had committed itself prior to 1994, starting in the 1970s. On 2 February 1990, De Klerk summarised these elements in his speech to the nation, in which he announced the unbanning of the African National Congress (ANC), the South African Communist Party (SACP) and other organisations. Perhaps overwhelmed by the unbanning of the liberation movement, very few people paid serious attention, if any, to the economic policy content of De Klerk's speech. Meanwhile, the apartheid regime was doing everything it could to protect the interests of its core constituency in the economy – the capitalist class being the principal beneficiary.

The last apartheid president premised the economic policy content of that speech on the rise of neoliberalism in the 1970s, which he referred to as 'structural adaptations' – from the neoliberal notion of structural adjustment programmes. De Klerk alleged that neoliberalism (the 'structural adaptations') had become 'inevitable' because the 1973 oil crisis had brought an end to the high economic growth rates of the 1960s, and the 1979 oil crisis had caused 'imbalances' in Western economies.

Relying on the rising wave of neoliberalism globally, De Klerk pursued the economic 'structural adaptations' agenda that the apartheid regime sought to achieve. These measures included reducing the role of the public sector and the government ('authorities') in the economy, giving the private sector full play, allowing market forces to set economic policy direction (determine 'adjustments'), restricting capital expenditure in state-owned enterprises (SOEs or 'parastatals'), undertaking privatisation and deregulation and curtailing government expenditure.

With the apartheid regime facing its demise and the country advancing towards a democratic dispensation, the neoliberal measures endorsed by the apartheid regime would conserve old-order patterns of control in the economy. These measures coalesced into curtailing space for the future democratic state and the publicly owned economic sector to play a significant role in the economy. This was going to allow the class forces that commanded economic control to not only keep their interests intact but also to perpetuate their economic hegemony. The situation would feed the root of racial supremacy, with the democratically elected government and the state kept out of the economy or playing a minimalist, delimited role going forward. It was exactly this that the ANC had warned against in its first Strategy and Tactics document adopted in Morogorogo, Tanzania, in 1969.

To many on the left, the adoption of GEAR amounted to a complete turn to the right.[1] GEAR advanced neoliberal economic policy measures that were essentially consistent with the template that formed the economic policy content of De Klerk's speech. In addition, this included a rigid inflation targeting policy regime – regardless of its cost to the workers, the poor and the economy – and an intransigent belief that tinkering with the supply side under a neoliberal macroeconomic framework would deliver adequate economic growth.

The trickle-down idea – that the unemployed would benefit from employment and move out of poverty and inequality and realise improved standards of living from capitalist growth – achieved dominance. Curtailing social spending, restricting capital expenditure in SOEs and in general following austerity countervailed the necessity to pursue employment creation, poverty eradication, radical inequality reduction and higher standards of living for the masses through direct, adequately funded, public policies.

---

1 For a detailed analysis of this point see, for example, Padayachee and Van Niekerk (2019).

Besides monetary policy instruments such as increasing interest rates, regardless of their impact on the workers and poor, and the expansion of domestic productive capacity, GEAR preferred moderating wage increases. This implied that wage increases for the poorly paid South African workers (the majority of whom were black) were a problem and had to be curtailed to control inflation, encourage investment and increase employment. GEAR targeted an economic growth rate of 6 per cent per annum and, from this, the trickle-down of 400 000 new jobs annually by the year 2000, thus reducing inequality and poverty. In this trickle-down growth orthodox, the interests of the masses would, in the main, follow from the government meeting the interests of the capitalist class.

There was virtually no alternative pursuit of policies that specifically target equitable distribution of the value created in production among those involved. Fiscal policy embarked on reducing corporate tax in a country that was characterised by extreme levels of income and wealth inequalities. Over time, the capacity of the state to advance sustainable redistribution weakened, threatening the erosion of important programmes that emanated from the Reconstruction and Development Programme (RDP) to support the workers and poor who needed those programmes. The RDP was a relatively left-thinking policy compared to GEAR, but it was abandoned, except for some programmes (such as 'RDP houses'), when GEAR was imposed. Over time, references to the RDP disappeared completely from the government's policy vocabulary, although, just after adopting GEAR, the government tried to use the RDP to justify its adoption of GEAR.[2] The intransigent pursuit of austerity in the medium-term expenditure frameworks, delivered to parliament annually by the National Treasury through the medium-term budget policy statements and budgets, eroded the capacity to adequately fund democratic transformation and development.

It was clear the thinking that informed GEAR was premised on the class aspirations of profit-seeking and private wealth accumulation interests, most of all finance capital – domestic and foreign – presented as the interests of the nation as a whole. The interests of

---

2   See, for example, Mbeki (1998).

the workers, such as achieving adequate remuneration, were seen as negative factors that weighed against the sentiments of the profit-seeking and private wealth accumulation interests (the 'investors'). Adopted merely two years after the 1994 democratic breakthrough, the policy stance to curtail wage increases was insensitive, especially for the formerly oppressed, black workers, against the background of persisting racially skewed high levels of labour market income and wealth inequalities. Instead, to end the apartheid income gap and establish a common standard of decent remuneration, it was essential to pursue a policy of redress-based wage increases and systematic elimination of economic exploitation, including racial and gender-based exploitation of workers.

GEAR propagated the idea that post-apartheid South Africa would achieve transformation and development through economic growth, which would result from a free market economy in the country (to be attained through liberalisation, among others).[3] The neoliberal policy regime, which emerged as a capitalist solution to the impediments of capital accumulation starting in the 1970s,[4] found its way into policy dominance within the ANC, ironically, an organisation that had played a key role in the liberation struggle.

In his third volume of *Capital*, Karl Marx (1894) writes that capitalist accumulation continually seeks to overcome its immanent barriers, but it does so only by means that again place such barriers in its way and on a more formidable scale. Instead of a solution, neoliberalism became the basis of the multiple crises of capitalism that were to follow.

In the 2000s, a global mineral commodity super cycle emerged. Mining houses laughed all the way to the bank. Annual economic growth rates averaged 4.4 per cent from 2000 to 2007. A low growth rate of 3.1 per cent was recorded in 2001 and 2003, compared to the high growth rate of 5.6 per cent in 2006, but with GEAR failing to achieve its growth rate target of 6 per cent.

The lowest unemployment rate, in terms of the narrow definition that excludes discouraged work-seekers in South Africa's democratic

---

3   For reflections on this score see, for example, Adelzadeh (2021).
4   After the Great Depression of 1929 to 1939 and the fall of the post-World War II capitalist Golden Age.

dispensation, was recorded in 1995, the year before the government imposed GEAR. This was 16.5 per cent, which was still high, however. Unemployment rose to crisis-high levels of above 20 per cent annually starting in 1996, the year in which the government imposed GEAR. Since then, it has never come down to 20 per cent, never mind any rate below that, and the unemployed population has grown over the years. A major economic policy failure developed. South Africa dismally failed to bring unemployment down and to ensure the right of all to work through full employment, a situation in which no workers are involuntarily unemployed.

The expanded unemployment rate, which includes discouraged work-seekers in its definition and scope of survey, continued to be higher than that of the officially preferred narrow definition of unemployment. With the government having placed South Africa's underdeveloped economy in shock therapy by implementing GEAR and thus exposing it to external shocks, every global crisis in the capitalist system has contributed to increasing unemployment in the country. This happened, for instance, following the outbreak of the global economic crisis that first developed in the United States in 2008. South Africa moved into stagnation, characterised by long-term low growth rates and frequent recessions, including technical recessions. Unemployment also increased after the 2011–2014 fall of the global mineral commodity super cycle of the 2000s. Its rise accelerated further under the global COVID-19 pandemic crisis.

Unemployment, having increased to levels above 20 per cent – and 46.6 per cent in terms of the expanded definition – affected approximately 12.5 million active and discouraged work-seekers in the third quarter of 2021.[5] The legacy of colonialism and apartheid prevailed in un/employment, as it did in other areas where it remained persistent. Unemployment for Africans not only remained the highest but also increased, reaching 51.1 per cent in terms of the expanded definition. With Africans overwhelmingly the worst affected, unemployment among all women reached 50 per cent. Unemployment was the lowest in terms of population groups among

---

5   For a detailed analysis of South Africa's unemployment in the third quarter of 2021, see the Quarterly Labour Force Survey report produced by Statistics South Africa (2021).

white workers, at 9.2 per cent in the narrow definition, and 11.5 per cent in the expanded definition of unemployment.

The racial unemployment dynamics are also an indicator that the capitalist legacy of uneven development forged during the colonial and apartheid era persisted.[6] This was evidenced by the fact that unemployment was at its highest in rural areas. The former bantustan areas, to which apartheid law confined Africans, were the worst affected. Except for improvements in areas such as household electricity connection, tarred access roads and water, there were no notable industrialisation and production development successes in the former bantustan areas post-1994.

In electricity provision, however, the government upset the impressive post-1994 massive household electrification expansion when, under its GEAR policy auspices, in energy at least dating back to the White Paper it adopted in December 1998, Eskom's productive capacity decayed, aged and started failing frequently with no successful replacement to ensure uninterrupted power supply (recall the neoliberal restriction of capital expenditure in SOEs). The decay and decline in electricity generation, transmission and consequently supply capacity, combined with corporate capture of and corruption at Eskom,[7] resulted in South Africa experiencing an electricity under-capacity crisis and, subsequently, load-shedding, starting in 2007 and worsening afterwards. This is but one example of how wrong – that is, neoliberal – policy choices and corrupt practices have destroyed state productive capacity, with private interests standing to benefit in economic terms from the proceeds of corruption and through profits from subsequent state procurement. In this scenario, government policy orientation made increasingly shifting to the procurement of electricity from private power producers ('independent power producers') a priority.

Beyond a policy regime, through economic restructuring neoliberalism developed to become the dominant variant of

---

[6] For a discussion of the concept of uneven development in South Africa, including its external dimensions, see Cronin and Mashilo (2017).

[7] For an exposition of corporate state capture and corruption at Eskom see Part IV of the report of the Judicial Commission of Inquiry into State Capture (2022).

capitalism, underpinned by imperialism, which Lenin (1917) found to be the highest stage of capitalism. Its other features affecting workers included increased labour flexibility – a code name for workforce restructuring – resulting in relatively secure permanent employment relationships being replaced with insecure forms of employment relationships, such as labour broking, casualisation and other forms of perpetual temporary and precarious employment relationships. The working class is always the worst affected by the exploitative capitalist mode of production and its crises, twists and turns.

As Adelzadeh (2021) concluded after an extensive review of evidence, the economic policy trajectory followed by South Africa post-1994, starting with GEAR in 1996, has consistently produced low economic growth rates (failing to achieve targets), high rates of unemployment, high rates of poverty, high inequality and de-industrialisation. This has meant that the productive sector of the country's economy, especially manufacturing, has shrunk in terms of its national significance and contribution to national output and employment.

In imposing GEAR, the government's liberalisation agenda comprised, in certain instances, more rapid and deep-going rates of trade liberalisation than the commitments under the World Trade Organization. In 2001, financial and capital markets liberalisation produced a currency crisis.[8]

Politically, imposing GEAR disrupted the unity of, and caused tensions within, South Africa's historical national democratic revolutionary front, the ANC-headed Alliance. While new iterations of the ANC's Strategy and Tactics asserted that it was a disciplined force of the Left, in reality, the ANC government's adoption of GEAR and other neoliberal policies contradicted this. This saw the SACP and the Congress of South African Congress of Trade Unions (COSATU) waging a fierce struggle, including against privatisation, to reassert a left agenda at the centre of the Alliance (Nzimande, 2021). To achieve organisational renewal and unity based on a revolutionary programme, the ANC will need to renounce, and become a dependable ally in the struggle against neoliberal policies.

---

8   For an analysis of the capital outflows or capital flight that occurred as a result of liberalisation under GEAR, see, for example, Mohamed (2010).

It might have been because of the apparent failure of GEAR, or perhaps partly because of the challenge from the Left, that in the mid-2000s the government adopted a policy called the Accelerated and Shared Growth Initiative of South Africa (AsgiSA). The government hoped this new policy would achieve what GEAR had failed to deliver: a reduction in unemployment and poverty, and annual growth rates of 6 per cent. In other words, faced with the failure of GEAR, the government extended the timeframe to achieve the 6 per cent annual growth rates by a decade from 2000 to 2010.

The measures adopted under AsgiSA included clearing infrastructure backlogs, addressing the skills shortage, improving international competitiveness of much of the manufacturing and tradable services sectors, addressing currency volatility, easing the regulatory environment for small and medium-sized enterprises, and boosting the capacity of the government to support economic development. These measures were important, but this depended on whether the theory behind them was revolutionary or reformist.

Sadly, the neoliberal thinking that continued to be dominant from GEAR stifled how the government saw the measures. For example, Phumzile Mlambo-Ngcuka, then deputy president, stressed that AsgiSA focused on microeconomic reforms and was not a replacement of GEAR.[9] This reaffirmed the neoliberal reformist path.

At this stage a new idea also emerged – the South African economy was no longer viewed as a single economy, but as two economies: the first a developed economy, and the second an underdeveloped economy characterised by substantial informality. The government embraced this notion and thus saw it as its key policy objective to develop the second economy so that it could be integrated into the first economy.

The notion of two separate South African economies was flawed. In reality, both theoretically and practically, the economy was a single economy characterised by uneven capitalist development.

---

9   See parliamentary media briefing by Deputy President Phumzile Mlambo-Ngcuka (6 February 2006). Available at: https://www.skillsportal.co.za/content/deputy-president-introduces-asgisa; https://omalley.nelsonmandela.org/omalley/index.php/site/q/03lv02409/04lv02410/05lv02415/06lv02417.htm (Accessed10 November 2022).

For example, when someone bought a motor vehicle to use as a taxi in the so-called second economy, that vehicle was manufactured or 'imported from' the so-called first economy, and it was probably purchased with a loan from one of the financial institutions at the centre of the so-called first economy – the banks. When that loan was repaid, the repayments and the interest rates received by the banks came from the taxi operations in the so-called second economy. The same principle applies to the alcoholic drinks produced by large multinational corporations in the so-called first economy, and sold in the shebeens in city centres, underdeveloped townships and rural areas. These alcoholic drinks are a major source of profit for the companies producing them in the so-called first economy. Like the motor vehicle used as an example here, these alcoholic drinks might as well be an import from North America, Western Europe or Japan, and not locally produced in the so-called first economy.

As can be seen from the methods used above, it was believed that under AsgiSA, high growth, employment creation and poverty reduction could be achieved under the macro-economic framework that essentially formed the heart of GEAR. It was therefore assumed that AsgiSA's objectives could be achieved only through supply side reforms. This was the context in which South Africa failed to address unemployment and poverty and to achieve high growth rates, even after extending the timeframe for GEAR's 6 per cent targeted annual growth rates by a decade, from 2000 to 2010.

If economic policy were based on science and not class interests, the dominant forces – whose ideas lie at the centre of the failed 1996 economic policy trajectory – would have long abandoned their stance. Instead, in contradiction, they assert more of the same measures and intensify this assertion with every major crisis. Following the 2008 economic crisis, the Organisation for Economic Co-operation and Development (OECD, 2017) pushed recommendations for neoliberal structural reforms in its publication titled *Economic Policy Reforms: Going for growth*.[10] The microeconomic liberalisation agenda especially targeted state infrastructure networks, to insinuate or

---

10 For a typical example, see the Organisation for Economic Co-operation and Development (OECD) (2017).

expand private capital accumulation in these spaces. Its measures coalesced into an agenda to liberalise network infrastructures, which in South Africa were under state control or state-owned enterprises, privatise the high radio frequency broadband spectrum, through an auction, and implement the unbundling of Eskom and Transnet.

In 2019, the National Treasury[11] released a paper, with the OECD neoliberal structural reforms making up its heart, claiming that it was South Africa's economic blueprint. In this way, the National Treasury served as a transmission channel for the International Monetary Fund (IMF)-backed neoliberal structural reforms. Notably, there was no focus in the paper on the content of the National Treasury's own mandate of macro-economic policy co-ordination. All the measures were sectoral or supply side reforms.

Pressed to produce a new macro-economic framework that would lead to the achievement of the desired results, the National Treasury[12] issued a revised paper merely rectifying the glaring miscalculations it had made in modelling the impact of the IMF-backed, OECD-driven measures, giving definitions of macro-economic concepts, and maintaining the failed macro-economic policy paradigm. Because of pressure from the Left, including trade unions, the National Treasury removed a section that sought to end the extension of collective bargaining agreements to non-parties. At most, the National Treasury was only prepared to maintain the neoliberal macro-economic paradigm or to deepen it with more of the same measures.

In contrast, to achieve the desired economic and broader social transformation and development outcomes, the challenge facing the Left in South Africa is to pursue an economic and social policy overhaul. This could include achieving changes in the macro-economic framework, fiscal and monetary policies, international trade policy, sectoral policies, provincial economic development strategies and local economic development plans, as well as contesting workplace change in favour of the working class and lifting the poor out of poverty. The way forward could include a

---

11   National Treasury, South Africa (2019a).
12   National Treasury, South Africa (2019b).

comprehensive social security system, inclusive of a minimum income guarantee to take care of the basic needs of the unemployed.

At the centre of a left programme and a left organisation are the interests and the quality of life of the workers and poor. A left programme should seek to eliminate the economic exploitation of the working class to achieve universal social emancipation, lift the poor out of poverty, establish and give practical effect to the right of all to work, and build a just and equal society. Equally important, a left programme should aim to eliminate uneven development between rural and urban areas. In South Africa's situation, a left programme should also comprise a dedicated focus on eliminating racial and gender inequalities. All of this requires building working-class unity, power and hegemony. This is a key organisational and political challenge facing the Left, which is not without its own problems that it has to address.

THE PROBLEM OF DIVISIONS

It is critical to highlight two works by Lenin at this stage. The first is '"Left-wing" childishness and the petty-bourgeois mentality' (1918). The second is '"Left-wing" communism: An infantile disorder' (1920a). These works can help trace some of the problematic tendencies by those falling into the category that Lenin characterised as the 'Left'.[13] For example, Lenin (1920a) found that by mistaking their desire, their politico-ideological attitude, for objective reality, the 'Lefts' in Germany committed the most dangerous mistake for revolutionaries to make. He argued that the tendency easily went to revolutionary extremes, but it was incapable of perseverance, organisation, discipline and steadfastness. This tendency is one of the sources of the divisions facing the Left in South Africa.

It is dangerous to propagate a politics claiming that everything is possible at a stroke. The self-proclaimed 'left', who propagate such claims, purport to be more revolutionary than the left they attack, the left with a proven track record of the qualities described by Lenin – that is, perseverance, organisation, discipline and steadfastness.

---

13 Meaning claiming to be the Left, or so-called.

Divisions are among the major challenges facing the Left. For instance, there are individuals who call themselves the Left but who do not mind dedicating most of their time and energy to attacking left organisations instead of contesting societal direction against class domination by the bourgeoisie.

Active on all fronts, and based on their economic control, the bourgeoisie have political parties, non-governmental or civil society organisations, foundations and institutions as part of their ideological, political and organisational apparatus. A clarification is necessary here, taking the sphere of civil society (organisations) as an example. By no means does the point suggest that all civil society organisations are at the service of the bourgeois domination of society. Rather, the point is that the sphere of civil society (organisations) is by no means immune from class contradictions and contestation.

SUBJECT TO CLASS CONTRADICTIONS AND CONTESTATION

To be sure, civil society organisations do not exist outside of the class divided society in which their members – that is, civil society members – live. No doubt there are examples of good civil society organisations. Indeed, there are some who are very committed to the counter-hegemonic left agenda. These civil society organisations are doing their best, and often without resources, to achieve the immediate aims and ultimate emancipatory goals of the workers and poor.

There are others, however, that act in the opposite direction or merely seek limited improvements, and within the bounds of the economic exploitation under the capitalist mode of production. It is to these that the spotlight has to turn, for left considerations.

Globally, the bourgeoisie (with those from imperialist bases and premises dominant) are actively involved as donors in the sphere of civil society (organisations). And, as Wallace (2004: 202) says, '[t]his process is fuelled by changing foreign policy positions'.

There are non-governmental organisations (NGOs) or civil society organisations that have become increasingly dependent on donors (Wallace, 2004; Wright, 2012; Steinberg and Wertman,

2018). In this reality, there are donors who attach conditionalities to their donations and/or make policy demands (Wallace, 2004), thus setting the agenda (Wright, 2012), seeking to influence the policies and politics of other states in a world in which millions of local and regional civil society organisations often work together with transnational ones (Steinberg and Wertman, 2018).

In the process, there are NGOs or civil society organisations that have transformed into political advocacy groups, blurring their self-described boundaries as formally independent actors (Steinberg and Wertman, 2018). This complex process is, essentially, class contestation:

> The funders that provide the source of power and influence are important elements... Funders are enablers, and when NGOs [based in the sphere of civil society] are supported by private and distant foundations to promote particular agendas, or when the primary donors are political officials in Western foreign ministries and development agencies and with no accountability in the target countries, the boundaries are blurred (Steinberg and Wertman, 2018: 2).

Steinberg and Wertman (2018) draw our attention to the fact that in many Western countries, millions of dollars, pounds and euros are allocated annually, directly to the NGOs or civil society organisations-cum-political advocacy groups actively seeking to influence policies and politics in other countries. In this complex process of class contradictions and contestation, there are NGOs or civil society organisations that have become the Trojan horses for global neoliberalism (Wallace, 2004) and part of the apparatus promoting Western hegemony in the developing world (Wright, 2012).

In South Africa, specifically, class contradictions and contestation emanating from the history of racial segregation in favour of white privilege play themselves out, also in the sphere of civil society (organisations). The origins of certain non-governmental or civil society organisations lay in activism to secure the inheritance and advantages acquired from that legacy. For example, the mindset and attitude as represented by AfriForum Jeug at UP [University of Pretoria] reveal that they claimed ownership and control over spaces that have been predominantly white and dominated by white power. Thus, when white spaces and white privilege are threatened, violence will be the norm. This is understood through their endorsement of and identification with [the colonialists] Rhodes and Van Riebeeck (Sooliman, 2022: 90–91).

Alive to the situation, the Left in the Global South, South Africa included, should avoid falling into the trap Wallace (2004) correctly cautions against – that is, an over-generalised picture that fails to capture the concrete mechanisms and specific effects of what is a complex and contradictory process. The Left needs to appreciate that the sphere of civil society, as well as its organisation, is a front on which the process of class struggle is not absent but continues. The sphere of civil society is among the key sites of power that the Left has to contest and win as part of the battle for democracy.

It is clear from the preceding summary that there is an enormous workload for the Left at the coalface of the class struggle. The tendency by the 'Left' who focus much of their time and energy attacking other left organisations instead of seeking left unity and contesting societal direction against class domination by the bourgeoisie, leaves much to be desired. It creates divisive inwardness in the Left and diverts attention from the real cause of the class struggle, which the workers and poor have to win to achieve final emancipation.

When you analyse the lexicon of the tendency, you will soon see that it pays lip service to the genuine struggle against the exploitative capitalist system of the bourgeoisie. Those involved in it are more preoccupied with criticising or opposing other left organisations and left efforts in the complex task of forging alliances or broad fronts in pursuit of the left cause. Meanwhile, they have little or nothing to show of their own achievements towards a breakthrough with and for the workers and poor from the capitalist mode of production. If those involved in this tendency were sincere, they would have demonstrably complied with the maxim '*Hic Rhodus, hic salta!*' used by Marx (2010: 177) to close his exposition of the contradictions in the general formula of capital.[14]

In South Africa, the largest organised, well-known left organisations, the SACP and COSATU, have been the major targets of attacks, not only by the apartheid regime[15] or right-wing forces, but also by the individuals who claim to be the Left, and similar sects.[16] Such negative attacks on the SACP, in particular, can be discerned as being propelled mainly from two angles, which are easily distinguishable by the conspiratorial allegations spread by them. From the one angle, the SACP is accused of having captured the ANC and are running it. In this angle there are those spreading scare stories about 'Communist take-overs', which dates back to the 1920s when the liberals who helped destroy the Industrial and Commercial Workers' Union raised the banner of anti-communism (SACP, 1976: 17).

Fast forward

In the face of its imminent defeat by the liberation struggle – in which the SACP had played a key role in alliance with the ANC and the progressive trade union movement – the apartheid regime made three demands as preconditions for negotiations. One of these was for the ANC to break with the SACP. Nelson Mandela rejected this demand and the right-wing allegation that the SACP controlled the ANC. As the SACP (1976) states, splinter groups also used this allegation to justify splitting from the ANC. Mandela said that deserting a lifelong alliance partner in the cause of the liberation struggle, a lifelong friend, at the insistence of a common opponent who rejected democratic majority rule, would result in losing credibility with the people (Mandela, 1994). The opponents Mandela referred to include those he described as virulent anti-communists.

---

14 Translated 'Rhodes is here, here is where you jump!' The maxim comes from the Aesop's fable *The Boastful Athlete*, who claimed that he had performed a stupendous jump when in Rhodes and had witnesses to back his story. A bystander intervened to this effect: Let us assume we are now in Rhodes, stop claiming and demonstrate your stupendous jump right here and now.

15 The Communist Party was the first organisation to be banned under the Suppression of Communism Act in 1950.

16 See, for example, the SACP (1976).

Meanwhile, from the other angle, the SACP is accused of following the strategy of the national democratic revolution allegedly developed by the ANC, depending on patronage, including career propping deployments from the ANC, and of having no track record of a socialist programme worthy of mentioning. This is the angle Kaaf asserts in Chapter 9 in this volume. The following is a different take from verifiable historical facts.

THE NATIONAL DEMOCRATIC REVOLUTION AND SOCIALISM

First, the strategy of the national democratic revolution has its roots in the Communist International (Comintern). This dates back to the 'Report of the Commission on the National and Colonial Questions'. Vladimir Lenin (1920b) presented the report on 26 July to the fifth session of the plenary of the Second Congress of the Communist International held in July and August 1920 in Petrograd and Moscow, Union of Soviet Socialist Republics (USSR). On the role of communist parties in advancing the anti-colonial and anti-imperialist liberation struggle and forging national liberation movements in colonised or oppressed countries, the commission unanimously adopted the term 'national-revolutionary' to characterise and distinguish revolutionary movements (and by virtue of this also their programme) from reformist 'bourgeois-democratic' movements and their programme.

The articulation of the strategy of the national democratic revolution concerning South Africa specifically emerged in the 'Resolution on the "South African Question"', first adopted by the Comintern (1928) after engagements with South African communists (SACP, 1981). The SACP, formerly the Communist Party of South Africa (and not the ANC) became, shortly after its founding in 1921, a South African affiliate of the Comintern. Thus, it was the SACP that first ratified the resolution in the country as the Communist Party of South Africa at the end of December 1928 and the beginning of January 1929 (SACP, 1981).

The anti-colonial and anti-imperialist struggle to achieve the liberation of the oppressed, being the black majority in South Africa, dismantle the legacy of colonialism and apartheid, and transform

South Africa into an independent democratic republic with equal rights for all, took centre stage in what became a South African elaboration of the strategy of the national democratic revolution by the Communist Party. This came out from what I call the 'black-cum-workers' and peasants' republic thesis', which the 'Resolution on the "South African Question"' advanced. This thesis was aimed at overthrowing colonial rule in, and imperialist domination of, South Africa, and transforming the country into an independent republic with democratic black majority rule based on equal rights for all, as an immediate stage towards the socialist republic – that is, the independent democratic workers' and peasants' republic.

Second, it was the Communist Party implementing the resolution that first played a leading role in establishing the alliance with the ANC and the progressive trade union movement. This was a key part of the effort to build a national-revolutionary movement, which the resolution saw as constituting one of the major tasks of the Communist Party. It was a necessary step in consolidating the widest possible patriotic unity to tilt the balance of forces in South Africa in favour of the liberation struggle, to defeat colonial rule in and imperialist domination of South Africa:

> The Party should pay particular attention to the embryonic national organisations among the natives, such as the African National Congress. The Party, while retaining its full independence, should participate in these organisations, should seek to broaden and extend their activity. Our aim should be to transform the African National Congress into a fighting nationalist revolutionary organisation against the white bourgeoisie and the British imperialists, based upon the trade unions, peasant organisations, etc. (Communist International, 1928: 96).

This approach proved to be formidable, as evidenced by the great role played by the Alliance, in finally defeating the apartheid regime in April 1994, with the support of an array of mass democratic formations and the majority of the people at large. SACP members were actively involved in all the key sites of the struggle, including holding senior positions and playing leading roles, not only in the

ANC but among others also in the high command of the liberation army, uMkhonto we Sizwe (Mandela, 1994). This was not the so-called patronage and career propping deployments by the ANC, but selfless dedication under extremely dangerous conditions.

The generalised allegation that the SACP continued with the alliance in 1994, and afterwards through a common ANC-headed Alliance electoral strategy and lists based on nothing but dependency on so-called patronage, including career propping deployments from the ANC, is therefore unhistorical and misleading.[17] At the centre of the strategy, based on agreed election manifestos, starting with the RDP in 1994, was the need to maintain the widest possible unity, as opposed to fragmenting the movement and its historical support bases when unity was essential to secure victory over the apartheid regime.

Achieved with invaluable selfless left contribution in the South African struggle for liberation and social emancipation, with the Alliance playing a formidable role at the forefront, the 1994 democratic breakthrough will go down in history, not as a failed 'old left' project but as victory over colonial oppression and the apartheid regime. It was this same movement that produced and adopted the Freedom Charter in 1955. This charter was drafted with the participation of communist cadres, both those who were organising underground and those who publicly formed part of the membership and leadership of the Congress Alliance partners.[18]

Third, the strategy of the national democratic revolution was

---

17 In Chapter IV of the Manifesto of the Communist Party addressing the position of the communists in relation to the various existing opposition parties, Marx and Engels (1848) recognised that communists, and this goes for their proposals as well, will not always receive acceptance but will also face hostile reactions and other challenges in other organisations with whom they necessarily had to build relations and even form part of in different national situations based on their historical contexts. As Marx and Engels state in the 1872 preface to the manifesto, while a greater portion of the political organisations they mentioned were swept from off the Earth by the progress of history, the principles they proposed for communists in that chapter remained correct.

18 For example, in 'South Africa's Way Forward', the SACP General Secretary Moses Kotane (1954) outlined a number of the key demands that went into the Freedom Charter when it was adopted the following year, in 1955.

refined and consolidated in November 1960 by the Meeting of Communist and Workers Parties in Moscow. Again, the SACP (and not the ANC) was and still is part of the Meeting of Communist and Workers Parties as a world movement. In defining national democratic tasks and the role of the working class, the statement adopted at the meeting by 81 communist and workers parties, including the SACP,[19] referred to the national democratic revolution as a national, anti-imperialist, democratic revolution:

> The working-class, which has played an outstanding role in the fight for national liberation, demands the complete and consistent accomplishment of the tasks of the national, anti-imperialist, democratic revolution (Meeting of Communist and Workers Parties, 1960b: 16).

The aim of this national, anti-imperialist, democratic revolution is to secure 'non-capitalist development ... [for the people to] free themselves from exploitation, poverty and hunger' (Communist and Workers' Parties, 1960b: 16). To this end, the democratic tasks included uniting all patriotic forces in a single national democratic front, to win national independence, uproot imperialist domination, accomplish far-reaching democratic transformations, including radical agrarian reforms, and create and develop national industry, improve the standard of living of the masses, democratise social life, and ensure social progress, broad democratic rights and freedoms – freedom of speech, press, assembly, demonstrations, establishment of political parties and social organisations, among others.

The Meeting of the Communist and Workers Parties saw the alliance of the working class and the peasantry as the basis of the broad, national democratic front, and the most important force in winning and defending these and other democratic tasks. In South Africa, it became the task of the alliance forged by the SACP with the ANC and the progressive trade union movement to implement the 'Resolution on the "South African Question"' adopted in 1928 and 1929 to strive to form that basis and serve as that force.

---

19 See the 'Communique' in the 'Documents of the Meeting of Representatives of the Communist and Workers' Parties (1960a: 6)

Last, but not least, the South African refinement and consolidation of the strategy of the national democratic revolution was subsequently first developed by the SACP (1962: 312–20) in its programme titled the 'Road to South African Freedom' (SACP, 1962: 284–320). The SACP adopted the programme at its fifth National Congress held underground in South Africa in 1962, within two years of the Meeting of Communist and Workers Parties held in Moscow in November 1960. Reaffirming the liberation of the oppressed black majority and the dismantling of the white supremacist minority rule and its legacy of discrimination as the immediate content of the national democratic revolution, the programme referred to the main aims and lines of the revolution as those enshrined in the Freedom Charter[20]. Under the historical conditions that obtained in South Africa, asserted the SACP, achieving the aims of the Freedom Charter, would answer the immediate needs of the people and lay the basis for advancing to the non-capitalist development path, socialism.

The first major reference to the national democratic revolution in the ANC appeared in its first Strategy and Tactics document it developed and adopted in Morogoro, Tanzania, in April 1969. This was seven years after the SACP adopted its 'Road to South African Freedom' programme in 1962.

The allegation that the SACP is doing nothing but following the strategy of the national democratic revolution developed by the ANC is, therefore, unhistorical and misleading. This does not mean that there were no tensions in the ANC-headed Alliance[21] regarding the meaning and direction of the national democratic revolution between the SACP (and COSATU), on the one hand, and the ANC, on the other, after 1994.

It was a revision of the content of the national democratic revolution, on the one hand, and an assertion of it, on the other, that saw rising tensions within the ANC-headed Alliance. These tensions were typified by the government's adoption of GEAR, which was later supported by the ANC, but strong opposition to it emerged from

---

20 Which is in line with the democratic tasks identified (above) from the statement of the Communist and Workers Parties.
21 See footnote 17.

the SACP and COSATU. The SACP 10th National Congress in July 1998 in Johannesburg became one of the fronts on which the tensions heightened, with ANC leaders defending GEAR and SACP members and leaders rejecting it, including in the final declaration of the congress.[22] In the declaration, the SACP called for an integrated industrial policy, an overarching employment creation strategy, social security nets and a reduction in interest rates, as opposed to raising interest rates in narrow inflation targeting pursued under the regime of global neoliberalism, regardless of national circumstances and its negative impact on the workers and the poor, as well as the economy in various ways.[23]

The call for an overarching employment strategy can at least be traced to the right of all to work, enshrined in the Freedom Charter. It was destined to give practical effect to the right to work, which can further be traced to the ten-point programme developed by Marx and Engels (1848) in Chapter II of the Manifesto of the Communist Party.

In its 10th National Congress declaration, the SACP also called for a different macro-economic policy that would be appropriate for our society, aligned with the objectives of the industrial policy and the overarching employment creation strategy that South Africa desperately needed. The new macro-economic framework had to support social deficit targets, including through social security nets. It was also in its response to GEAR that the SACP adopted, and together with COSATU, the anti-privatisation campaign that it drove.

Going back to the early 1990s, the SACP had adopted a decisive break with the 'two-stagism' embedded in the 'black-cum-workers'

---

22 See, for example, the 'Statement of the President of the African National Congress, Thabo Mbeki at 10th Congress of the SACP'. Available at: https://www.sacp.org.za/content/statement-president-african-national-congress-thabo-mbeki-10th-congress-sacp (Accessed 12 December 2022) and the 'Declaration of the 10th SACP National Congress'. Available at: (https://www.sacp.org.za/content/declaration-10th-sacp-congress (Accessed 12 December 2022).

23 See, for example, Saad-Filho (2010), who shows that in pursuing its policy prescript of narrow inflation targeting, the global neoliberal regime exaggerates the costs of inflation while underestimating the negative impact of the policy, including on output, employment, incomes, distribution, finance and balance of payments.

and peasants' republic thesis' by developing the programmatic theme 'Socialism is the future, build it now!' (Cronin and Mashilo, 2017). In April 1995, its 9th National Congress consolidated the decisive break in the strategic perspectives it amended and adopted under the title 'Socialism is the future, build it now!'[24] This underlined the immediate imperative of intensifying the struggle for socialism. In contrast, those who left the SACP from the early 1990s to pursue a reformist agenda, which was to include GEAR, notably after the dissolution of the USSR, erroneously argued that socialism was no longer necessary or the struggle to achieve it should follow in a distant future after the completion of the national democratic revolution (SACP, 2022). The programmatic theme 'Socialism is the future, build it now!' brought to the fore what had underpinned the interrelationship between the national democratic revolution and socialism, viewed dialectically. This can be summarised roughly as follows:

On the one hand, it was intensifying the struggle for socialism in the here and now that would guarantee a socialist advance from the national democratic revolution. This required building capacity for, momentum towards, and elements of socialism amid the national democratic revolution. On the other, but mutually reinforcing hand, it was advancing, deepening and defending the 'revolutionary content' in the 'national democratic revolution', which would ensure its advance to socialism. This articulation could be summed up from the 'Position of the communists in relation to the various existing opposition parties', defined in Chapter IV of the Manifesto of the Communist Party as follows:

> The Communists fight for the attainment of the immediate aims, for the enforcement of the momentary interests of the working class; but in the movement of the present, they also represent and take care of the future of that movement (Marx and Engels, 1848: 518).

---

24 SACP Strategic Perspectives: As adopted and amended by the SACP 9th National Congress, April 1995. Available at: https://www.sacp.org.za/content/strategic-perspectives-adopted-9th-national-congress-0 (Accessed 16 December 2022)

It was the concrete struggle to advance the programmatic theme, 'Socialism is the future, build it now', that guided the SACP's critique of and opposition to GEAR and the alternatives it put forward. These alternatives included the, yet to be won, long-haul battle for a change in the macro-economic framework. Also included were a call for the government to adopt an industrial policy that would develop domestic productive forces as rapidly as possible to create employment at scale and meet the material needs of the masses. In the process, the national health insurance to provide quality health care for all, as well as financial sector transformation, formed part of the proposals the SACP put forward and initiated struggles to achieve. There were some important achievements in a context in which the struggle still had to continue towards final victory by the working-class, with the SACP playing its role. The generalised, unsubstantiated allegation that the SACP's critique of and opposition to GEAR was devoid of left content, and not guided by any socialist programme, is unhistorical and misleading.

The Mzala Nxumalo Centre for the Study of South African Society took the important step to organise the Conference on the Future of the Left in June 2017 in Durban. Similar efforts intended at widening and consolidating left unity in South Africa from elsewhere, including the SACP, were in the past upset by, amongst others, those who came pushing the tendency to attack other left organisations and write them off as not being left or socialist. The attacks on, and attempts to, expunge the SACP from the Left or organisations engaged in the struggle for socialism, typify this tendency.

Centres such as the Mzala Nxumalo Centre for the Study of South African Society continue to provide opportunities in the form of research and conferences to address a wide range of issues facing the Left.

The effort to widen and consolidate left and broader working-class unity in South Africa needs to be strengthened, sustained and deepened. To succeed, this effort will have to overcome divisive tendencies.

Those genuinely left need to foster, promote and intensify solidarity and build maximum working-class unity based on a revolutionary programme. Tendencies that promote rivalry, instead of principled unity and cohesion of the Left, do not serve the working class and must be avoided and discouraged on all fronts.

In the same vein, denialism of internal weaknesses and problems should be avoided. For example, the Left needs to confront the fact that there are elitist, corrupt and even petty bourgeois tendencies that have found their way into the ranks of some of its organisations, including trade unions. Some of these tendencies have actually gained dominance in the top echelons of some organisations and are more pronounced during internal elections through factional contests.

Some trade union investment companies, established for the good of their members, were, to some extent, repurposed by unscrupulous elements who exploit them to advance private interests, linked with factions and associated patronage networks. Privately owned companies, called service providers, have in some respect gained an upper hand in the affairs of some of these organisations, including through sponsoring certain candidates to win elections. When elected, those candidates serve the commercial interests of the private companies that sponsored their election campaigns.

The destructive tendencies, including abuse of office to serve private interests, have contributed to the fragmentation that has badly affected many trade union organisations. In this unfortunate scenario, it is not uncommon for some elements, who are caught with their pants down, literally, to break away and form splinter trade union organisations. This reached a point where some organisations, established as a result of these splits, are akin to privately owned companies. From certain perspectives, they position themselves to appear leftist.

The Left must avoid such destructive tendencies and develop clarity on what makes up its common principles, immediate tasks and long-term strategy. Against such tendencies, the Left needs to take its cue from the caution by Marx (1852) in the 'The Eighteenth Brumaire of Louis Bonaparte'. We must distinguish, he says, the phrases and notions of organisations in historic struggles from their real organism, and their real interests, their notions and their reality, as in private life where we should distinguish between what a person thinks of themselves and says, from who that person is in reality and what they do in practice.

Neither can one be left by attacking other left organisations, nor can the real left be an abstract article of faith (a 'new left'), and worst, in opposition to historically existing left organisations. Several new projects have truly been unsuccessful in South Africa. Calling themselves the new left, they appeared positioned, notably with the aid of the anti-left media, in opposition to historically existing left organisations, especially the SACP, labelled as the so-called failed old left.

For example, there was a 'Democratic Left Front' that was framed in that way. It did not take a long time before less and less was heard about it or before it disappeared. Similarly, there was a 'Workers and Socialist Party' that went to the ballot immediately after its formation, but it did not return with a single parliamentary seat. Likewise, it did not emerge again. Other examples followed, while the SACP not only remained but also grew. These and other examples of unsuccessful cases of a similar politics cannot be a cause for celebration for anyone who is genuinely left, but they should be studied to draw lessons from them and to avoid repeating their errors. Obviously, there were internal weaknesses within those 'new left' projects which contributed to their failure.

The Left has to take history seriously and prioritise programmatic unity. In no way does this imply there should be no criticism within the ranks of the Left as a broader category or movement. Criticism, if any, should be constructive and respectful. To be genuinely left, such criticism has to be scientific.

TOWARDS A POPULAR LEFT FRONT PLATFORM AND MOVEMENT

The preceding text includes some principles and programmatic proposals for the Left. To the extent that some of these proposals appear again in this section, they represent matters for emphasis towards the conclusion. These proposals are not exhaustive, however.

The SACP (2017) adopted a resolution to build a popular left front movement, besides pursuing the struggle to reconfigure the ANC-headed Alliance, to resolve policy tensions, ensure democratic consensus-seeking policy consultation towards agreed upon policies on all major questions under the principles of collective leadership and accountability. In addition, the SACP (2022) resolved to build a powerful, socialist movement of the workers and poor. The SACP is clear: the popular left front movement and the powerful, socialist movement of the workers and poor require democratic consultation and working together with other left and worker organisations to build. In addition, while the popular left front movement and the powerful, socialist movement of the workers and poor are not electoral projects, they cannot be excluded from considerations as modalities in future electoral contests, without the reconfiguration of the ANC-headed Alliance. Therefore, the SACP is not confining itself to the ANC-headed Alliance and its reconfiguration, contrary to yet another misleading allegation levelled against it in the attacks it has seen.

Out of their own considerations, some organisations or individuals may choose to be part of the popular left front movement comprising an array of national, provincial, district and local organisations pursuing various campaigns based on left solutions. Others may choose to form part of both the popular left front movement and the powerful, socialist movement of the workers and poor. Yet others may choose to support particular campaigns led by either the popular left front movement or the powerful, socialist movement of the workers and poor or both, without structurally forming part of either or both of the movements. Any organisation or individual in these movements can still choose to belong to other alliances or coalitions as well. In addition, these movements need not take the form of, or rush to become, unitary formations. To succeed, this movement formation process has to be thoroughly democratic and also respect the autonomy or independence of its constituent elements or members.

The key tasks – organisational, political and strategic – facing the Left, including the progressive trade union movement, is to unite and build the popular left front movement and the powerful, socialist movement of the workers and poor to address, and finally resolve, the problems created by the exploitative system of capitalism, such as class inequality, unemployment and poverty (together with their racial, gender and spatial dimensions, both internal and external[25]) and to strive to overcome the system itself as the fundamental problem.

Unless all forces in the Left appreciate that class inequality, unemployment and poverty form the conditions of existence and are the products and levers of the accumulation of wealth on a capitalistic basis, as Marx (1867) found in his examination of unemployment, they will not all go to, and proceed from, the root of the matter. This means that the Left has to be radical in search of the way forward and the solutions it puts to the front. The Left will need to confront capitalism's latest imperialist agenda, neoliberalism,[26] among the systemic drivers of the problems and crises facing the workers and poor.

One more challenge the Left will have to address, having coalesced around a common programme distinct from the Right, is to develop and unite behind, to borrow from Marx and Engels (1848), the struggles to achieve the immediate aims of the working class and enforce its momentary interests, while taking care of its future. This future is a social formation in which the exploitation of one person by another will systematically be eliminated.

The Freedom Charter, particularly its clauses on economic transformation and land redistribution, thematically features frequently and prominently as the premise of such a common programme in many calls made by a number of left formations. It must be taken seriously, while opening space for innovation, creativity and dynamism.

The South African situation is changing. Class interests and the class content of the national struggle are coming to the fore, sharpening within the national content of the class struggle. The working class must become more and more assertive, based on its interests and aims, but without being sectarian. It must not allow other class elements to clothe their private wealth accumulation

---

25 Global North–South inequality.
26 See, for example, Adelzadeh (2021) on the failures of the economic policy adopted by the South African government post-1996.

aspirations and pursue them in the name of the historically oppressed and the previously and continuously disadvantaged, Africans, in particular, and black people in general.

Among the apex priorities, around which the Left needs to unite, is the need to tackle corruption, corporate rule and state capture and rent seeking, and ensure improvements in the quality and delivery of public goods and services. This is crucial to overcome the challenges of economic and broader social transformation and development in South Africa. It is inconceivable that the Left will achieve success without overcoming the factors that weaken its organisational capacity and unity, and building the strategic discipline required to confront the class adversary of the working class.

There is a wide range of policy considerations that have also emerged over the past two decades, including structural economic transformation to develop national production by expanding and diversifying manufacturing, industrialising. There is a widely shared left perspective that we must make use of our mineral and marine resources as a strategic advantage to localise the production of finished products, instead of continuing to rely on colonial economic features, namely the significant dependency on imports of finished goods and exports of our mineral resources, mainly as raw materials.

The question of adequate support for innovation, research and development has come to the fore as well. Linked with this is the imperative to drive curriculum transformation to meet the needs of the people and increase total productive forces as rapidly as possible, including through decisively rolling out free quality education at all levels for students from working-class and poor households who cannot afford to pay fees.

A correct approach to curriculum transformation has a key role to play if South Africa is to develop its productive capacity and achieve a breakthrough against the ideas of the capitalist rulers of the economy. The country needs an emancipatory curriculum system at all levels, as opposed to having its classrooms and lecture halls serving as the transmission belts for neoliberal straitjacketing.

LEARNING FROM PRACTICAL LEFT EXAMPLES
Financial Sector Transformation Campaign

Experiences gained from practical examples such as the Financial Sector Campaign started by the SACP in 2000 provide insights into uniting the Left and other progressive forces in action. While not all the organisations or individuals that joined in to support the campaign characterised themselves as left organisations or individuals, the campaign was left in content. Its aims included waging the struggle against exclusion and financial exploitation, including reckless and predatory lending practices. This was in the category of consumer protection and seeking non-exploitative inclusion of the unbanked and excluded in the financial sector. The objectives of the campaign included fighting against high financial services fees, including high bank charges and interest rates.

In terms of structural transformation, the objectives of the campaign included waging the struggle for de-monopolisation, transformation and diversification of the financial sector. The alternatives advanced in this category included fighting for an enabling legislative framework and adequate policy support for worker and community owned co-operative banks and financial institutions to thrive and grow as a sector.

A wide range of organisations, including trade unions, community-based organisations and taxi associations, to name but a few, joined in the Financial Sector Campaign. The results included the extension of banking services through the Mzansi Account, which offered affordable inclusion of the previously unbanked who were excluded by the banks.

The National Credit Act of 2005 was passed, among others, to clamp down on reckless and predatory lending practices and the National Credit Regulator was established. This approach was to serve as a key factor in cushioning against the worst effects of the 2008 global economic crisis in the financial sector in South Africa. The crisis first manifested in the financial sector in the United States in 2007, because of a so-called subprime meltdown, which was the result of unsustainable debt and rapid increases in the number of defaults in what was a high-risk mortgage market. The National Credit Act in South Africa discouraged this problematic financial sector conduct, which grew rampantly under liberalisation and deregulation in countries such as the United States, the epicentre of many global financial products and dealings.

While the Financial Sector Campaign registered achievements, it did not attain its ultimate goals. For example, the banking sector is still dominated by a handful of oligopolies. The South African Reserve bank relies on these few commercial banks for its monetary policy transmission channels, yet not one of them is developmental with the interests of the people at heart. All the banking oligopolies belong to profit-seeking, private wealth accumulating interests. This is their agenda, which is one reason why financial services fees, including interest rates, are high in the banks for many South Africans, more so for the workers and poor. The problematic interest rate hikes by the South African Reserve Bank are another factor. The central bank does not set developmental interest rates across the entire landscape of interest rates. In fact, it uses increases in interest rates as a narrow inflation-targeting policy instrument.

Besides, the state, which is a major depositor of funds and financial transactor of note in the South African economy, does not have its own footprint in the banking sector. The development of co-operative banks and financial institutions is suffocated by the financial architecture that underpins the dominance of the banking sector by oligopolies.

The Financial Sector Campaign is one strategic initiative that needs the broad unity of the Left and other progressive forces to take forward and intensify, to end all forms of financial exploitation and domination, build a people's financial sector and ensure developmental financial services. This is a key issue in the Freedom Charter's economic clause, which, among its goals, refers to people's ownership of banks. In this, building a developmental state banking sector is an imperative.

China is one country that has a strong developmental state banking sector from which we can draw important lessons. Almost every major sector of the Chinese economy has a developmental state bank. Some, for example the Industrial and Commercial Bank of China, the China Construction Bank, and the Agricultural Bank of China, have made it into Forbes Global 2000 List.[27] This shows that state ownership can thrive under decisive leadership, based on good governance, and with the interests of the people at heart. This includes dealing corruption a decisive blow, as the Chinese state does when corruption rears its ugly head. It is also interesting to note that the Industrial and Commercial Bank of China acquired a 20 per cent stake in the Standard Bank of South Africa in 2007.[28] Meanwhile, the South African state is either indecisive or drags its feet regarding establishing its presence and participation, on behalf of the people, in the banking sector.

Mawubuye Umhlaba Campaign

The transformation of land ownership is another key imperative for the Left. This should be anchored in the wider effort to ensure equitable access to our country's natural resources, transform agriculture, ensure food production, and systematically eliminate inequality, including in access to land. These were among the key demands of the major land campaign, *Mawubuye Umhlaba*, loosely translated as 'Let the land return'. The SACP (2004b) initiated this campaign in the early 2000s, through its flagship annual Red October Campaign. This was, arguably, the first major campaign in South Africa post-1994 on land redistribution. The campaign culminated in a National Day of Action, with national and provincial marches across the country, in 2004.[29]

The demands of the campaign included a national land summit within 12 months, which did occur in 2005.[30] The campaign also challenged the 'willing buyer, willing seller' approach to land redistribution, which the SACP General Secretary Blade Nzimande

---

27 See Murphy *et al.* (2021).
28 See the Standard Bank (2021).
29 The author was one of the co-ordinators and mobilisers of the campaign in the Tshwane metropolitan area, where the national march through the capital city took place on Saturday, 6 November 2004.
30 See the Briefing by the Minister of Agriculture and Land Affairs Thoko Didiza to the Land and Environment Select Committee on 13 September 2005, National Council of Provinces (2005).

(2004) summarised as a law-governed and coherent expropriation policy.

The success of the campaign involved its capacity to bring together an array of organisations. By the time the SACP convened a press briefing on 15 October 2004 to announce the details of a consultative conference with other organisations that supported the demands for land redistribution, it had received confirmations of attendance from over 43 organisations, including COSATU, the Food and Allied Workers Union, the National Land Committee, the Land Access Movement of South Africa, the Landless People's Movement, the Pan-Africanist Congress of Azania, and the Azanian People's Organisation (SACP, 2004a).

Land ownership transformation, as an apex priority for the Left, should include accelerated land redistribution and technical capacity building, including skills training and support in the form of equipment, materials and funding for the working class to use land productively, build and expand access to productive work and sustainable livelihoods, and advance poverty eradication. In driving the radical land redistribution campaign, the Left should target building collective worker ownership and control in the entire land-based economy instead of limiting itself to agriculture, important as it is. The land-based economy is vast. It includes, but it is not limited to, agriculture, forestry, mining, hospitality and tourism, game farming, human settlement, and fisheries sectors.

CONCLUSION

The proposals in this chapter are an attempt to build a foundation for a broader left platform, whose strategic objective should be to advance, deepen and defend a thoroughly democratic national revolution to advance towards a socialist transition. Considering this, the Left needs to unite and consolidate a coherent and comprehensive left programme and overarching strategy. This should be characterised by measures, which advanced and deepened, will systematically eliminate the economic exploitation of labour, give practical effect to the right of all to work, eradicate poverty, systematically eliminate inequality and build a just and equal democratic society.

Given the problem of imperialism, including its interference in national policy spaces through institutions hegemonised by imperialist states, such as the IMF, the Left needs to defend national independence and democratic policy sovereignty, and intensify the struggle to achieve freedom from imperialism. This struggle stands a better chance of succeeding if it is waged as an international struggle and not merely a national one. This approach is consistent with the character of the working-class struggle as an internationalist struggle against the exploitative capitalist world-system, the imperialist global regime and its iterations, including neoliberalism. Building the unity of the working class beyond and across national borders, and strengthening left movements globally is essential for success, as opposed to tendencies that sow divisions and concentrate attacks on other organisations within the Left.

REFERENCES

Adelzadeh, A. (2021). 'South Africa's long term policy options beyond 2021'. Pretoria: Presentation to the Human Science Research Council Macro-economic Policy Dialogue Series.

African National Congress. (1969). 'Strategy and Tactics of the ANC', *Marxist Internet Archive*. Available at: (Accessed 14 December 2022).

Communist International. (1928). 'Resolution on "The South African Question" adopted by the Executive Committee of the Communist International following the Sixth Comintern Congress', in South African Communist Party. (1981). *South African Communists Speak: Documents from the History of the South African Communist Party 1915–1980*. London: Inkululeko Publications, pp. 91–97.

Commission of Inquiry into State Capture. (2022). *Judicial Commission of Inquiry into State Capture Report: Part IV, Vol. 4: The Capture of Eskom*. Johannesburg: Commission of Inquiry into State Capture. Available at: https://www.gov.za/sites/default/files/gcis_document/202204/state-capture-commission-report-part-iv-vol-iv.pdf (Accessed 10 December 2022).

Cronin, J. and Mashilo, A.M. (2017). 'Decentring the question of race: Critical reflections on colonialism of a special type', in E. Webster and K. Pampallis (eds). *The Unresolved National Question in South Africa: Left thought under apartheid and beyond*. Johannesburg: Wits University Press, pp. 20–41.

Kotane, M. (1954). 'South Africa's Way Forward', statement by Moses Kotane, published in *Advance* (successor to the banned *Guardian*) on 6 and 13 May 1964. In South African Communist Party (1981). *South African Communists Speak: Documents from the history of the South African Communist Party, 1915–1980*. London: Inkululeko Publications, pp. 231–42.

Lenin. V.I. (1920a). '"Left-wing" communism: An infantile disorder', in V.I. Lenin (1974). *V.I. Lenin Collected Works, Vol. 31: April–December 1920*. Moscow: Progress Publishers, pp. 17–118.

Lenin, V.I. (1920b). 'Report of the Commission on the National and the Colonial Questions, July 26', in V.I. Lenin (1974). *V.I. Lenin Collected Works Vol. 31: April–December 1920*. Moscow: Progress Publishers, pp. 240–45.

Lenin, V.I. (1918). 'Left-wing childishness and the petty-bourgeois mentality', in V.I. Lenin. (1974). *V.I. Lenin Collected Works Vol. 27: February–July 1918*. Moscow: Progress Publishers, pp. 323–54.

Lenin, V.I. (1917). 'Imperialism, the highest stage of capitalism. A popular outline', in V.I. Lenin (1970). *V.I. Lenin Selected Works in Three Volumes: Volume 1*. Moscow: Progress Publishers, pp. 667–768.

Mandela, N.R. (1994). *Long Walk to Freedom: The autobiography of Nelson Mandela*. London: Little, Brown and Company.

Marx, K. (1867). *Capital: A critique of political economy, Vol. I*. In K. Marx and F. Engels. (2010). *Marx and Engels Collected Works, Vol. 35: Karl Marx–Capital Volume I*. London: Lawrence & Wishart.

Marx, K. (1894). *Capital: A Critique of Political Economy. Vol. III*. In K. Marx and F. Engels (2010) *Marx and Engels Collected Works, Vol. 37: Karl Marx – Capital Volume III*. London: Lawrence & Wishart

Marx, K. (1852). 'The Eighteenth Brumaire of Louis Bonaparte', in. K. Marx and E. Engels (2010). *Marx and Engels Collected Works, Vol. 11: Marx and Engels 1851–53*. London: Lawrence & Wishart, pp. 99-197.

Marx, K. and Engels, F. (1848). 'Manifesto of the Communist Party', in K. Marx and F. Engels. (2010). *Marx and Engels Collected Works,*

Vol. 6: Marx and Engels 1845–48. London: Lawrence & Wishart, pp. 477–519.

Mbeki, T. (1998). Statement of the President of the African National Congress, Thabo Mbeki at 10th Congress of the SACP.

Meeting of Communist and Workers' Parties. (1960a). 'Communique', *Peking Review*, 49 and 50, 13 December, 1960, p. 6

Meeting of Communist and Workers' Parties. (1960b). 'Statement', *Peking Review*, 49 and 50, 13 December, 1960, pp. 7–22

Mohamed, S. (2010). 'The state of the South African economy', in D. Pillay, J. Daniel, P. Naidoo and R. Southall. (eds). *New South African Review 1*. Johannesburg: Wits University Press, pp. 39–64.

Murphy, A., Haverstock, E., Gara, A., Helman, C. and Vardi, N. (2021). 'Global 2000: How the world's biggest public companies endured the pandemic', *Forbes*. Available at: https://www.forbes.com/lists/global2000/#6bf42eb65ac0 (Accessed 12 December 1922).

National Council of Provinces, Land and Environment Select Committee. (2005). 'Land Summit Recommendations: Department Briefing'. Parliamentary Monitoring Group. Available at: https://pmg.org.za/committee-meeting/5522/ (Accessed 18 December 2022).

National Treasury, South Africa. (2019a). 'Economic transformation, inclusive growth, and competitiveness: Towards an Economic Strategy for South Africa'. Pretoria: Economic Policy, National Treasury.

National Treasury, South Africa. (2019b). 'Economic transformation, inclusive growth, and competitiveness: A contribution towards a growth agenda for the South African economy'. Pretoria: National Treasury.

Padayachee, V. and Van Niekerk, R. (2019). *Shadow of Liberation: Contestation and compromise in the economic and social policy of the African National Congress, 1943–1996*. Johannesburg: Wits University Press.

Nzimande, B. (2004). 'Land reform, the market and the constitution', *Umsebenzi Online*, 3(21), 3 November.

Nzimande, B. (2021). 'SACP Centenary: 100 Years of Unbroken Struggle. Put People Before Profit: Socialism is the future, build it now! Statement of the South African Communist Party Central

Committee, *African Communist*, Second and Third Quarters 2021, 205: 3–38.

Organisation for Economic Co-operation and Development (OECD). (2017). *Economic Policy Reforms 2017: Going for growth*. Paris: OECD Publishing. Available at: http://dx.doi.org/10.1787/growth-2017-en (Accessed 12 December 2022).

Saad-F, A. (2010). Monetary Policy in the Neo-liberal Transition: A Political Economy Critique of Keynesianism, Monetarism and Inflation Targeting. In R. Albritton, B. Jessop and R. Westra (eds). *Political Economy and Global Capitalism: The 21st century, present and future*. London: Anthem Press, pp. 89–119.

South African Communist Party. (2022). 'Towards the 15th Party Congress: The South African struggle for socialism', *Bua Komanisi*, 14(1), April 2022.

South African Communist Party. (2017). '14th National Congress, 10–15 July 2017: Declaration and Resolutions'. Johannesburg: South African Communist Party.

South African Communist Party. (2004a). 'SACP to host consultative conference on its Red October Campaign on Land and Agrarian Reform'. Available at: https://www.sacp.org.za/content/sacp-host-consultative-conference-its-2004-red-october-campaign-land-and-agrarian-reform (Accessed 17 December 2022).

South African Communist Party (2004b). 'The Programme of Action of the 2004 Red October Campaign'. Available at: https://www.sacp.org.za/content/programme-action-2004-red-october-campaign (Accessed 17 December 2022).

South African Communist Party. (1998). 'Declaration of the 10th SACP Congress'. Available at: https://www.sacp.org.za/content/declaration-10th-sacp-congress (Accessed 12 December 2019).

South African Communist Party. (1981). 'Editorial note', in South African Communist Party. (1981). *South African Communists Speak: Documents from the history of the South African Communist Party 1915–1980*. London: Inkululeko Publications, pp. 89–90.

South African Communist Party. (1976). 'The enemy hidden under the same colour', *African Communist*, 65, Second Quarter: 16–40.

South African Communist Party. (1962). '*The Road to South African Freedom*, programme of the South African Communist Party adopted at the fifth national conference of the Party held inside the country in 1962'. In South African Communist Party. (1981). *South African Communists Speak: Documents from the history of the South African Communist Party 1915–1980*. London: Inkululeko Publications, pp. 284–320.

Standard Bank. (2021). 'Top 10 shareholders. Standard Bank of South Africa'. Available at: https://reporting.standardbank.com/shareholder-info/shareholder-information/ (Accessed 12 December 2022).

Statistics South Africa. (2021). *Quarterly Labour Force Survey, Quarter 3: 2021*. Pretoria: Statistics South Africa.

Steinberg, G. and Wertman, B. (2018). 'Value clash: Civil society, foreign funding, and national sovereignty', *Global Governance*, 24: 1–10.

Van Niekerk, R. and Padayachee, V. (2019). *Shadow of Liberation: Contestation and compromise in the economic and social policy of the African National Congress, 1943–1996*. Johannesburg: Wits University Press.

Wallace, T. (2004). 'NGO Dilemmas: Trojan Horses for global neoliberalism?' In L. Panitch and C. Leys. *The Socialist Register 2004: The new imperial challenge*. New York: Monthly Review Press, pp. 202–19.

Wright, G.W. (2012). 'NGOs and Western hegemony: Causes for concern and ideas for change', *Development in Practice*, 22(1): 123–34.

EIGHT

GLOBAL ECONOMIC IMPERIALISM AND THE POLITICS OF (UNDER)DEVELOPMENT: STREET TRADERS, DOMESTIC WORKERS AND SEX WORKERS

Pat Horn

INTRODUCTION

Street traders, domestic workers and sex workers are three of the principal categories of women workers in the informal economy in Africa. Research has shown that the informal economy comprises over 70 per cent of non-agricultural employment on the continent. The figure is even higher in the agricultural sector. The reality at the moment is that most new employment is taking place in the informal economy (Horn, 2008). As long as many African countries have most of their labour force carrying out survivalist economic activities in the informal economy, poverty will continue and worsen.

The disproportionate number of women at the survivalist end of the informal economy, who are trapped there by the social discrimination against women in most societies, the lack of skills development or access to credit, and the child-care responsibilities, which are foisted on them by society, deepens inequalities in the labour market (particularly those between formal and informal workers). Trade unions are in no position to address these inequalities or the poverty that they constantly reinforce, without organising those who work in the informal economy. The challenge for the trade union movement is to ensure that increased employment is decent work,[1] whether it be in the formal or informal economy. However, unless trade unions are active in the informal economy, they are not in a position to ensure this. Some unions have become painfully aware of this, and what it means for them as representative working-class organisations.

Employment in the formal economy continues to drop as a result of deregulation, privatisation, structural adjustment and other neoliberal programmes designed to boost economic growth without due regard for their employment implications. Growing unemployment in the formal economy and the absence of unionisation in the informal economy carry major implications for trade unions and their representivity. As their traditional base of full-time permanent employees shrinks, the section of civil society that they represent becomes increasingly more marginal. In countries where economies are underpinned by informal traders, street vendors and mobile hawkers, small-scale agricultural producers, home-based producers of goods and services, own-account workers, casual and sub-contracted workers, and what is euphemistically referred to as 'family labour', none of these sectors are unionised in any significant numbers. As a result, the trade unions often find themselves representing a small (usually rather elite) group of workers in the formal labour market who have better wages and working conditions (even where these are bad relative to workers in other countries) than the rest of the working population. Such a marginal group cannot in all seriousness hope to properly represent the entire workforce, no matter how strong they were in the past or what proud history of their struggle remains in the memory of workers and civil society. However, trade unions usually have systems of direct democracy

---

1 'Decent work' is work that complies with basic labour standards, by workers who have access to social security, and enjoy the basic rights of organisation and representation (Horn, 2008: 2).

(either working or lapsed in practice), which provide a stronger basis for democratic and representative civil society actions than do many other kinds of civil society organisations. For this reason, the rest of civil society often looks to trade unions for leadership in broad civil society actions and campaigns.

There have been substantial, well-established developments on organising workers in the informal economy (including at international level), notably the following:

- recognition by local government authorities and, in some cases, also national government;
- voice and representation for informal workers, even if ad hoc;
- means for informal workers to exercise their rights in respect of International Labour Organization (ILO) Convention 87 (Freedom of Association) and Convention 98 (the Right to Organise and Collective Bargaining Convention);
- means for informal workers to affiliate internationally and enjoy international solidarity (for example, when street vendors are being harassed); and
- means for informal workers to be represented in international forums (such as the International Labour Conferences of the ILO).

Internationally, a number of existing organisations represent previously marginalised or new forms or labour, as described below.

Domestic workers[2]

The International Domestic Workers' Federation (IDWF) was established in Montevideo, Uruguay, on 28 October 2013. As of October 2018, the IDWF had 69 affiliates from 55 countries, representing over 600 000 domestic/household workers. Most are organised in trade unions, and others in associations, networks and workers' cooperatives. Prior to this, in June 2011, a new ILO Convention 189, 'concerning decent work for domestic workers',[3] developed with

---

2   Available at: http://www.wiego.org/informal-economy/occupational-groups/domestic-workers
3   Available at: https://www.ilo.org/dyn/normlex/en/f?p=NORMLEXPUB:12100:0::NO::P12100_ILO_CODE:C189

intensive participation of organised domestic workers, was adopted. This Convention (C189) has resulted in significant advances in the legal protection of domestic workers in many ILO member states, at least in theory.

Street vendors[4]

StreetNet International was established in Durban, South Africa, on 14 November 2002. As of January 2019, StreetNet had 51 affiliated membership-based organisations (MBOs) in 47 countries in Africa, Asia, the Americas and Eastern Europe, representing over 550 000 street vendors, informal market vendors and hawkers. Most of the workers in this sector are own-account workers, defined in Clause 4 of the ILO's Conclusions[5] on Decent Work and the Informal Economy as follows:

> Workers in the informal economy include both wage workers and own-account workers. Most own-account workers are as insecure and vulnerable as wage workers, and move from one situation to the other. Because they lack protection, rights and representation, these workers often remain trapped in poverty.

In June 2015, a new ILO Recommendation 204 (R204) on 'transitions from the informal to the formal economy'[6] was developed – with intensive participation of organised workers in the informal economy – and adopted. R204 broke some important new ground and so was a victory for workers in the informal economy. Pressure should be exerted on ILO member states to implement it.

The strong rights-based approach of R204 makes it a useful tool for initiating favourable formalisation processes in the interests of workers in the informal economy. However, in certain areas, organised informal workers will need to strive for results beyond

---

4   Available at: http://www.wiego.org/informal-economy/occupational-groups/street-vendors
5   Available at: www.ilo.org/public/english/standards/relm/ilc/ilc90/pdf/pr-25res.pdf
6   Available at: https://www.ilo.org/dyn/normlex/en/f?p=NORMLEXPUB:12100:0::NO:12100:P12100_ILO_CODE:R204:NO

those contained in R204. The two most obvious of these are the struggle for direct participation in collective negotiations and collective bargaining, and pressurising local governments to play a leading role in implementing the provisions of the transitions from the informal to the formal economy.

In relation to social protection, the approach of R204 is to extend the existing provisions – rather than providing new forms of protection – which are particularly crucial to workers in the informal economy, such as food security and the provision of quality public services. There is no reason why organised groups of informal workers should not demand that their governments reconceptualise the forms of social protection to be instituted as part of the transitions from the informal to the formal economy.

Because of the broad application of R204 to all sectors of the informal economy, every organised group would be able to use it in the way that is most useful to their sector. It was not deemed necessary to list all the different sectors and groups of informal workers who should benefit from the R204 – this would have run the risk of some groups being left out. In one of the preparatory discussions in the SADC region,[7] there was a debate about the fact that organised sex workers, while not specifically mentioned anywhere in the text, are also technically covered by the R204 according to the broad description provided, even in countries where sex work has not been legalised. Indeed, any group of informal workers could benefit from the provisions of R204 – but this is far more likely in cases where they organise collectively to make demands about implementation of particular provisions.

Sex workers

In addition to all the challenges of marginalisation faced by all workers in the informal economy, sex workers face the additional challenges of the criminalisation of their work and profession. This makes it difficult to organise openly without putting their members at risk by exposing their identities. Despite this, there is a Global Network of Sex Work Projects (NSWP) whose membership, as of mid-

---

7   Gaborone, April 2015.

2019, comprised 237 sex worker-led organisations in 71 countries across the globe, including local organisations and national and regional networks. Regional networks in the Global South and Global North represent thousands of sex workers, who actively oppose the criminalisation and other legal oppression of sex work.

In 2013, following a global consultation process with members, the NSWP issued a 'Consensus Statement on Sex Work, Human Rights and the Law' on behalf of the NSWP members and the sex workers they represent. The consensus statement identifies and focuses on eight rights that have been recognised and ratified by most countries as fundamental human rights. These eight rights are established in various international human rights treaties, as well as many national constitutions, but are too often denied to sex workers. The fundamental rights identified by sex workers as most at risk of being denied were:

1. Right to associate and organise
2. Right to be protected by the law
3. Right to be free from violence
4. Right to be free from discrimination
5. Right to privacy and freedom from arbitrary interference
6. Right to health
7. Right to move and to migrate
8. Right to work and to free choice of employment.

Having described new formations that allow or provide for trade union activities for formerly under-represented groups, the following sections explore how established trade unions might interface with, as well as support, nascent organisations at the local level.

ORGANISATIONAL PROGRESS – DIFFERENT APPROACHES

Community-based vs workplace-based approaches to organising

In 'Creating Opportunities for Fair Globalisation in Southern Africa: A response to the ILO's World Commission on the Social Dimension of Globalisation', Edward Webster and Andries Bezuidenhout of the

Sociology of Work Unit, University of the Witwatersrand, suggest that trade unions should 'consider developing a dual organising strategy, including a "community based" approach to organising, in conjunction with other "shopfloor" organising methods'. This suggestion is made in recognition of the fact that representing workers in the informal economy requires 'new organisational forms and new strategies'. However, another (more direct) way would be for unions to develop a new approach to the workplace of workers in the informal economy (where the workplace is the streets, the homes of workers, or any other place where informal workers work) and for unions to define their organising activities and strategies according to the types of workplaces in which their members are working – still organising their members primarily as workers rather than as community members or consumers.

The question has been raised as to whether workers in the informal economy could be represented in tripartite structures such as the ILO, or whether they should be part of a fourth social partner, such as the Community Constituency of the National Economic Development and Labour Council (Nedlac) in South Africa. However, the constant marginalisation of the Community Constituency in Nedlac does not provide much encouragement for the adoption of the latter approach. As stated in the report of the Committee on the Informal Economy at the 90th International Labour Conference of the ILO in 2002, participating informal economy organisations were not 'in favour of a fourth social partner being introduced to the tripartite structures of the ILO, namely non-governmental organisations (NGOs). (We are in favour of) promoting representation through independent, democratic and representative membership-based organisations of workers in the informal economy'.[8] Such organisations need to form an integral part of the ILO Workers' Group or the labour constituency of tripartite bargaining forums.

While this section has focused on the role that unions or representative organisations can play in terms of providing for access, representation and voice in various fora, the next section

---

8   Para. 37 of the report of the Committee on the Informal Economy to the 90th Session of the International Labour Conference, June 2002. Available at: www.ilo.org/public/english/standards/relm/ilc/ilc90/pdf/pr-25.pdf

focuses similarly on the role that businesses play in relation to the representation of organisations in the informal economy.

'Leaving the informal economy to business and not to organised labour'

This notion (popular in some circles) assumes that everybody in the informal economy and the small business sector has the same class interest – a questionable assumption.

The business sector occupies itself with the needs and interests of the business component of the informal economy, for example, small entrepreneurs and employers, intermediaries (including sub-contractors, labour brokers, etc) rather than the workers. Clauses 31 to 34 of the ILO's Conclusions on Decent Work and the Informal Economy[9] are very clear about the roles of both trade unions and employers' organisations, with Clause 33 focusing on the specific business support services that employers' organisations can offer.

A social movement of the self-employed proletariat as agents of social transformation

An innovative approach to organisation is that of the Nicaraguan Confederación de Trabajadores por Cuenta Propia (CTCP), based on its analysis of the political macro-economy within which it operates as a representative organisation of own-account workers. This approach was documented in the First Self-Employed Workers' Manifesto of the CTCP-FNT (Soto, 2011), which describes 'the birth of what today has become a self-employed proletariat which now seeks a place in anti-establishment theory and practice, rather than merely being counted as poor or as an electoral mass when an election year comes around' (Soto, 2011: 37). The manifesto also emphasises the importance of organising self-employed workers into:

> [A] social movement which aims to improve the correlation of

---

9   Para. 37 of the report of the Committee on the Informal Economy to the 90th session of the International Labour Conference, June 2002. Available at: www.ilo.org/public/english/standards/relm/ilc/ilc90/pdf/pr-25.pdf

forces in their country of residence, struggling to improve their standard of living, not only in terms of their own income, but also by gaining access to national surpluses – specifically to the nation's budget, as they are the group that proportionally pays the highest taxes. This is so because in their countries indirect taxes are far higher than direct ones, a burden which must be carried by the vast majority of the population, among them the self-employed proletariat. But most important, as mentioned, is to advance toward the individual and associative control of production, transport, local and international trade, distribution and consumption (Soto, 2007: 38–39).

Own-account workers were mobilised to join CTCP as part of this strategy, which is consciously differentiated from the way in which CTCP perceives mainstream development strategies. The latter objectify the poor as being in need of social aid instead of recognising them as impoverished 'worker–producers' capable of being the agents of social transformation. Having described forms, roles and possibilities for the organisation and representation of labour, the next section considers challenges experienced by unions and workers when organising labour in the informal economy.

ORGANISATIONAL CHALLENGES

Trade unions world-wide face the challenge of either finding and applying strategies for effectively organising workers in the informal economy, or remaining helpless to prevent the slow attrition of being reduced to very small, weak organisations as their traditional membership base dwindles away to little or nothing.

How can trade unions know what issues and demands to put forward to create decent work in the informal economy, if they have never organised workers in the informal economy? With the best intentions, all they can do is take a guess at the interests and demands of workers in the informal economy and put these issues forward. But this is no better than those heads of state who formulate policies around what they think their people need, instead of engaging in proper consultation with civil society.

Trade unions can confront these challenges by tackling the following practical issues:
- *Political will*: motivating trade union leadership to prioritise the organisation of workers in the informal economy and making human and financial resources available to implement this.
- *Legal changes*: where the laws of a country obstruct or prevent workers from organising in the informal economy, unions need to lobby for the necessary changes to the laws.
- *Constitutional changes*: changing trade union constitutions where this is the obstacle to organising informal workers.
- *New organising strategies*: learning strategies that are more appropriate for workers in the informal economy. This could mean identifying new negotiating partners (such as municipalities instead of employers in the case of street vendors) and new collective bargaining strategies and demands.
- *Women leadership*: overcoming the traditional male bias in formal sector trade unions in order to have significant leadership by women (who are in the majority, especially in the lowest income-earning work) in many sectors of the informal economy.
- *Learning from those doing it already*: by means of exchange visits or other engagement, unions can learn from the experiences of those who are already organising in the informal economy, avoid some of the mistakes and replicate the more successful strategies – rather than try to reinvent the wheel. There are many different models operating in different African countries, so sometimes a combination of different models can be applied where no single one fits exactly.
- *Organising workers in the informal economy as workers and as equals*: because of the greater marginalisation of workers in the informal economy, and their often lower levels of formal education, there is frequently a tendency for formal workers to want to do things on their behalf instead of organising for them to represent themselves and set their own organisational agenda. Formal workers need to consciously avoid this tendency – remembering the struggles they previously have had to wage to represent themselves instead of being represented by others – and to respect the principle of 'nothing for us without us!'

- *Joint campaigns*: for successful joint campaigns, there must be demands set by the workers in the informal economy, as well as the demands of the formal workers. If the formal workers set all the demands and the agenda, and expect the support of workers in the informal economy when there is nothing in it for them, it will not work on a sustained basis.
- *Tackling globalisation*: workers need to confront the negative consequences of globalisation in a unified way (that is, formal and informal workers should identify their common ground and organise around this) to find ways of influencing or acting on the way in which they are affected by globalisation.
- *Taking a lead in civil society*: if trade unions are sufficiently representative of the working people in any society, they are the natural leaders of any civil society or social movement. They become much more representative of the wider working class if they genuinely represent the workers in the informal economy, and are then much better equipped to take up a leading civil society role.

The strength of trade unions lies in their ability to represent the interests of members to whom they are directly accountable and from whom they obtain a direct mandate. It is not adequate for formal sector trade unions, just because they define themselves as working-class organisations, to claim the right to represent informal economy workers who are not their members and have not given them a direct mandate. The only way to genuinely represent workers in the informal economy and put forward their demands for decent work is by organising them, and enabling their elected representatives to participate directly in negotiations and policy dialogue. This forms the focus of the following section.

POLICY CHALLENGES

Eradication of poverty and inequality

Poverty eradication should not be merely a question of pushing for more welfare grants, but of raising the levels of work security, income security and social security for the working poor. The working poor are situated both in formal waged employment and in the informal economy. Unfortunately, many of the working poor in the informal economy (particularly home-based workers, the vast majority of whom are women) are counted in unemployment figures and their work is not recognised in the official statistics. This results in inappropriate policies, which view them solely as potential recipients of welfare grants instead of as a part of the informal labour market, whose working conditions need to be improved so that they can earn more income for the work they do. Trade unions with a strong formal economy bias sometimes become culprits in promoting such inappropriate measures, in their eagerness to pressurise governments to do more to eradicate poverty.

However, by organising these socially invisible workers in the informal economy, and proactively collaborating in solidarity with their self-organised, membership-based organisations, trade unions can obtain proper mandates from them for the kinds of measures they would like to see in place for the eradication of their own poverty. This enables trade unions to speak with greater authority on the demands of the working poor, backed by organised workers in the formal as well as the informal economy.

Policy interventions

What are the areas of policy intervention that need to be undertaken in the interests of decent work in the informal economy? The following recommendations, reflecting the areas of policy intervention that need to be considered for creating an enabling policy environment for decent work, were presented by the Community Constituency of Nedlac to the Minister of Labour in South Africa as far back as in June 2006.

Labour legislation

Labour legislation needs to take into account the 'realities of modern organisation of work' (Clause 16 of the ILO Conclusions on Decent Work and the Informal Economy).[10] This means that labour legislation needs to focus distinctly on the situations of both vulnerable wage workers and own-account workers in the informal economy, in order to address the realities on the ground with a greater degree of precision.

Wage workers

A new ILO Recommendation concerning the employment relationship was adopted at the 95th session of the International Labour Conference on 15 June 2006.[11] This Recommendation provides guidelines for the protection of workers in an employment relationship in situations of disguised employment, ambiguous employment and, to some extent, triangular employment relationships. Since informal workers are often found in sectors and occupations where these types of employment relationships prevail, our labour legislation could become more applicable and enforceable for most informal wage workers by introducing a package of further labour law and policy reforms in accordance with the new ILO Recommendation concerning the employment relationship.

Own-account workers

This category of workers presents a conceptual challenge to legislators because of the absence of an employment relationship in their case. New ground needs to be broken regarding the protection and legal rights of own-account workers, whose status as workers was officially recognised by the ILO for the first time in Clause 4 of the Conclusions on Decent Work and the Informal Economy in 2002.

The following approach was proposed to start making headway in how to most appropriately extend labour legislation and regulation to own-account workers:

---

10 Available at: www.ilo.org/public/english/standards/relm/ilc/ilc90/pdf/pr-25res.pdf

11 Available at: www.ilo.org/public/english/standards/relm/ilc/ilc95/pdf/pr-21res.pdf

- Reform our labour legislation (in line with previous reforms to the labour legislation in Ghana) to use the term 'worker/s' throughout rather than the term 'employee/s', so that the general rights and protections in the labour legislation should apply to own-account workers and wage workers in the informal economy, as well as the more traditional categories of formal employees.
- Commission a study into the dynamics and relationships of economic dependence of own-account workers on other economic actors (other than employers) such as suppliers, public authorities and buyers of products or services, etc. The aim would be the development of a conceptual framework for legal definitions, which make a precise distinction between own-account workers and small entrepreneurs, in line with the existing realities on the ground, without effectively excluding own-account workers from labour legislation, as is currently the case.

Other laws and policies for decent job creation for informal workers

A major achievement of the 2002 Conclusions on Decent Work and the Informal Economy was that it enabled the international debate to move away from a polarised 20-year-old impasse between the employers' project to 'grow the informal economy' and the workers' project to 'formalise the informal economy' – towards a consensual framework focusing on the situation of workers who find themselves working in informality, rather than the 'size' of the informal economy and whether it could be made to increase or decrease. Clause 27 of the Conclusions on Decent Work encourages the adoption of a policy and legal environment that 'increases the benefits of legal registration, facilitating access to commercial buyers, more favourable credit terms, legal protection, contract enforcement, access to technology, subsidies, foreign exchange and local and international markets' in order to 'discourage businesses in the formal economy from shifting into the informal economy', to help 'new businesses to start and smaller businesses to enter the formal economy and to create new jobs, without lowering labour standards [which] also increases state revenues'.

In line with this framework, the following practical measures were proposed:

- Establish a simple one-stop registration system for all informal workers to register and get ID cards identifying them as workers in a simply defined trade (for instance, street vendor, market vendor, waste collector, minibus taxi conductor, etc), which could provide the administrative basis for benefits such as social security schemes and social insurance schemes. This would be an incentive for compliance.
- Develop an appropriate taxation system (based on the principle of progressive taxation) suited to the particular conditions of wage workers and own-account workers in the informal economy. Employers in the informal economy (including intermediaries, in accordance with the principle of joint and several liability) would also need to be taxed in line with their particular reality. A study of functioning tax systems in some of the marketplaces in West Africa would provide good ideas for simple and effective methods of tax collection in the informal economy.
- Extend trade policies to remove the unnecessary obstacles faced by informal cross-border traders to increase the access of informal workers to foreign markets and reduce their dependence on intermediaries. The latter's trade in large volumes of certain products (relying on the availability of many vulnerable informal workers willing to sell anything that is supplied to them) produces distortionary effects on sectors of our economy (such as the trade in foreign-donated second-hand clothing).
- Commission a national review of municipal bylaws that impact directly on the work and livelihoods of workers in the informal economy, such as street trade bylaws, and produce legal guidelines to bring such bylaws into compliance with the ILO's 2002 Conclusions and the country's Decent Work Programme.
- Financial and non-financial support measures for informal workers are an obvious way, if accurately targeted, for informal workers to formalise and regularise their work situation. This should include legal services and skills training.

Social security

Clause 28 of the Conclusions on Decent Work and the Informal Economy[12] states that:

> the conclusions concerning social security adopted by the 89th Session of the International Labour Conference in 2001 should be supported and implemented... Policies and initiatives on the extension of coverage should be taken within the context of an integrated national social strategy.

Representation

Clauses 31 to 34 of the Conclusions on Decent Work and the Informal Economy[13] focus on the importance of extending representation, both of employers and workers, throughout the informal economy. These clauses provide extensive guidelines for employers' and workers' organisations, including trade unions, on how to do this. The Community Constituency has extensive information on efforts by trade unions and other informal workers' organisations who have been increasingly joining a growing movement to organise workers in the informal economy. This has been happening in Africa, Asia and Latin America in particular (since the 1970s in the case of the pioneers in India and Ghana) but gaining substantial momentum in other countries in these regions in the past five years. We know less about the organisation of employers in the informal economy – but we hope that the employers' organisations are taking care of this.

However, even where workers in the informal economy are becoming organised, they find themselves in the situation – unlike workers in the formal economy – of having no statutory labour market institutions through which they can engage the relevant authorities in collective negotiation. They have to set up ad hoc negotiating arrangements, which means that none of their

---

12 Available at: www.ilo.org/public/english/standards/relm/ilc/ilc95/pdf/pr-21res.pdf
13 Available at: www.ilo.org/public/english/standards/relm/ilc/ilc95/pdf/pr-21res.pdf

negotiated agreements or contracts are secure, and the continuity of any negotiated arrangement is a major problem.

THE CHALLENGES OF REPRESENTATION IN THE INFORMAL ECONOMY AND NEW FORMS OF WORK

One of the main obstacles to the organisation of workers in the informal economy and in new forms of non-standard work is that these works are usually not part of the labour force recognised by law – especially own-account or self-employed workers. Contrary to the popular belief that such workers cannot be organised, there are real possibilities for workers in the informal economy and new forms of work to organise themselves (whether or not the laws recognise them as workers) and fight for their legal recognition as workers, and for new laws and policies that will eventually grant them all the basic rights and core labour standards to which other workers are entitled. This is already happening extensively.

Workers in the formal economy and their trade unions are not the most suitable representatives for workers in the informal economy and in non-standard work. In the words of an informal worker at a seminar held in Lusaka, Zambia, in 2001 to determine the representational needs of workers in the informal economy, 'If you want to know what a crocodile eats, you don't ask a monkey.' The most acceptable 'voice-regulation' (Standing, 1999)[14] mechanisms for workers in the informal economy, including new forms of non-standard work, are trade unions and workers' organisations that have organised these workers as their members, and in which informal economy and non-standard workers regularly elect their own representatives. Formal sector unions can genuinely represent informal and non-standard workers only when they, too, start actually organising them and having them elect their own leadership in their unions.

---

14 'Voice regulation' is one of three forms of labour regulation, the other two forms being statutory regulation and market regulation. The term 'voice regulation', derived by Albert Hirschman, 'implies that labour relations, practices and changes are managed through bargaining between representatives of potentially conflicting interests' (Standing, 1999).

Unless workers in the informal economy and new forms of non-standard work are brought into the system of voice regulation, labour market inequalities between workers in the formal and informal economy, and between workers in increasingly varied forms of work, will deepen. In all likelihood, the relatively privileged situation of workers in the formal economy will eventually undermine their own employment security unless they form alliances with organised workers in the informal economy and new forms of work, and engage jointly with them in new inclusive and integrated voice-regulation systems.

Historically, struggles for trade union rights and representation in any system of voice regulation have lasted many decades. It has been through independent, democratic worker-controlled organisations that current systems of voice regulation have been achieved. For workers in new forms of work and the informal economy to be able to participate in – and sustain – an appropriate system of voice regulation, they also need to be organised in independent, democratic organisations controlled by and accountable to themselves. These workers' organisations may need to have different characteristics from traditional trade unions, and different organising strategies – and they need to be democratically run by and accountable to the workers in the informal economy and in new forms of non-standard work who are their members, who elect their own spokespeople to represent them in collective bargaining and social dialogue.

Workers often find themselves having to organise outside of existing legal frameworks, and their struggles include demands for the establishment of a legal framework that would include them. However, during the years leading up to this, many other gains are won on the way, bringing about short-term improvements in their wages and working conditions. The short-term victories are also important for helping to strengthen their organisation and build alliances to fight for their rights to be properly represented in national (and eventually international) voice-regulation systems.

Workers worldwide in the informal economy and in new forms of non-standard work are normally not recognised as workers in terms of labour legislation. Some trade unions perpetuate the myth that 'they are not defined as workers in law – therefore we cannot organise them'. These trade unions feel that they can only organise workers who have been defined as workers in labour legislation. On the contrary, however, as has been amply demonstrated in many African countries, workers can organise themselves whether or not they have been recognised as workers in the labour legislation – as long as they recognise themselves as workers. When they organise, however, they need to organise not only for improvements in their working and living conditions, but also to shape new laws that will recognise and protect all workers in the informal economy and in new forms of work. They also need to develop laws to usher in an appropriate voice-regulation framework within which all workers in the informal economy and new forms of work can be represented through their own directly elected representatives.

Where governments make policies and legislation to deal with the challenges of promoting decent work in the informal economy and in new labour markets, there is invariably a strong organisation which has been putting pressure on government and policymakers. For example, the government of India had a lot of living examples and new initiatives (especially in the area of social security) that they were able to bring into the discussion on Decent Work in the Informal Economy at the 90th session of the International Labour Conference in June 2002. India has had the Self-Employed Women's Association (SEWA) since 1972, actively lobbying for policies and measures to address the needs of workers in the informal economy. For workers in the informal economy and in new forms of non-standard work in other countries, there is a clear message: do not wait for legislators and policymakers but get organised and start pressurising them to introduce appropriate laws and policies.

Struggles to win small victories also help organisations to strengthen their capacity to work together and develop their organisational and collective bargaining skills. Workers in the informal economy and in new forms of non-standard work need to be engaging in alliances with traditional formal sector workers and their trade unions. Learning how to effectively work together and run joint campaigns for small victories has proved to be an important step on the way to building towards the longer-term vision of full organisational and representational rights for all workers, including those in new forms of work and the informal economy – as was seen in the successful general strike action in Guinée Conakry early in 2007 for the removal of the Prime Minister and introduction of reforms in formal labour laws and informal trade regulation. The success of this action was generally attributable to the full participation of both formal and informal economy workers, and the leading role taken up by women street vendors.

REFERENCES

Horn, P. (2008). 'Realising decent work in Africa: A shared vision of growth and improved quality of life in a globalizing world'. Unpublished paper for presentation to the IIRA 5th African Regional Conference, Cape Town, 26–28 March 2008.

Horn, P. (2017). 'Nicaragua and the social solidarity economy', in *African Communist*, 194, 1st Quarter.

Soto, O.N. (2011). 'The solidarity social economy in proleterianised nations and the role of the self-employed proletariat in the transformation of the system', 4th edition. CTCP, Managua, Nicaragua: EDINTER (International Editions). Available at: https://streetnet.org.za/wp-content/uploads/2012/03/CTCPSSEmanifesto_en.pdf (Accessed 21 April 2023).

Standing, G. (1999). *Global Labour Flexibility: Seeking distributive justice*. London: Palgrave MacMillan and ILO.

NINE

SOCIAL AND ECONOMIC CHALLENGES FROM A LEFT PERSPECTIVE

Gunnett Kaaf

INTRODUCTION

The major social and economic challenges for the Left stem primarily from two phenomena of contemporary social reality. One is the deepening crisis of global capitalism and how it manifests on the local scene, both economically and politically. The second is the weakness of the Left and its failure to pose a meaningful challenge to a capitalism that is in deep crisis and to push for social transformation, particularly in the countries on the periphery of global capitalism in the Global South, like South Africa. This chapter attempts to analyse these two challenges separately and then concludes by analysing them jointly and examining the dynamic interplay they express.

THE CRISIS OF GLOBAL CAPITALISM THAT IS IMPLODING

The deepening crisis of global capitalism did not start in 2008 with the Great Recession that resulted from the financial meltdown but goes back further to the 1970s. Following the end of World War II, from 1945 up until 1975, global capitalism experienced the highest levels of growth and high rates of profit. This was a 'Golden Age' that was spurred by the reconstruction efforts following the destruction caused by war. Huge investments went into the reconstruction efforts and production to meet the vast demand for goods and services, spurred by a big expansion in industries such as automobile, appliance and military equipment manufacturing, and housing. As Paul Sweezy (1982) has pointed out, a great investment boom was triggered in all the essential industries of a modern capitalist society: steel, automobiles, energy, shipbuilding, heavy chemicals and many more. Capacity was built up rapidly in all the leading capitalist countries and in a few of the more advanced countries of the developing world, such as Mexico, Brazil, India and South Korea.

But contrary to the illusions of proponents of supply-side economics, even though investment can initially create demand, it relies on a growing demand for further growth. Although demand is essential for ongoing growth, it is objectively limited because capitalism's tendency is to supress increases in workers' wages, which are the main source of income for household consumption. Yet capitalism is predicated on endless capital accumulation, which presupposes never-ending growth. When post-war aggregate demand became exhausted in the 1970s, economies slipped into recession and a crisis of overproduction, with the result that firms had to cut back on production and investment. Thus, levels of investment and profits were reduced and growth in output declined and never went back to precrisis levels. The post-war boom had come to an end in the early 1970s, and the global capitalist economy was back in the stagnation of the 1930s.

This stagnation of the 1970s was never really resolved. Instead, capitalists resorted to globalisation and financialisation, while industrial production was outsourced to the Global South. The slump of the 1970s, as Samir Amin (1998) points out, was like all other downturns, manifested through surplus capital unable to find sufficiently profitable outlets in the expansion of productive capacity. Capitalist management of the stagnation was therefore aimed at providing alternative profitable outlets in the financial arena, and that very fact has made the preservation of capital values its main priority, even when this is detrimental to economic growth. This new hegemony of the capital markets has acted through a variety of means, notably floating exchange rates, high interest rates, the privatisation of formerly state-owned enterprises, huge deficits in the United States' balance of payments, and policies by international financial institutions forcing Third-World countries to put the servicing of their foreign debt above all other considerations. As usual, such policies confined the world economy to a stagnant, vicious cycle out of which there is no escape.

Amin (1998b) points out further that, for most of the 1980s and 1990s, this stubborn stagnation affected mainly the United States, Europe and Japan, and their Latin American, African and Middle Eastern dependencies, which were forced to undergo the measures adopted by the capital markets to manage the slump. East Asia (especially China), followed by Southeast Asia and, to some degree, India, have in contrast experienced a speeding up of their economic growth, and to that extent they escaped the impact of the slump.

When the democratic breakthrough of 1994 occurred in South Africa, it was against the background of the hegemony of financial capital in the neoliberal capitalist era, which came about in the 1970s and was consolidated in the 1980s and early 1990s. What was needed, therefore, were some audacious policies that would delink from the neoliberal management of the global economy and build a sovereign economy. This required a radical restructuring of the production system, away from the generalised monopolies in mining, energy, industry, agriculture and finance, towards building a state-led sovereign industrial production system with strong manufacturing sectors and an agricultural sector to secure the sovereignty of food production. Instead, the Growth, Employment and Redistribution policy (GEAR) of 1996 marked the official consolidation of neoliberal economic policy in post-apartheid South Africa. GEAR promoted neoliberal policy positions, such as a contractionary fiscal policy and a tight monetary policy, the liberalisation of financial and capital controls, privatisation, trade liberalisation, the liberalisation of the exchange rate, tax reductions for corporates and high-income earners, and labour market flexibility.

The discourses of mainstream economists, corporate boardrooms and chambers of political power still maintain a state of denial with regard to the vulnerabilities of the South African economy emanating from trade and financial liberalisation. Their talk stuck to more comforting themes: an economy full of verve, 'solid fundamentals', the maturity of the banking sector, and so on. They ignored the chronic balance of payment problems and periodic currency crashes, such as the 2001 nosedive that stripped 35 per cent off the value of the rand against the US dollar in a matter of weeks. Even now, more than 13 years after the 2009 recession, the South African economy has not reached prerecession growth levels and continues to show vulnerabilities. Hein Marais (2011) provides a powerful analysis of these vulnerabilities in his seminal book, *South Africa Pushed to the Limit: The political economy of change*.

As far as insertion into the global capitalist economy is concerned, the delinking position of Amin (1990) seems appropriate. This does not mean autarky but rather refusal to bow to the dominant logic of the world capitalist economy, which promotes the building of economies on the periphery of the global system through domination by foreign capital. The contradictions that come with opening up an economy on the periphery, like South Africa's, cannot be resolved through the kind of extreme polemical opposition between openness and closure to which supporters of neoliberalism usually try to reduce the debate.

To benefit from openness, one must know how to manage it. To speed up development so that it involves a degree of catching up, it is necessary to borrow the most advanced technologies and, in some cases, even to import whole plant – which has to be paid for out of exports so as to avoid balance of payment problems. What can actually be offered by world markets, at this stage of development, is obviously goods that enjoy a 'comparative advantage' by virtue of their high labour intensity. But those who opt for such exports have to understand that they are being exploited by the unequal exchange, even if they accept it for the time being because they lack any alternative.

RADICAL ECONOMISTS SAW TROUBLE COMING BUT WERE IGNORED

As an aside to the narrative concerning stagnation, it must be said that some economists were not caught unaware by the financial meltdown and the Great Recession of 2008/09, which was caused by the stagnation and financialisation of the global economy and was the deepest slump since the 1929 Great Depression. Unlike mainstream economists, who have no sense of reality in their economic analysis, many radical economists such as Paul Sweezy, Henry Madgof, Samir Amin, Dani Wadada Nabudere, Steve Keen and others foresaw the financial crisis and wrote about it continually, even though they were ignored by mainstream economics.

Despite the wake-up call of 2008, the crisis of global capitalism has not receded. Even mainstream economists such as Larry Summers and Paul Krugman admit that the global economy is experiencing stagnation, which is a prolonged period of low growth. Emmanuel Wallenstein (2011) argues that this crisis is going to deepen for the next 20 to 40 years, and that capitalism is not going to get out of it alive.[1] Capitalists are aware of this, he says, so they are not trying to save capitalism; instead, they are trying to build another social system that still has the class hierarchy and exploitation of capitalism, even though it will not be capitalism as we have it today.

Amin (2011) says we should not attempt to save capitalism, which is in a deep crisis, but should rather save humanity from a capitalism that is prone to crises. To paint the stark picture and tragic crisis of late capitalism, and the necessity of posing left alternatives, Amin invokes Rosa Luxemburg's retort: we are reaching the age of either 'barbarism or socialism'.

---

[1] It is interesting how Wallerstein, back in 2011, already called out the structural crisis of global capitalism and how it was playing out in 2020/21. He directly mentions pandemics as one of the big moments of the deepening global capitalist crisis. 'The primary characteristic of a structural crisis is chaos. Chaos is not a situation of totally random happenings. It is a situation of rapid and constant fluctuations in all the parameters of the historical system. This includes not only the world economy, the interstate system, and cultural-ideological currents, but also the availability of life resources, climatic conditions, and pandemics.'

THE WEAK LEFT CHALLENGE TO CAPITALISM

The dramatic dissolution of the Soviet Union in 1991 was the biggest event that shifted world political affairs unfavourably for the Left and bolstered the United States and its imperialist allies of Europe and Japan. The United States became more confident about imposing its unilateral hegemony over the globe, to the point that it invaded Iraq during the first Gulf War of 1991. Here, the liberal view that claims the United States acts for the good of the world is not supportable – it acts to pursue its imperialist interests that are shared with its junior partners, Europe and Japan. It is a unilateralist project of US hegemonism to promote a world in which the sovereign national interests of the United States should hold sway over all other principles defining what is regarded as legitimate political behaviour, and has led to systematic distrust of all international law.

The US ruling class is on an offensive to impose US leadership over its triad partners and over the globe, involving a conception of 'military control of the planet' worked out by whoever is the president of the United States at the time. The triad manages the economic dimension of capitalist globalisation through the institutions at its service (the World Trade Organization, the International Monetary Fund, the World Bank and the Organization for Economic Co-operation and Development). It also exercises the political–military dimension through NATO, whose responsibilities have been redefined so that it can, in effect, substitute itself for the United Nations.

In his book, *Beyond US Hegemony: Assessing prospects for a multipolar world*, Amin (2006) provides a splendid analysis in this regard. Even though the Soviet Union was a major countervailing force during the Cold War period from 1945 to 1990, the view that portrays this period as a purely bipolar world between the United States and its Western Allies, on the one hand, and the Soviet Union and its Eastern Europe bloc and other Third World allies, on the other, is not an accurate reading of history. There were four main players in world affairs: the United States, the Soviet Union, China (remember the Sino–Soviet split of the 1960s) and Bundung (initially made up of countries from Asia and Africa), which later became the Non-Aligned Movement (including Latin America, with Cuba playing an active role).

Political models of the old Left, comprising the communists and the social democracy and national liberation movements, have since become exhausted and failed. The social democracy model ran out of steam when the post-war boom came to an end, which is unsurprising given its origins. The social democracy movement, which started at the end of World War II, resulted from a class compromise between the working classes and the bourgeoisies of developed countries of the Global North. The bourgeoisies of the Global North, preoccupied with preventing a socialist revolution, made concessions that extended the social wage, guaranteed jobs and paid workers higher wages. Objectively, they could afford these concessions with workers because of the imperialist rent they extracted from dominating world trade and the global economy (Wallerstein, 1998; Harvey, 2006; Yates, 2016).

The national liberation project was unsuccessful mainly because these movements failed to effect meaningful social change in colonial societies once they came to power after the victories of anti-colonial struggles. Failure to transform and develop colonial economies in a way that builds sovereign industrial production systems and redistributes incomes and wealth, was behind the failure to deliver any meaningful social change.

In recent years, the South African Communist Party (SACP) has grown increasingly critical of the African National Congress (ANC) but remains committed to the Alliance (the SACP and COSATU) and has not forged an independent programme guided by the social demands of the workers and the poor. The question is: Why does the SACP lack courage? The answer to this should go beyond the trappings of patronage networks, wherein they rely on ANC deployment to prop up political careers.

The main reason the SACP lacks courage is that it has no political independence from the ANC. It also has no independent socialist programme worth the name. For most of post-1994, the party continued the sterile mode, inherited from the exile years, of operating within the ANC without a truly independent socialist programme. They have continued to pursue their struggle for socialism within the ANC's political framework of the National Democratic Revolution (NDR).

The Alliance has failed because it is based on the ANC's political strategy, the NDR, which is not radical, despite the radical-sounding rhetoric. The ANC itself is not radical, in that it is not anti-capitalist, and does not support socialism or any other form of egalitarian society. Rather, the ANC is trapped within the capitalist framework. Its social wage policies have been useful in alleviating extreme poverty, but have been held back by the neoliberal fiscal policy adopted by government. For instance, tax revenue was intentionally kept below 25 per cent of gross domestic product (GDP) during the boom years (1999–2007), through tax cuts for high-income earners and corporates. If these tax cuts had not been implemented, the country's tax revenue would have increased to 33 per cent, as Dick Forslund (2016) shows in his study. That would have made more funding available for government to spend on the poor.

The ANC has not always been quasi-capitalist. Historically, particularly during the struggle against apartheid, the ANC was revolutionary, in that it fully opposed apartheid and understood that apartheid could not be merely reformed – it had to be destroyed. There was a potential to be radical if the ANC had elaborated a post-apartheid South African society from an anti-capitalist stance, with a meaningful social transformation perspective beyond political conquest. The ANC did not do this, and thus, after 1994, it made a full bourgeois capitulation and embraced neoliberalism.

The other potential for radicalism on the part of the ANC stemmed from its popular social base of black workers and township and rural communities. The SACP, COSATU, the Youth League, ANC branches, students, civics and other mass formations could have insisted on a radical social transformation programme that has a strong economic redistribution element for workers and other poor strata from the black community. Sadly, that did not happen. Now the ANC has become fully bourgeois and, on top of the neoliberal policy embrace, increasingly corrupt.

If the SACP had had an independent political programme

for advancing socialism, it could have used it to meaningfully bargain within the Alliance. It could have insisted on radical policy measures for the whole Alliance. Instead, the SACP mainly sought accommodation within the Alliance. Even their criticism of the GEAR policy and neoliberalism did not come from the firm standpoint of a sound socialist programme, which is why they were easily co-opted after Polokwane into the conservative Zuma inner circle. They then defended the neoliberalism and rotten ways of the Zuma years. The SACP appears to be trapped in a quagmire from which only courage and bold measures will save it. If it does nothing, the party will almost certainly perish from the political scene, as the ANC continues to implode like an 'Empire of Chaos' (Amin, 1992).

Over the past 25 years, the old Left outside the ANC, including the Trotskyites of different formations, the Workers Organisation for Socialist Action, the Pan-Africanist Congress and the Azanian People's Organisation – has receded further and further into the peripheral margins of politics. The new left has been emerging in intellectual circles (universities and think-tanks), in NGOs, around anti-privatisation campaigns and in some grass-roots movements. For the most part, the new left has not been coherent, failing to connect the issues around which they mobilise, with the broad political questions of radical social transformation.

The Economic Freedom Fighters (EFF) is one of the new left forces. Ideologically, it combines some version of Marxism with Black Consciousness. The party has been successful in bringing radical questions, such as land and economic transformation, back to mainstream politics. It has also been effective in holding the ANC accountable, particularly in relation to the scandals linked to former president, Jacob Zuma (Nkandla and so on). Yet, the EFF is strategically limited and ideologically confused in terms of articulating a clear political vision and a political strategy that leverages its mass character. It is becoming an electoral machine with no mass activities in communities. The fact that the EFF is built largely around the character of Julius Malema has positive and negative dimensions, in that it inhibits the party from growing beyond 'Juju's' charisma.

THE WAY FORWARD: ON THE POLITICAL ECONOMY

The implosion of capitalism is leading to the disintegration and weakening of the liberal establishment in most of the West. In the absence of left alternatives, the right is on the rise, from the more extreme and dangerous (for example, former US President Donald Trump) to the perhaps less dangerous but dogmatic supporters of neoliberalism (for example, French President Emmanuel Macron). The Left has made headway in Spain, with the Podemos party, which was built around an anti-austerity campaign, winning 22 per cent of the vote in the 2016 elections, only two years after it was formed. In Greece, the Syriza party initially won in January 2015, but then capitulated on the austerity of the Troika, against which they had been campaigning fiercely.

In Latin America, leftist parties that initially won elections in the early 2000s were removed from power in the middle of that decade through elections and other means of public pressure. Despite the weaknesses of these parties, the big business that is linked to the United States is taking advantage of the economic slump and is actively involved in their removal. The major weakness of these parties seems to have been the failure to transform their economies and create new sovereign productive industries; instead, they redistributed incomes accruing from the boom in the commodities markets, through government transfers to households and higher minimum wages. A second wave of the electoral ascendency of left parties is underway in the Latin America, with Lula da Silva back as the elected president of Brazil.

If the ANC continues to deteriorate as a viable, credible political organisation and there are no left alternatives, and given the weak parliamentary opposition, South Africa may easily slip into a tragic impasse as a country.

The way forward for the Left lies in breaking away from the futile and failed political models of the old Left. Even if it still moves from the basic premises of Marxism, as formulated in the Second and Third Internationals, the Left must go much further. It must be creative and imaginative enough to formulate a social vision and a political strategy that expresses the social demands of popular classes, based on the values of emancipation, solidarity and equality.

The Left's political strategy must respond adequately to the contemporary challenges of a crisis-ridden capitalism. Instead of being trapped in the sterile concept of historical Marxism–Leninism of an abstract class struggle between the proletariat and the bourgeoisie, the Left must elaborate on the strategies of mobilising and expressing the social demands of the popular classes. The Left must present tangible strategies that respond to the worsening levels of poverty and inequality, particularly in South Africa as a country on the periphery. We urgently need to build a sovereign industrial production system that has strong manufacturing sectors, which can produce goods that compete in global markets, without relying on captured markets – as in the case of commodities or trade deals with unequal power relations, such as the African Growth and Opportunity Act (AGOA) enacted by the United States in 2000 to give eligible sub-Saharan countries duty-free access to US markets.

Such a sovereign production system must also integrate an agricultural sector that secures food sovereignty by promoting smallholder and subsistence farming for both rural and township communities. Too much reliance on big agribusiness, which is integrated into global capitalism and subject to market fluctuations, has led to increasing levels of hunger and food insecurity. This also means abandoning the current conservative monetary and fiscal policies that are worsening the economic crisis. A progressive monetary policy could support a sovereign industrial policy by repositioning the Public Investment Corporation (which manages the biggest financial asset made up of workers' pensions) and by creating state banks to avail capital for the sovereign industrialisation project, and by imposing capital controls so as to curb capital flights that result from abandoning the futile inflation targeting monetary approach. With regard to fiscal policy, apart from also directly funding the sovereign industrial effort, there should be fiscal expansion – instead of the current fiscal austerity – for investment in health services, education, housing, public transport and infrastructure. Public investment should be undertaken to offset the persistent decline in private investment and employment to create public sector jobs.

Pursuing these ideas cannot occur without audacious measures aimed at radically restructuring the production system away from the dominant monopolies in mining, energy, industry, agriculture and finance. The role of the state in reordering the production system and in managing the aggregate demand is going to be very decisive in this regard. This also means pursuing a redistribution of wealth and income in favour of the lower strata of the black communities. We need to push for decent wages and ensure that they grow in parallel with the productivity of social labour. Building the movement towards socialism should entail unity in diversity and a strong component of autonomous mass movements. We must abandon the notion of vanguardism as a central nexus to building a socialist movement, and instead build a popular socialist movement that embraces notions of both representative and participatory democracy in a mutually reinforcing way. The participatory aspect of democracy should be thought of as the more decisive.

A WAY FORWARD ON THE MOVEMENT BUILDING STRATEGY: POPULAR MOVEMENTS TOWARDS SOCIALISM

Communist parties no longer offer a viable model for effective left parties and movements to challenge capitalism and pose revolutionary advances in today's world. Instead, I propose that we should build new movements, which should be popular movements towards socialism. These should allow for an open-ended approach on how to build socialism from below, instead of a vanguardist approach that has it 'all figured out' through the Marxist–Leninist template.

I use the concept of 'the Left' to refer to political forces that adopt an anti-capitalist dimension in their pursuit of social transformation to address the plight of the popular classes, who make up the majority. These popular classes are largely black, reflecting the racist past of our country, the history of colonialisation and apartheid, and how it adds to the post-1994 social crisis of governance and social transformation failures.

The anti-capitalist dimensions of the South African left fall into two broad categories. First, there are those from the various communist and socialist traditions who frame their visions and strategies around resolving the basic contradiction of capitalism between labour and capital, and going beyond capitalism towards socialism. Second, there are those who fight for the immediate social demands of popular classes without going too far into the future. While their social transformation measures do not seek to replace capitalism outright, as in the case of communists, they still challenge the foundations of South Africa's capitalism, which has shaped the economy and social relations since the mining industrial revolution of the late 19th century. Activists and organisations that are part of this second category include liberation movements, feminists, environmental justice activists, and those struggling for radical reforms in community development in urban township and rural areas, and for public and basic services such as housing, electricity, transport, youth development, health care and education.

There is a need to rethink the vision and strategy of the Left for anti-capitalist struggles and for building socialism. The starting point is to give up the old position of communist parties, which is to conquer state power first and then build socialism. Instead, social and political conditions that allow for an advance toward socialism should be fostered. Hence, as in Latin America, we need to build 'popular movements toward socialism'. This entails abandoning an approach to building socialism derived from the Soviet experience, which focused on nationalisation and state planning. In contrast, 'popular movements toward socialism' leave open the question of the methods to be used in socialising the modern economy and the ongoing democratisation of society.

As Marxists, we only have to start with Marx – we do not necessarily have to end with him, because although he was a genius, he did not develop a template that we should simply apply eternally. Instead, Marx's opus remains open ended and incomplete, which is why we have to advance it and develop it further in light of the changing historical and social reality.

Changes in contemporary capitalism require that we update our definitions and analyses of social classes, class struggles, political parties, social movements and the ideological forms in which they express their modes of action in the radical social transformation of society amidst the deepening crisis. The Left will succeed if it meets this challenge and invents new approaches to organising effective struggles that lead to victories of the popular classes. We need to lay bare the reality of neoliberal capitalism in South Africa and its integration in the global economy. Here I borrow from Samir Amin again (2013): 'We need to encourage diverse lines of descent in the formation and advancement of socialist thought and action, unity and diversity of the left forces.'

There is a need to rethink and renew trade union organisation in light of the changes brought about by the neoliberal restructuring of the workplace and the capitalist economic crisis, particularly its impact on the Global South with its already underdeveloped industrial bases. Poverty is worsened by the closure of factories and industries, which leads to massive unemployment. The drastic decline of trade unions in the post-1994 period can be partly explained by their failure to adapt to these changes.

Worsening unemployment and poverty emphasise the need to connect deeper factory struggles with community struggles for survival, livelihood and social change driven from within the townships. The demand for a basic income grant (BIG) of R1 400 – as per the upper-bound poverty line determined by Statistics South Africa (StatsSA) – should feature prominently in these struggles. Alongside the demand for BIG, should be other key demands that challenge the neoliberal capitalism in South Africa. These demands should include (1) public employment schemes; (2) quality public services such as health, education, housing and transport; (3) an end to fiscal (budget cuts of public sector workers and public services) and monetary (inflation targeting) austerity; (4) fixing our municipalities; and (5) addressing the Eskom energy crisis in an ecologically sustainable way that keeps Eskom under public ownership instead of the looming privatisation. This type of discussion on movement building amidst the deepening capitalist crisis – made worse by the COVID-19 slump – is exemplified by the 'Movement building in the shadow of COVID-19' paper by the COVID-19 Working Class Campaign (2020), which is made up of grass-roots organisations and NGOs.

The Left's way forward out of the current political crisis is not to form a workers' party or a vanguard party with a socialistic manifesto to contest elections in the hope of winning parliamentary seats. Any preoccupation with a centralised party of the left will be a serious distraction. Rather, there is much to learn from Prabhat Patnaik's (2009) argument that the old model of centralised communist parties has to be abandoned:

> The idea of a centralised party running an economy and guiding society in the interest of a class, which in the process gets depoliticised, has to be abandoned. It is not enough to say 'democracy'; we need an activation of the people, which has to be institutionalised. Thus, from this point of view, when we think of socialism today, we have to think in terms of structure, parties and strategy, all of which really empower people to decide their own destiny (Patnaik, 2009: 101).

Instead, the Left should work with the popular classes to build strong grass-roots and sector movements to fight for the immediate social demands of these classes on health, education, housing, food, women, youth, decent jobs, sports, arts, culture and so on. While the struggles should be about immediate social demands, they must have a clear anti-capitalist outlook and seek to go beyond the limits of the current capitalist society. They must express a yearning for a better society that is not capitalist. The struggles and mass movements must be connected through a coherent vision and political efforts to build an anti-capitalist and anti-neoliberal historic bloc in South Africa. These should also connect with other struggles of popular classes in Africa and the wider world.

This is not to lose sight of political power that results from elections, but rather to build popular power on the ground, on the base of which genuine left political alternatives should be advanced. Rebuilding a new left alternative political pole should be based on mass struggles and the vision of democratic eco-socialism. The mass political party or parties that come out of such efforts should be non-vanguardist, open ended and long term, and linked to mass movements without controlling them. A left electoral victory based authentically on a radical programme is possible only after the victory of popular struggles, not before.

Struggles for reforms in the here and now to ameliorate people's conditions are going to be essential in building the long-term momentum for a genuine left renewal. These struggles should be based on the Constitution and other democratic rights and demands, including challenging the power and the regulation of the private sector.

Struggles for alternatives and transformation will be essential in grounding the Left and mass movements in an anti-capitalist and anti-neoliberal outlook. These struggles should address matters concerning development in townships and rural areas, including issues such as seed banks; a solidarity economy; and public goods and services such as education, health, transport, housing, a social wage and renewables. Workers struggles in the workplace, in new inventive ways, are also included.

Popular struggles to characterise the left renewal must be made up of both protest and developmental work. Community development activities could cover art, culture, the media (including magazines), literature, cultural movements, people's heritage and knowledge production from below (including research, studies and publications of all types). These efforts should seek to build a popular movement for meaningful social transformation based on a coherent anti-capitalist, anti-neoliberal vision. However, none of this is possible without sustained activist development and political education to build a critical mass of conscious, confident, capable and effective activists who can carry out the tasks at hand.

The forms of activity and organisation proposed here, predicated on popular struggles and popular inventiveness, cannot be decreed in advance through a sanctified doctrine. Revolutionary advances are possible on the basis of developing a real and new people's power to drive away the power of political elites and monopoly capital, which are responsible for protecting and reproducing the social crisis of post-1994 South Africa. Marx did not expound any theory of 'the great day of revolution and definitive solutions'; on the contrary, he insisted on an open-minded approach, believing that a revolution is a long transition marked by a conflict between social powers – the former powers in decline and the new ones on the rise. Let the power and organisation of the popular classes rise for a meaningful left renewal in South Africa.

REFERENCES

Africa Growth and Opportunities Act. (2000). Public Law 106, 200th Congress of the United States of America.

Amin, S. (2013). *The Implosion of Contemporary Capitalism.* New York: Monthly Review Press.

Amin, S. (2011). *Ending the Crisis of Capitalism or Ending Capitalism.* Cape Town: Pambazuka Press.

Amin, S. (2006). *Beyond US Hegemony: Assessing the prospects for a multipolar world.* London: Zed Books.

Amin, S. (1998). *Spectres of Capitalism: A critique of current intellectual fashions.* New York: Monthly Review Press.

Amin, S. (1992). *Empire of Chaos.* New York: Monthly Review Press.

Amin, S. (1990). *Delinking: Towards a polycentric world.* London: Zed Books.

COVID-19 Working Class Campaign, *Movement building in the shadow of COVID19.* Available at: https://karibu.org.za/movement-building-in-the-shadow- of-covid19/ (Accessed 21 April 2023).

Forslund, D. (2016). *Personal Income Taxation and the Struggle against Inequality and Poverty: Tax policy and personal income in South Africa since 1994.* Cape Town: Alternative Information and Development Centre (AIDC).

Harvey, D. (2006). *The Limits to Capital.* London: Verso Books.

Marais, H. (2011). *South Africa Pushed to the Limit: The political economy of change.* Cape Town: University of Cape Town Press.

Patnaik, P. (2009). 'Chapter 6: Interview Prabhat Patnaik, India,' in V. Satgar and L. Zita (eds). *New Frontiers for Socialism in the 21st Century: Conversations on a global journey.* Johannesburg, COPAC: 101.

Sweezey, P.M. (1982). 'Why stagnation?' in H. Magdoff and P.M. Sweezy. *Economic History as it Happened, Volume IV, Stagnation and the financial explosion*. New York: Monthly Review Press.

Wallerstein, I. (2011). 'Structural crisis in the world-system: Where do we go from here?' *Monthly Review*, 62(10) March: 31. DOI:10.14452/MR-062-10-2011-03_2

Wallerstein, I. (1998). *Utopistics: Or historical choices of the twenty-first century*. New York: The New Press.

Yates, M.D. (2016). *The Great Inequality*. New York: Routledge.

TEN

AFTER REVISIONIST MARXISM: REANIMATING THE CRITIQUE OF CAPITALISM IN SOUTH AFRICA[1]

Bernard Dubbeld

INTRODUCTION

Contemporary leftism has come to mean opposing inequality and struggling against it, whenever it might be found to occur. This might involve the diagnosis of what produces inequality or the sustained expression of disagreement aimed at broadening political conversations and recognising new forms of inequality.[2] The intersecting imperatives of diagnosing inequality and the expression of disagreement have enabled the possibility of identifying new inequalities and making them part of shared struggles to overcome

---
1 The first version of this paper was presented at the Mzala Nxumalo Future of the Left conference in Durban in 2017, and subsequently revised, presented again, revised and published in *Transformation*, 100. It has been slightly revised and is republished with the permission of *Transformation*.
2 This would allow all kinds of inequalities to become the subject of activism. The political standpoint of disagreement as the basis of rendering visible inequalities, is articulated most clearly by Jacques Ranciere (1999).

them. Whether we talk of inequalities faced by black and other indigenous groups that many in former colonies have connected to racism and xenophobia in the Global North, or various kinds of public and private inequalities suffered by women in different locations, or the inequalities suffered by those identifying with non-normative sexual and gender subjectivities, all inequalities can be the basis of struggle. Despite the recent turn to the right politically in the Global North, this leftism has yielded significant successes in terms of a more general recognition of inequalities, especially at the level of the state, and in an emerging global liberal consensus that forbids discrimination on the basis of race, gender and sexual orientation. One strategy of the Left today would see it defending the gains that have been made, and continuing the work of diagnosing inequalities and disagreeing with political orders that silence these inequalities.

Although there is a significant history of scholarship and political activism in South Africa engaging Marxism, in scholarly circles this work has been dismissed over the last two decades for offering 'grand narratives' that fail to recognise local accounts and for prioritising class over race and gender.[3] While some of the languages of Leninism persist in ruling ANC circles, and there is a growing recognition, both inside and outside the party, that formal political and legal equality has not translated into economic equality, it is not clear that those advocating an explicitly Marxist politics have any answers. Once a bastion of political support for the ruling party, the trade union federation has fragmented and it is less clear that a politics based on the working-class struggle has much traction in shaping the political direction of the country.

---

3 Established leftist thinkers and analysts, from Steven Friedman and Colin Bundy to Bill Freund and Andrew Nash, acknowledged as early as 1986 that the influence of Marxism was on the wane (Freund, 1986: 118; Bundy, 1991: 65). By 1999, Nash blamed political urgency of transition and the Soviet character of the Communist Party for undermining a robust debate about Marxism in South Africa (Nash, 1999: 77–78), with Friedman concluding that mainstream debate in the country consigned Marxist theorisation to oblivion (Friedman, 2015: 283). Perhaps ironically, debates on racial capitalism emanating predominately from the academy in the United States continue to acknowledge a certain South African revisionist Marxist tradition of the 1970s, alongside Du Bois, Robinson and others as a starting point (Fraser, 2019; Ralph and Singhal, 2019; White, 2020; Go, 2021).

All at once, international leftist politics, and South African scholarship and left politics seem to have moved away from Marxist approaches. And yet, what all of these approaches appear to neglect is capitalism and its effects on social life, including how some of its recent transformations may have reshaped society. Instead, the focus has largely become about the power and its formations – often expressed in gendered or racial terms, but also in relation to heterosexuality, generation and class. While necessary to engage such formations, such a focus might be complemented by a reframed Marxian reading of capital, especially insofar as such a reading seeks to understand the source of inequality and social domination as immanent to the operation on capital – understood as a form of value production that structures society – rather than perpetuated by one group over another. This is what I hope to show in this chapter.

To do this, it is necessary to explain some of the important criticisms of Marxist thought in South African studies and the way these sought to challenge how Marxism itself had become limited. It is also necessary to traverse some theoretical terrain to reread Marx in a manner that I suggest is useful for understanding the present. Indeed, I offer Moishe Postone's reading as a way to think Marx in the post-Fordist present, notably by recognising the abolition of labour as an important condition in the struggle against capitalism. Diverging from a Marxism that seeks to champion workers against exploitative capitalists, this reading seeks to recognise capitalism as a formation in the present that mediates all in society. It shifts attention from those who focus on domination and resistance as a matter of political will, and from identity-inspired responses to social domination to the mediation of social, cultural and political life by value.

MARXISM AND THE STUDY OF SOUTH AFRICA AT THE MOMENT OF THE ANTI-APARTHEID STRUGGLE

The early 1970s marked a moment in the growth of Marxist scholarship of South Africa across the social sciences: political theory, history, economics, sociology and anthropology all felt the influence of Marxism by the end of that decade. In Britain, political exiles from apartheid connected to scholars, especially at the universities of Sussex and Essex and SOAS, led to seminar papers, articles, dissertations and monographs broadly engaging Marxism. In South Africa, renewed worker struggles and political protest emerged together with Marxism and Black Consciousness movements, even when texts by Marx were banned by the government. The connection between capitalism and the racist state, the transition to capitalism in agriculture, and worker consciousness were energetically theorised and studied empirically. For a time, South Africa became the place from which to rethink the terms of Marxism, even in parts of the metropole, with journals such as *Economy and Society*, *Capital and Class*, *Socialist Register* and *New Left Review* featuring theoretical engagements with South Africa (Morris, 1988: 60).

This scholarly energy around Marxist thought differed explicitly from the exiled South African Communist Party (SACP) position. Receiving aid primarily from the Eastern Bloc, and in alliance with the African National Congress (ANC), in 1962 the SACP developed a theory of 'colonialism of a special type'. This theory sought to address racial domination and proposed a two-stage theory of revolution, where anti-apartheid struggle would lead to a 'national democracy' that would be followed by a second stage of socialist revolution. The SACP thus made the overcoming of racist state domination a primary political goal but it did not specify its position on the probable post-apartheid emergence of a black elite or middle classes who might become invested in the continuation of capitalism, let alone what might spark the second stage of revolution. Indeed, a common refrain in relation to the contemporary Communist Party is to ask what happened to the second stage of revolution!

The 1970s revisionist Marxist scholarship addressed itself to these problems of relating racial inequality to class difference and the particular form of capitalist profitability in South Africa. Most explicitly, it targeted a form of white liberalism that regarded capitalist interests as innocent of apartheid government racism and held that white and black South Africans inhabited two different economies, with the implication that the latter could be modernised with the appropriate development interventions. In 1972, Harold

Wolpe theorised the articulation of these two economies in an early issue of *Economy and Society*. He argued that by confining black South Africa to rural subsistence agriculture, white capitalists profited from the racial regulation of black migrant workers because it allowed them to pay black workers less than the costs of the social reproduction of black households, as women and children were covered by the rural subsistence economy. Government regulation of the labour market did not protect workers: instead, it gave white capitalists a steady supply of workers to whom it could pay the lowest possible wages. In effect, the rural subsistence economy – in tribal or quasi-feudal form – subsidised the urban capitalist economy. Even as the rural subsistence economy declined, as it did from the 1940s, capitalist profitability was maintained by the increasingly repressive apartheid regime. By the 1970s, with the migrant labour system increasingly expensive to police, Wolpe noticed the relocation of some capitalist enterprise to 'border industries' – spaces alongside bantustans where the apartheid state offered tax incentives to continue capitalism's reliance on cheap black labour power.

Wolpe's work was followed by several other theoretical accounts. Legassick (1995[1972]) questioned the equation of South African racism and Afrikaners by considering the relation between the Cape Liberal Tradition and segregation. Morris (1976) drew on Lenin to suggest a Prussian path to the transition to capitalism in South African agriculture, arguing that the apartheid state settled the class struggle between white farmers and black tenants, destroying the autonomy of the latter as independent producers. Bundy (1979) showed how an independent class of African peasants emerged in the Eastern Cape during the 19th century, only to be systematically deprived of land and robbed of the possibilities of profitable agriculture. Johnstone (1978) theorised how the control of living and working conditions of black miners in Johannesburg was a condition for immense mine-owner profitability. Hemson (1976) and Webster (1985) showed how working-class consciousness grew among African urban workers and how they were capable of challenging their white employers and racist laws. O'Meara (1983) showed how Afrikaner capitalists developed in the 1920s and 1930s and their role in establishing and entrenching apartheid. And Guy (1990) offered a class analysis of precolonial Zulu households, showing how its economic basis involved patriarchs exploiting the labour power of women.

Together, this work gained the appellation 'Marxist revisionism', and it became a prominent force in the South African academy in the late 1970s and the 1980s. While some of the revisionists were connected to grassroots worker organisatiosn and emerging trade unions, their relationship with the Communist Party in exile was limited by mutual suspicions: the SACP was considered Stalinist by some revisionists, while the revisionists in turn were regarded as armchair intellectuals, whose limited political involvement was seen as external to the working class.[4] Theoretically the SACP was regarded as failing to convincingly establish the relationship between race and class and being too allied to nationalism, whereas the revisionists were viewed as ignoring the national question and even making racism secondary to the class struggle. Such suspicion was expressed mostly directly by the suspension from the ANC of four revisionists, including Martin Legassick and David Hemson for 'factionalism' – a charge that stemmed from their involvement in a group called the Marxist Workers Tendency, which explicitly aimed to advocate for socialism and worker struggle within the ANC.

These revisionists certainly engaged 'Western Marxist' contemporaries, left-wing scholars at universities in the Global North, including Perry Anderson, Brenner, Hindness and Hirst, Laclau, Ralph Miliband, Althusser, Polantzas, Laclau and Arrighi. Yet if some of these debates have been forgotten over four decades, arguably Legassick and Hemson's 1976 pamphlet 'Foreign investment and the reproduction of racial capitalism' has had the most contemporary resonance. The pamphlet repeats the shared revisionist position that capitalism in South Africa, through racial exploitation and the rendering of blacks as a working class, has put them in a far more oppressed and subordinate position than the white working classes elsewhere. It then goes on to argue that international capitalist investments in business, and its promise to reform apartheid in early 1970s, needs to be understood within

---

[4] The accusation of Stalinists gained more credence with the expulsion of four prominent Marxists from the ANC-in-exile in 1980.

a longer history of international investment and colonialisation in South Africa; hence racial capitalism was not a product of white Afrikaner domestic capital but rather intimately tied to colonialism. Low wages to African workers – stagnant for most of the century – had benefitted international capitalists, including during the 1960s when South Africa proclaimed independence from the Commonwealth. Thus, the promise of the 1970s reform led by international capitalist firms had to be viewed extremely sceptically: it was they who profited all along from racial capitalism, and promises to increase wages and welcome worker representation had to be seen as a more sophisticated 'ideological defence' of the perpetuation of racial capitalism.

This discussion of racial capitalism was picked up in the early 1980s by Stuart Hall in the United Kingdom and Cedric Robinson in the United States, and has become a concept widely discussed over the last decade (see, for example, Ralph and Singhal, 2019; White, 2020). Apart from this very important concept, a more general point about the revisionists is important. They attempted to offer an analytical framework that could encompass different aspects of experience and explain their interconnection in a manner that related capitalism to politics and to domestic life. While this promise of a more totalising account did prove attractive to some, it was one that was slowly picked apart during the 1980s and 1990s by pointing to the limits of various of its claims, as the next section will show.

THE DECLINING INFLUENCE OF MARXISM IN THE ACADEMY

If Marxism established itself in the academy by disputing liberal readings of racism, asserting the necessity of recognising the capitalist profit from racism, and attempting to show the articulation of different modes of production and forms of existence, its decline in the 1990s and 2000s was the effect of a changing society, both at the level of scholarly concepts and of political economy.

At the conceptual level, four distinct challenges to the revisionist brand of Marxism emerged in the South African academy, even if these are not altogether discrete positions epistemologically. The first of these, which might retrospectively be regarded as a 'black radical' response, is captured in Archie Mafeje's[5] review of a collection of essays edited by Wolpe (1980) entitled *The Articulation of Modes of Production*. Engaging the work of Wolpe and Morris in particular, Mafeje developed a critique that expresses many commonly held concerns.

Mafeje (1981: 134) argued that there was a limit to the need for cheap labour by capitalists, and, therefore, the shift that Wolpe charts between the period of segregation and apartheid was not merely a matter of the African reserves (later called bantustans) becoming agriculturally unviable as their population grew, leading to their inability to subsidise the cheap wages of workers. Instead, the need for cheap labour itself diminished, and a demand for differently skilled African labour power emerged, together with a growing number of unemployable Africans (from the perspective of South African capitalists).

Mafeje also argued that the particular conditions of South Africa needed to be given more prominence than Wolpe and Morris' theories offered. African ownership of cattle could not be adequately understood as marking a precapitalist or feudal mode of production (Mafeje, 1981: 129); instead, it was the basis of social prestige and value for many Africans and often purchased with cash wages. This led Mafeje to conclude that reading economic data alone was not enough to understand South African capitalism; it was necessary to understand the forms of mediation of subjects and objects *by* capital, as well as their mediation *of* capital, which together produce the form of local capitalism (Mafeje, 1981: 137). In Mafeje's own terms, a Marxism that relied primarily on 'nomothetic enquiry' at the expense of 'idiographic enquiry' ended up failing to understand the role that particular cultural and social forms played in enabling

---

5   Mafeje is not the only black radical thinker to engage Marxism during the 1980s but the directness of his critique of revisionists makes his essay a useful illustration. Nyoka's intellectual history of Mafeje suggests that Marxism was a method for him through which to analyse African society, albeit with the proviso that he understood that 'the problematic that it [Marxism] sets itself was mainly Europe'; and that 'while Marxism has "universalistic pretentions", it is in fact a product of European history at a particular juncture' (Nyoka, 2017: 115, 311).

capitalism in any given society.[6]

Instead, Mafeje proposes that we need a theory of mediation, in which culture and capital might be understood as shaping each other. Approaching capitalism as a singular structural force that proceeds identically everywhere is Eurocentric as it is unable to account for variations in cultural forms from the European forms taken for granted by Marx's analysis. In making this argument, Mafeje finds a kind of abstraction to be the problem with revisionist Marxism, complaining that in both Wolpe's and Morris's work, 'capital or capitalism is often talked of as a noun agent with an inexorable logic such as an insatiable quest for unlimited supplies of labour and raw materials, or as being driven to gobbling up all antecedent modes of production so as to realise itself universally' (Mafeje, 1981: 134).

Another influential objection came from feminism, well captured by Bozzoli's 1983 essay.[7] Her article confronted the revisionist position directly, taking Wolpe to task for naturalising the subordination of women, and for subsuming this subordination within both pre-capitalist and capitalist society without explaining it adequately (Bozzoli, 1983: 143–45). She argued that structural analyses do not account for the variation of patriarchal forms in South African life, proposing instead that analyses should take as its starting point domestic struggle, and consider the different contexts in which capitalism has interacted with a range of patriarchies, without assuming that those patriarchies were subordinated to capitalism. Indeed, even if one assumes proletarianisation as a central way to understand capitalist accumulation in southern Africa, Bozzoli draws attention to how various kin formations – expressing differing patriarchies – interact and shape how proletarianisation happens and mediates the experience of capitalism.

---

6 Both of these criticisms that, on the one hand, Wolpe and Morris misunderstood some of the dynamics of capital accumulation in South Africa and, on the other, they disregarded how particular social-cultural forms shaped the experience and trajectory of capital in South Africa, are part of the broader charge Mafeje levels against revisionist Marxists. That is, that their structural accounts are unable to account for either changing circumstances within the country or with differentiation and variation that can only be established with richer empirical analysis.

7 Bozzoli's article has approximately nine times as many citations as Mafeje's.

Bozzoli correctly challenges revisionist Marxists for attempting to subsume gender relations to those of class – that is, for assuming the priority of class identity – as well as for failing to recognise the mobility and urban presence of black women in particular, throughout much of apartheid. But while she explicitly calls for a general historical theory that considers the place of gender with the forms of race and class oppression theorised by the revisionists (Bozzoli, 1983: 171), her insistence on the importance of understanding the workings of a range of different patriarchies and on domestic struggles, implicitly pushed research towards accounts of particular local contexts rather than towards theorising more generally.[8]

This position is explicitly nurtured by the third conceptual challenge to Marxist revisionism, from a version of social history that became especially prominent in South African social sciences from the mid-1980s onwards. These social historians took inspiration from E.P. Thompson's *Making of the English Working Class* to rescue 'the poor stockinged, the "obsolete" hand-loom weaver, and the "utopian" artisan ... from the enormous condescension of posterity' (Thompson, 1963: 12), as well as from US historians such as Vito Genovese and Carolyn Montgomery. From the early 1980s, studying popular and working-class lives drew historians and sociologists of South Africa to urban peripheries, small towns and into the countryside, requiring them to learn African languages and to embrace a range of non-archival sources (Breckenridge, 2004; Hyslop; 2016). Many of these scholars may have been inspired by an interest in class consciousness, but increasingly argued that the revisionists did not have sufficient empirical evidence to sustain their theoretical categories. While the successes of these studies of informal economies, domesticity and leisure changed the academy through providing elegant descriptions of 20th century South African life, today local social historians are generally impatient with any kind of theory, and where E.P. Thompson is read, it is for his justification of the study of the experience and agency of ordinary people, not for his cultural Marxism (Delius, 2017). In some ways,

---

8   This echoes Mafeje's caution about abstraction and his insistence on the importance of idiographic enquiry to counter Eurocentric categories.

social historians have embraced a position similar to that demanded by Mafeje, and over the last two decades, much scholarly interest has turned to reconstructing the writings and social lives of previously neglected African intellectuals, to better capture epistemologies and even ontologies of black life.

The fourth major challenge to Marxist revisionism in the study of South Africa was by an amalgam of post-structural and postcolonial theory across the social sciences. Like Bozzoli's version of feminism, and unlike the social historians, post-structuralists disputed the adequacy of the theoretical terms used to study South Africa, rather than rejecting the impulse to theorise. This group of scholars privileged Foucauldian readings of subjectivity and power/knowledge. They foregrounded institutional domination and disputed Marxist claims to totality and teleology in favour of more fragmented and contingent performances of history (Witz, 2004; Lalu, 2009). Some studies made violence into an analytical object and rejected Marxist attempts to explain violence in relation to the market or class (Crais, 2002). While seldom disputing that capitalism had some influence on social life, these scholars did not regard capital as generative of domination, turning the focus to the state and other institutions (Robinson, 1996).

Although these challenges have not led to the total erasure of Marxism in South Africa, they have made the weaknesses of Marxist revisionism clear, essentially confining Marx to either a 'classical' role – a figure relevant only to intellectual history – or, at most, as relevant only to a field of economic history or radical political economy. Despite the complexities of some of the revisionist analyses, Marx is received in contemporary South African scholarship as insisting on class domination as the primary relation (subsuming gender, race, culture and sexuality into class). This 'Marxism' grasps neither historically variable racist regimes nor contemporary state failures in their own terms, offering class explanation as the answer, no matter the distance of such explanations. In addition, concepts associated with Marxism, including 'grand narratives', 'teleology', 'determination', 'necessity' and even 'structure' are largely regarded as inadequate, with contingency, local histories, African experience and agency affirmed as alternatives. In radical political economic circles, Marx continues to be engaged to explain the shape of the contemporary South African economy and to assess the growth of finance capital (Fine and Rustomjee, 1996; Bond, 2001; Marais, 2011). But at most, these analyses are held by many to be partial, proper to the domain of political economy but of limited salience for the contemporary social analysis of South Africa.

CHANGING SOCIAL AND POLITICAL CONDITIONS

In addition to the inadequacies of Marxist revisionism on intellectual grounds, concrete social transformations in South Africa since the late 1980s have shaped thought in decisive ways. This is perhaps most clearly seen in the transformations of capitalism and labour. If it was plausible during the most productive period of revisionist analyses – the 1970s and early 1980s – to recognise the existence of a small industrial working class in South Africa, accompanied by pressures on urbanisation that many believed would lead to proletarianisation, that working class has changed quite dramatically over the last 30 years. Industries employing the greatest numbers of workers, in mining, manufacturing and agriculture, have shed or casualised workers, either becoming more mechanised or – as in the case of textiles – declining dramatically. Public sector employment, along with tourism, retail and financial services have grown significantly but much of this employment is flexible and has not produced anything resembling a stable, urban working class. Indeed, the trade unions that during the 1980s successfully mobilised many thousands of workers against apartheid have become smaller and more fragmented, and are largely unable to engage the outsourcing and casualisation of labour or forge solidarity across professional occupations. If the working class is regarded as central to Marxism, the fragmentation of such a class, materially and politically, makes the theory less plausible.⁹

Since the end of apartheid, there has also been considerable public attention paid to the Constitution and the law, and rights more generally, as mechanisms through which injustice might be successfully fought. The commitment to political equality is enshrined in the Constitution, and even if the law is limited to the extent that it might be able to broker large-scale social transformation, the legal contestation of the denial of rights and, indeed, the claiming of rights that may previously have been obscured, has become a mode of leftist politics. This extends from the early recognition of same-sex marriage and the right to claim anti-retroviral drugs from the state, to contestations over the right to housing for the poor (including the location of that housing) and the use of the law to police discrimination, wherever it may occur and in whatever form (Comaroff and Comaroff, 2006; Davis and Le Roux, 2019). Of course, the law has not only been used by those with leftist political inclinations – it has also become a space in which a politics that is committed to fighting a range of inequalities can be actualised. This social transformation of politics away from aspirations to overthrow the state and capital, and towards the fighting of local inequalities appears to find a counterpart in scholarship, which since the 1990s has turned to the local or the particular in search of rich accounts of oppression, experience and identity.

If these changing social conditions suggest moves away from the concept of working class and from structural accounts of the relationships between capital and race towards contingent local struggles, which allow for previously marginalised groups to gain representation and even some measure of restitution, there has

---

9   I have argued that emphasis on the success of the mobilisation of the working class during the 1980s by left-wing trade unions misses the extent to which capitalism was already taking on a global, neoliberal form, and the working class was already in decline. Unlike others, who regard a stark break between apartheid and democracy (Webster and Von Holdt, 2005) or those who blame the ANC for having sold out to neoliberal capitalism in the early 1990s (Bond, 2001; Marais, 2011), I suggest that shifts in capital already transformed the grounds of politics in the 1980s and limited the possibilities for the ANC's enactment of socialism, prior to the negotiations to end apartheid (Dubbeld, 2015).

been one prominent exception. In 2017, two related concepts gained public attention, which promised to connect the conditions of capitalist accumulation in South Africa to broader social experience: 'white monopoly capital' and 'radical economic transformation'. The scholar associated most closely with these terms, Chris Malikane, defined these terms by locating them within the genealogy of SACP thought (Malikane 2017a, 2017b, 2017c). From the SACP's *Road to South African Freedom* (1962), he quotes whites as having monopoly interests in mining, industry and agriculture, as well as banks and finance houses, and as having a monopoly on skilled jobs. From the 1985 ANC document, 'The Nature of the South African Ruling Class', he draws the idea that the ruling class is exclusively white; a minority who relies on an ideology of white supremacy and on imperialist backers. From the ANC's 'Strategy and Tactics' document (1997), he takes the notion that some white monopolists are drawing black propertied classes into their monopoly but ensuring that they maintain economic power in the country. Having established this genealogy, Malikane argues that despite black empowerment and democracy, 'White monopoly capitalists ... own and control monopolies in mining, banking and other industries [as well as] own a disproportionate share of land' (April, 2017). This can be challenged by Radical Economic Transformation, which would involve the nationalisation of mines and banks, including the South African Reserve Bank, and the state expropriation of all land without compensation.

Following Malikane's appointment in 2017 as adviser to Zuma's new finance minister, Malusi Gigaba, many dismissed this as Zuma's attempt to justify the capture and pillage of the state. The concepts were further discredited as details surfaced of Bell Pottinger's involvement in a media campaign to shift the image of Zuma away from corruption and to cast him as a figure fighting white monopoly capital.[10]

Despite their instrumental deployment to preserve Zuma's power, these concepts represented an explicit return to a kind of structural analysis that related capital and race, and one that continues to be invoked by some in the ruling party and by the Economic Freedom Fighters (EFF) as expressing a necessary step in the transformation of South African society.[11] Indeed, popular support for this kind of explanation is symptomatic of the absence of a theory that can account for the contradiction between a society that continues to generate massive inequality, on the one hand – within with racial inequality persists but which traditional Marxist class categories do not capture – and, on the other, a set of progressive state and legal apparatuses that simultaneously invest in infrastructure for the upliftment of the poor black majority and attempt to overturn formal inequalities and fight injustice using the law.

REREADING MARX AFTER THE DEMISE OF THE WORKING CLASS

The dominant understandings of Marx in the 20th century, including those offered by the South African revisionists and those in communist parties across the globe, shared an assumption about Marx's theory of capitalism. This was that capitalism should be understood in productive terms as the exploitation of labour

---

10 In March 2017, the *Sunday Times* (Skiti and Shoba) reported on Bell Pottinger's hire by the Guptas and the campaign to shift the media focus to 'white monopoly capital' and away from state capture. This was followed by vehement threats to sue the newspaper, as well as much public debate over the term. In May 2017, e-mail leaks revealed the extent of the Gupta's involvement in state-owned entities. Zuma was replaced as president in February 2018, and his successor initiated a commission of inquiry into state capture, presided over by Judge Raymond Zondo in August 2018.

11 The South African Communist Party (2017) responded to Malikane by accusing him of mobilising a set of radical terms to misread the post-apartheid character of capital and class. Pointing to the public sector as a significant source of employment and wealth, as well as black ownership of significant portions of the mining sector and real estate, they suggested that Malikane's account of value, as being created by white capitalists and income tax payments ('white monopoly capitalists'), presented too limited a picture of the economy.

power by capitalists, and in social terms by the domination of the proletariat by the bourgeoisie. Class is the primary analytical category because it grasps the basis of exploitation, and the processes of proletarianisation are critical for understanding capitalism's development, because it creates a working class that depends almost exclusively on wages for survival and the bourgeoisie who grow rich based on their ability to generate surplus value through capitalist production. There is a trajectory to capitalism, in which more and more people have to be drawn into the labour process and the value of their labour power exploited. At stake in the question of value is distribution: it is a question of who owns capital enterprise, and who profits from it. It imagines emancipation as a theoretical and political task of (1) overcoming the ideological obfuscations of capitalism and showing the exploitation of labour for what it really is, and (2) spreading this consciousness among workers who will be the forces of emancipation. The content of this emancipation imagines work and its proceeds being distributed equally across society.[12]

This basic understanding is what Moishe Postone (1993: 43–83) terms 'traditional Marxism' and, as I have suggested, seemed to be less and less able to describe conditions where the working class is fragmented, precarious and, indeed, where many are not working at all. Postone, by contrast, seeks to develop a reading of Marx that shows how his theory can be adequate to these changed conditions of capitalism, and in which the attempts by 'actual' socialist regimes to overcome capitalism through state-regulated distribution have failed. Postone's analysis develops in the wake of the publication of Marx's *Grundrisse* in English in 1973, and considers the nature and trajectory of capitalist value. In so doing, he makes clear that Marx's theory of capitalism depends on the reality of abstraction as a feature of social life, and not simply an analytical move that does not recognise the lived realities of people in a capitalist society.

Postone starts with the premise that, for Marx, capitalism is more

---

[12] While the SACP's criticism of Malikane's Radical Economic Transformation does point to how the economy has changed since 1994, it shares with him the presupposition that the creation of value is a product of ownership of capitalist enterprise.

than only an economic system: it is a social system of production that expresses a particular kind of society. It does so by establishing a new set of relations between people and people, and people and things, and cannot be generalised across all time. The implication is that forms of life and forms of knowing are specific to a particular time.

From this standpoint, he argues that it is not arbitrary that Marx begins *Capital* with the category of commodity (Postone, 1993: 18, 135–43). The commodity, and its double-sided character, is not merely an economic dimension of life, but expresses categories of existence in capitalism: that our existence in this society has to constantly reckon with the usefulness of things and their economic value, and that at times we may experience these as a tension, and at others we measure the usefulness of things through their exchange value. In so doing, everyday life in capitalism involves abstraction: rather than a figment of a philosopher's imagination, our abstraction of the value of our labour and the value of things is a necessity for survival in capitalism.

Moreover, the commodity expresses our relations with others because it is at once a material thing with use and, at the same time, a social thing through which our relation with others is expressed – not only a means of sociality that makes us recognisable as people in relation to the value of the things we have, but also because the value of commodities expresses a veiled sociality between ourselves and the numerous people who made the things we consume. It is at this point, of course, in the first few papers of *Capital*, that labour appears. Like the commodity, it appears in double-form: at once the concrete labour of exercising energy to produce an object (whether physically or virtually), and as abstract labour. Abstract labour enables the measurement of different kinds of activity and their calibration on a single scale; this measurement, in turn, reduces concrete labour to a number, a quantitative measure through which value can be decided.[13]

In effect, this points to a tautology: labour that is more financially lucrative is rendered more valuable, and as value mediates how we engage in labour, it shapes what kinds of labour we need to do. Indeed, unlike other societies, labour is the means through which we are able to survive; it is the direct basis of our consumption, and of all of our social ties. As Postone noted informally, 'in other societies the nature of your work did not directly determine whether and how you ate and lived, other social relations mediated between the work you did and how you consumed'. The role of labour in capitalism is historically specific. Its form, as necessarily generating economic value as a condition of its continued existence, is also historically specific.

It is at this point that the differences between Postone's reading of Marx and other readings become especially sharp. Postone argues that labour in capitalism is intrinsically alienating: that it cannot be redeemed by improving wages, job security, altering the structure of ownership, or even attempting to make all in society

---

13 Abstraction for Postone is a key part of what is specific to capitalism. In an interview (Blumberg and Nogales, 2008) he said, 'I don't think that abstract labour is simply an abstraction *from* labour, that is, it's not labour in general, it's labour acting as a socially mediating activity. I think *that* is at the heart of Marx's analysis: Labour is doing something in capitalism that it doesn't do in other societies. So, it's both, in Marx's terms, concrete labour, which is to say, a specific activity that transforms material in a determinate way for a very particular object, as well as abstract labour, that is, a means of acquiring the goods of others. In this regard, it is doing something that labour doesn't do in any other societies. Out of this very abstract insight, Marx develops the whole dynamic of capitalism. It seems to me that the central issue for Marx is not only that labour is being exploited – labour is exploited in all societies, other than maybe those of hunter-gatherers – but, rather, that the exploitation of labour is effected by structures that labour itself constitutes. So, for example, if you get rid of aristocrats in a peasant-based society, it's conceivable that the peasants could own their own plots of land and live off of them. However, if you get rid of the capitalists, you are not getting rid of *capital*. Social domination will continue to exist in that society until the structures that constitute capital are gotten rid of.'

equal at an economic level.¹⁴ Instead, labour in capitalism needs to be overcome. While traditional interpretations are made from the standpoint of labour, this reading is offered from the standpoint of the critique of labour in capitalism. The implication is that while Marx is sympathetic to the plight of the working class, who are necessarily exploited in the process of capitalist production, for capital to be overcome it is the form of labour in capitalism that must be abolished. The moment of post-Fordism may, thus, be grasped politically as an opportunity to overcome labour and not just a moment to lament the end of the working class.

Postone approaches the production of value as tied to labour time, understood once again in concrete and abstract dimensions. In his reading, time itself becomes abstracted from task – following E.P. Thompson (1967) – and takes on a universal character. This enables Postone to argue that a Marxian analysis approaches time not only descriptively, but also critically: time in capitalism becomes a normative measure for activity, a standard around which capitalist production has reorganised society over two centuries (Postone, 1993: 186–216). For capitalist production, reducing labour time is the basis of surplus value, so for people living in a capitalist society, there is an experience of constantly having to work harder in less time. Hence the production of value is itself problematic: not only does it rest on extracting more time from labour than it can fully remunerate – the necessary exploitation of the valorisation process – but it is also an ongoing, ceaseless process in which the production of surplus is not necessarily tied to the quantity of material wealth that is produced. Instead, individual capitalists must find ways to produce more efficiently or risk falling behind the production time of their competitors and going out of business. This is what Postone (1993: 289) calls the 'treadmill effect', which sees capitalists face an ongoing struggle to continue their enterprises. Such increasing

---

14 'A forcing up of wages ... would therefore be nothing but better payment for the slave, and would not conquer for the worker or for labour either human status or dignity. Even the Equality of Wages demanded by Proudhon only transforms the relationship of the present-day worker to his labour into the relationship of all men [sic] to labour. Society is then conceived as the abstract capitalist (Marx (1973 [1844]): 80).

efficiency of production relies ever more on science and technology, and less on direct labour power.

While the exploitation of labour remains the basis of value, there are continual attempts to cheapen the cost of labour, to erode benefits and job security and to extract as much as possible from workers. Simultaneously, the increasing efficiency of production, and the fact that it relies more on machinery than workers, opens up the potential for capitalism to be overcome from within: that is, hyper-efficient production, from the vantage point of the material goods produced, no longer requires human labour power. This form of production, freed from labour power, could be the basis for allowing people to establish relations with one another, and between things, that no longer depend on their capacity to work for money, since enough is produced to enable the possibility of a different system of distribution to take effect.

Postone's reading has important theoretical and political implications in relation to the contemporary moment. At the theoretical level, his emphasis on value as the basis of existence in capitalism means that whether production is accomplished in labour-intensive factories or in technologically advanced industries, and whether large numbers of people are employed or are without wage work, we can continue to learn from Marx. This focus also emphasises that capitalism does have a directional dynamic, a *telos*, but that this is not a crude teleology associated with Marxism, which regarded each society as having to pass through stages of history in order to reach communism. Rather, teleology, in Postone's understanding, is specific to capitalism: for capitalism to persist it must produce value, and as it attempts to produce value, so it attempts to make labour more efficient, ultimately seeking to mechanise the labour process. In so doing, it produces more material wealth and relies less on labour power. Given unequal distribution, this means that class divides are likely to sharpen rather than diminish as capitalism expands. It is to this dynamic of 'all that is solid melts into air', of the constant attempts by capitalists to revolutionise production, that Postone suggests Marx is referring to in the *Communist Manifesto* (1848).

Such a focus also means that Marx's salience does not depend on having two classes – one owning the means of production and others working in it for wages. The empirical existence of a more varied class structure with a greater proportion of people under- or unemployed, does not invalidate Marx's analysis, especially insofar as these people remain dependent on money as the material embodiment of abstract human labour to survive.

Politically, Postone's (1999) reading of Marx distances itself from the need to defend 'actually existing socialism' in China, in Eastern Europe between 1945 and 1990, or in the Soviet Union. He suggests that, despite significant differences, key similarities in respect of the role of labour in production in these countries and the United States during the 20th century points to a shared and deeper historical dynamic at work: in other words, these countries never fully managed to escape capitalism, often employing authoritarian techniques to implement similar kinds of production regimes. Indeed, Postone warns (1996) of what he calls 'romantic anti-capitalism', by which he understands as nostalgic the promise of utopian arrangements in which everybody knows their place, where the unpredictability of the market is brought under control, and people are not estranged from one another. Romantic anti-capitalism is at its most dangerous when it becomes a political movement with its eye on capturing state power. This is central to Postone's analysis of the Holocaust as a promise by the Nazis to institute a *Reich* in which the purported purveyors of capitalist alienation – the Jews – are eliminated entirely.

This interpretation of Marx differs sharply from a conspiratorial notion that regards capitalism as a system run by a few elite capitalists in London and New York, and that challenging this elite would be adequate to overcome capitalism. Indeed, capitalists are themselves structured by the dynamics of capital: they are definitely not aristocrats, and their businesses can and do fail, and when they do, they become like everybody else, forced to sell their labour power. This emphasises Marx's understanding of capitalism – that it is a social form, not only a political regime or economic system, and it mediates both of these. The implication of this analysis is that politics as such becomes a more restricted sphere, which can improve people's conditions within capitalism, but if society cannot develop the technological possibilities to overcome capitalism, politics cannot, on its own, shift an entire epoch.

TRANSLATING POSTONE'S MARX: SOME PRELIMINARY THOUGHTS

While I have shown that Postone's interpretation of Marx differs in substantial theoretical terms from what is held to be Marxism in South Africa, the translation of the conceptual apparatus that he offers into the country's particular historical experience is not self-evident. At the outset, I would suggest that his theory decisively challenges any accounts that are satisfied with local narratives as expressions of different individual experiences by insisting that these are located within a global context of capitalism as a social form. Unlike traditional Marxist accounts, however, the point of this approach is not to subsume all difference into a universal expression of class. Instead, the challenge is acknowledging that a range of differing social positions and experiences are possible within capitalism without according them complete autonomy from capitalism. An example here would be not to view 'tradition' as a holdover from pre-capitalist society – as the revisionists largely did – but to recognise that the desire for 'tradition' might be a response to capitalism and to see the ways in which tradition might take place through capitalist forms of value, without tradition ever being obviously 'invented' by any of its adherents.

Crucially the point of departure is that capitalism mediates social relations. This is not the same as determining them in a one-to-one fashion: the tensions internal to capitalism do express themselves subjectively, but these expressions are broad ranging and not knowable prior to their expression.[15] In this sense, Postone's analysis would be in line with Mafeje's insistence that we need idiographic inquiry to recognise how capital exists in any particular society, and we cannot know concretely in advance what capital will look like. At the same time, however, Postone's analysis would insist that we need to take the abstract dimension of value production seriously as a form of compulsion. Otherwise, value production seems like the outcome of decisions made by particular capitalists rather than decisions made under a structure that demands continued value production.

In relation to our contemporary moment, Postone's analysis does not inspire a politics that regards left-wing political parties championing worker rights (whether in Europe, Brazil or South Africa) as sufficient politically to claim the overcoming of capitalism. Indeed, this theory would respond to the paradox of present-day South Africa in which inequality continues to be produced despite progressive laws attempting to overcome it and an administration attempting to ameliorate this inequality. Postone's theory suggests it is likely that capitalism will continue to produce additional inequality that will move increasingly far from traditional concepts of class, and that every effort to produce employment or to industrialise will be susceptible to the same dynamic.

Efforts to escape this dynamic politically are fraught with danger. Indeed, Postone's contribution is at its most trenchant when it points to how the attempts to escape from capitalism – from Eastern Bloc socialism to Nazism – end up grasping only one dimension of

---

15 Crucially, this mediation places all of us within capitalism, and subject to its forces. The analyst cannot adopt a set of concepts free of the mediation of capitalism. Mistaking the attempt to improve workers' conditions with a transcendence of capitalism is to mistake the nature of capitalism. There are good grounds – of human dignity in the first instance – of supporting high wages and improved working conditions for all workers, but there is a limit here, akin to the limit that feminists long ago pointed to: while they showed how focusing on workers misses the unpaid labour that is integral to the reproduction of society, what the focus on workers does here is to miss the trajectory of capitalism that will continue to create divisions between workers and the unemployed and, by assuming that capitalism can be kept static politically, it misses how its own progress may lead ever closer to the possibility of its overcoming.

capitalism and how these political attempts to overcome it fail, often with catastrophic human consequences.

It is promising from this perspective to re-examine the relations between capitalism and race. Instead of explaining race in terms of class, both may exist in relation to the movement of capital at a given historical moment. The projection of forms of value onto particular races, especially in relation to the political promise to overcome some of the alienating effects of capitalism, might be a fruitful basis from which to re-evaluate anti-black racism in the 20th century, including in relation to apartheid. Such an approach would not regard racism as instrumental to capital development in an economic sense (which it was at certain moments, and less so at others), but rather that racism was imposed as a promise to resolve the social problems introduced by capitalism, problems that were expressed economically at certain moments and at others in psychological and even political terms.

Where determination (and necessity) does appear in Postone's analysis is more strictly with respect to the trajectory of capitalist social life, insofar as its *telos* is towards the production of value by reducing the cost of necessary labour time, while continuing to make the sale of labour time the condition of acquiring value, and, indeed, the condition of personal and social reproduction. How this appears in different concrete circumstances will vary, but for Postone this internal contradiction of capitalism – where work is at once necessary for survival and at the same time increasingly superfluous for production – drives it forward. What makes South Africa especially interesting in this regard is the extent of un- and under-employment, since so many people depend on the few who are working to acquire the means of their own survival. Across the political spectrum, including many Marxists, multiple actors aim to find ways to increase employment. However some, such as James Ferguson (2015), have suggested that government grants may offer the basis for a different set of post-wage–work social relations. Such mechanisms are not yet substantial enough to seriously challenge wage-earning as the primary – and most desired – source of survival and prosperity for many South Africans.

Approaching the political potentials of overcoming wage work in South Africa once again reminds us of feminism, which has long demanded that Marxism analytically account for priority of paid labour against the unpaid work of social reproduction. In making paid labour the problem that needs to be overcome if capitalism is to be overcome, Postone partially responds to this problem by refusing to affirm work as the solution to overcoming domination.

A fuller response is offered in recent work undertaken by Nancy Fraser (2009), which bears more than a family resemblance to Postone's reading of Marx. She argues for grounding feminist analysis in an analysis of capitalism and its effects in the world today, tracing how second wave feminism of the 1960s developed a critique that connected gender injustice at the economic, cultural and political levels. This critique revealed the kinds of patriarchal gender norms at the heart of the welfare state's family wage, called attention to the state organisation as bureaucratised and androcentric, demanded that the gendered division of labour be overcome, and that caregiving be recognised as socially valuable. This foundational intersectional critique was transformative of culture and society, at least in the Global North, producing legislative changes and opening political and social space for women to occupy more prominent public and occupational roles than ever before.

Yet Fraser shows that as neoliberalism took hold in the late 1970s and 1980s, the ambition of second wave feminism to systematically challenge capitalism fell away, as did their attempts at a more encompassing mode of analysis. Curiously, the arguments about women's equality and their critique of the state flourished during this later period, and Fraser points out that the success of their arguments dovetailed neatly with the rolling back of the welfare state and the rejection of the family wage. This leads her to argue – as she admits, 'disturbingly' – that 'second wave feminism provided a key ingredient to neoliberalism ... with the dream of women's emancipation ... harnessed to the engine of capital accumulation' (Fraser, 2009: 110–11). The position that once drew attention to the hidden labour of unpaid social reproduction that ensured the stability of state-led capitalism – that is, the personal as political – became one justifying that the state should bear no responsibility (other than ensuring formal equality) for the reproduction of the household, and facilitated the entry of flexible, deregulated, mobile capitalism, ensuring maximum productivity founded on the 'cornerstone of women's waged labour' (Fraser, 2009: 133). This has reduced feminism's capacity to engage capitalism and diminished feminism's social critique to a question of individual lifestyle choice where, in effect, the political becomes personal.

CONCLUSION

I have briefly reviewed the moment of revisionist Marxism in South Africa, and the conceptual positions and social conditions that lead to its waning. I have no intention to resuscitate that form of Marxism and have recounted its limits, even as I recognise some of the importance of its contributions. Yet I have suggested that a reading of capitalism is important to understand contemporary conditions at a moment when the demands of the main current of leftist politics to address racial and gender inequalities seem to have eschewed them.

I have suggested that a focus on the relations of capitalism remain important, with the recognition that commodities still mediate social relations – including those that produce race – and that the position of the working class has shifted and become radically flexible and insecure. In 21st-century conditions, my analysis points to the need to rethink political possibilities in light of capitalism, if a truly transformed future is our goal.

I have argued that the advantages of such an analysis lie in its reflexivity – recognising our common predicament is with our mediation by capital – and in its refusal to regard a particular subject position as the standpoint from which emancipation might arise. Instead, it suggests a focus on the fraught conditions of existence today, and asks us to reconsider how a politics beyond wage work, provided it can be socially generalised, could be the direction of a future emancipation.

REFERENCES

African National Congress (ANC). (1997). 'Strategy and Tactics'.

Document adopted at the ANC's 50th National Conference. Available at: https://www.anc1912.org.za/wp-content/uploads/2021/07/Umrabulo-Issue-4-Special-Edition-1997.pdf (Accessed 10 April 2022).

African National Congress (ANC). (1985). 'The Nature of the South African Ruling Class'. This document is one of a series of National Preparatory Committee Documents from the ANC National Consultative Conference at Kabwe, Zambia, in June 1985. Available at: https://www.marxists.org/subject/africa/anc/1985/nature-ruling-class.htm (Accessed 10 April 2023).

Blumberg, B. and Nogales, P. (2008). 'Marx after Marxism: An interview with Moishe Postone', *Platypus Review*, 3(1). Available at: https://platypus1917.org/2008/03/01/marx-after-marxism-an-interview-with-moishe-postone/ (Accessed 20 March 2023).

Bond, P. (2000). *Elite Transition: From apartheid to neoliberalism in South Africa*. London: Pluto Press.

Bozzoli, B. (1983). 'Marxism, feminism and South African studies', *Journal of Southern African Studies*, 9(2): 139–71.

Breckenridge, K. (2004). 'Promiscuous method: The historiographical effects of the search for the rural origins of the urban working class in South Africa', *International Labor and Working-class History*, 65: 26–49.

Bundy, C. (1979). *The Rise and Fall of the South African Peasantry*. London: Heinemann.

Bundy, C. (1991). 'Marxism in South Africa: Context, themes and challenges', *Transformation*, 16: 56–66.

Crais, C. (2002). *The Politics of Evil: Magic, state power and political imagination in South Africa*. Cambridge: Cambridge University Press.

Comaroff, J. and Comaroff, J. (2006). *Law and Disorder in the Postcolony*. Chicago, IL: University of Chicago Press.

Davis, D. and Le Roux, M. (2019). *Lawfare: Judging politics in South Africa*. Johannesburg: Jonathan Ball.

Delius, P. (2017). 'E.P. Thompson, "Social history", and South African historiography, 1970–90', *Journal of African History*, 58(1): 3–17.

Dubbeld, B. (2015). 'Capital and the shifting grounds of emancipatory politics: The limits of radical unionism in Durban Harbour, 1974–

1985', *Critical Historical Studies*, 2(1): 85–112.

Ferguson, J. (2015). *Give a Man a Fish: Reflections on the new politics of distribution*. Durham, NC: Duke University Press.

Fine, B. and Rustomjee, Z. (1996). *The Political Economy of South Africa: From mineral-energy complex to industrialisation*. London: Zed Books.

Fraser, N. (2019). 'Is capitalism necessarily racist?' Available at: http://quarterly.politicsslashletters.org/is-capitalism-necessarily-racist/ (Accessed 12 October 2021).

Fraser, N. (2009). 'Feminism, capitalism and the cunning of history', *New Left Review*, 56: 97–117.

Freund, B. (1986). 'Some unasked questions on politics: South African slogans and debates', *Transformation*, 1: 118–29.

Friedman, S. (2015). *Race, Class, and Power: Harold Wolpe and the radical critique of apartheid*. Pietermaritzburg: University of Kwazulu-Natal Press.

Go, J. (2021). 'Three tensions in the theory of racial capitalism', *Sociological Theory*, 39, 1. DOI.org/10.1177/0735275120979822CES

Guy, J. (1990). 'Gender oppression in South African's precapitalist societies', in C. Walker, (ed.). *Women and Gender in Southern Africa to 1945*. Cape Town: David Philip, pp. 33–47.

Hemson, D. (1979). 'Class consciousness and migrant workers: Dock workers of Durban'. PhD thesis, University of Warwick.

Johnstone, F. (1976). *Class, Race, and Gold: A study of class relations and racial discrimination in South Africa*. London: Routledge.

Lalu, P. (2009). *The Deaths of Hintsa: Post-apartheid South Africa and the shape of recurring pasts*. Pretoria: HSRC Press.

Legassick, M. (1995 [1972]). 'British hegemony and the origins of segregation in South Africa, 1901–1914', in W. Beinart and S. Dubow (eds). *Segregation and Apartheid in Twentieth Century South Africa*. London: Routledge, pp. 43–60.

Legassick, M. and Hemson, D. (1976). 'Foreign investment and the reproduction of racial capitalism in South Africa'. Foreign investment in South Africa: A discussion series, No. 2. London: Anti-Apartheid Movement.

Malikane, C. (2017a). 'The unfettered power of white monopoly capital', *Sunday Independent*, 16 April. Available at: https://

www.iol.co.za/news/opinion/the-unfettered-power-of-white-monopoly-capital-8680007 (Accessed 12 October 2021).

Malikane, C. (2017b). 'How to break monopoly white capital', *Sunday Independent*, 23 April. Available at: https://www.iol.co.za/news/opinion/how-to-break-monopoly-white-capital-8779291 (Accessed 12 October 2021).

Malikane, C. (2017c). 'Some notes on white monopology capital: Definition, use, denial'. Unpublished presentation, 23 June. Available at: https://docs.google.com/viewer?a=v&pid=forums&srcid=M-DcxMzc1ODAwMjQzMTA4MDUyNzYBMTUyMTczMjA0OTMyO-DIxODk2MDgBQmdIeU1wSUhBZ0FKATAuMQEBdjI&authuser=0 (Accessed 12 October 2021).

Marais, H. (2011). *South Africa Pushed to the Limit: The political economy of change*. Cape Town: UCT Press and London: Zed Books.

Marx, K. (1978 [1844]). 'Economic and philosophical manuscripts', in R.C. Tucker (ed.). *Marx–Engels Reader*. New York: Norton Press.

Mafeje, A. (1981). 'On the articulation of modes of production: Review article', *Journal of Southern African Studies*, 8(1): 123–38.

Morris, M. (1988). 'Social history and the transition to capitalism in South African agriculture', *Review of African Political Economy*, 15(41): 61–72.

Morris, M. (1976). 'The development of capitalism in South African agriculture: Class struggle in the countryside', *Economy and Society*, 5(3): 292–343.

Nash, A. (1999). 'The moment of Western Marxism in South Africa', *Comparative Studies of South Asia, Africa and the Middle East*, XIX(1): 66–81.

Nyoka, B. (2017). 'Archie Mafeje: An intellectual biography'. PhD Dissertation, University of South Africa.

O'Meara, D. (1983). *Volkskapitalisme: Class, capital and ideology in the development of Afrikaner Nationalism, 1934–1948*. Johannesburg: Ravan Press.

Postone, M. (1999). 'Contemporary historical transformations: Beyond post-industrial theory and neo-Marxism', *Current Perspectives in Social Theory*, 19: 3–53.

Postone, M. (1996). 'The Holocaust and the trajectory of the twentieth century', in M. Postone and E. Santner (eds). *Catastrophe and Meaning*. Chicago, IL: University of Chicago Press, pp. 81–114.

Postone, M. (1993). *Time, Labour and Social Domination*. Cambridge: Cambridge University Press.

Ralph, M. and Singhal, M. (2019). 'Racial capitalism', *Theory and Society*, 48(6): 851–81.

Robinson, J. (1996). *The Power of Apartheid: State, power, and space in South African cities*. Durban: Butterworths.

Smith, M.N. and Jankie, R. (2019). 'On identity and its discontents: What of politics?', *Mail & Guardian*, 15 June. Available at: https://mg.co.za/article/2019-06-15-00-on-identity-and-its-discontents-what-of-the-politics/ (Accessed 12 April 2023).

Skiti, S. and Shoba, S. (2017). '"White monopoly capital" chosen distraction in PR strategy to clear Guptas: report', *The Sunday Times*, 19 March. Available at: https://businesstech.co.za/news/government/165231/white-monopoly-capital-a-pr-stunt-to-protect-zuma-and-the-guptas-report/ (Accessed 12 April 2023).

South African Communist Party (SACP). (2017). 'Chris Malikane and the Gupterisation of Marxism'. Available at: http://www.polity.org.za/article/sacp-chris-malikane-and-the-gupterisation-of-marxism-2017-05-11 (Accessed 10 April 2023).

South African Communist Party (SACP). (1962). *Road to South African Freedom*. Available at: https://www.marxists.org/history/international/comintern/sections/sacp/1962/road-freedom.htm (Accessed 10 May 2023).

Thompson, E.P. (1967). 'Time, work-discipline, and industrial capitalism', *Past and Present*, 38(1): 56–97.

Thompson, E.P. (1963). *The Making of the English Working Class*. London: Vintage.

Webster, E. (1985). *Cast in a Racial Mould: Labour process and trade unionism in the foundaries*. Johannesburg: Ravan Press.

Webster, E. and Von Holdt, K. (2005). *Beyond the Apartheid Workplace: Studies in transition*. Pietermaritzburg: University of KwaZulu-Natal Press.

White, H. (2020). 'How is capitalism racial? Fanon, critical theory and the fetish of antiblackness' *Social Dynamics: A Journal of African Studies*, 46(1): 22–35.

Witz, L. (2004). *Apartheid's Festival: Contesting South Africa's national pasts.* Cape Town: David Philip.

Wolpe, H. (1980). *The Articulation of the Modes of Production: Essays from Economy and Society.* London and Boston, MA: Routledge and Kegan Paul. Published online by Cambridge University Press (2009).

Wolpe, H. (1972). 'Capitalism and cheap labour power in South Africa', *Economy and Society*, 1(4): 425–56.

ELEVEN

EMERGING POWERS AND THE POLYCENTRIC WORLD

Vladimir Shubin

INTRODUCTION

This chapter begins with a critique of the term 'emerging powers', which I regard as an expression of Eurocentrism. I question the belief that the bipolar world that allegedly existed during the 'Cold War' was replaced by a unipolar one on the threshold of the 1990s. Moreover, I question the traditional history of the Cold War itself, both its beginning and its end. In the second part of this chapter, I consider the correlation between internal and domestic policy, with South Africa and Russia as case studies. The final section is devoted to considering the cooperation between South Africa and Russia as members of BRICS (Brazil, Russia, India, China and South Africa).

I place the words 'emerging powers' in inverted commas because I believe this is an expression of Eurocentrism, as if one believes that China or India, or Russia for that matter, have not existed for centuries – it is as if only Western countries existed and we are 'emerging' only now. The same applies to 'emerging economies' or 'emerging markets', as if there were no economies or markets before.

As for the second part of my title, 'polycentric world', I cannot say that like this term and we are more accustomed to a 'multipolar world', but according to physics, that there can be only two poles and hence my use of the word polycentric. Both the terms polycentricism and multipolarity have historic antecedents worth exploring in some detail as a means of contextualising some of my later comments about the discourse concerning multiparty democracies, such as South Africa. The theory of polycentrism was coined by Palmiro Togliatti in 1956. Initially understood as a means of describing different centres sharing the commonality of socialism in the post-Stalin era (see Abse, 1999), polycentricism has been advanced by other scholars such as Perlmutter (1969) to refer to many forms of governance arrangements. The emphasis includes difference and diversity of arrangements without necessarily excluding the links and connections between different political, economic or legal systems. The terms are often regarded as synonymous, although some political scientists believe that polycentrism should be distinguished from multipolarity.

> While the latter refers to a specific distribution of material power that has periodically prevailed in international affairs, often centring on the interaction between great powers, the former is an idea for organizing the global system that enjoys more persistent and universal appeal across time and space (Paikin, 2020).

In the following sections I provide some examples of this with a view to illustrating how poles can become 'poles apart', while polycentres can suggest affinities and opportunities for better collaboration.

When considering conventional histories of the Cold War, the usual approach is to speak about the bipolar world, which existed during the 'Cold War', then about the unipolar world that allegedly appeared after it had ended, although some speak about the formation of the multipolar world nowadays.

However, in the Soviet Union, we did not regard the world developments as the Cold War – for us it was an anti-imperialist struggle that the socialist countries were waging in alliance with the working class of the capitalist countries and the national liberation movement. Nevertheless, for convenience I will use these terms in my chapter.

THE 'COLD WAR'

Now we have to take a step back and discuss the Cold War itself, in particular, when it began. Usually, people say that the Cold War began soon after the end of World War II, around 1946, but my late senior comrade and good friend Brian Bunting used to say that it actually began in early 1920s, immediately after the end of the civil war in our country and the foreign intervention of 14 countries (almost forgotten now) against Soviet Russia.

Another question is, how did the Cold War end? Boris Yeltsin's late close associate, Yegor Gaidar, claimed that our country had lost and, therefore, Russia was in a bad state in the 1990s. In this way, he tried to justify the disaster caused by his initiation of so-called 'reforms' in the 1990s. According to Evgeny Primakov, Russian Prime Minister from 1998 to 1999, these 'liberal' reforms caused losses to our country's economy that were more than twice as high as those suffered in World War II (Makarov, 2016).

Rather peculiar is the opinion of some academics in the United States, who believe that 'we all lost the Cold War' (Lebow and Stein, 1993). They refuse to agree with the 'conventional wisdom ... that would interpret the end of the Cold War as an endorsement of American policy' (Hodgson, 1994).

I personally believe that if one uses military language, we could say that at the threshold of the 1990s, a ceasefire of some kind was reached through mutual compromise, although some of the agreements included were probably unnecessary concessions by Mikhail Gorbachev. Then one side – the USSR – to the surprise of the other, committed suicide, or rather its leaders of the day killed it.

What happened later? Expressing 'conventional wisdom', political commentators and scholars refer to a now unipolar world, dominated by Washington; however, recently some of them have 'noticed' the formation of the multipolar world. Nevertheless, I personally believe that the world was bipolar for a relatively short period – from the 1950s to the mid-1960s – after the revolution in China and the formation of the alliance between Moscow and Beijing. Then serious problems arose in their bilateral relations, and a so-called Sino-Soviet conflict became an important factor in world politics for over 15 years.

In the military sense, the world definitely became multipolar and, when viewed from that perspective, also much more polarised. The relations between the USSR and China deteriorated so badly that military skirmishes even took place on the borders in 1969. On the other side, General Charles De Gaulle withdrew France from the military structures of NATO, and the alliance had to move its headquarters from Paris to Brussels. In the economic sense, the 1960s witnessed a remarkable economic upsurge in Japan, and the creation of the European Economic Community, which was later transformed into the European Union. In the political sense, the situation could not be reduced to the two 'blocs' either; the Non-Aligned Movement, born at the conference in Belgrade in 1961, became a formidable factor in international relations, even if some of its members were closer to Moscow – for example, Cuba – and others, such as Indonesia, after its 1965 coup, closer to Washington. Therefore, in those decades, we could speak about a bipolar world only in the sense of the existing two ideological and political systems, although many discrepancies could be found in each of them. Hence the issue nowadays is not the creation of the multipolar world, but rather the strengthening of it, and the rebuff of attempts to transform it into a US-dominated unipolar one.

Before coming to the second part of this chapter, let me comment on some the discourse concerning the leadership of the United States after the Cold War period. In what sphere does it lead? Take public debt, for example. Here it really is the world leader, with around US$31.42 trillion in public debt in January 2023 (Duffin, 2023). Washington owes money not only to China, but to Russia as well. Unfortunately, over many years, Moscow has been buying US Treasury bonds, and although there was a strong feeling in Russia that we had to stop helping the American economy, the process of getting rid of them has started too late.

Is the United States a leader in the number of mass public

shootings? Maybe, but this is definitely not an example to follow. The leader in the illegal occupation of the highest legislative body in the country? Hardly so, because the bizarre events on 6 January 2021 in Capitol Hill, Washington, were preceded by the shelling of the Russian Parliament building by Boris Yeltsin's tanks before its illegal occupation in October 1993.

Now, concerning the much-praised multiparty democracy: is it always real or sometimes illusory? Consider Ethiopia, for example, where officially proclaimed multiparty democracy found contradiction in its political reality. Prior to the elections in 2015, there was only one independent deputy to the Ethiopian Parliament, the House of Peoples' Representatives, and not a single one from the opposition parties. After the 2015 election, the composition of the Ethiopian Parliament changed to all of the deputies belonging to the then ruling Ethiopian People's Revolutionary Democratic Front and its allies. Then in the 2021 election, the new ruling Prosperity Party received over 90 per cent of the vote and 410 out of 436 seats, but over 100 seats remained vacant since no elections took place due to 'a lack of security' in Tigray and three other regions. In addition to this, a number of opposition parties boycotted the election. Officially, however, the country has remained a 'multiparty democratic state' all these years, although participation in that system seems to suggest domination by one party purporting to representing a group, in the absence of representation of other key groups within the state.

THE CORRELATION BETWEEN INTERNAL AND FOREIGN POLICY

The third theme concerns the correlation between internal and foreign policy, and I will take South Africa and Russia, two 'emerging countries', as case studies.

In this book race and gender appear as the new foci, but class has not attracted the attention it ought to receive as part of a Marxist analysis. Officially, the ANC classifies itself as a multiclass organisation of an anti-imperialist nature, so it is very important to determine (maybe through future research by the Mzala Centre) what these classes are, and, further, the parts of these classes and their strata. I believe researchers should 'dissect' the words of Cyril Ramaphosa (2013), now president of the ANC and of South Africa:

> The ANC is a political organisation that welcomes everyone. It welcomes socialists, communists, capitalists, rural people, urban people, the poor, the wealthy, the professionals ... all of those people are all welcome within the ANC. What binds us all together is the objective that the ANC is seeking to achieve.

But what is the correlation and balance of these forces within the ANC? Do these people really have the same objective?

The ANC has never proclaimed socialism as its aim, at least in official documents, although in the 1970s and 1980s the majority of its leaders did support it. It has to be noted, however, that the ANC is a member of the Socialist International and one of its then vice-presidents, former president of the ANC and South Africa, Jacob Zuma, has more than once reaffirmed the character of the ANC as 'a disciplined force of the left, a multiclass mass movement and an internationalist movement with an anti-imperialist outlook' (2011), with 'a strong bias towards the working class and poor' (2013). However, it remains to be seen whether this 'bias' is still typical for the South African ruling party today. In any case, if the organisation is 'multiclass', its politics – both internal and external – can be stable only if the interest of different classes and social strata coincide, but this does not and cannot always happen. In fact, some difficult questions arise.

The term 'social cohesion' is often used in South African political vocabulary. However, is there 'social cohesion' between, say, owners of villas in Clifton and shack dwellers in Philippi? Moreover, is social cohesion at all possible in a class society? It may be possible when interests coincide, but what if they differ? And I am afraid this is often the case. The point to emphasise here is that although the discourse of the state enables a shared notion of what social cohesion ought to entail, and how it can address the challenges of race and economic polarisation, the differences between experiences of polarisation based on class, make both the social and the cohesion aspects of the terms, unreal – or perhaps idealistic rather than real. Such experiences of disparity and polarisation are also not accidental; they derive from unequal relations of economic power that find expression in how the economy is organised and who participates in it.

Let me quote from a prominent South African intellectual (even if he is not often quoted nowadays), Pallo Jordan. In 1997, on the eve of the ANC's 50th national conference, he wrote, in his article titled 'The National Question in post-1993 South Africa':

> Since 1994 the multiclass character [of the] ANC itself is undergoing transformation. Whereas in the past there were no captains of industry in the leading organ of the ANC, today at least one NEC member heads one of the largest conglomerates trading on the Johannesburg Stock Exchange. This corporation moreover employs thousands of other ANC members as well as ANC supporters (Jordan, 1997).

I am not aware of whether there is still only one such person in the ANC's leading organ or if there are more, or (which is highly unlikely) none. What is certain, however, is the changing nature of social structures and the need for deep research on these issues, and I believe that this could be done by the Mzala Centre for the Study of South African Society.

One more point: to the best of my memory, the term 'class struggle' was not been mentioned at the inauguration conference of the Mzala Centre; it does not seem to be 'fashionable' nowadays but, nevertheless, it is inevitable in a class society. Let me quote this time from a very different source, Warren Buffet, an American billionaire, who was not shy at all to say: 'There's class warfare, all right, but it is my class, the rich class, that's making war, and we're winning' (Buffet, n.d.). The point to be made with reference to such triumphalist statements is that these utterances do not recognise the relationships between classes that make triumph and defeat seem axiomatic, when in fact they are not.

Now for some words on the situation in Russia. Professor Alexey Vassiliev, a long-serving director of the Institute for African Studies, and now its honorary president, wrote 20 years ago:

> Russia is a split society. There exist various social groups, or, if you wish, class interests, which are reflected in its foreign policy. Quite real interests of certain social groups, which became a part of the Russian economic and political elites, caused a chimerical orientation to integration with the West. These are exporters of raw materials, big financial speculators, who export a considerable part of their capital to the West (Vassilev, 2003: 169).

Unfortunately, this characteristic of Russian society remained by and large valid until recently, although the political expression of West-oriented forces became much weaker, and openly pro-Western parties are no longer represented in the State Duma. We have to speak about intraclass differences and the appearance of forces within the ruling class that (maybe with reservation) could be called the 'patriotic bourgeoisie' (using South African political vocabulary), while some 'tycoons' have moved to the United Kingdom and other Western countries.

The political situation in Russia is rather peculiar. The 'United Russia' party, which Vladimir Putin was officially heading before becoming president again, could not even get 50 per cent of the vote in the general election in 2011. It received over 53 per cent in the 2016 election, but the number of its supporters decreased, because the number of voters was much lower. Then in the 2021 election its percentage of the electorate decreased again to 49.82 per cent and it lost 14 seats in the State Duma. However, Putin's support increased after the peaceful reunification of the Crimea in March 2014 from 63.6 per cent in 2012 to 76.7 per cent in 2018 and it remains stable.

Most people – including the left-wing opposition – back his line in foreign and defence policies. Nevertheless, in the field of economics, his government has hardly deviated from the notorious 'neoliberal' course chartered during 'Yeltsin's era', although the pressure to change it is increasing, both from the working class and from a part of the bourgeoisie. In any case, whether it is South Africa or Russia, achievements and failures cannot be attributed or reduced to one person. We have to see a social side to them, to understand whose interests this or that politician represents.

Coming to bilateral relations between Russia and South Africa, we should underline the identity or closeness of views on major international issues. The principal stand of both countries is to protect their own independence, but not to quarrel with others. Relations were enhanced when South Africa became a member of BRICS. True, most BRICS members nowadays are experiencing serious economic problems and their rapid economic growth is no more, but this association has already created a versatile structure of sectoral cooperation, and both Russia and South Africa actively participate in it.

However, we cannot but see a paradox: these bilateral relations are very good in the political sphere, but weak in the economic and cultural fields. One of the reasons for this is a lack of genuine information about each other and much misinformation. The knowledge of Russia in South Africa is rather distorted or simply non-existent. I cannot forget when, a few years ago, a porter in a Johannesburg hotel told me: 'I know Russia; men are wearing skirts there.' But another one corrected him: 'No, Russia is Brussels.'

Even more alarming are the results of the poll published by the Pew Research Centre in Washington. A favourable attitude towards Russia was expressed by only 25 per cent of South Africans compared, for example, with 35 per cent in Kenya, 39 per cent in Nigeria and 56 per cent in Ghana; 24 per cent of respondents in South Africa were undecided, and more than half – 51 per cent – expressed a non-favourable assessment (Stokes, 2015). Russophobia flourished in South Africa especially during a rather dirty anti-Moscow campaign around a so-called 'nuclear deal'. For example, a prominent South African businessperson (a former 'comrade', by the way) scared his listeners by saying: 'We'll work for the Russians for the rest of our lives. Our children would be slaves of the Russians' (News24, 2017). On the contrary, the conditions suggested by Rosatom State Nuclear Energy Corporation for an expected tender were to be extremely advantageous for South Africa – the payment for each unit would begin only after its completion, when the energy production would start.

The bilateral document signed by Russia and South Africa in November 2013 was not a 'deal' but just a framework agreement; moreover, critics of Russia 'forget' that the bilateral intergovernmental agreements were concluded with the United States, South Korea, China and France as well.

It looks as though both the media and the general public in South Africa overestimated Moscow's interest in the nuclear project. After his meeting with Putin in July 2018, when Cyril Ramaphosa explained that owing to 'huge financial constraints', his government was 'not able to proceed with a nuclear build programme', he told a press-conference: 'President Putin was quite relaxed about this. He said you deal with your issues and when the situation changes, we can keep talking about this' (Reuters, 2018). (By the way, Rosatom now has 34 projects abroad at different stages of implementation.)

All of this despite many events that link the two countries: the participation of Russian volunteers in the Anglo-Boer War, the joint struggle against Nazism during World War II and, of course, the support rendered by the Soviet Union to the struggle against the apartheid regime over several decades.

What is behind this attitude? There are several reasons: for decades, intensive anti-Soviet propaganda was aimed not only at the white minority, but also at the black majority; and there has been a lack of information on Russia and its cultural activities, even after 1994. In the almost three decades since the elimination of the apartheid regime, Moscow has not been able to open a single cultural centre in the country, and relevant draft documents have been 'frozen' in South African administrative structures for several years.

However, perhaps the most important reason is the negative influence exerted by the Western media, and the media in South Africa, which bases its reports on Western sources. According to Blade Nzimande (2015): 'South Africa is consistently portrayed always five minutes to midnight, always on the verge of collapse and transformation into a "failed state".' Yet this can be said about the coverage of Russia by so-called 'international mass media' as well. In Russia itself, the mass media by and large is controlled by alien forces; until recently, 62 per cent of them were owned by non-Russian citizens (Nikonov, 2012). It should be noted that a distorted picture of Africa, with a racist flavour, is often painted by the 'liberal' press, by the true heirs of John Locke, the racist father of liberalism.

Mutual understanding and cooperation between the two countries is especially valuable now, when both of them have become targets for 'regime change' by certain external forces. The experience of so-called 'coloured revolutions' demonstrated the danger of foreign interference, in particular of the dependence of the NGOs on external funding. Nevertheless, whatever the interference from outside, these 'revolutions' – be they in Africa, Central Asia or South America – can succeed only when the local conditions are conducive for them.

A new anti-Moscow campaign was unleashed by South African media and some NGOs after the beginning of – as the Kremlin calls it – 'a special military operation' in Ukraine. These tragic developments, of course, are beyond the scope of this article. One can only assume that those who criticise the South African attitude to the conflict are either ignorant or cynical. 'We are already involved in this war,' proclaimed John Steenhuisen, the Democratic Alliance's leader. 'South Africa is on the wrong side of history,' and even 'Russia is a pariah state,' write South African papers.

Some critics explain Tshwane's refusal to 'condemn' Russia's actions as being the result of longstanding relations with Moscow forged during the liberation struggle. But another factor was no less important. Pressure exerted by the US and its allies to tow their line boomeranged. Speaking at the SACP's 15th National Congress, Cyril Ramaphosa clearly said that South Africa had been threatened and blackmailed but that it would not be moved or shifted from its stand, and that the solution of the conflict should be through dialogue and negotiations (SABC News, 2022).

As Elizabeth Sidiropoulos of the South African Institute of International Affairs (SAIIA) wrote: 'Many in the West were baffled by the lack of overwhelming support from the Global South.' As to South Africa, she continued: 'The [South African] government does not consider the war as one between Russia and Ukraine, but as a proxy war between Russia and NATO – a war that has its roots in NATO's eastward expansion despite Russia's legitimate security concerns' (Sidiropoulos, 2022).

The peoples of both Russia and South Africa need an objective knowledge of each other's domestic and foreign policies. The situation could be improved, in particular, by the work of academics, but although South Africa is being studied at several Russian universities and research institutes, Russian studies practically do not exist in South Africa.

The Russian researchers fully understand the importance of enhancing mutual knowledge. Having completed a three-year research project on 'South Africa, a strategic partner of Russia' and published a book (in Russian) titled 'South Africa Today', our team, which consists mostly of young post-doctoral researchers and doctoral candidates of the Moscow Institute for African Studies, began work on a joint Russia–South African project on the historical memory in the two countries about the struggle against apartheid and international solidarity, funded by the Russian Foundation for Basic Research and the National Research Foundation. The results are expected to be covered in a book published in Moscow and Tshwane.

Naturally, we would be glad to co-operate in our studies with South African colleagues, including the 'unapologetically left' Mzala Centre.

REFERENCES

Abse, T. (1999). 'Togliatti and 1956: A response to Sassoon', *Journal of Southern Europe and the Balkans*, 1(1): 39–48, DOI: 10.1080/14613199908413986

Buffet, W. (n.d.) Quotes. Available at: http://www.goodreads.com/quotes/123058-there-class-warfare-all-right-but-it-s-my-class-the (Accessed 12 May 2023).

Duffin E. (2023). 'United States – public debt by month 2021/22'. Available at: www.statista.com (Accessed 11 January 2023).

Central Election Commission of the Russian Federation. Results of Russian Presidential Elections. (2018). www.cik.rf.

Lebow, R.N. and Stein, J.G. (1993). *We All Lost the Cold War*. Princeton, NJ: Princeton University Press.

Hodgson, G. (1994). 'Book review: Wise owls, dangerous asses: We all lost the Cold War', *Independent*, 30 March. Available at: http://www.independent.co.uk/arts-entertainment/books/book-review-wise-owls-dangerous-asses-weall-lost-the-cold-war-richard-lebow-janice-stein-princeton-1430144.html (Accessed 10 April 2023).

Jordan, Z.P. (1997). 'The national question in post-1994 South Africa'. African National Congress. Available at: http://www.anc.org.za/content/national-question-post-94-south-africa-discussion-paper-preparation-50th-national-0 (Accessed 11 January 2023).

Makarov, B. (2016). 'Krizis ili "Apokalipsis"' ['Crisis or "apocalypse"'], *Sovetskaya Rossiya*. Available at: http://www.sovross.ru/modules.php?name=News&file=print&sid=602088 (Accessed 10 April 2023).

News24. (2017). 'If Zuma gets hands on Treasury, it's game over for SA – Pityana'. Available at: https://www.news24.com/fin24/if-zuma-gets-treasury-it-will-be-game-over-for-sa-pityana-20170202 (Accessed 10 April 2023).

Perlmutter, H.V. (1969). 'The tortuous evolution of multinational enterprises', *Columbia Journal of World Business*, 1: 9–18.

Ramaphosa, C. (2013). 'Interview with CNN's Christiane Amanpour', aired 8 January. Available at: http://edition.cnn.com/TRANSCRIPTS/1301/08/ampr.01.html (Accessed 10 April 2023).

Reuters. (2018). 'South Africa's Ramaphosa says to discuss nuclear with Putin in future'. Available at: https://www.reuters.com/article/us-safrica-brics-nuclear/south-africas-ramaphosa-says-to-discuss-nuclear-with-putin-in-future-idUSKBN1KH1ZG (Accessed 10 April 2023).

Nikonov V. (2012). 'Vybor Posle Vyborov' ['Choice after elections']. *Rossiskaya Gazeta*, 22 March. Available at: https://rg.ru/2012/03/22/vybor.html (Accessed 10 April 2023).

Nzimande, B. (2015). 'SACP Central Committee Report to the 3rd Special National Congress as delivered by the General Secretary Dr Blade Nzimande'. SACP.org.za, 8 July. Available at: http://www.sacp.org.za/main.php?ID=4810 (Accessed 11 January 2023).

Paikin, Z. (2020). 'Polycentrism in the era of great power rivalry'. Valdai Discussion Club, 17 August 2020. Available at: https://valdaiclub.com/a/highlights/polycentrism-in-the-era-of-great-power-rivalry/ (Accessed 10 April 2023).

SABC News. (2022). 'ANC President Cyril Ramaphosa addresses 15th SACP National Congress'. Available at: https://www.youtube.com/

watch?v=ppCUKhnOyHs (Accessed 10 April 2023).

Sidiropoulos, E. (2022). 'How do Global South politics of non-alignment and solidarity explain South Africa's position on Ukraine?' Brookings Institute, 2 August 2022. Available at: https://www.brookings.edu/blog/africa-in-focus/2022/08/02/how-do-global-south-politics-of-non-alignment-and-solidarity-explain-south-africas-position-on-ukraine/ (Accessed 10 April 2023).

Stokes, B. (2015). 'Russia, Putin held in low regard around the world'. Pew Research Center, Global Attitudes and Trends. Available at: http://www.pewglobal.org/2015/08/05/russia-putin-held-in-low-regard-around-the-world/ (Accessed 10 April 2023).

Vassilev, A. (2003). 'Afrika: Padcheritsa Globalizatsii' ['Africa: A stepchild of globalisation']. Moscow: Vostochnaya Literatura, p. 169.

Zuma, J. (2013). 'Workers' rights should never be taken for granted', SAnews.gov.za, 1 May. Available at: http://www.durban.gov.za/Resource_Centre/new2/Pages/Workers'-Rights-Should-Never-Be-Taken-For-Granted--Zuma.aspx (Accessed 11 January 2023).

Zuma, J. (2011). 'Discipline must be enforced at all levels', *SA News*, 9 January. Available at: https://www.sanews.gov.za/south-africa/discipline-must-be-enforced-all-levels-zuma (Accessed 10 April 2023).

TWELVE

ECOCIDE OR SOCIALISM: ECOLOGICAL CHALLENGES AND NEOLIBERAL CAPITALIST CONSTRAINS ON RADICAL TRANSFORMATION[1]

Rasigan Maharajh and Sigfried Tivana

INTRODUCTION

The possibility of constructing a truly united, democratic, non-racial and non-sexist Republic of South Africa (RSA) emerged out of the first elections to be premised on the basis of universal suffrage in 1994. That year, the African National Congress (ANC) had also commemorated its 82nd anniversary and its 8 January statement declared 1994 as the 'Year of Liberation for all South Africans' (ANC, 1994). The putative 'democratic breakthrough' was achieved consequent to approximately 342 years of struggle against corporate state capture, colonial subjugation, imperial incorporation into world systems, racial capitalism and apartheid

---

1 This chapter is based on a presentation to 'The Future of the Left – South Africa in a Global Context Conference', held on 10 June 2017, at the Mzala Nxumalo Centre, Pietermaritzburg, and the various comments subsequently received from fellow participants and peer reviewers.

by the overwhelming majority of south Africans. Notwithstanding the Portuguese claim that they were the first European travellers to venture past the southern-most territories of the continent of Africa, it was the Dutch East India Company[2] (DEIC or VOC) that would initially come to occupy the land through the violent expropriation of the indigenous inhabitants. The DEIC enclosed a portion of land in Cape Town whereupon they constructed a fort and later a castle. It was during the European transition from the feudal mode of production into capitalism that the origins of private property relations were established in southern Africa.

Karl Marx had noted in Volume 1 of *Capital* that,

> The discovery of gold and silver in America, the extirpation, enslavement and entombment in mines of the aboriginal population, the beginning of the conquest and looting of the East Indies, the turning of Africa into a warren for the commercial hunting of black skins, signalised the rosy dawn of the era of capitalist production. These idyllic proceedings are the chief momenta of primitive accumulation (Marx, 1887: 703).

For Marx, the DEIC effected a form of corporate capture of the hitherto feudal state at the early onset of capitalism. Thus, Marx identifies Holland as the 'head capitalistic nation of the 17th century' (Marx, 1887: 704). Merchant capital, according to Marx, arose because

> (t)he system of public credit, i.e., of national debts, whose origin we discover in Genoa and Venice as early as the Middle Ages, took possession of Europe generally during the manufacturing period. The colonial system with its maritime trade and commercial wars served as a forcing-house for it. Thus, it first took root in Holland (Marx, 1887: 706).

It is upon this conceptualisation of 'primitive accumulation' that Marx notes that '(t)he treasures captured outside Europe by

---

2 The Verenigde Oostindische Compagnie (VOC) or Dutch East India Company (DEIC in English) was established as an archetypical vertically integrated corporation and chartered by a patent granted to it by the Republiek der Zeven Verenigde Nederlanden on 20 March 1602.

undisguised looting, enslavement, and murder, floated back to the mother-country and were there turned into capital' (Marx, 1887: 705). Primitive accumulation and the violent expropriations underpinning it were never remediated nor were the victims compensated. Thus, the origins of private property relations in South Africa retained the heavy imprint of corruption, and as observed by Marx: '(g)reat fortunes sprang up like mushrooms in a day; primitive accumulation went on without the advance of a shilling' (Marx, 1887: 704).

One of the national liberation movements, the ANC received 62.65 per cent, or approximately 12 237 655, of the votes cast and deployed Nelson Rolihlahla Mandela to serve as the inaugural head of state of the post-apartheid South Africa. On the occasion of his inauguration on 10 May 1994, Mandela declared that, '(w)e have, at last, achieved our political emancipation. We pledge ourselves to liberate all our people from the continuing bondage of poverty, deprivation, suffering, gender, and other discrimination' (Mandela, 1994).

The opening up of a transition away from colonial corporate capture, imperial subjugation, racial capitalism and apartheid towards the construction of a national democracy was the result of valiant resistance, and heroic struggles against expropriation, subjugation, oppression and exploitation by the overwhelming majority of the peoples of South Africa, often in co-operation and solidarity with most of the peoples of the world. Numerous lives were sacrificed in pursuit of a better life for all in a united, democratic, non-racial and non-sexist South Africa.

One such hero of the liberation struggle was Jabulani Nobleman Nxumalo (Mzala). Sixteen years after Mandela's swearing-in as the first president of post-apartheid South Africa, Mzala was awarded the Order of Luthuli in Silver for his contribution to the struggle for a free and democratic South Africa by the seventh government in 2010. The citation acclaimed that, among his other attributes, Mzala's 'biting and at times provocative criticisms did not always please everyone. But nobody could doubt his fierce commitment to the oppressed and exploited masses of our country' (RSA, 2010).

The citation recognises Mzala's indomitable analytical abilities and consequent revolutionary criticism that served to inspire, motivate and nurture the generation of young lions and other cadres in their active struggles that rendered the apartheid apparatus ungovernable, and hastened the fall of the regime in the mid to late 1980s. According to Mzala,

> the emergence of the national movement of the oppressed in South Africa was in a very direct way influenced by the development of capitalism. It was the colonialists that introduced the capitalist mode of production, thereby greatly disorganising and destroying the African people's hereditary means of subsistence. In this way, they were forced, under the threat of starvation, into proletarians – producers and consumers within the capitalist system of the British Empire (Nxumalo, 1988: 9).

Mzala also drew our attention to the strong parallels with Marx and Engels' famous description in the Communist Manifesto that showed how '(t)he bourgeoisie compels all nations, on pain of extinction, to adopt the bourgeoisie mode of production; it compels them to introduce what it calls civilization into their midst, i.e. become bourgeois themselves' (cited in Nxumalo, 1988: 9).

The current Minister of Science, Technology and Innovation, Bonginkosi Emmanuel 'Blade' Nzimande also acknowledged Mzala's massive and invaluable impact on the national liberation struggle but also alluded to his critical contributions to the theoretical and empirical dimensions of 'revolutionary-scholarly' discourse, dialogue and debate. According to Nzimande, '[Mzala's] life is an inspiration to young academics and intellectuals who are committed to honest intellectual endeavour, rigorous research and socio-political analysis that can contribute centrally to the total liberation of South Africa – and indeed all countries' (Nzimande, 2015).

All critical analysis of the contemporary conjuncture in South Africa demands a robust engagement with the facts that characterise our current conditions, and a serious engagement with a critique of the political economy. As this will necessarily require understanding transformations, transitions and other changes, if any, to the relations of production, it becomes fundamentally important to also intensify our study of the emergence and establishment of the materiality of our historical circumstances through the periods of corporate state capture, imperialism, colonialism, racial capitalism, and apartheid over the long duration of nearly four centuries. This affords us better opportunities to reflect critically on the progress in post-apartheid reconstruction and development, while accounting for post- and neo-colonial challenges.

The adoption of a materialist conception of history also serves to focus our attention on the articulation between developments within forces of production, the relations of production that serve to extend and expand capital accumulation, and our environmental relationship with the ecology of southern Africa. Any tendency seeking to transcend the dominance and hegemony of the capitalist mode of production must be capable of understanding its origins, current dynamics and future trajectories.

This chapter comprises five sections. After this introduction, we present the long history of the five mass extinctions on Earth prior to the emergence of our species-being. In section three we discuss the sixth mass extinction as characterising our contemporary conjuncture. In section four, we briefly consider the impacts of climate change expected in southern Africa. The concluding section emphasises the urgency of radical transformation beyond the currently corrupted, corporate-state-captured, and predatory neoliberal capitalism festering in South Africa.

OUR LONG PAST: FIVE MASS EXTINCTIONS AND EVOLUTIONARY CHANGE

Our collective scientific, technological and innovative (STI) capacities, capabilities and competences are, indeed, awesome to behold and it is awe-inducing to consider our development from a precarious primordial emergence to our contemporary precarity as a species-being with a global population exceeding eight billion people (UN, 2022). Even though we remain largely earth-bound, two technological artefacts produced on the basis of our collective global knowledge commons and constructed through the application of human creativity and labour, namely Voyager 1 and 2, have ventured into interstellar space beyond our solar system, whilst remaining in contact with us on earth. Human-made electromagnetic signals also permeate deep into the infinite bounds of space and across the cosmos. Under the current globally hegemonic mode of production, however, our advanced STI prowess primarily serves to maintain the unequal political economy of capitalism, while extending socio-economic inequalities, expanding ecological damage, accelerating climate change, and constantly clawing back against any democratic gains of the majority of people.

Constant improvements in our cognitive capacities, our capabilities for learning, and our social competences have afforded us the opportunity to peer deeply into our past and begin appreciating the circumstances within which we were all forged. We can, with high levels of confidence, speculate that the first living cells appeared approximately between 3.8 and 4.3 billion years ago, during the Eoarchean Era (Dodd *et al*, 2017). From this shared source, living cells constitute the basic unit of life and have reproduced themselves into the variety of living organisms with whom we share planet Earth. Earth, itself, has been determined to be about 4.543 billion[3] years old (Dalrymple, 1991).

Thus, life on Earth has a long history that nearly encapsulates the age of the planet itself. Various living organisms adapted themselves to their environments and changed over time through processes of natural selection, which conferred to their offspring certain physical and psychological traits[4] that allowed them to occupy ecological niches and thereby populate the contemporary biodiversity of life (Darwin, 1859). Engels wrote positively about Darwin's book to Marx, declaring that 'Darwin, by the way, whom I'm just reading now, is absolutely splendid,' in the year of its original publication (Engels, 1859). Marx noted that 'Darwin's book is very significant, and I like it as a scientific-natural basis for the historic struggle of classes' (1861).

While we do not know the precise number of species that have emerged since our common ancestry as 'living cells' in the 'primordial sludge' around hydrothermal vents, some scientists

---

3   Standard error: 70 million years.
4   Genetically determined characteristics.

have utilised statistical tools to estimate the planet's biodiversity to number approximately 8.7 million[5] species globally (Mora *et al*, 2011). Carl Linnaeus, a founder of taxonomy, began the naming and classification of plants and animals in the mid-18th century. More than 260 years later, humanity is still discovering new forms of life on the planet that we share with others. With approximately 18 000 'new' species being recorded in 2016, it could be said that we realise approximately 50 new species per day. Mora and colleagues further speculate that 86 per cent of the species on Earth, and 91 per cent in the ocean have not yet been described or catalogued (Mora *et al*, 2011). Notwithstanding our incomplete knowledge, research suggests that natural selection and accelerated environmental change have contributed to 'biological annihilation' over time (Ceballos *et al*, 2017).

Scientists have calculated at least five previous *mass extinctions*[6] over the history of life on Earth. The first mass extinction is estimated to have occurred when a severe ice age led to sea levels falling by 100 meters, wiping out 60–70 per cent of all species that were prominently ocean dwellers at the time. Soon after, nearly 445 million years ago, the ice melted, leaving the oceans starved of oxygen (Ceballos *et al*, 2017). The second mass extinction, approximately 360 million years ago, also followed a prolonged climate change event, hitting life in shallow seas very hard, killing 70 per cent of species, including almost all corals (Ceballos *et al*, 2017).

The third mass extinction destroyed 90 per cent of species when massive volcanic eruptions in Siberia caused a savage episode of global warming about 250 million years ago (Brannen, 2017). The fourth mass extinction is also believed to be the result of volcanism, which reaped nearly 75 per cent of species 201 million years ago (Brannen, 2017). The fifth mass extinction is thought to have been caused when an asteroid or meteor, which measured 10 kilometres across, hit Earth and generated an explosion that caused the 180-kilometre-wide Chicxulub crater in the Gulf of Mexico about 65 million years ago. This also resulted in volcanic eruptions across the planet, which

---

5 Standard error: 1.3 million species.
6 Mass extinctions are defined as periods during which a large percentage of all known species living at the time goes extinct or is completely exterminated.

together caused the release of approximately 300 gigatons of sulphur and 420 gigatons of carbon dioxide into the atmosphere.[7]

According to Artemieva and Morgan (2017), the surface temperature of Earth was reduced by more than 20 °C and it took over 30 years to recover. It is suggested that the dinosaurs and other species that lived on the surface would have been decimated within hours or weeks, while those that lived in burrows or hibernated, might have survived. It is this mass extinction of the giant dinosaurs that may have paved the way for the emergence of small primitive mammals, which have to come to occupy their current scale and scope across the planet.

Common to all mass extinction events have been massive volcanic activity that caused global warming of the atmosphere, together with acidification and oxygen depletion in the Earth's oceans (Bond and Grasby, 2017). For Bond and Grasby (2017), the other mechanisms that decimated the species of living organisms were acid rain, damage to the ozone layer, enhanced ultraviolet radiation and toxic metal poisoning. In hindsight, we have learned that all the five mass extinctions were essentially driven by rapid climate change, and the inability or incapacity of the hitherto living organisms to adapt in time to the emergent new environment.

OUR SHORT PRESENT: THE SIXTH MASS EXTINCTION AND RISING PRECARITIES

Consensus is rapidly emerging among scientists that we are currently experiencing a sixth mass extinction. While for every 10 000 vertebrate species, two became extinct over the course of a period of 100 years before the year 1500 CE, almost 500 vertebrate species have become extinct in the last century, which indicates an extinction rate 100 times higher than the background rate (Ceballos *et al*, 2015). According to Ceballos and colleagues (2015), 'an exceptionally rapid loss of biodiversity over the last few centuries [indicates] that a sixth mass extinction is already under way'. Counterfactually, it would

---

[7] In comparison, the International Energy Agency estimates that total carbon emissions reached 'a historical high' of 32.5 gigatons in 2017 (IEA, 2018).

have *ordinarily* taken between 800 and 10 000 years for the Earth to experience such a loss of biodiversity ((Ceballos *et al*, 2015).

Mammals, largely prey for the giant reptiles (dinosaurs), emerged during – and prospered after – the extinction of the dinosaurs. Among contemporary mammals are tiny bats and enormous blue whales, which are now found across the globe. Human beings emerged more recently in our long evolutionary path to the present. Utilising the genealogical heuristic of the most recent common ancestor (MRCA), it is conservatively estimated that anatomically, modern human beings are the contemporary progeny of nearly 6 billion ancestors (Rohde *et al*, 2004).

Such an estimation, however, is prone to the vagaries of the actual human and social dynamics as they emerged and were adapted in the evolutionary path to the present. While we have still not fully determined our exact and precise evolutionary history, our species continues to expand at an accelerated pace. The total world population was estimated at approximately 7.9 billion people as at the end of December 2021 (United Nations, 2018).

Our scale and distribution, however, is dwarfed by the complex and intertwined set of plants and other animals that we have domesticated, and thereby also genetically modified for our growth purposes. According to Harari (2015: 298):

> If you took all the people in the world and put them on a large set of scales, their combined mass would be about 300 million tons. If you then took all our domesticated farm animals – cows, pigs, sheep and chickens – and placed them on an even larger set of scales, their mass would amount to about 700 million tons. In contrast, the combined mass of all surviving large wild animals – from porcupines and penguins to elephants and whales – is less than 100 million tons.

Thus, while we definitely do not constitute the bulk of the mass of living animals, people occupy an almost apex-predator-type relationship with the rest of the planet's life forms. Our species requires a biomass of more than double our combined weights while we have reduced that of those not domesticated to less than a third of ours. Concerns about the ecological consequences of human activities have a long history in the literature. These concerns expand across the range of requirements for the reproduction of the human species and our production of material life.

The demise of carbon-based life forms over the history of the planet and their burial in the earth has allowed their subsequent sequestration in geophysical process, which resulted in the creation of fossil fuels and included naturally occurring unprocessed hydrocarbons in the form of crude oil and products derived from the refining of the extracted crude oil. While evidence exists of its existence and utilisation from two millenniums ago in China, petroleum as an industry began to 'take-off' with the production of paraffin[8] from an unidentified seepage near Manchester in 1847/48. Kerosene emerged in 1846 and Jan Józef Ignacy Lukasiewicz designed an oil refinery in 1856 (Gesner, 1861). It is precisely within the space of that decade that Marx and Engels would include reference to environmental degradation in the *Communist Manifesto* of 1848.

Oil rigs began to be deployed to extract the crude oil from below the surface from 1859. George Perkins Marsh published *Man and Nature: Or, physical geography as modified by human action* in 1864. Marsh's text also challenged the benign relationship between people and nature. According to Marsh (1864), the environment was affected by and became a product of human agency and, therefore, was dependent on social relationships.

With industrialisation following agriculture, nearly a century later, the American Petroleum Institute (API) created its Smoke and Fumes Committee in 1954 because it sought to forestall 'passing the wrong law [which] can also often be the most expensive and irritating way to approach the problem as far as both the public and industry are concerned' (Jenkins, 1954: 145). In seeking to meet a mandatory emission target, Jenkins argued that the willingness of the petroleum industry not to cheat was

> good evidence that the petroleum industry is managed by men who want to be good neighbours, by men who will go more than

---

8   James Young obtained a patent for the extraction of paraffin from shale in 1850.

half way in cooperating with enforcement agencies in order to be good neighbours, even when the laws under which they operate are not believed to be wisely drawn' (Jenkins, 1954: 149).

Roger Revelle from the Scripps Institution of Oceanography testified in the US Congress that '(f)rom the standpoint of meteorologists and oceanographers we are carrying out a tremendous geophysical experiment of a kind that could not have happened in the past or be reproduced in the future' (Revelle, 1956).[9] Revelle worked with Hans Suess, a chemist, and published a paper on the ocean's capacity to absorb carbon dioxide and determined that 'the average lifetime of a carbon dioxide molecule in the atmosphere before it is dissolved into the sea is of the order of 10 years' (Revelle and Suess, 1957: 18). They also suggested that 'most of the carbon dioxide released by artificial fuel combustion since the beginning of the industrial revolution must have been absorbed by the oceans' (Revelle and Suess, 1957: 19). Notwithstanding their empirical research, they are now popularly remembered for raising alarm that '(w)ithin a few centuries we are returning to the atmosphere and oceans the concentrated carbon stored in sedimentary rocks over hundreds of millions of years. The experiment if adequately documented may yield a far-reaching insight into the processes determining weather and climate' (Revelle and Suess, 1957: 9–20).

As we proceed further into the 21st century, the 'experiment' has indeed yielded insights into the relationship between the concentration of carbon dioxide in the atmosphere and climate change. Just two years after Revelle and Suess, Bert Bolin and Erik Eriksson argued that 'industrial production would expand exponentially, and that the concentration of carbon dioxide in the atmosphere would probably rise 25% by the end of the [20th] century' (Bolin and Eriksson, 1959: 142). In a further prophetic text, an official of the US Bureau of Land Management, Eugene Peterson, also researched the effects of increased atmospheric carbon dioxide concentrations on plant growth and populations. Peterson found that

---

9   Testimony of Roger Revelle, US Congress, House 84 H1526-5, Committee on Appropriations, Hearings on Second Supplemental Appropriation Bill, Washington DC.

'(t)hrough rapid exploitation of fossil fuels, mankind is inadvertently triggering major changes in the carbon cycle unprecedented in rapidity in known geologic history' (Peterson, 1969: 1162).

Forty-nine years ago, Peterson had astutely forecast and warned that:

> These changes may drastically affect world weather and global ecology within the next 30–80 years. We should avoid being misled because such other factors as dust, sunspots, or changes in local weather patterns may temporarily offset the long term, and perhaps irreversible, effects of [carbon dioxide]' (Peterson, 1969: 1164).

According to Peterson:

> These alternative projections to the year 2020 and beyond could be reasonably accurate if preliminary research findings prove to be a firm estimate of the rate of absorption of carbon dioxide by the oceans and the amount of heat trapped by carbon dioxide and water vapour in the atmosphere. If they prove to be substantially correct, whenever the optimum carbon dioxide level (from the standpoint of human welfare) over the centuries is reached (if it has not already been reached), additional carbon dioxide input through the burning of fossil fuels should cease. Other energy sources should be substituted. In fact, atmospheric carbon dioxide could prove to have such an effect upon the environment that it will be a major limiting factor for several centuries upon both industrial development and world population (Peterson, 1969: 1167).

It is on this evidence-based prescience, that Peterson demanded that a 'fully-fledged research programme to determine with certainty the many diverse and complex interrelationships that are involved in the build-up of both atmospheric carbon dioxide and particulate matter is essential to [humankind's] future welfare' (Peterson, 1969: 1169).

With the clarity of hindsight, it may be seen that confronting climate change denial has not been easy and, notwithstanding the contemporary global consensus that accelerated climate change is the consequence of human activities, transnational corporations such as Imperial Oil 'knew' that '(s)ince pollution means disaster to the affected species, the only satisfactory course of action is to prevent it – to maintain the addition of foreign matter at such levels that it can be diluted, assimilated or destroyed by natural processes – to protect man's environment from man' (Holland, 1970: 3). Besides not accounting for growth and interdependence of the variables, the petroleum industry continued to advocate that 'a problem of such size, complexity and importance cannot be dealt with on a voluntary basis' (Holland, 1970: 3).

A decade after such confessions, Imperial Oil (69.6 per cent owned by Exxon Mobile) argued that '(i)t is assumed that the major contributors of carbon dioxide are the burning of fossil fuels... There is no doubt that increases in fossil fuel usage and decreases in forest cover are aggravating the potential problems of increased carbon dioxide, in the atmosphere' (Imperial Oil, 1980). Thirty-six years later and the Union of Concerned Scientists (UCS) reported that the Alliance for Automobile Manufacturers had submitted a report 'calling into question impacts of climate change and tailpipe pollutants in an effort to undercut the need for fuel economy regulation' in February 2018 (UCS, 2018). According to the UCS, this 'follows a familiar pattern, generally calling into question the science behind the health impacts of [insert pollutant here], frequently based on a convoluted and biased modelling effort masquerading as science' (UCS, 2018).

Richard York, Brett Clark and John Bellamy Foster note that,

> (w)here [orthodox economists] primarily differ is not on their views of the science behind climate change but on their value assumptions about the propriety of shifting burdens to future generations. This lays bare the ideology embedded in orthodox neoclassical economics, a field which regularly presents itself as using objective, even naturalistic, methods for modelling the economy. However, past all of the equations and technical jargon, the dominant economic paradigm is built on a value system that prizes capital accumulation in the short-term, while de-valuing

everything else in the present and everything altogether in the future (Foster, Clark & York, 2010: 98).

According to calculations by the Organisation for Economic Cooperation and Development (OECD), the economic damage caused by air pollution is expected to cost US$2.6 trillion, due to the costs of sick days, medical bills and reduced agricultural output, while the human price is approximately six to nine million premature deaths per year by 2060 (OECD, 2016).

Pacifici and colleagues studied global hotspots of species at risk from climate change and, while maintaining that 'the Northern Hemisphere is likely to be more subject to global climate change than the Southern Hemisphere', they did include north-eastern South Africa in their listing (Pacifici, Piero and Rondinini, 2018). They specifically note that 'the areas hosting large numbers of vulnerable species are mostly concentrated in eastern Sub-Saharan Africa, specifically in the eastern side of the Democratic Republic of Congo, southern South Sudan and Ethiopia, Kenya, Tanzania, Zambia and north-eastern regions in South Africa' (Pacifici, Piero and Rondinini, 2018). According to the World Bank, 85 million people or nearly four per cent of sub-Saharan Africa's total population will become 'internal climate migrants' as they are 'forced to move within their own countries to escape the slow onset impacts of climate change' (World Bank, 2018).

SOUTH AFRICAN IMPACTS AND THE URGENT NEED FOR A JUST TRANSITION AND RADICAL TRANSFORMATION

Francois Engelbrecht and Pedro Monteiro draw on the Sixth Assessment report of the UN's Intergovernmental Panel on Climate Change (IPCC) to contend that 'the southern African region is likely to become drier, even under 1.5 °C of global warming (Engelbrecht and Monteiro, 2021: 2). They argue further that 'the observed rate of warming in recent decades is about twice the global average, and further drastic warming is projected for the region as the level of global warming increases'. It is on this empirical basis that the southern Africa region is rendered as a 'climate change hotspot'[10] (Engelbrecht and Monteiro, 2021). These scientists also warn that while multi-year droughts would become more prevalent generally, the eastern territories of the country would experience 'increases in heavy precipitation, despite the region projected to become generally drier' (Engelbrecht and Monteiro, 2021). Accompanying the warming would be heat waves and consequent heat stress. If we cross the threshold of 3 °C of global warming, we can expect that 'both the maize crop and the cattle industry in southern Africa are likely to collapse' (Engelbrecht and Monteiro, 2021: 3).

Gina Ziervogel and five colleagues who participated in the IPCC assessments contributed to an invited commentary in the *South African Journal of Science* and noted that '(i)ncreasingly strong intersectoral relationships between food production, water supply, energy generation and space for natural ecosystem function are emerging in South Africa and southern Africa at large' (Ziervogel *et al*, 2022). They also recognise that the increasing demand for urban residencies also magnifies climate change impacts. Accordingly, Ziervogel *et al* (2022) encourage a focus on the 'most at-risk urban residents'. Notwithstanding such a suggested orientation, they argue that

> because the just transition threatens existing development pathways and the status quo, climate justice will be hard to achieve in practice. In addition, the feasibility and effectiveness of many urban adaptation actions are currently constrained by limited institutional, financial and technological access and capacity' (Ziervogel *et al*, 2022: 3).

These six scientists argue further that:

> In the South African context, it is critical to consider justice, because of the country's apartheid history, its stark levels of inequality, and the future challenges related to a just transition, such as prioritising decarbonisation and a move away from fossil

---

10 When a region that is naturally dry and warm becomes drastically warmer and drier, the options for adaptation are limited.

fuels without reducing economic development and individual well-being' (Ziervogel et al, 2022: 3).

These science-based assessments find resonance in the report of CIVICUS[11] on the flooding in KwaZulu-Natal in 2022. According to CIVICUS,

> Scientists have linked the record-breaking downpour to climate change and warn of increasingly extreme weather events to come. These are putting strain on the ability of countries to prevent and respond to disasters. In South Africa, the scale of the crisis left the government struggling to mount an adequate response, while civil society played a vital role in leading recovery efforts on the ground (CIVICUS, 2022).

Ecological changes resulting from human and social actions are endangering our environment and thereby increasing our precarity as a species-being. As we are essentially located within the sixth mass extinction, the need for a just transition and radical transformation is becoming increasingly more urgent and desperate.

On 9 February 2023, the South African President and President of the ANC delivered the 29th State of the Nation Address (SONA) since the democratic breakthrough of 1994. In the 2023 SONA, 'climate change' was mentioned thrice, and a national state of disaster was declared to respond to the electricity crisis and its effects (RSA, 2023a; 2023b). A mere four days later, the Minister of Co-operative Governance and Traditional Affairs declared a further national state of disaster as a result of 'the magnitude and severity of the impact of the flooding incidents which caused devastating impact in Eastern Cape, Free State, Gauteng, KwaZulu-Natal, Limpopo, Mpumalanga, and North West provinces that resulted in the loss of life, missing persons, damage to property, infrastructure and the environment' (RSA, 2023c). Engaging with the challenges of energy generation, transmission, and universal accessibility while simultaneously

---

11 CIVICUS, which means 'of the community', was established in 1993. Although it has its head office in South Africa, it is part of a global alliance dedicated to strengthening citizen action and civil society around the world.

confronted by the disastrous impacts of climate change does pose serious problems for understanding our contemporary conjuncture and the contestation over a fundamentally just transition. The deteriorating environmental situation is contributing to accelerated climate changes and this is further escalating misery in the environment. While the country's financialised minerals–energy complex remains at the core of ecological catastrophe, the crisis is also co-located within the context of international, continental and national forces that are characterised by the consequences of corporate state capture, neoliberal fiscal and monetary orthodoxies, hollowed-out state capacities, and austerity-restrained public service capabilities.

Between ecocide and socialism, our major transformational imperative is in itself a battle for our very survival and our continued existence as a species-being. The need to remain focused on the primary contradictions that give rise to the manifestations being experienced is proving to be extremely difficult in the global and domestic battle of ideas. The totalising ideological capture of those leading institutions of power and their advisers poses further challenges to those seeking solutions that open pathways beyond the genocidal tendencies of capitalism. We sorely miss the courage and discipline of Mzala to challenge the current thinking beyond the simplistic and formulaic towards a deeper and more serious critique of the current form and dynamics of capitalism in South Africa. The sixth mass extinction may prove to be our ecocide should we relegate ourselves to mere reformist initiatives framed within the currently dominant capitalist relations of production rather than seeking to advance socialist reconstruction and development.

CONCLUSION

Data continues to reaffirm that we are failing to redress the metabolic rift and thereby are increasing the existential risk to our species. As Fidel Castro famously warned at the Earth Summit in 1992: 'Enough of selfishness. Enough of schemes of domination. Enough of insensitivity, irresponsibility, and deceit. Tomorrow will be too late to do what we should have done a long time ago'

(Castro, 1992). Mzala had long recognised that '(t)he theory of the South African revolution aligns its approach to the national question to the social content of our epoch, the epoch of the transition from capitalism to socialism; it aligns itself with the stage of social development and the special features of South Africa' (Nxumalo, 1988: 17). In seeking to affect such a just transition, we are assisted by noting that '(s)ocialism for the twenty-first century, in short, is not capitalism' (Lebowitz, 2016). This guidance should help us resist the temptation to endure endless reforms of the existing catastrophic mode of production under the beguiling promise of trickled-down benefits, while our very existence is further threatened at the altar of increasing extraction of surplus values and the continuance of the accumulation of capital.

Class struggle and the nurturing of various post-capitalist alternatives within the belly of the neoliberal capitalist regime would help to usher in socialism, which would of necessity and circumstances be instilled with South African characteristics. Counterfactually, seeking to reform neoliberalism through the agency of corrupt private–public partnerships, an ostensibly hollowed-out state, and absent a socialist orientation from the top down will further the violence of austerity and hasten precarity under the spectre of ecocide. To save ourselves, together with all of the life forms constituting the biodiversity on the planet of our birth, we must redress the metabolic rift and, without disdain, clearly, coherently and cogently advance our collective demand for the establishment and defence of 'an association, in which the free development of each is the condition for the free development of all' (Marx and Engels, 1848).

REFERENCES

African National Congress (ANC). (1994). Statement of the National Executive Committee on the occasion of the 82nd Anniversary of the ANC, African National Congress, Johannesburg.

Artemieva, N., Joanna M. and Expedition 364 Science Party. (2017). 'Quantifying the release of climate-active gases by large meteorite impacts with a case study of Chicxulub', *Geophysical*

Research Letters, 44(20): 1–9.

Bolin, B. and Eriksson, E. (1959). 'Changes in the carbon dioxide content of the atmosphere and sea due to fossil fuel combustion', in B. Bolin (ed.). *The Atmosphere and the Sea in Motion*. New York: Rockefeller Institute Press.

Bond, D.P.G. and Grasby, S.E. (2017). 'On the causes of mass extinctions, paleogeography, palaeoclimatology', *Paleoecology*, 478: 3–29.

Brannen, P. (2017). *The Ends of the World: Volcanic apocalypses, lethal oceans, and our quest to understand Earth's past mass extinctions*. New York: Ecco Books.

Brent, G.B. (1991). *The Age of the Earth*. Standford, CA: Stanford University Press.

Castro, F. (1992). 'Speech at the Earth Summit', Rio de Janeiro, 12 June.

Ceballos, G., Ehrlich, P.R. and Dirzo, R. (2017). 'Biological annihilation via the ongoing sixth mass extinction signaled by vertebrate population losses and declines', *PNAS*, 114(30): E6089–96. DOI.org/10.1073/pnas.1704949114

Ceballos, G., Ehrlich, P.R., Barnosky, A.D., García, A., Pringle, R.M. and Palmer, T.M. (2015). 'Accelerated modern human-induced species losses: Entering the Sixth Mass Extinction', *Science Advances*, 1(5): e1400253. DOI: 10.1126/sciadv.1400253

CIVICUS. (2022). 'South Africa: The deadly impacts of climate change', *CIVICUS Lens*, 24 May. https://lens.civicus.org/south-africa-the-deadly-impacts-of-climate-change/ (Accessed 26 May 2023).

Dodd, M.S., Papineau, D., Grenne, T., Slack, Rittner, M., Pirajno, F., O'Neil, J. and Little, C.T.S. (2017). 'Evidence for early life in Earth's oldest hydrothermal vent precipitates', *Nature*, 543(7643): 60–64.

Engelbrecht, F.A. and Monteiro, P.M.S. (2021). The IPCC Assessment Report Six Working Group 1 report and southern Africa: Reasons to take action', *South African Journal of Science*, 117(11/12). DOI:https://doi.org/10.17159/sajs.2021/12679

Engels, F. (1883). *Dialectics of Nature*. New York: International Publishers [1979].

Engels, F. (1876). *The Part Played by Labour in the Transition from Ape to Man*. New York: International Publishers [republished 1950].

Engels, F. (1859). 'Letter to Marx', 12 December.

Foster, J.B., Clark, B. and York, R. (2010). *The Ecological Rift: Capitalism's*

War on the Earth, Monthly Review Press, New York City.

Gesner, A. (1861). *A Practical Treatise on Coal, Petroleum and Other Distilled Oils*. New York: Bailliere Brothers.

Golubski, C. (2017). 'Even before the U.S. left the Paris Agreement, Africa stepped up to the plate on climate change'. Brookings Institute, 2 June.

Harari, Y.N. (2015). *Sapiens: A Brief History of Humankind*. Toronto: Signal.

IEA. (2018). *Global Energy and CO2 Status Report 2017*. Paris: International Energy Agency.

Imperial Oil. (1980). 'Review of environmental protection activities for 1978–1979'. Toronto: Imperial Oil Archives.

Jenkins, V.N. (1954). 'The petroleum industry sponsors air pollution research', *Air Repair*, 3(3): 144–49.

Lebowitz, M.A. (2016). 'What is socialism for the twenty-first century?' *Amandla Magazine*, 22 November.

Marsh, G.P. (1864). *Man and Nature: Or physical geography as modified by human action*. New York: Charles Scribner.

Marx, K. (1861). 'Letter to Lassalle', 16 January, in *Marx and Engels Collected Works, Vol. 41*. London: Lawrence Wishart. [1985].

Marx, K. (1887[1984]). *Capital, Vol. 1*. Moscow: Progress Publishers. [1984].

Marx, K. and Engels, F. (1998 [1848]). *Manifesto of the Communist Party*. London: Verso.

Mora, C., Derek P.T., Sina A., Alastair G.B.S. and Worm, W. (2011). 'How many species are there on earth and in the ocean?' *PLoS Biolog*, 9(8): e1001127.

Nxumalo, J.N. (1988). 'The national question in South Africa', in M. van Diepen (ed.). *Revolutionary Theory on the National Question in South Africa*. London: Zed Books.

Nzimande, B.E. (2015). Speech by the Minister of Higher Education and Training at the Launch of the Mzala Nxumalo Centre, Pietermaritzburg.

OECD. (2016). *Economic Consequences of Outdoor Air Pollution*. Paris: Organisation for Economic Cooperation and Development.

Pacifici, M., Piero, V. and Rondinini, C. (2018). 'A framework for the identification of hotspots of climate change risk for mammals', *Global Change Biology*, 24(4): 1626–36.

Peterson, E.K. (1969). 'Carbon dioxide affects global ecology', *Environmental Science and Technology*, 3(11): 1162–69.

Revelle, R. and Suess, H.E. (1957). 'Carbon dioxide exchange between atmosphere and ocean and the question of an increase of atmospheric carbon dioxide during the past decades', *Tellus*, 9(1): 18–27.

Rohde, D.L.T., Olson, S. and Chang, J.T. (2004). 'Modelling the recent common ancestry of all living humans', *Nature*, 431: 562–66.

RSA. (2023a). State of the Nation, Parliament of South Africa, Cape Town.

RSA. (2023b). Declaration of National State of Disaster: Impact of Severe Electricity Supply Constraint, Disaster Management Act, Act No. 57 of 2002, Government of South Africa, Tshwane (9 February).

RSA. (2023c). Declaration of National State of Disaster: Floods due to Inclement Weather, Disaster Management Act, Act No. 57 of 2002, Government of South Africa, Tshwane (13 February).

Ryder, G. (2017). 'A greener future will not be decent by definition, but by design'. Geneva: International Labour Organization.

Steffen, W., Broadgate, W. Deutsch, L. Gaffney, O. and Ludwig, C. (2015). 'The trajectory of the Anthropocene: The great acceleration', *The Anthropocene Review*, 2: 81–98.

Strauss, M. (2016). 'Our Universe is too vast for even the most imaginative sci-fi'. Aeon Media, published in association with Princeton University Press. Available at: https://aeon.co/ideas/our-universe-is-too-vast-for-even-the-most-imaginative-sci-fi (Accessed 12 April 2023).

Union of Concerned Scientists (UCS). (2018). 'Automakers turn to climate deniers in quest to lower fuel economy regulations', 19 March. Boston, MA: Union of Concerned Scientists. https://blog.ucsusa.org/dave-cooke/automakers-turn-to-climate-deniers-in-quest-to-lower-fuel-economy-regulations/ (Accessed 26 May 2023).

World Bank. (2018). *Groundswell: Preparing for internal climate migration*. Washington, DC: World Bank.

Ziervogel, G., Lennard, C., Midgley, G., New, M., Simpson, N.P., Trisos, C.H. and Zvobgo, L. (2022). 'Climate change in South Africa: Risks and opportunities for climate-resilient development in the IPCC Sixth Assessment WGII Report', *South African Journal of Science*, 118(9/10): 1-5.

CONCLUSION

THE FUTURE OF LEFTIST THOUGHT IN A NEW CENTURY

Robert J. Balfour

This book is both a tribute to and a reflection on the intellectual work of Mzala Nxumalo – a scholar and activist who has influenced a Marxist scholarship, not only of apartheid, but also the use of Marxist analysis to deal with the complexities of societies in which socialist as well as capitalist influences compete, sometimes within the same political organisation, and sometimes seemingly within political figures and leaders. Context remains a significant factor in assessing the efficacy to date of approaches to social organisation and the economy. To be sure, most of the issues confronting South Africa and the globe have their legacies in practices and approaches developed over the course of the past two centuries, not least of which are capitalism and industrialisation. Mzala Nxumalo's contribution to Marxist analysis has evidently inspired analysis not only of the South African context in which neoliberalism has been evidenced, but also further afield. That this book consists of contributions that acknowledge the scholarly legacy and intellectual debt owed to him, is not to suggest a debt to history, but rather to show how Mzala wrestled with questions that are still relevant today, and how his work has provoked a series of new questions about the future of socialism in this still new century.

Humanity's capacity to generate devastating social and financial disasters astounds (for example the global financial meltdown of 2007 and the devastation of resource-motivated wars, as seen in the Syrian and Iraqi conflicts). These developments result in diasporas that will continue to be felt by present and future generations, and cloud claims concerning the diminishment of violent conflict (Pinker, 2011). Even if less deadly than the world wars, smaller-scale conflicts between states increased between 2010 and 2020 (Roser *et al*, 2016).

The parallels and links between the unintended impact of natural and human disasters speak to our collective incapacity to regulate – let alone control – ourselves without resorting to violence (see Shaw, 2003, on this theme) or the destruction of the environment. Oppression and concomitant inequality invariably continue to accompany the extraction and accumulation of wealth, without accountability, and poverty remains unacceptably normalised. This volume touches on the experience of the above at the national level of South Africa, as well as globally, in its consideration of the future of leftist thinking in an age of catastrophe and crisis. Migrancy of labour and migrancy of capital (speculative or financial capital in particular) are features of globalisation, but not by accident (Balfour, 2010). Both forms of migrancy are enabling of a global elite under terms and conditions. In general, we see that if labour becomes intransigent, the migration of capital can cause both the former and the latter to move, often with devastating outcomes for people and the planet.

In Africa, Mzala was conscious that the notion of the state is nebulous given the legacy of colonialism; it comprises groups that extend beyond its marked borders, and the impact of these borders has been to create false practices of othering, which deny commonalities between peoples. In the context of borders that have been imposed and divisions that have been created, and continue to be created, the struggle of the oppressed remains an international one, which extends beyond as well as within national borders. Migrancy is an imagined condition of the state, which, if seen from a Weberian perspective, is used to include and exclude people depending on changed political conditions, which in turn are influenced by changed economic conditions (Barrow, 1993). To be sure, contemporary analyses from the perspective of capital and socialism are not in short supply (Cudworth, 2007).

The first section acknowledges contributions to the interpretation of Marxism made by illustrious African and other scholars (Mzala counts among them), South American scholars (consider the impact of Paulo Freire's famous work on education) who have strived to reimagine fundamental concepts such as class and struggle in the context of changes in society. Such changes pertain, for example, to decolonisation (consider Ngũgĩ wa Thiong'o's [1994] work on language and culture), as well as feminism and the struggles concerning gender equality (Lewis, 2022). The chapter contributions are surveyed and linked to demonstrate not only the development and application of Marxism on social and economic matters, but also to reveal where perspectives are either dated or in need of revision.

This leads to the second section of the chapter, in which the post-human features more prominently in the future of sustainable life on the planet. As such, the relationship between human consciousness and the planet is widened to acknowledge that antagonisms exist not only between classes of people, but also between species and the planet, as life and resources become more precarious. These developments are linked again to chapters to illuminate the continuities between concerns addressed in both the first and second halves of the book by way of situating Mzala's contribution to the scholarship of Marxism, history and political and cultural analysis in both the previous and the new century. The chapter is framed at the outset with reference to the analysis of Naomi Klein and Elizabeth Povinelli, among others. The choices are purposeful because of the different and illustrative ways in which they define and focus on the conditions that produce 'context'.

Povinelli's (2012, 2017) work extends the focus of Marxism and accounts – in a sophisticated manner – for the aberrations of 21st-century capitalism, not least of which is the recognised capacity of humanity to alter the sustainability of life on the Earth. Povinelli explains this in the following terms:

> Marx thought the social dialectic was leading to the purification of the fundamental opposition of human classes. But many believe we are now witnessing a new war of the world as an antagonism between humans and all other classes of existence take center stage (Povinelli, 2017: 294).

Klein has been concerned with the uses to which natural and human disasters are put, by governments and related agencies. Klein (2007) has aptly described the intimate and distressing relationship between crises and the abuse of power in late 20th-century capitalism. Klein, in her book *The Shock Doctrine* (2007), suggests that crisis, whether provoked or accidental, provides an excellent occasion for change. She considers over 40 disasters globally, and finds that these have been used by powerful lobbies within and outside of government, in opportunistic ways to neutralise opposition and threats, and marginalise critique such that accountability for impact is eroded.

With an abundance of information at our disposal and an enhanced capacity to compress and organise big data, we cannot claim ignorance about the impact of our actions, as men abuse women in their homes, as corporations or government abuse cheap labour, as young people neglect older people, as rich disregard poor. As a species, we know well how to be aware and how to be indifferent, and how to make an impact on the world, and yet we conduct ourselves as though we were not of, or indeed, in it (Klein, 2007). Humans are collectively skilled enough to enhance industrial methods of extraction, and through extraction, manufacture and create a related financial 'services' sector that enables capital to exit and enter labour markets depending on where labour can be had, most cheaply. Capital has demonstrated its capacity to form privilege (its development, maintenance or destruction), to create cheap labour, to maintain and reinforce marginalisation (through stigmatisation, othering and stereotyping) which is critical to defining cheap labour, and to concentrate the power in necessarily few hands to enable an easy denial of the humanity of both the oppressing and the oppressed. Dispossession, distortion and disfigurement are well-used and understood devices in our collective skills set and when these are applied, they are applied differently depending on race, gender and class, and the intersectionalities of these identity markers.

RETHINKING MARXISM AND THE NEED FOR A CONTINUED CRITIQUE OF CAPITAL

Amilcar Cabral (1924–1973) argued that history began with class, but that such an understanding denied whole epochs of human history in which class was not yet an evident social form of organisation. Other African theorists such as Leopold Senghor (1906–2001) argued that the class struggle, as defined by Marx, was not relevant to Africa, and suggested rather that African socialism be based on spiritual values. Kwame Nkrumah (1909–1972) similarly critiqued the notion of African socialism as a romantic invention of leftist intellectuals, residing mostly abroad, whose ideas were taken up by Western publicists, and therein lies the dilemma of its not dealing with imperialism and the legacy of colonialism. Ayi Kwei Armah (1939–) went on to critique Marx and Engels (1820–1895) for not recognising that Africa has its own history and that this was not accounted for in their analysis: the fact of European supremacy and violence was seen as axiomatic, and thus not needing reflection.

Such examples are not limited to African scholars or only to past writings. Pearson (1999), an Australian Aboriginal activist, argued that state welfare, when applied to indigenous peoples, is a technique of numbing indigenous and non-indigenous people to the radical 'state of dysfunction' in Aboriginal communities. This echoes a point made by Povinelli (2012: 387) who argues that, 'in the wake of liberal forms of multiculturalism's failure to equalize structures of racial inequality ... the singular largest problem with addressing the fetid nature of these communities is that indigenous [peoples] are so destroyed and so used to their destitution that it is unclear how to fix their life-worlds'. The history of black and non-Eurocentric Marxist analysis thus serves to illuminate and provide critical points of scrutiny that contribute to national economic as well as social dialogues. Having described possibilities for the further renewal and revision of Marxist theory, the paragraphs that follow link this to developments in the critique of both capitalism and Marxism.

In considering the scope and contributions this book makes to leftist thought in general, and to socialism in particular, it is useful to understand how other scholars have explored the asymmetry of meaning and power in contexts where this asymmetry has profound implications for interpretation. In other words, how can alterity be crafted in contexts in which the spaces are so hegemonically possessed as to make it is almost impossible to see alternative perspectives on power and its abuses?

The search for a cogent critique of capitalism remains relevant, not so much for reasons associated with the fall of Marxism as much as for the evidence, politically, socially and economically, for the continued excess associated with capitalism in its latest guise: neoliberalism. The demise of communism and the collapse of communist states was heralded in the West as irrefutable evidence of the unsustainability of socialism. Theorists and commentators (Francis Fukuyama, 1992, being one such prominent proponent) contested that the fall of communism (as a form of statist socialism) was sufficient grounds to declare capitalism as the only viable form of social organisation; this despite abundant catastrophic examples of the devastation associated with an insufficiently regulated capitalism on the environment and on population groups too old, or too young, to be of use for reproductive labour. What becomes of populations surplus to the requirements of labour is not simply the problem of post-industrialised society, but also the developing society. And this problem is a fundamental issue relevant to every group that is removed from the mechanisms of participation in government as well as industry, and relevant to those groups qualified (by virtue of age or education, or means) who are active in government and industry.

If capitalism has been seen to erode the welfare and socialist state, there is also recognition that the investment of hope placed in the state, and its related institutions, as the primary stakeholder or the most effective agent of change, is perhaps overemphasised (as argued by Foucault *et al*, 2009). What do we do with the state and how might the limits of statism (Bakunin, 1990) be debated without falling into liberal categories of public and private sector investment as though these were mutually exclusive? The expectation of all citizens is that the state, and its related institutions, should and is able to deliver on the needs of the most vulnerable majority and minority groups (as suggested by Schreiner) and to do so it must also be an economic role-player (through systems of benefit, as well as through regulation of the economy (as suggested by Habermas) (Cook, 2004). The state has to be viewed in terms of its birth: by conquest, conquering, reconquered and unconquered. The independence moment (especially for postcolonial societies) is not entered without a decision to either destroy it or perpetuate it. Furthermore, because of this Marxist proposition, the question arises as to whom the state belongs? It must be depersonalised, reconstructed and rehabilitated – but it is not clear how this is to occur. What is clear in the 21st century is an increase in lack of accountability: all over the world, there are too many examples of the state that neither respects its own laws nor enacts its own polices. Decisions are made (too) often without consent yet end up being accommodated or accepted.

Simply put, while a statist form of socialism (communism) has been revealed to be inadequate as a means of social organisation, an unregulated form of capitalism (neoliberalism) is evidently ineffective in addressing any of the pressing social questions of the 21st century. Socialism remains relevant as a means to organise societies, not on the basis of ideological comparison, but rather because it is possible to see socialist values underpinning stated (though possibly not realised) aspirations of even 'capitalist' industrialised societies, when explored for example, in constitutions, bills of rights and other high-level policy framing documents. Socialism as theory and discourse is concerned with social and transformative justice (the recognition of inequality and redress). This justice entails protection of the poor from exploitation by the rich, protection of the weak from the aggression of the strong, protection of vulnerable labour in the face of unaccountable capitalist profit, protection of local manufacture from drive-down profiteering free markets, and a stated commitment to the common good.

Any modern state (comprising government and industry) is measured in terms of its capacity and effectiveness to support and protect its most vulnerable groups, even as it provides for all its citizens. The success of industry at the expense – or to the exclusion – of a government's capacity to deliver on and account for its commitments, is the failure of the state. Similarly, the failure of industry to recognise its accountability to employed and unemployed citizens alike, is a failure of the state to develop itself and protect its resources. The state is all within it. It is for this reason that accountability for the delivery of services and for prospects of honest employment are the responsibility of both government and industry. It is mistaken to imagine that government is accountable to itself or to the narrow definition of that part of an electorate that placed it in office; it is the contributions of all working adults, whether they supported a ruling party or not, that support programmes of public spending, and these should benefit all the citizens of a state, not merely those who supported a ruling party. The role of government and its commitment to the delivery of services is contested in this book, with many references to corruption, which is an attendant feature of the neoliberal state's reliance on dependent elites (commonly referred to in Marxist theory as the bourgeoisie, and in its tenderpreneurial form, as the petite bourgeoisie). There are particular insights in this book arising from its focus on Mzala's reflections on colonialism and apartheid (as colonialism of a special form), which also occur in analysis of the impact of colonialism as a form of imperialism. The national bourgeoisie is regarded with scepticism arising from its devotion to self-enrichment, because its agenda is not devoted to the most vulnerable groups in terms of access to services and support. Our economy is thus a bourgeois enterprise in which the 'trickle down' of wealth has evidently not occurred, and hence the national question remains unaddressed. The insights regarding capitalism should also be accompanied by self-critique by Marxists. Self-critique is an incredibly important aspect of elevating thinking about the 'how and why' South Africa has come to this point of self-recognition.

The South African Communist Party recognised the colonial and imperial nexus in the 1960s. A second shift in thinking occurred in the 1990s when the negotiations took place to lay the foundations of a new South Africa, but almost 30 years later, the socialist revolution has not happened. Instead, globalisation and neoliberalism emerged to curtail its possibilities as both developments undervalue the need for social and economic justice in favour of a commitment to the unregulated accumulation of wealth at the continued expense of the economically and socially disenfranchised. Corporate state capture is another way to describe the systemic state-based corruption that has occurred – a collusion of economic and political elites in plunder. Struggling against this development is not only a national struggle – we see similar developments and similar resistance globally, as wealth is repatriated to metropolitan centres on the basis of old imperial practices. The postcolonial state is not sufficiently different from the colony, despite the struggle for liberation and independence having gathered momentum during the 1960s. There remains a disturbing intransigence of labour practices between colony and postcolony in which the conditions for marginalisation seem continuous.

Part 1 of this book explores perspectives on the national question, from the perspective of Mzala himself, as well those who have been influenced by him. Ngonyama argues that Mzala was a keen intellectual whose analysis of figures like Gatsha Buthelezi revealed the extent to which hegemonic systems like apartheid and capitalism could distort those resisting it, as well as key leftist policy initiatives, even after the occurrence of national liberation. That Mzala was non-sectarian in his approach to politics, did not detract from the systematic approach he took to the struggle against the inhumane system of capitalism. His intellectual and social activism can be seen not only in his approach to history, but also in his ability to extrapolate from Marxist theory to the national question, evident in his writing about a wide range of issues inclusive of economic, political and social conditions. Mzala's contribution is not, according to Unterhalter, only of academic interest, because of the direct links between scholarly debate, history and activism. Linking analysis to policy implications in post-apartheid South Africa, Radebe describes how, for Mzala, the connections between national and class oppression needed to be made evident. Class was integral to the national question in the struggle against apartheid, but also in precolonial and postcolonial societies, globally. The national question could thus, in Mzala's view, be contextualised against precolonial, colonial histories, as well as the contemporary bourgeois democratic period, where the black working class remains 'subalternised'. In Chapter 4, Houston and Davids extend this focus on the national question across race and class lines. They use SASAS data to demonstrate that those least trusting of one another in a post-apartheid South Africa are the upper classes across both race and gender lines. Further, they argue that the first transition had the effect of exacerbating the underlying negative issues instead of growing national unity by focusing on measures that, although designed to increase economic participation of hitherto excluded groups, had the effect of creating a bourgeoise, which is seemingly unconcerned about the longevity of issues, inclusive of race polarisation, by focusing more on race rather than the creation of a more equal society. The focus on race, rather than the ongoing class struggle, is a theme addressed further by Mataise, who argues that the focus on greed and individualism, as associated with capitalism, detracts from the forgotten origins of the leftist struggle for the rightful place of a focus on the common good of the community.

The discrepancy between aspirations and lived experience is also addressed by Solani, who describes a fundamental disconnect between constituencies' expectations of government and the mandate that successive democratically elected governments have gone on to execute. This accounts, at least in part, for the persistence of deep structural economic issues like poverty and unemployment. Mzala's analysis of apartheid's coercive structures and strategies provide a platform and impetus to prioritise programmatic unity in the face of capitalism's enablement of only the bourgeoise, who even if formerly part of the class struggle, have somehow forgotten any obligations to create employment for the working classes and precariat. This important point is extended by Horn, who notes that while structures like trade unions have long established systems of direct democracy, there is a need to organise people who are not formally employed so that participation can be widened beyond a relatively small 'working class'. In this vein, Kaaf extends Horn's analysis to consider how to increase democratic participation, across organisations and classes, in key issues concerning employment, work and social services for vulnerable groups. Kaaf suggests that Mzala's work provides a basis for breaking away from the futile and failed political models of the 'old' Left and that new strategies are needed, which are creative and imaginative enough to galvanise people across class and race lines to commit to emancipation, solidarity and equality. The role of class elites in the debates concerning capitalism and Marxism have tended to mask the underpinning tenets of capitalism in which mobility into and out of such elites is dynamic. Capitalism – as a social as well as economic form – has to be scrutinised, argues Dubbeld, to understand that politics is a restricted area of activity and that policies and state interventions cannot in themselves shift an entire epoch. Understanding the impact of capitalism throughout the epoch brings to full circle the influence of Mzala, who was always eager to describe and analyse the impact of capitalism not only on people, but also on communities, society and the environment, with reference to the colonial period and the bantustans created in South Africa. Marxist analysis demonstrates that bantustans are not the only regions to which the dispossessed can/could be removed, and retrieved at will to the metropolitan centres, depending on labour needs, without any prospects of developing economic liberation – let alone political liberation. This state of vulnerability is described variously in the literature as 'surplus populations' or the precariat, and in this book it is shown how Mzala's work contributes to an understanding of precarity, and how it is linked to, and dependent on, a system that generates accumulation and gross disparities. Maharajh and Tivana extend this analysis to the South African and international situations to demonstrate how the austerity measures of neoliberalism hasten precarity and the spectre of ecocide.

MARXISM, HUMAN CONSCIOUSNESS AND THE POST-HUMAN TURN

Despite the hegemony of neoliberal discourse and the pervasiveness of its policies in everything from health care to education, from defence to transport, the capitalist insistence on a forced cohabitation of worth and value has met with resistance, and has been fractured even as it was merged. Indeed, the cracks within the current policy regimes reveal to us the humanity of our differences; the wealth generated through solidarity and collaboration could produce healing and exceed the limits of both hopes and expectations of the political mainstream characterised by increasing tax and land grabs, more system dysfunction and yet higher civil servant salaries, more education and yet high unemployment. In some ways it is reassuring to note that within the lingo of neoliberalism, with its well-known epithets such as 'the free market', 'market justice' and 'deregulation', socialist values have continued to attract people in a world dominated by spectacular conspicuous consumption and waste.

And, in a post-Cold War world, the debates about what constitutes imperial practices are cloudy, precisely because it is no longer possible to ascribe, believe in or reasonably articulate the meaning of the labels: capitalist, communist, socialist and imperialist. These debates are to some extent overtaken by the impact of climate change on the present and future sustainability of humans as well as other species. This point is also made by Chakrabarty (2009: 201) who suggests that the conditions of anthropogenic climate change have dissolved the 'age-old humanist distinction between natural history and human history'. This theme, addressed towards the end of this book, creates another dimension of complexity to the relationship between capital and labour.

That noted, there is a danger in the conflation of values and the actions that seem to undermine them, by the very same actors/agents articulating them. The danger is not limited to scepticism or disbelief, but also touches on something much deeper: people have lost their sense of credibility and confidence in the capacity of the state to proclaim and support truth. Double-speak or speak left, walk right politics underly the development of semiocapital: 'And insofar as it is effective in this capture, semiocapital pushes beyond labor power into soul power – not merely a consumption of human labor but a pneumaphagia, a spirit-eater' (Povinelli, 2017: 299). The capture of discourse and ideas – and their misuse

– is only one dimension of the seriousness of the struggle against neoliberalism as a phase of capitalist development, made more insidious by the grafting and appropriation of terms associated with socialism. This makes the terrain of debate more complex than it was in the early 20th century because the struggle concerning ideas risks drift from the practices to which ideas speak, a matter noted in the introduction of this book, where reference is made to China, and how to understand China's approaches to loans, investment and the extraction of raw materials from former (European) colonies. Political control may not be evident, but its seeming absence should not suggest the absence of terms under which the extension of assistance occurs – terms that remain asymmetrical, even as they do benefit the old elites. Influence and power require organisation to find effective expression in policy, and the effectiveness of capital, in its continued evolution, similarly requires renewal and reflection on the forms of organisation and alliance needed by socialists and allies, and elaborated on in the sections that follow.

What is compelling in this book is not only deep reflection on the insights offered by Marxism, but also the need for socialist reorganisation. The value of Marxism is that it underscores the importance of looking behind and beyond changes in the economic structure. New forms of work compel a revision of ideas about the working class, because in the period of globalisation, own-account workers are not the same as entrepreneurs: the latter being more economically dependent than the former. Old paradigms concerning industrialisation and manufacturing give rise to the social solidarity economy, which can combine formal and informal economies, using new technologies associated with the 'gig economy'. These open source and app-based technologies provide many exciting possibilities for connection, organisation and support.

An understanding of work also requires more nuance than a purely sectoral and mainstream progressive economic analysis of capitalism. This nuanced understanding provides for a richer account of industrialisation and de-industrialisation, which, if plotted empirically, shows that these are not phase or stage determined. In developing countries de-industrialisation has occurred, for example, without these societies ever having been industrialised. If stagism perceives development as being linked to progress and perceives capitalism as only one stage leading to the development of socialism, which is regarded as the benign and political end-point of social organisation, rethinking this analysis is critical. Even if Marxists hold that socialism is a more benevolent political arrangement as it does not focus purely on the support of the elite, but also the workers, rethinking stagism remains relevant because anti-colonial struggles do not always land up weakening imperialism or leading to better lives (Keefer, 2010). Efforts still have to be made to find new forms of solidarity, not only among the working class and precariat but also among left-thinking intellectuals.

Systems, whether bureaucratic or economic, are not simply abstractions: in essence they are forms of organisation. One of the myths of capitalism is that the free market operates almost independently of people, and that worth drives value. In this myth, human agency is obscured and the global movement of capital occurs almost invisibly, except that its impact on the ground is visible, and tangible insofar as people lose their jobs, then they lose their homes and remain unprotected and unsupported; unemployment grows almost in proportion to the incapacity of the state to support welfare systems. Capitalism's discourse is concerned with sectors. Marxist analysis takes the underlying social relationships that give rise to activities, rather than sector classification. In Marxist terms, commodities are not necessarily physical. Services can also be considered as commodities. Services, which might be classified in terms of their 'sectors', may in fact be related in terms of the underpinning social relationships. Industrialisation produces growth and progress but it also produces surplus value and accumulation, not without human misery. Manufacturing, and its pace, has a special place in a Marxist understanding of accumulation.

The informal economy provides a fascinating terrain for workers to organise themselves, whether as street traders, domestic workers or sex workers. Trade unions need to acknowledge that, although the informal economy comprises many women and is constrained by domestic labour inequalities, they have an obligation to support organisational efforts of the unemployed for the unemployed. Irrespective of membership, the organisation of labour cannot depend only on the formal notion of a 'job'. Workers, whether formal or informal, have rights, need protection and are capable of giving rise to effective leadership, which helps create better conditions for work, through recognition. Unionisation at the level of this economy is difficult but necessary because the formal economy is shrinking and because the informal economy is growing.

The three components of this informal economy are worthy of analysis concerning efforts to organise workers. Domestic workers, for example, have an international federation grown from the ground up, but some sectors of the economy remain difficult to organise. While Street Vendors International was formed in 2002, sex workers have to deal with criminalisation, which makes open organisation difficult. Unpaid labour is a site for gender differentiation. Gender in this context involves an understanding of human relationships, which may involve women and men in power relations through structures, rituals and routines that are proximal and relational. The requirement for organisation needs also to demonstrate an awareness that capitalism responds to and evolves in relation to changing labour practices. Social relationships emerge from the messy material realities of reproducing human life, but these relationships are unequal within a capitalist system. In *The Capital* (1867), Marx shows how everything can be viewed in terms of functions and capacities – bodies have the capacity to produce labour. Marxist analysis attends to the need for a systemic understanding of capital and how it functions, without losing focus of the need for the humanisation of identity. Gender and the family pretend to be natural but derive from the modes of production.

This noted, capital responds to changes in strategy in relation to pressures to pay hitherto unpaid forms of labour. Bernardi (2009: 186), in describing the development of a European-wide autonomist refusal to subjugate life to labour power, notes that this seems to have provided more impetus to the automation of technology to replace workers, the rise of deregulation and what Povinelli terms 'the reorganization of relations between economy and society, and the disorganization of the coordinates of left critical discourse' (2017: 298). This section described the need for organisation in light of a necessary revision of key thought concerning stagism and the development of organisation. The following sections explore a further series of changes that have occasioned a turn away from the Anthropocene towards a recognition that future conflicts will not only be between classes of people, but also between the environment and species.

Human consciousness is in a state of crisis. State and global systems demonstrate that this crisis is constructed yet not controlled. The experiences of colonialism and neocolonialism, together with the experiences of Marxism and communism the world over, and in Africa in particular, have revealed the very damaging nature of dependence. Attempts at violent revolution or clean breaks from that dependence have historically not been successful because the liberation movements were not socialist to begin with, but rather nationalist in impulse. Sometimes the 'nationalist impulse' contains a romanticisation of socialist principles and values. Thus, liberation movements, if considered within a historical perspective, are not the ideal vehicles for creating the socialist state (a point also made by Mamdani, 2018). There are disturbing similarities between industrialisation of communist states and industrialisation of capitalist states, making comparisons weak and a defence of communism difficult.

As noted earlier in this chapter, the hot politics (with acknowledgement to Povinelli's phrase) of climate change has also changed the nature of debates within socialist circles:

> The illusions of our epoch are the autonomous and antagonistic. Other illusions may be better suited. Viruses, gassings, toxins – these are the names we give to manners of appearing and spreading; tactics of diverting the energies of arrangements of existence in order to extend themselves; strategies of copying, duplicating, and lying dormant even as they continually adjust to, experiment with, and test their circumstances; manoeuvres to confuse and level every difference that emerges between regions while carefully taking advantage of the minutest aspects of their differentiation (Povinelli, 2017: 308).

The alternative for socialism, in terms of the future, is to focus on the value it adds to the healing of people and the planet that needs to occur in the aftermath of colonialism: that value concerns education. Socialism is a process in which transformation is entailed, but this must take account of the need to deal with and exit capitalism. The retreat from socialism has to be confronted, as does the problematic of capitalism and this entails introspection on the part of Marxist and socialist thinkers, and reflection. The question concerning how to build an African socialism, or indeed an international socialism, in a post-neoliberal world (assuming here that we do not head towards mass extinction, as some of the chapters in this volume suggest is inevitable), demands a rigorous and detailed response of socialism in this period of fragmentation and reintegration in this global century. Why? Because it is not yet post-neoliberal and it is certainly not post-capitalist. What remains clear is that global and local elites collude to maintain and further the interests of capitalism in the pursuit of profit without accountability for how this is generated, and to which purposes it is employed.

REFLECTIONS

This book began with Pampallis and Radebe's exploration of Mzala's key contribution to understanding, defining and analysing the national question in the context of South Africa, at the point at which the scales had tipped and national liberation was only a near horizon away. The perspectives on capital expressed in the first half of the book, although discussed in the context of South Africa, are linked to the global context in which imperialism, far from ebbing, has taken on new and more insidious forms. Polycentrism, as Shubin suggests, is the presence of multiple and equally rapacious centres of power, which, while not necessarily acting in unison, nevertheless constitute an 'imperium'. Nzimande notes that a related and fundamental condition of such hegemony is underdevelopment, the collective actions and impact of which are made evident in uprising conflict.

Within these constellations of imperial economic and military hegemony, the role of the Left in general, and the radical left in particular, remains vital and Mzala's contribution to the scholarship of the former and the activism of the latter, rings true for both the previous and the new century. Who Mzala was (see Unterhalter in Chapter 2) and who he remains in terms of his influence on thinking is demonstrated in the insights shared from around the world by contributors who either knew him or whose work has been influenced by him. Thus, while his contributions to the national question are explored across several contributions (see chapters 4 and 6), his role in the Left extends well beyond the end of the 20th century. The end of the first half of the book anticipates scholars rethinking this contribution to South Africa in the 21st century – a South Africa in which so many issues remain unresolved largely because challenges are not sufficiently responded to in terms of government policies concerning the economy and the social order. These issues (unemployment, poverty, extremes of wealth and inequality) and challenges (redress, redistribution, equality, economic inclusion, participation and accountability – see chapters 7 and 9) are not particular to South Africa, even if the gross inequality of the society means that they are most acutely felt by the population excluded by the neoliberal policies of the state (see, for example, chapters 5 and 6).

In spite of these challenges, this book demonstrates, through examples and scholarship, that economic development is not only the province of the employed (be this employers or government), but also the responsibility of those sectors that are formally considered to be 'unemployed'. In addition, in the second part of the book, the need for solidarity, recognition and organisation is revealed to be pressing and possible to achieve, even in contexts in which resources may be withheld, are not accessible or are simply not shared. Thus, while South Africa is an imbricated society, insights gained from around the globe and arising from the transnational, indeed global, networks of labour to which South Africans belong or in which they are represented, suggest that agency can achieve impact if solidarity is formed and maintained across the borders of nations, and across the barriers and limitations of narrow understandings of class, gender and race (see chapters 8 and 10 in the volume). It is for this reason that dilemmas of communities and the challenges of inclusive and sustainable approaches to development – to which capitalist forms of value need not be axiomatic – can be developed in one context and be the best examples worthy of emulation in many others. Polycentric powers do provoke solidarity and common purpose, especially where inequity, abuse and oppression are their consequences. Reanimating the critique of capitalism in South Africa and beyond is shown to be not merely a necessary response to the severe and damaging impact of neoliberalism, but also a critical need in the face of ecocide (see Chapter 12) as the consequence of humanity's incapacity to regulate itself and better sustain life, not only of humans, but of all species on our planet.

Acknowledging that there is awareness, among some capitalists and socialists alike, that the capitalist trajectory with regard to exploitation, extraction, wealth accumulation and oppression has reached the ontological end-point, is not prescient of the onset of a global acceptance of socialism. So, what becomes of the idea of revolution? What is needed is for organised movements of related leftist interests to forge alliances to work towards restoring human consciousness as part of a continuity of life on this planet, and radically transforming values away from the accumulation of surplus wealth. However, it is clear from the example of even formerly communist states that there is not the longevity of Marxist ideas of solidarity adequate to resist new forms of political particularism or essentialism away from the unscrupulous accumulation of surplus wealth towards a balance for future life on this planet. Far from suggesting cause for pessimism, this awareness provides a renewed impetus, urgency and relevance to the need to counter and provide alternatives, as well as activism, to the agendas of capitalism.

REFERENCES

Balfour, R.J. (2010). *Culture, Capital, and Representation: 1700–2000*. London: Palgrave-Macmillan.

Barrow, C.W. (1993). *Critical Theories of State: Marxist, Neo-Marxist, post-Marxist*. Madison, WI: University of Wisconsin Press.

Bakunin, M. (1990). *Statism and Anarchy*. Cambridge: Cambridge University Press.

Berardi, F. (2009). *Precarious Rhapsody: Semiocapitalism and the pathologies of the post-alpha generation*. (Translated by Arianna

Bove *et al.*) London: Minor Compositions.

Chakrabarty, D. (2009). 'The climate of history: Four theses', *Critical Inquiry*, 35(2): 197–222.

Cook, D. (2004). *Adorno, Habermas, and the Search for a Rational Society*. London: Routledge.

Cudworth, E. (2007). *The Modern State: Theories and ideologies*. Edinburgh: Edinburgh University Press.

Freire, P. (1972). *Pedagogy of the Oppressed*. London: Penguin Books.

Foucault, M., Senellart, M., Ewald, F. and Fontana, A. (2009). *Security, Territory, Population: Lectures at the College de France, 1977–1978*. New York: Picador/Palgrave Macmillan.

Fukuyama, F. (1992). *The End of History and the Last Man*. London: Penguin Books.

Keefer, T. (2010). 'Marxism, indigenous struggles, and the tragedy of "stagism"', *Upping the Anti: A Journal of Theory and Action*, (10). Available at: https://uppingtheanti.org/journal/article/10-marxism-indigenous-struggles-and-the-tragedy-of-stagism (Accessed 22 March 2022).

Klein, N. (2007). *The Shock Doctrine: The rise of disaster capitalism*. Toronto: Knopf Publishers.

Lewis, H. (2022). *The Politics of Everybody: Feminism, queer theory, and Marxism at the intersection*. London: Zed Books.

Mamdani, M. (2018). *Citizen and Subject: Contemporary Africa and the legacy of late colonialism*, 2nd edition. Princeton, NJ: Princeton University Press.

Marx, K. (1976 [1867]). *The Capital: A critique of political economy*, Vol. 1. London: Penguin Books.

Pearson, N. (1999). 'Aboriginal Australia at a crossroad: Reciprocity, initiative and community'. Edited text of an address to the Brisbane Institute, 26 July 1999. Available at: http://www.mrcltd.org.au/uploaded_documents/ACF1277.htm (Accessed 25 June 2009).

Pinker, S. (2011). *The Better Angels of our Nature*. New York: Viking.

Povinelli, E.A. (2017). 'The ends of humans: Anthropocene, autonomism, antagonism, and the illusions of our epoch', *The South Atlantic Quarterly*, 116(2): 293–308. DOI 10.1215/00382876-3829412.

Povinelli, E.A. (2012). 'Beyond the names of the people: Disinterring the body politic', *Cultural Studies*, 26(2-3): 370–90. DOI http://dx.doi.org/10.1080/09502386.2011.636206

Roser, M., Hasell, J., Herre, J. and Macdonald, B. (2016). *War and Peace*. Published online at OurWorldInData.org. Available at: https://ourworldindata.org/war-and-peace' (Accessed 4 April 2022).

Shaw, M. (2003). *War and Genocide: Organized killing in modern society*. Cambridge: Polity Press in association with Blackwell.

wa Thiong'o, N. (1994). *Decolonising the Mind: The politics of language in African literature*. Nairobi: EAEP Publishers and Oxford: James Currey Publishers.

ABOUT THE CONTRIBUTORS

ROBERT J. BALFOUR

Robert Balfour is Deputy Vice-Chancellor for Teaching–Learning at North-West University (NWU), South Africa. Until 2017 he was Professor and Dean of Education Sciences, also at the NWU, having worked previously at the University of KwaZulu-Natal and as Registrar at St Augustine College of South Africa. Robert has held fellowships at the Institute of Commonwealth Studies (University of London), Clare Hall (Cambridge University) and the Institute of Education (University College, London). He teaches courses in Applied Language Studies and specialises in language policy design and research. His book, *Education in South Africa: Crisis and change*, was published by Cambridge University Press in 2015. In literary cultural studies, his book *Culture, Capital and Representation* was published by Palgrave in 2010 to critical acclaim. Balfour holds degrees from the universities of Rhodes, Natal and Cambridge and is a published writer and poet and an exhibited painter.

YUL DEREK DAVIDS

Dr Yul Derek Davids is a Research Director in the Developmental, Capable and Ethical State (DCES) division at the Human Sciences

Research Council (HSRC) and an advisory member of the Department of Applied Legal Studies at Cape Peninsula University of Technology (CPUT). He holds a PhD in Political Studies from the University of Stellenbosch and an MA in Research Psychology from the University of the Western Cape. He specialises in the area of democracy, governance and social cohesion, and has also done work on the socio-economic conditions of vulnerable people. Yul previously worked at the Institute for Democracy (Idasa), where he managed the Public Opinion Service (POS) and the Afrobarometer survey project. He has done consultancy work for Management Systems International (MSI) in Nigeria and USAID in Tanzania, as well as for the International Foundation for Elections Systems (IFES) in Uganda. He co-edited *South African Social Attitudes 2nd Report: Reflections on the Age of Hope* (HSRC Press, 2010) and currently manages the State of the Nation book publication. Yul recently contributed to the HSRC–University of Johannesburg COVID-19 Democracy Survey project.

BERNARD DUBBELD

Dr Bernard Dubbeld is Associate Professor in the Department of Sociology and Social Anthropology at Stellenbosch University. Prior to teaching, he was involved with the South African Students Congress in KwaZulu-Natal. His ongoing interests include social theory, capital and labour, governance and citizenship, housing, race, and South African social sciences. He is the editor of *Social Dynamics*, and has recently published on contemporary capitalism, on housing struggles and on the future of work. He is currently completing a book on the experience of democratic transformation in RDP settlements in KwaZulu-Natal.

PAT HORN

Pat Horn is currently based in Durban (eThekwini), South Africa, and is responsible for the Women in Informal Employment Globalizing and Organizing (WIEGO) project on collective bargaining in the informal economy (www.wiego.org). She worked in the South

African trade union movement from 1976 to 1991 and began organising women workers in the informal economy in the 1990s. Pat is the founder of the Self-Employed Women's Union (SEWU), which represented women workers in the informal economy in five provinces of South Africa from 1994 to 2004. She was also a founder of StreetNet International (www.streetnet.org.za), a global federation of street vendors and informal traders, launched in Durban in November 2002. Pat has aided and led active affiliation with similar organisations in Africa, Asia, Eastern Europe and Latin America. She has been a member of the South African Communist Party (SACP) since 1991 and became a member of the Party's Central Committee in 2019.

GREGORY HOUSTON

Dr Gregory Houston is a chief research specialist at the Human Sciences Research Council (HSRC) and a research fellow of the Department of History at the University of the Free State. Before joining the HSRC in 1998, he lectured in the Department of Political Studies at the University of Transkei (now Walter Sisulu University) for 12 years. Gregory was seconded to the South African Democracy Education Trust (SADET) in 2000 until he returned to the HSRC in 2010. He played a key role in commissioning, managing and editing the first four volumes of *The Road to Democracy in South Africa*, published by SADET, and contributed chapters to five of the volumes. He authored *The National Liberation Struggle in South Africa: A case study of the United Democratic Front, 1983–87* (Ashgate, 1999), and has co-authored or co-edited numerous books, most recently *Society, Research and Power: The history of the Human Sciences Research Council from 1929 to 2019* (HSRC Press, 2021), with Craig Soudien and Sharlene Swarts.

GUNNETT KAAF

Gunnett Kaaf is a Marxist activist and a writer (in the fields of politics and economics) based in Bloemfontein. He is a long-standing political activist of more than 30 years. Previously an activist of the African

National Congress and the South African Communist Party, he is now active in community organisations, as he simultaneously explores new left politics and alternatives. Kaaf is the Board Chairperson of Zabalaza Pathways Institute, which is an NGO that walks and works with social movements to win transformative change through support for movement-building, activist development, and radical people-driven transformative initiatives. He works as a fiscal policy analyst at the Free State Provincial Treasury.

RASIGAN MAHARAJH

Rasigan Maharajh is an activist scholar who is concurrently the founding Chief Director of the Institute for Economic Research on Innovation at Tshwane University of Technology; Associate Research Fellow of the Tellus Institute in Boston; and an elected Member of the Academy of Science of South Africa. Rasigan was awarded a Doctor of Philosophy degree by the School of Economics and Management, Lund University, Sweden, and is also an alumnus of the University of KwaZulu-Natal, and the Harvard Business School. He further serves as Ministerial Representative on the Council of Rhodes University, is an elected Senator of Tshwane University of Technology, and a member of the Education Sub-Committee of the National Education, Health, and Allied Workers Union. Having occupied leadership roles in both the mass democratic and the national liberation movement, he served as national coordinator of the science and technology transition programme of the first post-apartheid government. Since 2004, Rasigan has contributed to more than 65 publications, and has presented his research in over 42 countries.

ALEX MOHUBETSWANE MASHILO

Alex Mohubetswane Mashilo was appointed as a visiting researcher at the Southern Centre for Inequality Studies at the University of the Witwatersrand (Wits) in 2020. His work experience started in the automotive industry in the late 1990s, when he was an apprentice. He obtained his trade certificate as an electrician and a National N Diploma in engineering while working in the automotive manufacturing industry. Alex was later elected a full-time shop steward for the National Union of Metalworkers of South Africa (NUMSA). From 2007, he served the union in various capacities as a full-time national official. In 2013, the South African Communist Party appointed him as its head of communications and spokesperson. He furthered his studies while working and holds a PhD from Wits. His research focus is on economic and social upgrading in areas such as technological change and the future of work in Global Production Networks.

SAM MATIASE

Sam Matiase is an activist and working-class member of parliament for the Economic Freedom Fighters (EFF). Since 2014, he has served on various portfolio committees such as Health, Justice and Correctional Service, Defence and Military Veterans, Agriculture, Land Reform and Rural Development. He previously worked as a public servant, including as a spokesperson in the Office of the MEC for Public Safety in the Free State and later as a senior manager for Support Services in Mangaung Municipality. Sam has been politically active since 1988, starting as a student activist in the Botshabelo Students Congress (BOSCO) and the Botshabelo Youth Congress (BOYCO). He was elected to various positions in the ANC Youth League and the Young Communist League in the Free State. In 2013, he became a founding member of the EFF and currently serves in its Central Command Team. Sam holds a BA in Management and Leadership and a post-graduate diploma and is in the second year of a MA in Public Administration.

PERCY NGONYAMA

A historian by training, Percy Ngonyama was a researcher at the Pietermaritzburg-based Mzala Nxumalo Centre for the Study of South African Society. At the time of his passing in 2019, Percy had just finished writing a political biography of the late Jabulani Nobleman Nxumalo. In the mid-1990s, he started the KwaZulu-Natal chapter of the South African Prisoners' Organisation for Human

Rights (SAPOHR) and in 1998 worked for the Ceasefire Campaign in Johannesburg, a lobby group that advocated for the removal and destruction of landmines in Mozambique and Angola. From 2003 to 2005, he again worked for SAPOHR and in the international section of the SADC Health Sector Unit. During this period, he toured countries such as Palestine and Australia to gain insight into how their correctional services systems functioned and what lessons could be learned from them. Percy's first degree was a BA in History and Politics from the then University of Natal. In 2006 he enrolled for the MA in History and worked at the Killie Campbell Library, University of KwaZulu-Natal.

BONGINKOSI EMMANUEL 'BLADE' NZIMANDE

Dr Bonginkosi Emmanuel 'Blade' Nzimande has been South Africa's Minister of Higher Education, Science and Innovation since May 2019. Prior to this, he was Minister of Transport (February 2018 to May 2019) and Minister of Higher Education and Training (May 2014 until October 2017). He is Chairperson of the Parliamentary Select Committee on Education, General Secretary of the South African Communist Party (SACP) and Deputy Chairperson of the Central Committee of the SACP, as well as Chairperson of the Financial Sector Campaign Coalition. Bonginkosi holds a Doctorate in Philosophy from the University of Natal. He started his career as a lecturer, first at the University of Zululand and then the University of Natal, and is a published researcher on education. His published work includes *Schooling in the Context of Violence in SA: The challenges of change* (Harare SAPES Books, 1993).

JOHN PAMPALLIS

John Pampallis is a teacher by profession and taught secondary school history before becoming an education policy analyst and researcher. Before he retired, he spent six years as Special Adviser to the Minister of Higher Education and Training. He recently published *A Brief History of South Africa* (Jacana Media, 2021), which he co-authored with Maryke Bailey.

MANDLA J. RADEBE

Mandla J. Radebe is an Associate Professor in the Department of Strategic Communication and the Director of the Centre for Data and Digital Communications at the University of Johannesburg. He is the author of *The Lost Prince of the ANC: The life and times of Jabulani Nobleman 'Mzala' Nxumalo 1955–1991* (Jacana Media, 2022) and *Constructing Hegemony: The South African commercial media and the (mis)representation of nationalisation* (University of KwaZulu-Natal Press, 2020).

VLADIMIR SHUBIN

Vladimir Shubin is Principal Research Fellow at the Institute for African Studies of the Russian Academy of Sciences. He has a DSc in History from the Moscow State University, a PhD in History from the Academy of Social Sciences, an MA in International Relations and Oriental Studies from the Moscow State Institute of International Relations and a PhD (Honoris Causa) from the University of the Western Cape. Before joining academia, he was involved in providing political and practical support for the liberation struggle in Africa in his capacity as Secretary of the Afro-Asian Solidarity Committee and Head of the Africa Section of the International Department of the Communist Party of the Soviet Union. Apart from Russian/Soviet state awards, he is a recipient of the South African Order of Companions of OR Tambo (silver) 'for excellent contribution to the struggle against apartheid and colonialism in Southern Africa'.

NOEL SOLANI

Noel Solani graduated from the universities of the Western Cape and Fort Hare and is interested in history, culture, heritage and social theory. He has worked for the Robben Island Museum, the Department of Higher Education, the Nelson Mandela Museum and the Mzala Nxumalo Centre for the Study of South African Society. He is currently associated with the DITSONG: Museums of South Africa, and has written on community struggles, liberation history, memory, heritage and museums. Noel continues to be concerned with issues of social change and how they are playing out. His latest publication, *Robben Island Rainbow Dreams: The making of democratic South Africa's first national heritage institution*, was co-edited with Neo Lekgotla Laga Ramoupi, Andre Odendaal and Kwezi ka Mpumlwana, and was published in 2021 by African Lives Best Red, an imprint of HSRC Press and the National Institute for the Humanities and Social Sciences.

SIGFRIED TIVANA

Sigfried Tivana is Assistant Director: Africa Multilateral Cooperation at the Department of Science and Innovation, responsible for facilitating and coordinating South Africa's participation in African Union–European Union research and innovation partnerships. He previously worked as a research assistant at the Human Sciences Research Council and the Open African Innovation Research Partnership, and remains a member of the New and Emerging Researchers Group under the OpenAIR Partnership. Sigfried served as a national policy guide to a team of South African senior policy-makers under the Global Innovation Policy Accelerator. While a student at the Tshwane University of Technology, he was the Student Representative Council President and General Secretary, the Postgraduate Forum General Secretary and a member of the South African Union of Students. Sigfried, who was a member of the ANC Youth League and was an active part of the #FeesMustFall movement, holds a MTech in Comparative Local Development from the Institute for Economic Research on Innovation.

ELAINE UNTERHALTER

Elaine Unterhalter is Professor of Education and International Development at University College London. She was born and educated in Johannesburg and studied at the University of the Witwatersrand, the University of Cambridge and the School of Oriental and African Studies (SOAS) of the University of London. From the 1970s, she was active in the Anti-Apartheid Movement in

ABOUT THE CONTRIBUTORS

the United Kingdom and the ANC in exile. From 1986 to 1995, Elaine worked as a researcher on the Research on Education in South Africa (RESA) project. She has written widely about education and social change, with studies in South Africa, Tanzania, Kenya and Nigeria. Her books include *Forced Removal: The division, segregation and control of the people of South Africa* (1987)' *Apartheid Education and Popular Struggles* (1990, co-edited with Harold Wolpe and Thozamile Botha); *Education in a Future South Africa* (1991, co-edited with Harold Wolpe and Thozamile Botha); *Gender, Schooling and Global Social Justice* (2007); *Education, Poverty and Global Goals for Gender Equality: How people make policy happen* (2018, with Amy North); and *Critical Reflections on Public Private Partnerships* (2020, co-edited with Jasmine Gideon).

INDEX

A
Abahlali baseMjondolo (translating as Shack Dwellers' Movement), 165
Accelerated and Shared Growth Initiative for South Africa (AsgiSA), 32, 138, 158, 179, 186, 187
ActionSA, 2
activism, 204, 337, 356
    community, 11, 93
    intellectual and social, 336
    of the radical left, 353
    scholarship and political, 257
activist, 59, 69, 71
    development, 265
    organisations, 61
    scholars, 65, 67, 83
    soldier, 23
activists, 265
    ANC and Communist Party, 83
    environmental justice, 249
    from the Third World, 53
    in exile, 57
    left, 61
    lesbian and gay, 54
    political, 45, 49
    socialist, 167
    young, 32
Africa, 243, 297
    great sons of, 135
African Communist, 3
African Growth and Opportunity Act (AGOA), 247
African Independent Congress (AIC), 167
African National Congress (ANC), 1, 3, 6, 9, 12, 21, 22, 23, 24, 25, 27, 28, 29, 31, 32, 33, 34, 36, 43, 49, 50, 55, 57, 60, 61, 69, 77, 79, 81, 85, 86, 87, 91, 97, 98, 99, 100, 107, 112, 118, 119, 120, 121, 122, 123, 131, 136, 137, 145, 156, 157,

158, 160, 161, 162, 163, 164, 167, 169, 171, 179, 180, 182, 185, 193, 194, 195, 196, 197, 198, 199, 243, 244, 245, 246, 256, 258, 260, 267, 291, 292, 293, 301, 316
  alliance partners, 131, 157, 159
  ANC-SACP-associated think tank *See* Mzala Centre
  ANC-SACP-COSATU alliance, 133, 137
  document 'The Nature of the South African Ruling Class' (1985), 268
  document Strategy and Tactics (1969), 180, 185, 198
  document Strategy and Tactics (1997), 268
  election manifesto (1994), 157
  Empire of Chaos, 245
  multiclass organisation, 160, 291, 292
  National Policy Conference, 5th (2017), 24
  neoliberal policy embrace, 244
  social base, 244
African National Congress Youth League (ANCYL), 22
Afrikaner, 72, 73, 89, 259
  belief, 36
  capitalists, 259
agricultural sector, 217, 239, 247
  agriculture, 209, 210, 239, 248, 258, 259, 266, 268, 310

big agribusiness, 247
AIC, *See* African Independent Congress
AIDS
  denialism, 32
  drugs, 32
Alliance, the (the SACP and COSATU), 122, 162, 185, 195, 196, 198, 243, 244, 245
  ANC-headed, 185, 196, 198, 204
Alliance for Automobile Manufacturers, 313
AMM, *See* Anti-Apartheid Movement
Amandla, 153, 154, 169
  see also liberation movements, slogan, 153
Americas, the, 220
ANC, *See* African National Congress
Anglo-Boer War, 296
antagonism
  class, 161
  racial, 161
Anthropocene, 338
anti-apartheid, 34
  activists, 57
  struggle, 99, 258
  thinking, 14
Anti-Apartheid Movement (AAM), 11, 46, 47
anti-austerity
  campaign, Podemos party (Spain), 246
anti-black racism, 278
anti-capitalism, romantic, 275

INDEX

anti-capitalist, 244, 248, 252
　dimensions, 248
　historic bloc, 251
　outlook, 251
　stance, 244
　vision, 252
anti-colonial
　liberation, 194
　struggles, 77, 194, 243, 336
　see also colonial
anti-colonialism, 48
　see also colonialism
anti-communist 193
　foreign policy, 46
　politics, 55
　see also communist
anti-establishment theory and practice, 224
anti-imperialist
　democratic revolution, 197
　Fanonist, 25
　liberation, 194
　nature, 291
　outlook, 292
　struggle, 194, 288
　see also imperialist
anti-left media, 203
anti-neoliberal *see also* neoliberal
　historic bloc, 251
　vision, 252
anti-privatisation
　campaign, 199, 245
　see also privatisation
anti-working-class *see also* working class
　economic programme, 159
　ideological shifts, 137
apartheid, 1, 4, 5, 6, 7, 9, 11, 13, 14, 15, 22, 23, 24, 27, 28, 29, 30, 31, 33, 37, 38, 39, 46, 48, 49, 50, 51, 52, 54, 57, 58, 69, 70, 71, 74, 78, 79, 83, 89, 91, 98, 99, 100, 103, 107, 109, 110, 112, 117, 118, 119, 120, 136, 137, 140, 145, 154, 156, 160, 161, 164, 165, 166, 177, 178, 179, 180, 182, 183, 184, 193, 194, 195, 196, 239, 244, 248, 258, 260, 262, 264, 266, 267, 269, 278, 281, 296, 298, 301, 303, 305, 315, 323, 330, 331, 332
　apparatus, 304
　end of, 267
　era, 178, 184
　government racism, 258
　income gap, 182
　law, 165, 184
　legal, 4
　liberation from, 12
　oppression, 98, 177
　regime, 1, 4, 52, 71, 78, 79, 178, 179, 180, 193, 195, 196, 259, 296
　state, 29, 30, 33, 46, 259
aristocrats, 275
armchair
　critics of capitalism, 146
　intellectuals, 260
Articulation of Modes of Production, The, 262
AsgiSA, *See* Accelerated and

357

Shared Growth Initiative for
South Africa
Asia, 220, 232, 243
   Beijing, 290
   Central Asia, 297
   East Asia, 134, 239
   South Korea, 238, 296
   Southeast Asia, 239
asylum seekers, 46
austerity, of the Troika, 246
authoritarian
   capitalism, 2
   techniques, 275
autonomy, 52, 204, 259, 276
Azanian People's Organisation,
   210, 245

B

bantustan, 51, 73, 77, 79, 89, 259,
   262, 333
   apartheid-created, 51
   areas, former, 184
   as nation-states, 79
   border industries, 259
   former areas, 184
   formerly known as African
   reserves, 262
   logic, 6
   notions, 37
   policy, 70, 71, 72
   structures, 6, 52
   system, 4
   thinking, 37
Bantu Affairs department, 50
Bantu education, abolishment
   of, 165
Bantu Education Act, No. 47 of
   1953, 165
basic income grant (BIG), 250
battle
   battleground, 137, 138
   for survival, 317
   of ideas, 130, 317
   over interpretation of
   national question, 58
BEE, *See* black economic
   empowerment
*Beyond US Hegemony: Assessing
   prospects for a multipolar
   world*, 242
BIG, *See* basic income grant
biodiversity, 306, 307, 308, 309,
   318
biological annihilation, 307
black
   advancement, concept of, 4
   capitalist class, 36, 138, 162
   elite or middle classes, 258
   empowerment, 268
   households, 139, 259
   labour power, 259
   life, 265
   majority (meaning African,
   Coloured and Indian
   citizens), 5, 156, 165, 198,
   269, 296
   middle-class community, 162
   migrant workers, 259
   miners, 259
   ownership, of JSE-listed
   companies, 139
   propertied classes, 268
   radical response, 262
   tenants, 259

women, mobility and urban presence of, 264
Black Consciousness, 33, 245, 258
black economic empowerment (BEE), 4, 121, 131, 136, 140, 164
    broad-based black economic empowerment (B-BBEE), 4
black Marxist analysis, 327
Black Republic Thesis, 34
black South Africa, 259
Blade, *See* Nzimande, Bonginkosi Emmanuel
Boers, the, 23, 73
bourgeois
    aspirations, 133, 135
    capitulation, 244
    enterprise, 330
    interests, 4
    national bourgeoisie, 330
    nationalists, 25, 35, 37
    patriotic bourgeoisie, 294
    petite bourgeois class, 8, 131
    petite bourgeoisie, 330
bourgeoise, 332
bourgeoisie, 25, 37, 38, 39, 77, 78, 80, 83, 84, 85, 86, 87, 91, 162, 190, 192, 195, 247, 270, 294, 304, 330
Brazil, 2, 15, 132, 238, 246, 277, 287
    Bolsonaro, Jair, 2
    da Silva, Lula, 246
Bretton Woods institutions, 10
BRICS (Brazil, Russia, India, China and South Africa), 15, 287, 295

Britain, 11, 45, 46, 53, 54, 55, 70, 258
    British Defence and Aid Fund for Southern Africa, 43
    British Empire, 45
    British Museum Library, 45
    United Kingdom, 46, 55, 92, 261, 294
Brotherhood Movement, 46
Brussels, 290, 295
Bundung, *See* Non-Aligned Movement
Buthelezi, Gatsha, 49, 51, 331

C

cadres, 22, 24, 27, 39, 130, 170, 196, 304
Canon Collins Education Trust for Southern Africa (CCETSA), 43, 44, 45
Cape Liberal Tradition, 259
Cape Town, 166, 302
capital
    accumulation, 182, 238, 305
    dynamics of, 275
    reframed Marxian reading of, 257
    controls, 239, 247
    development, 278
    enterprise, 270
    expenditure, 180
    flights, 247
    markets, new hegemony of, 239
    values, 239
Capital, The (1894), 182, 271, 302, 337

see also Marx, Karl
Capital and Class, 258
capitalism, 5, 9, 10, 11, 12, 14, 38, 58, 70, 71, 79, 80, 81, 86, 87, 88, 89, 90, 92, 98, 99, 130, 131, 133, 134, 135, 137, 138, 142, 143, 144, 146, 147, 148, 149, 163, 164, 177, 182, 185, 205, 237, 238, 241, 246, 248, 249, 250, 256, 257, 258, 259, 260, 262, 263, 265, 266, 267, 269, 270, 271, 272, 273, 274, 275, 276, 277, 278, 279, 280, 302, 304, 317, 318, 323, 326, 328, 329, 330, 331, 332, 333, 335, 336, 337, 339, 341
- attempts to escape from, 277
- attempts to produce value, 274
- autonomy from, 276
- barbarism of, 136
- conspiratorial notion, 275
- contemporary, 9, 249
- crises of, 182
- crisis-ridden, 247
- directional dynamic (telos), 274
- effects on social life, 257
- form of local, 262
- global context of, 276
- ideological obfuscations of, 270
- imperialist agenda, 205
- implosion of, 246
- in agriculture, 258
- Marxian theory of, 15
- myths of, 336
- productive terms, 269
- relations of, 280
- role of labour in, 272
- social problems introduced by, 278
- social terms, 269
- state-led, 279
- tendency, 238
- tensions internal to, 276
- transformations of, 266

capitalist
- accumulation, 182, 263, 268
- alienation, 275
- by night, 136
- class interests, 138
- class, 7, 163
- countries, 238, 289
- crisis, 250
- democracy, US-style, 132
- economy, 163
- enterprise, relocation of, 259
- exploitative social relations, 134
- forms of value, 276, 340
- globalisation, 242
- influences, 323
- legacy, 184
- mode of production, 305
- production, 10, 81, 270, 273, 302
- profit, 261, 329
- profitability, 258, 259
- relations of production, 317
- rulers, 206
- social life, 278
- society, 84, 146, 163, 238, 251, 263, 270, 273, 276

solution, 182
system, 5, 8, 11, 13, 36, 38, 137, 149, 183, 192, 337
trajectory, 341
value, 270
without capital, *See* black aspirant bourgeoisie
captains of industry, 164, 170, 293
carbon-based life forms, 310
CCETSA, *See* Canon Collins Education Trust for Southern Africa
Charles Johnson Memorial Hospital, 49
China, 10, 11, 15, 144, 147, 208, 209, 239, 242, 275, 287, 290, 296, 310, 335
    Agricultural Bank of China, 209
    China Construction Bank, 209
    economy, 208
    Industrial and Commercial Bank of China, 209
    revolution in, 290
    rise of, 10
    world affairs, main players, 242
Christian
    liberal left, 47
    transnational networks, 46
civic
    movements, 12
    organisations, 165
civil rights, 90, 155
civil society, 12, 90, 148, 149, 157, 163, 190, 191, 192, 218, 219, 225, 227, 316
    actions and campaigns, 219
    organisations, 12, 157, 163, 190, 191, 219
class
    antagonism, 161
    aspirations, 181
    compromise, 243
    consciousness, 87, 264
    -divided society, 7
    divides, 274
    domination, 190, 192, 265
    elites, 333
    hierarchy, 241
    identity, 264
    interest, 161, 162, 224
    lines, 333
    neutral, 8
    oppression, 34, 77, 264, 331
    traditional concepts of, 277
    universal expression of, 276
class struggle, 69, 70, 71, 84, 85, 86, 192, 205, 211, 260, 293, 318, 327, 332
    abstract, 247
    between white farmers and black tenants, 259
    struggle, South Africa, 3
climate change, 143, 305, 306, 307, 308, 311, 312, 313, 314, 316, 317, 334, 338
    climate crisis, contemporary, 15
    hot politics, 338
    hotspot, 315
Cold War, 12, 15, 54, 132, 242,

287, 288, 289, 290, 334
bipolar world, 15, 242, 288, 290
era, 12
multipolar world, 288, 289, 290
multipolarity, 288
polycentric world, 288
post-Cold War world, 334
traditional history of, 287
unipolar world, 287
collective
bargaining, 14, 188, 226, 234, 235
negotiation, 232
Colombia, 132
colonialisation, 248, 261
colonialism, 9, 28, 38, 48, 61, 119, 141, 142, 178, 183, 194, 258, 261, 305, 324, 327, 330, 338, 339
colonisation, 58, 177
Committee on the Informal Economy, 223
commodities, 138, 142, 246, 247, 280, 336
commodity, 182, 183, 271
common ancestry, 306
common citizenship, 171
Commonwealth, 261
communism, 136, 143, 189, 193, 274, 329, 338
demise (fall of), 328
spectre of, 136
communist
cadres, 196
parties, 48, 194, 248, 249, 251, 269
states, collapse of, 328
traditions, 249
Communist Manifesto, The (1848), 161, 274, 304, 310
see also Marx, Karl
communities
black, 54, 55, 118, 248
ethnic, 89
exile, 60
indigenous, 327
local, 13
mass activities in, 245
poor and lower middle-class, 158
poor and working-class, 163, 170
rural, 244
working-class, 54
community
activism, 7
protests, 7, 164
struggles, 7, 13, 154, 156, 164, 165, 168, 250
Community Constituency of Nedlac, 178, 223, 228, 232
Conclusions on Decent Work and the Informal Economy (2002), 224, 228, 229, 230, 232
Conference on the Future of the Left (2017), 201
Congress Alliance, 154, 155, 196
Congress of South African Congress of Trade Unions (COSATU), 26, 32, 52, 131, 135, 137, 139, 145, 157, 159, 160, 170, 185, 193, 198, 199,

210, 244
Congress of the People, 3, 154
Consensus Statement on Sex Work, Human Rights and the Law, 222
Constitution of the Republic of South Africa, 156
Constitution, the, 121, 166, 170, 252, 267
consumer protection, 207
consumerism, 131, 142
consumerist Western culture, 134
Convention (C189), 220, *see also* ILO Convention
corporate state capture, 15, 301, 305, 317, 331
COSATU, *See* Congress of South African Congress of Trade Unions
COVID-19
   pandemic, 139, 183
   slump, 250
COVID-19 Working Class Campaign (2020), 250
Creating Opportunities for Fair Globalisation in Southern Africa: A response to the ILO's World Commission on the Social Dimension of Globalisation, 222
crony capitalism, 131
cronyism, 136
CTCP, *See* Nicaraguan Confederación de Trabajadores por Cuenta Propia

currency
   crashes (2001), 240
   crisis (2001), 185
   volatility, 186

D

DA, *See* Democratic Alliance
Darwin, Charles, 306
Dawn and Sechaba, 3
De Klerk, Frederik Willem, 13, 123, 179, 180
   speech, 179, 180
Decent Work in the Informal Economy, 235
Decent Work Programme, 231
decolonisation, 16, 25, 325
DEIC, *See* Dutch East India Company
de-industrialisation, 335
democracy
   direct, 218, 332
   multiparty, 291
   national, 85, 258, 303
   participatory, 248
   political, 138
   representative, 248
   social, 243
democratic
   breakthrough, 13, 91, 153, 154, 178, 182, 196, 301, 239, 316
   dispensation, 11
   eco-socialism, 251
   era, 34, 100, 118, 124
   gains, of the majority of people, 306
   government, 137

national sovereignty, 178
participation, 333
rights and demands, 252
rule, first 23 years of, 154
rule, South Africa, 163
Democratic Alliance (DA), 162, 297
Democratic Left Front, 203
Democratic Republic of Congo, 314
Department of Public Works, 167
deregulation, 11, 180, 208, 218, 334, 337
developed and developing countries, 10, 11, 243, 335
developed economy, 186
diasporas, 324
Dlangezwa High School, 3
dominant ruling class, 8
Durban, 201, 220, 255
Dutch East India Company (DEIC or VOC), 302

E
Earth, 37, 196, 305, 306, 307, 308, 309, 326
Earth Summit (1992), 317
　Castro, Fidel, speech, 317
Eastern Cape, 167, 259, 316
eastern Sub-Saharan Africa, 314
ecocide, 15, 317, 318, 333, 341
ecological
　catastrophe, 15, 317
　changes, 316
　consequences, 310
　damage, 306

niches, 306
ecology of southern Africa, 305
economic
　actors, 170, 230
　data, 262
　development, 8, 13, 29, 31, 32, 134, 186, 188, 316, 340
　dimension of life, 271
　emancipation, 135
　empowerment, 136
　equality, 256
　exploitation, 182
　form, 333
　freedom, 119, 170
　growth, 32, 137, 160, 179, 180, 181, 182, 185, 218, 239, 295
　hegemony, 180
　level, 273
　liberation, 333
　meltdown, 168
　participation, 332
　power, 4
　redistribution element, 244
　role-player, 329
　slump, 246
　system, 145, 164, 165, 168, 170, 271, 275
　upsurge, 290
　value, 271, 272
Economic Freedom Fighters (EFF), 91, 129, 133, 135, 138, 141, 145, 245, 269
　Founding Manifesto, 133
economic policy
　direction, 179
　failure, 183

trajectory, South Africa post-
     1994, 185
economies
     Western, 179
Economy and Society, 258, 259
economy, two, 186
eco-socialism, 251
Ecuador, 132
     Correa, Rafael, 132
education, crisis in, and quality
     of, 140
EFF, *See* Economic Freedom
     Fighters
efficiency of production, 274
Eighteenth Brumaire of Louis
     Bonaparte, The, 202
Ekurhuleni, 167
electoral
     contests, 204
     mass, 224
     projects, 204
     system, 168, 169
electromagnetic signals, 306
elite capitalists, 275
elites, dependent, 330
emancipation, 83, 85, 118, 140,
     141, 189, 192, 196, 247, 270,
     279, 280, 333
emergent new environment,
     308
emerging
     economies, 287
     markets, 287
     powers, 15, 287
employment relationship
     ambiguous, 229
     disguised, 229
     triangular, 229
employment security, 234
Endlovini, 166
Engels, Friedrich, 45
English bourgeoisie, 163
eNgotshe, 21
environment, 27, 89, 112, 143,
     147, 158, 159, 186, 230, 310,
     312, 313, 316, 317, 324, 328,
     333, 338
environmental
     change, accelerated, 307
     degradation, 310
     justice activists, 249
     relationship, 305
     situation, deteriorating, 317
Eoarchean Era, 306
equality
     economic, 256
     formal political and legal,
          256
Eskom,
     corporate capture/
          corruption, 184
     energy crisis, 250
     unbundling of, 188
     White Paper (1998), 184
Ethiopia, 291, 314
     Ethiopian Parliament, 291
     Ethiopian People's
          Revolutionary Democratic
          Front, 291
ethnic
     affiliations, 6, 52
     chauvinism, 34
     dimensions, 77
     groups, 35, 81

nationalism, 90
policies, 89
separation, 79
stereotypes, 35
ethnicity, 5, 12, 26, 34, 35, 37, 45, 60, 71, 89, 90, 99
ethno-nationalist parties, 2
e-tolls, 168, 169
Europe, 3, 45, 53, 88, 187, 239, 242, 262, 275, 277, 302
Eurocentric, approach to capitalism, 263
Eurocentrism, 15, 287
European
colonies, 335
supremacy and violence, 327
transition, 302
travellers, 302
European Union, previously European Economic Community, 290
evolutionary
history, 309
path, 309
exile
community, South African, 47
South African exiles, 47
years, 243
existential
crisis, 10
risk, 317
exploitation, 35, 70, 80, 83, 84, 85, 86, 87, 98, 131, 134, 141, 145, 182, 189, 190, 197, 205, 207, 208, 210, 241, 269, 270, 272, 273, 274, 303, 312, 329, 341
expropriation, 15, 85, 122, 123, 210, 268, 302, 303
extinction, 304, 308, 309
asteroid or meteor crash,
fifth mass extinction, 307
climate change event,
second mass extinction, 307
ice age, , first mass extinction, 307
mass extinction, 307, 308, 316, 317, 339
volcanic eruptions, third mass extinction, 307
volcanism, fourth mass extinction, 307
Exxon Mobile, 313

F

factionalism, 260
factions, 30, 202
family
labour, 218
wage, 279
feudal
mode of production, 302
state, 302
financial
capital, 3, 239, 324
crisis, 241
meltdown, 163, 237, 241
Financial Sector Campaign (2000), 207, 208
Mzansi Account, 207
financialisation, 238
First Self-Employed Workers' Manifesto of the CTCP-FNT,

224
fiscal
　austerity, 247
　expansion, 247
　policy, 181, 247
Forbes Global 2000 List, 209
forced removals, 166
foreign capital, 240
foreign markets, 231
formal economy, 16, 218, 220, 221, 228, 230, 232, 233, 234, 337, *see also* informal economy
formal education, 226
formal equality, 279
formal labour
　laws, 236
　market, 218
formal sector, *see also* informal sector
　trade unions, 226, 227
　unions, 233
　workers, 235
formal waged employment, 228
forms
　of existence, 261
　of knowing, 271
　of life, 271, 307
　of value, 278
　of work, 233, 234, 235, 335
fossil fuels, creation of, 310
Foucauldian readings, 265
Founders, The (2012), 155
France, 296
　Charles De Gaulle, 290
　Macron, Emmanuel, 246
　Paris, 163, 290

free market, 13, 29, 31, 54, 132, 134, 182, 334, 336
　economic policies, 132
　market economy, 182
　trickle-down effect, 31
Free Market Foundation, 121
Free State, 166, 316
　Ficksburg, 166
　killing of Tatane, Andries, 166
Freedom Charter, 3, 31, 33, 38, 60, 74, 99, 154, 155, 156, 158, 160, 196, 198, 199, 205
Freedom Front Plus, 2
free-market
　economic model, 22
　system, 137

G
Gaidar, Yegor, 289
Gatsha Buthelezi: Chief with a double agenda (1988), 3, 34
Gauteng, 167, 168, 316
GDP, *See* gross domestic product
GEAR, *See* Growth, Employment and Redistribution Programme
gender
　differentiation, 337
　equality, 325
　gendered division of labour, 279
　inequalities, 189, 280
　injustice, 279
　relations, 264
genocidal tendencies, of capitalism, 317

Germany
　Leftists, 189
　Nazi Germany, 61
　Nazis, 275
　Nazism, 277, 296
Ghana, 230, 232, 295
gig economy, 335
global capitalism, 14, 35, 237, 247
global capitalist
　system, hegemonic, 8
　economy, 238, 240
global economic
　crisis (2008), 163, 183, 207
　environment, 168
　system, 168
global economy, 55, 239, 241, 243, 250
global elite, 324, 339
global financial meltdown (2007), 324
global hotspots, 314
global imperialist regime, 178
global inequality, 2
global knowledge commons, collective, 305
global markets, 247
global mineral commodity super cycle, 182, 183
global nationalism, 2
global neoliberalism, 199
global population, 305
global system, 240
global warming, 308, 314
global world, 2
Global Network of Sex Work Projects (NSWP), 221
Consensus Statement on Sex Work, Human Rights and the Law, 221
Global North, 205, 222, 243, 256, 260, 279
　bourgeoisies of, 243
　recent turn to the right politically, 256
Global South, 9, 14, 192, 222, 237, 238, 250, 297
　industrial production (1970s), 238
globalisation, 5, 34, 37, 227, 238, 324, 331, 335
Golden Age, 238
Gordhan, Pravin, 161
governance arrangements, 288
government grants, 278
Government of National Unity (GNU), 156
Gqeberha, 166
grass-roots
　movements, 251
　organisations, 251
　worker organisation, 260
Great Depression (1929), 241
Grootboom case, 166
Gross Domestic Product (GDP), 157, 244
Group Areas Act, No. 41 (1950), 165
growth crisis, 137
Growth, Employment and Redistribution Programme (GEAR), 13, 31, 32, 86, 137, 138, 139, 154, 158, 159, 160, 178, 179, 180, 181, 182, 183,

184, 185, 186, 187, 198, 199, 200, 201, 239
    COSATU envisaged objectives, 159
    economic policy, 13
    macro-economic framework, 137
    policy, 159, 245
    primary principle, 137
Grundrisse (English, 1973), 270
Guinée Conakry, strike action (2007), 236
Guptarisation, 131, 136
Gwala, Harry, *see also* intellectual giants, 132, 133

H
Hani, Chris, 135, 141, 142, 143, 145
Hemson, David, 260
Holland, 302
Holocaust, the 275
Honduras, 132
House of Peoples' Representatives, 291
    Ethiopian Parliament, 291
housing situation, 157
human
    activities, 310, 313
    agency, 336
    beings, modern, 309
    consciousness, 325, 338, 341
    history, 81, 327, 334
    labour power, 274
    rights, 147, 165, 171, 222
    species, 10, 310
humanisation, 337

hybrid governance system, 169

I
ideological capture, institutions of power, 317
idiographic inquiry, 277
IDWF, *See* International Domestic Workers' Federation (IDWF)
Ikamvalihle, 166
ILO, *See* International Labour Organization (ILO)
imperial
    incorporation into world systems, 301
    practices, 331
    subjugation, 303
Imperial Oil, 313
imperialism, 9, 10, 11, 34, 74, 84, 141, 149, 178, 185, 211, 305, 327, 330, 336, 339 *see also* neo-imperialism
imperialist
    backers, 268
    domination, 197
    rent, 243
India, 2, 15, 45, 232, 235, 238, 239, 287, 302
Indonesia, 290
industrial
    action, 154
    production system, 239
    revolution, 311
    working class, 266
industrialisation, 55, 143, 156, 162, 184, 185, 247, 310, 323, 335, 338

of capitalist states, 338
of communist states, 338
see also de-industrialisation
inequalities
   faced by black and other indigenous groups, 256
   formal, 269
   local, 267
   suffered by those identifying with non-normative sexual and gender subjectivities, 256
inequality, 1, 3, 13, 69, 87, 99, 119, 124, 137, 139, 158, 164, 168, 171, 180, 181, 185, 205, 209, 210, 227, 247, 255, 257, 269, 277, 315, 329, 340
   concomitant, 324
   new forms of, 255
   racial, 258
informal
   labour market, 228
   market vendors, 220
   settlements, 157, 162, 166
   trade regulation, 236
   traders, 218
informal cross-border traders, 231
informal economy, 7, 14, 217, 218, 219, 220, 221, 223, 224, 225, 226, 227, 228, 229, 230, 231, 232, 233, 234, 235, 236, 336, 337
   business sector, 224
   developments, organising workers, 219
   marginalisation of workers, 221
   methods of tax collection in, 231
   national review of municipal bylaws, 231
   needs of workers in, 235
   organisations, 223
   representation throughout, 232
   representational needs of workers, 233
   survivalist economic activities, 217
   workers, 233
injustice, 36, 48, 62, 85, 118, 267, 269
Inkatha, 2, 35, 36, 51, 72
Inkatha Freedom Party, 2
Institute for African Studies, 293
institutional domination, 265
intellectual
   circles, 245
   giants, of the revolution, 132, 133
Intergovernmental Panel on Climate Change (IPCC), 314
   Sixth Assessment report, 314
Interim Constitution (1993), 155, 156
internal climate migrants, 314
international
   debate, 230
   financial institutions, 138, 239
   forums, 219
   human rights treaties, 222
   law, 242

leftist politics, 257
monopolist capitalist associations, 9
relations, 290
socialism, 339
solidarity, 219
international capitalist
  firms, 261
  investments, 260
International Domestic Workers' Federation (IDWF), 219
International Labour Organization (ILO), 219, 220, 223, 224, 228, 231
  Conclusions on Decent Work and the Informal Economy, 220
  Convention 87 (Freedom of Association), 219
  Convention 98 (the Right to Organise and Collective Bargaining Convention, 219
  ILO Convention 189 (2011), 219
  ILO Recommendation, new, 229
  ILO Workers' Group, 223
  International Labour Conference, 90th (2002), 223, 235
  International Labour Conference, 95th (2006), 229
  International Labour Conferences, 219
  Recommendation 204 (R204), 220
  tripartite structures of, 223
International Monetary Fund, 35, 188, 242
interstellar space, 305
intraclass differences, 294
investment boom, 238
Iraq, 242
  Gulf War (1991), 242

J

Japan, 187, 239, 242, 290
Jews, the, 275
Jinnah, 46
job security, 61, 272, 274
Johannesburg, 139, 166, 199, 259, 293, 295
Johannesburg Municipality, 169
Johannesburg Stock Exchange (JSE), 139
joint campaigns, 227, 235
Jonas, Mcebisi, 161
Jordan, Pallo, 133
Judicial Commission of Inquiry into Allegations of State Capture, 1
Juju *See* Malema, Julius

K

Kenya, 295, 314
Kenyatta, Jomo, 46
Khama, Seretse, 46
Khayelitsha, 166
Khumalo, Ngacambaza
  Mzala pseudonym, 35
Kliptown, 3, 154
KwaZulu-Natal, 2, 9, 21, 49, 167, 316

CIVICUS report (2022), 316
flooding in (2022), 316

L

labour
    abstract, 271, 272
    coercion, 162
    concrete, 271
    cost of, 274
    exploitation of, 270, 274
    family labour, 218
    flexibility, 185
    force, African countries, 217
    in capitalism, 273
    legislation, 228, 229, 230, 234, 235
    movements, former, 132
    outsourcing and casualisation of, 266
    paid labour, 279
    power, 173, 260, 269, 270, 274, 275, 337
    process, 270, 274
    role in production, 275
    social labour, 248
    time, 278
    transformations of, 266
    value of, 271
    vulnerable, 329
labour market
    flexibility, 240
    government regulation of, 259
    inequalities, 218, 234
land ownership, territorial separation of, 162
Latin America, 130, 131, 132, 134, 232, 243, 246, 249
League Against Imperialism, 46
Left, the, 9, 10, 11, 12, 13, 14, 45, 54, 55, 130, 131, 132, 133, 135, 136, 142, 143, 147, 148, 149, 185, 186, 188, 189, 190, 192, 193, 201, 202, 203, 204, 205, 206, 207, 208, 209, 210, 211, 237, 242, 246, 247, 248, 249, 251, 252, 255, 256, 301, 339, 340
    anti-capitalist, 248
    future of, 130
    old, 333
    organised, 135
    political strategy, 247
    revival of, 130
    rise of, 132
    the way forward, 246
    tragic death of, 133
    way forward, 251
    weakness of, 237
left
    renewal, 252
    old Left, 243, 245, 246
    agenda, 185
    alternatives, 246
    formations, largest, 170
    organisations, 46, 160, 170, 171, 190, 192, 193, 201, 203, 207
    parties, 246, 248
    thoughts, 7, 8
leftism, 256
Leftist
    alternatives, 132
    governments, 132

ideas, 9
intellectuals, 327
parties, 131
policy initiatives, 331
political inclinations, 267
politics, 257, 267, 280
struggle, 332
thinking, 324
thought, 328
traditions, 132
left-thinking intellectuals, 336
left-wing
   opposition, 294
   organisations, 160
   political parties, 277
   scholars, 260
Legassick, Martin, 260
liberal
   model of capitalism, 130
   tendency, 73, 76
   theory, 90
   thinking, 137
   view, 242
liberalisation
   agenda, 185
   currency crisis (2001), 185
   of financial and capital controls, 239
   of the exchange rate, 239
   trade and financial, 239, 240
liberalism, 132, 258
liberation, true or genuine, 134
liberation movement, 3, 13, 25, 74, 81, 194, 243, 249, 338
   former, 132
   left leaning sections, 34
   slogan, 153
   unbanning of, 179
liberation struggle, 12, 36, 80, 82, 85, 97, 100, 140, 161, 178, 182, 193, 194, 195, 297, 303
Limpopo, 165, 316
Linnaeus, Carl, 307
local government elections, South Africa (2021), 2
London, 3, 4, 6, 11, 21, 45, 46, 47, 48, 49, 50, 51, 53, 55, 57, 275
Lonmin Platinum Mine, 162
Lonmin striking mineworkers (2012), 139
Louwsburg, 2, 21, 49

M

macro-economic
   framework, 201
   strategy, 137, 139
Mahube Valley, 162
mainstream
   economics, 241
   economists, 240, 241
Makhado Municipality, 166
Making of the English Working Class, 264
Malamulele, 165, 166
Malema, Julius, 245
Mamelodi, 162
Man and Nature: Or, physical geography as modified by human action (1864), 310
Manchester, 46, 310
Mandela, Nelson Rolihlahla, 303
Mantashe, Gwede, 24
Manuel, Trevor, 137
Marikana massacre (2012), 162,

163
see also Lonmin striking mineworkers (2012)
marked borders, 324
market justice, 334
Marx, Karl, 45, 136, 182, 202, 205, 249, 252, 269, 274, 275, 302, 304, 306
   texts, 258
   theory of capitalism, 269, 270
Marxian analysis of time, 273
Marxism, 12, 14, 70, 71, 72, 78, 80, 88, 90, 130, 147, 245, 246, 256, 257, 258, 261, 262, 263, 264, 265, 266, 270, 274, 276, 279, 280, 325, 328, 333, 335, 338
Marxism-Leninism, 12, 247
Marxist
   accounts, traditional, 276
   analysis, 323
   approaches, 257
   claims, to totality and teleology, 265
   class categories, traditional, 269
   concepts, fundamental, 16
   ideas of solidarity, 341
   intellectuals, 1
   Marxist Workers Tendency, 260
   Marxist–Leninist analysis, 8
   Marxist–Leninist essentials, 129
   Marxist–Leninist template, 248
   Marxist–Leninist tradition, 22
   politics, 256
   proposition, 329
   revisionism, 260, 264, 265, 266
   scholarship, 257, 258, 323
   theory, 328, 331
   thinking, 179
   thought, 257, 258
   Western Marxist contemporaries, 260
Matatiele, 167
Mawubuye Umhlaba
   Let the land return, 209
MBOs, *See* membership-based organisations
mechanisms of participation, 328
media
   anti-left media, 203
   international mass media, 296
   South African, 296, 297
   Western media, 296
mediation, theory of, 263
membership-based organisations (MBOs), 220, 228
Merafong, 167
Mexico, 132, 238, 307
   Chicxulub crater, Gulf of Mexico, 307
migrancy, 324, 325
migrant labour system, 162, 259
Millennium Development Goals (MDGs), 32

mining industrial revolution, 249
minority
    groups, 100, 116, 329
    national groups, 90
    population, 99
    white, 9, 117, 198, 296
Mlambo-Ngcuka, Phumzile, 186
mode of production, 79, 81, 134, 177, 178, 185, 190, 192, 261, 302, 304, 306, 318
    capitalist, 178, 185, 305
    colonially imposed, 177
    precapitalist or feudal, 262
Modi, Narendra, 2
monetary policy, 86, 181, 208, 239, 247
monopolies, 9, 239, 248
monopolists, white, 268
monopoly
    capital, 252, 268
    classes, 8
    interests, 268
Montevideo, Uruguay, 219
Msimang, Solly, 162
Mzala Nxumalo Centre for the Study of South African Society, 201
    conference (2017), 129
    Mzala Centre, 131, 291, 293, 298

N
narrow
    ethnic chauvinism, 6
    ethno-nationalistic politics, 3
    nationalism, 2, 6, 35, 48, 87, 103
National Credit Act (2005), 207, 208
National Credit Regulator, 207
national democratic
    revolution, 9, 134, 196, 198, 200
    revolutionary front, 185
    struggle, 171
National Democratic Revolution (NDR), 99, 164, 244
National Development Plan (NDP), 32, 138, 154, 158
    Vision 2030, 154
National Economic Development and Labour Council (Nedlac), 178, 223, 228
    Nedlac Act (1994), 178
national government, 108, 109, 169, 219
national liberation, 6, 12, 36, 54, 69, 71, 78, 81, 84, 85, 90, 91, 98, 147, 194, 197, 243, 289, 303, 304, 331, 339
    movement, 69, 71, 78, 90, 91, 243, 289
    project, 243
    struggle, 6, 304
national question, 1, 2, 3, 5, 6, 11, 12, 23, 25, 31, 34, 35, 36, 37, 38, 45, 48, 49, 52, 53, 56, 58, 59, 60, 61, 62, 69, 70, 71, 72, 73, 74, 75, 76, 77, 78, 79, 80, 81, 82, 83, 84, 85, 86, 87, 88, 89, 90, 91, 95, 97, 98, 99, 106, 107, 117, 118, 119, 122,

123, 124, 260, 318, 330, 331, 332, 339, 340
National Treasury, 181
National Union of Metalworkers of South Africa (NUMSA), 32
Cloete, Karl, 160
national unity, 2, 6, 12, 35, 36, 91, 97, 98, 101, 104, 116, 332
nationalisation, of mines and banks, 268
nationalism, 2, 5, 23, 35, 38, 48, 72, 81, 83, 85, 86, 87, 89, 90, 91, 98, 99, 260
nationalist impulse, 338
nationalist parties, 2
NATO (North Atlantic Treaty Organization), 242, 290, 297
natural and human disasters, 326
natural selection, 306, 307
NDP, *See* National Development Plan
NDR, *See* National Democratic Revolution
Nehru, Jawaharlal, 45
neo-colonial challenges, 305
neocolonialism, 338 *see also* colonialsim
neo-imperialism, 10 *see also* imperialism
neoliberal
    capitalism, 2, 10, 15, 137, 250, 305
    capitalist 11, 239, 239
    course, 294
    economic policies, 136, 180, 239
    fiscal and monetary orthodoxies, 317
    fiscal policy, 244
    macroeconomic framework, 180
    management, 239
    orientation, 138
    policy, 13, 137, 178, 179, 182, 185
    politics, 12
    programmes, 218
    reformist path, 186
    restructuring, of the workplace, 250
neoliberalism, 2, 25, 39, 133, 134, 137, 143, 178, 179, 182, 184, 191, 205, 211, 240, 244, 245, 246, 279, 318, 323, 328, 329, 331, 333, 334, 335, 341
new forms of work, 233, 234, 235, 236
New Growth Path (NGP), 158
new left alternative political pole, 251
New Left Review, 258
new world order, 129
Ngawethu, 153
Ngoje, 2, 49
NGOs, *See* non-governmental organisations
Nicaragua, 132
Nicaraguan Confederación de Trabajadores por Cuenta Propia (CTCP), 224
Nigeria, 295
Non-Aligned Movement, 243, 290

non-agricultural employment, 217
non-governmental organisations (NGOs), 190, 191, 223, 245, 251, 297
non-racialism, 171
non-vanguardist, mass political party or parties, 251
North West provinces, 316
north-eastern South Africa, 314
Northern Hemisphere, 314
Nqutu, 49, 50
NSWP, *See* Global Network of Sex Work Projects
Ntshayisa, Lulama, 167
NUMSA, *See* National Union of Metalworkers of South Africa
Nzimande, Bonginkosi Emmanuel 22, 209, 296, 304

O
Odendaal, Andre, 155
OECD, *See* Organisation for Economic Cooperation and Development
oil crisis (1973), 179
Open University, 4
oppression, 1, 36, 48, 61, 70, 71, 73, 80, 82, 83, 85, 86, 87, 88, 91, 98, 153, 177, 222, 267, 303, 341
Order of Luthuli in Silver, 303
Organisation for Economic Cooperation and Development (OECD), 314
organisational agenda, 226
organised
    informal workers, 220
    workers, 221, 225, 228, 234
Organization for Economic Co-operation and Development, 187, 188, 242, 314
Ortega, Daniel, 132

P
Pan-African
    conferences, 46
    left, 47
    thinkers, 47
Pan-African Congress (PAC), 33, 46, 245
paradox, 51, 295, 277
Parliament, marches to, 161
parliamentary
    committee, 121
    formations, 170
    opposition, 246
patriarchies, 263, 260
Patriotic Alliance, 2
patronage networks, 202, 243
Peru, 132
petroleum industry, 310, 313
Philippines Communist Party, 23
Podemos party, 246
policy
    dominance, 182
    environment, 228
    intervention, 228
    vocabulary, 181
political
    activists, 45, 47
    alternatives, genuine left,

377

251
careers, 243
conquest, 244
conversations, 255
crisis, 251
discourse, 28, 35
economy, 261, 304, 306
education, 252
elite, 135, 252
equality, 267
exiles, 45, 46, 59, 60, 61, 258
forces, 248
formations, 169
framework, 244
incumbency, 135
independence, 243
liberation, 333
macro-economy, 224
models, of old Left, 243
movement, 275
power, 4, 251
reality, 291
regime, 275
scientists, 288
spectrum, 278
strategy, 244, 245, 246, 247
support, 256
unrest, 140
vocabulary, 292, 294
will, 257
polycentricism, 288, 339
popular
classes, 247, 248, 249, 250, 251, 253
struggles, 252
traditions, 132
Portuguese claim, 302

post-apartheid
community struggles, 7
emergence, black elite or middle classes, 258
era, 31, 117, 165, 166
government, 156
protests, 166
reconstruction and development, 305
South Africa, 1, 22, 23, 58, 65, 117, 154, 156, 160, 182, 239, 303, 331, 332
South African society, 244
post-capitalist alternatives, 318
postcolonial
societies, 329, 332
state, 331
theory, 265
post-Fordism, 273
post-GEAR policy period, 158
post-industrialised society, 328
post-neoliberal world, 339
post-structural theory, 265
post-structuralists, 265
post-wage-work social relations, 278
poverty 170, 227, 228
Prague, 3
pre-capitalist society, 263
precariat, 7, 332, 333, 336
precolonial societies, 77, 332
Pretoria, 26, 31, 33, 54, 120, 162, 192
previously marginalised groups, 267
Primakov, Evgeny, 289
private sector, 29, 134, 139, 150,

179, 252, 329
privatisation, 170, 180, 185, 199, 218, 239, 245, 250
see also anti-privatisation
pro-colonial challenges, 305
producers
    home-based, 218
    small-scale agricultural, 218
production
    forces of, 305
    of material life, 310
    of value, 273, 278
    regimes, 275
    relations of, 305
    system, 239, 248
productive capacity, expansion of, 238
professional occupations, 266
proletarianisation, 263, 266, 270
proletariat, 35, 36, 86, 88, 144, 147, 163, 224, 247, 270
Prosperity Party (Ethiopia), 291
protests
    Endlovini (Monwabisi Beach, Khayelitsha), 166
    mass demonstrations, 154
    mass struggles, 251
    Middelplaas (Mpumalanga), 166
    protest movements, 170
    protesters, 166
    strike action, 236
    student protests, #FeesMustFall, 33, 168
    Vuwani residents, 165
    Witzenberg Municipality, 166
    Wolseley, 166
pro-Western parties, 294
public debt, 290
Public Investment Corporation, 247
public sector, 29, 179, 247, 250, 269

Q
quality public services, 221, 250
quasi-capitalist, 244

R
race
    lines, 332, 333
    polarisation, 332
racial
    antagonism, 161
    capitalism, 15, 261, 301, 303, 305
    domination, 140, 258
    exploitation, 260
    inequality, 269, 280, 327
    oppression, 34, 36, 52
    regulation, 259
    supremacy, 180
    unemployment dynamics, 184
racialised inequality, 5
racism, 35, 256, 258, 259, 260, 261, 278
racist
    laws, 259
    regimes, 31, 265
    state, 258
    system, 34
radical

economic transformation, 268
economists, 241
policy measures, 245
political economic circles, 265
programme, 252
questions, 245
reforms, 249
transformation, 245, 250, 305, 316
Radical Economic Transformation, 27, 268, 270
radicalism, 244
rainbow nation, 2, 65
Ramaphosa, Cyril, 292, 296, 297
RDP, *See* Reconstruction and Development Programme
recession
Great Recession (2008), 237, 241
technical, 183
Reconstruction and Development Programme (RDP), 13, 31, 112, 137, 154, 157, 158, 181, 196
RDP document (1994), 157
RDP houses, 181
Red October Campaign, 209
reformist
agenda, 200
initiatives, 317
strategy, 134
refugees, 46, 371
Reich, 275
Republic of South Africa (RSA), 156, 301

RESA, *See* Research on Education in South Africa
Research on Education in South Africa (RESA), 3, 43, 50
Reservation of Separate Amenities Act, No. 49 of 1953, 165
revisionist
analyses, 265, 266
Marxism, 263, 280
Marxists, 263, 264
position, shared, 260
revisionists, 260, 261, 262, 264, 276
armchair intellectuals, 260
South African, 269
revolution, 3, 12, 23, 26, 31, 58, 69, 71, 80, 84, 85, 87, 88, 90, 130, 132, 134, 135, 163, 177, 178, 194, 195, 197, 198, 200, 210, 252, 253, 258, 290, 318, 338, 341
revolutionaries, 133
revolutionary
activities, 3
advances, 248
alternatives, 132
circles, 131
devotion, 133
party, 130
programme, 185
strategy, 134
tasks, 130
theory, 170
transformation, 178
right-wing influences, 132
Riverlea, 166

Road to South African Freedom (1962), 268
Rosatom State Nuclear Energy Corporation, 295
ruling class, 92, 162, 164, 242, 268, 294
ruling party, 122, 162, 170, 256, 269, 292, 330
rural subsistence
   agriculture, 259
   economy, 259
Russia, 15, 287, 289, 290, 291, 293, 294, 295, 296, 297
   alliance between Moscow and Beijing, 290
   anti-Moscow campaign, new, 295, 297
   anti-Soviet propaganda, 296
   credibility gap, 25
   Eastern Bloc, 242, 258, 277
   Gorbachev, Mikhail, 25, 289
   Kremlin, 297
   Lenin, Vladimir, 9, 45, 79, 80, 81, 84, 85, 86, 88, 91, 130, 135, 147, 161, 163, 185, 189, 259
   Leninism, 70, 71, 72, 256
   Meeting of Communist and Workers Parties, Moscow (1960), 197, 198
   Moscow, 194, 197, 198, 290, 296, 297, 298
   Moscow Institute for African Studies, 298
   post-Stalin era, 288
   Prussian path, transition to capitalism, 259
   Putin, Vladimir, 294, 296
   researchers, 298
   revolution, 135
   Russia–South African project, joint, 298
   Russophobia, 295
   Siberia, 307
   Sino-Soviet conflict, 290
   Sino–Soviet split (1960s), 242
   society, 294
   Soviet bloc, 132
   Soviet experience, the, 249
   Soviet Russia, 289
   Soviet Union, 3, 25, 132, 134, 242, 275, 288, 296
   studies, 298
   United Russia party, 294
   USSR, 194, 200, 289, 290
   volunteers, in Anglo-Boer War, 296
   Yeltsin, Boris, 289, 291
   Yeltsin's era, 294
Russian Foundation for Basic Research and the National Research Foundation, 298
Russian Parliament building, 291

S

SACP, *See* South African Communist Party
SADC region, 221
Sandinista National Liberation Front, 132
SASAS data, 332
scientific, technological and innovative (STI), 305
Scripps Institution of

Oceanography, 311
Second Internationals, 246
segregation, 162, 191, 259, 262
self-critique, 330
Self-Employed Women's Association (SEWA), 235
self-recognition, 330
semiocapital, 334
service delivery issues, 7
SEWA *See* Self-Employed Women's Association
single economy, 186
Slovo, Joe, 131, 133
slump of the 1970s, 238
small business sector, 224
Smoke and Fumes Committee, 310
social
  aid, 225
  and economic justice, 331
  base, 244
  change, 243
  classes, 168, 249
  cohesion, 15, 35, 106, 124, 292
  competences, 306
  conditions, 267
  crisis, 248, 252
  demands, 243, 246, 247, 249, 251
  dialogue, 234, 328
  domination, 257
  dynamics, 309
  form, 275, 276, 327
  historians, 264, 265
  justice, 2
  life, 14, 90, 197, 257, 265, 270
  movement, 224, 227
  order, exploitative, 134
  organisation, 323, 328, 329, 336
  powers, 253
  protection, 221
  questions, 329
  reality, contemporary, 9
  reform, 333
  relations, 134, 249, 272, 276, 278, 280
  relationships, 310, 337
  reproduction, 259, 278, 279
  sciences, 61, 257, 264, 265
  security, 189, 199, 218, 228, 231, 232, 235
  separation, 45
  solidarity economy, 335
  strata, 292
  system, 241, 271
  transformation, 8, 14, 84, 91, 177, 188, 206, 225, 237, 244, 248, 249, 252, 267
  unrest, 140
  vision, 246
  wage policies, 244
socialism, 3, 12, 15, 31, 70, 71, 83, 84, 85, 86, 88, 91, 92, 98, 99, 130, 131, 132, 133, 135, 136, 138, 141, 142, 143, 144, 145, 147, 148, 149, 150, 159, 160, 164, 198, 200, 201, 241, 244, 245, 248, 249, 260, 267, 275, 288, 292, 317, 318, 325, 328, 329, 335, 336, 338, 339, 341
  commonality of, 288
  enemy of, 136

future of, 324
retreat from, 339
under democracy, 136
unsustainability of, 328
weaknesses of, 136
Socialism is the future, build it now!, 200, 201
socialist
countries, 288
culture, 130
forces, 129
influences, 323
movement, 204, 248
orientation, 318
politics, 133
programme, 201, 243, 245
reconstruction and development, 317
regimes, 270
reorganisation, 335
revolution, 129, 134, 243, 258, 331
society, 160, 163
state, 338
struggle, 83, 85, 171
systems, 134
thinkers, 339
traditions, 249
values, 329, 334
Socialist International, 292
Socialist Register, 258
socialistic manifesto, 251
socialists by day, 136
sociality, veiled, 271
socio-economic
inequalities, 306
challenges, 1, 2, 7

SONA *See* State of the Nation Address
South Africa Pushed to the Limit: The political economy of change, 240
South African academy, 260, 261
South African Communist Party (SACP), 1, 3, 9, 21, 22, 24, 29, 31, 34, 36, 38, 46, 60, 69, 70, 79, 84, 87, 98, 99, 100, 131, 135, 145, 157, 160, 164, 170, 171, 179, 185, 193, 194, 195, 196, 197, 198, 199, 200, 201, 203, 204, 207, 209, 210, 243, 244, 245, 258, 260, 270, 330
SACP National Congress, 10th (1998), 199
SACP National Congress, 9th (1995), 200
SACP National Congress, fifth (1962), 198
SACP Road to South African Freedom (1962), 198
SACP thought, genealogy of, 268
SACP's 15th National Congress, 297
South African
revolution, 318
scholarship, 257, 265
South African Institute of International Affairs (SAIIA), 297
South African Journal of Science, 315
South African Reserve Bank, 208, 268

South America, 297
Southern Hemisphere, 314
southern South Sudan, 314
sovereign economy, 239
sovereign industrial
    effort, 247
    policy, 247
    production system, 243, 247
    project, 247
sovereign national interests, 242
sovereign productive industries, new, 246
sovereignty of food, 239, 247
Soweto, 1, 3, 154
space, 306
Spain, 246
    Podemos party, 246
stagism, 85, 199, 335, 336, 337
stagnation, 241
    of the 1930s, 238
    of the 1970s, 238
    of the 1980s and 1990s, 239
Stalinist, 260 *see also* neo-Stalinist
Standard Bank of South Africa Industrial and Commercial Bank of China stake (2007), 209
State Duma, 294
State of the Nation Address (SONA) 9th (2023), 316
state
    coffers, 164, 167
    control, 159, 188
    expropriation of all land, 268
    grants, 157, 171
    ownership, 209
    power, 137, 148, 249, 275
    procurement, 184
    productive capacity, 184
    resources, 133
    revenues, 231
    the role of, 248
    banks, 208, 247
state capture, 136, 206, 301, 305, 317, 331,
state-based corruption, 331
state-led capitalism, 279
state-owned enterprises (SOEs or 'parastatals'), 180, 239
state-regulated distribution, 270
statist socialism, 328
Statistics South Africa (StatsSA), 163, 250
STI, *See* scientific, technological and innovative
street traders, 217, 218, 336
Street Vendors International, 337
street vendors, 218, 219, 220, 226, 236
structural
    adaptations, 179
    adjustment, 179, 218
    analysis, 269
    problems, 178
    of ownership, 272
struggle
    against apartheid, 244
    anti-apartheid, 258
    anti-imperialist, 288
    for liberation and independence, 331
    of the oppressed, 324

theory and tactics, 23
working-class, 256
struggles, 9, 13, 14, 28, 39, 54, 58, 61, 129, 133, 147, 155, 156, 160, 161, 165, 168, 170, 171, 201, 202, 205, 226, 234, 249, 250, 251, 252, 258, 267, 303, 304, 325
  anti-colonial, 243
  concerning gender equality, 325
  domestic, 264
  for alternatives and transformation, 252
  for reforms, 252
  popular, 252
  popular, 252
  shared, 255
  workers, in the workplace, 252
students, 33, 165, 206, 244
subjugation, 15, 56, 81, 303
sub-Saharan Africa, 314
sub-Saharan countries, 247
surplus populations, 333

T
Tambo, Oliver (OR), 4, 22
Tanzania, 180, 198, 314
Tau, Parks, 167
tautology, 272
tax
  cuts, 244
  incentives, 259
  reductions, 239
  revenue, 244
taxation system, 231
taxonomy, 307

technological artefacts, 305
  Voyager 1, 305
  Voyager 2, 305
telos, 274, 278
tenderpreneurship, 137, 142
Third Internationals, 246
Third World
  allies, 242
  countries, 239
trade liberalisation, 11
trade policies, 231
trade union
  activities, 222
  constitutions, 226
  federation, 256
  leadership, 226
  movement, 54, 55, 157, 193, 195, 197, 204, 218
  organisation, 250
trade unions, 14, 54, 55, 155, 188, 195, 202, 207, 218, 219, 222, 223, 224, 225, 226, 227, 228, 232, 233, 234, 235, 250, 260, 266, 267, 332
  drastic decline of (post-1994 period), 250
  dual organising strategy, 223
  formal sector, 226, 227
  practical issues, 226
  strength of, 227
tradition, 29, 39, 72, 73, 74, 90, 91, 141, 256, 276
traditional
  concepts of class, 277
  formal sector workers, 235
  male bias, 226
transformation, land and

economic, 245
transnational corporations, 313
Transvaal, 167
treadmill effect, 273
trickle down, of wealth, 330
trickle-down
   growth orthodox, 181
   idea, 180
tripartite
   bargaining forums, 223
   structures, 223
Tripartite Alliance, 22
Troika, 246
Trotskyites, 245
Tshwane, 298
Tutu, Desmond, 2

U

UCS, *See* Union of Concerned Scientists
Ukraine, 297
uMkhonto we Sizwe (MK), 3, 21, 196
unemployment, 1, 13, 32, 35, 119, 124, 137, 139, 140, 151, 156, 159, 160, 163, 164, 168, 170, 171, 182, 183, 184, 185, 186, 187, 205, 218, 228, 250, 332, 334, 336, 340
   unequal distribution, 274
   relations of economic power, 293
Union Buildings, marches to, 161
Union of Concerned Scientists (UCS), 313
unionisation, 218, 337
United Nations (UN), 242
United States (US), 2, 60, 77, 92, 207, 208, 239, 242, 246, 247, 256, 261, 275, 289, 290, 296
   American economy, 290
   American Petroleum Institute (API), 310
   Capitol Hill, Washington, 291
   Congress, 311
   Gulf War (1991), 242
   historians, 264
   imperialist allies, 242
   imperialist hegemony, 132
   leadership, 242, 290
   markets, 247
   New York, 77, 144, 275
   Pew Research Centre, Washington, 295
   ruling class, 242
   Treasury bonds, 290
   Trump, Donald (former US President), 246
   US Bureau of Land Management, 311
   US-dominated unipolar world, 290
   Washington Consensus, 132
   Washington, 132, 289, 290, 291, 295, 311
   Western Allies, 242
universities, of Sussex and Essex and SOAS, 258
University of the Witwatersrand, 223
University of Zululand, 3, 50
urbanisation, 162, 266

V

valorisation process, 273
value
    of commodities, 271
    of things, 271
    production, 277
vanguard party, 251
vanguardism, 248
vanguardist approach, 248
Venezuela, 132
    Chavez, Hugo, 131
violence, 38, 48, 75, 192, 222, 265, 324, 327
voice regulation 233, 234, 235

W

war
    Cold War, 242
    Iraqi conflicts, 324
    post-war aggregate demand, 238
    post-war boom, 238, 243
    Syrian conflict, 324
    World War II, 162, 238, 243, 289, 296
    world wars, 9, 324
wealth
    accumulation, 181, 182, 205, 324, 331, 341
    distribution, disarticulated, 4
    inequalities, 182
    material, 273, 274
    redistribution of, 248
    unequal distribution, 86
welfare
    state, 279
    systems, 336

West Africa, 231
Western
    countries, 191, 287, 294
    culture, 134
    economies, 179
    hegemony, 191
    nations, 10
    powers, 9
    publicists, 327
West-oriented forces, 294
white
    Afrikaner domestic capital, 261
    capital, 138
    capitalism, 36
    capitalist, 4, 139, 259, 269
    employers, 259
    farmers, 123, 259
    hands, control of the economy, 139
    supremacy, 87, 165, 268
    working classes, 260
women
    domestic workers, 156, 219, 220, 336
    equality, 279
    feminism, 16, 72, 263, 265, 279, 280, 325
    inequalities 256
    labour power of, 260
    leadership, 226
    political and social space for, 279
    sex worker-led organisations, 222
    sex workers, 221, 222, 336, 337

social discrimination,
  against women, 217
street vendors, 236
subordination of, 263
waged labour, 280
workers, 217, 347
  black, 182, 244, 259
  formal workers, 226, 227
  informal workers, 218, 219, 220, 221, 223, 226, 227, 229, 231, 232, 233
  own-account workers, 225, 229, 233
  self-employed workers, 233
  wage workers, 220, 229, 230, 231
  wage work, 278, 280
Workers and Socialist Party (WASP), 203
Workers Organisation for Socialist Action, 245
workforce, 109, 185, 218
wages, 218, 234, 238, 243, 246, 248, 259, 261, 262, 270, 272, 273, 275, 277
working class, 6, 7, 12, 15, 25, 35, 36, 37, 38, 52, 71, 82, 83, 84, 85, 86, 87, 88, 89, 91, 92, 103, 106, 109, 112, 114, 115, 117, 118, 130, 133, 134, 135, 138, 141, 142, 146, 148, 149, 153, 158, 160, 163, 167, 168, 170, 178, 185, 188, 189, 197, 200, 202, 205, 206, 210, 211, 227, 243, 260, 266, 267, 270, 273, 280, 289, 292, 294, 332, 335, 336

working-class
  black, 6, 260, 332
  communities, 163
  consciousness, 259
  internationalism, 71, 86
  leadership, 91
  lives, 264
  majority, 138
  organisations, 218, 227
  politics, 83
  programme, 160
  solidarity, 37
  struggle, 133, 211, 256
  unity, 189, 201
world affairs, main players, 242
World Bank, 35, 242, 314
World Economic Forum, 35
World Marxist Review, 3
World Trade Organization, 35, 185, 242

X

xenophobia, 5, 35, 37, 256
xenophobic messages, 2

Y

Yale University, 4
Young Communist League, 36
young lions, 28, 304
Youth League, 244
youth unemployment rate, 140

Z

Zambia, 50, 233, 314
Zondo, Justice Raymond, 1
Zulu
  history and culture, 3

    households, precolonial, 260
    nationalism, 34
    people, 35
Zuma, Jacob, 31, 131, 161, 167,
    268, 292
    government, 32
    inner circle, 245
    Nkandla, 245
    presidency, 161
    Pottinger, Bell media
    campaign, 268
    scandals, 245
    years, 245

www.ingramcontent.com/pod-product-compliance
Lightning Source LLC
Chambersburg PA
CBHW032008220426
43664CB00006B/181